Passion's Fortune

The Story of Mills & Boon

Passion's Fortune
The Story of Mills & Boon

Joseph McAleer

OXFORD
UNIVERSITY PRESS

OXFORD
UNIVERSITY PRESS

Great Clarendon Street, Oxford OX2 6DP

Oxford University Press is a department of the University of Oxford.
It furthers the University's objective of excellence in research, scholarship,
and education by publishing worldwide in

Oxford New York

Athens Auckland Bangkok Bogotá Buenos Aires Calcutta
Cape Town Chennai Dar es Salaam Delhi Florence Hong Kong Istanbul
Karachi Kuala Lumpur Madrid Melbourne Mexico City Mumbai
Nairobi Paris São Paulo Singapore Taipei Tokyo Toronto Warsaw

and associated companies in Berlin Ibadan

Oxford is a registered trade mark of Oxford University Press
in the UK and certain other countries

Published in the United States
by Oxford University Press Inc., New York

British Library Cataloguing in Publication Data
Data available

Library of Congress Cataloging in Publication Data
Data applied for

ISBN 0-19-820455-8

1 3 5 7 9 10 8 6 4 2

Typeset by J&L Composition Ltd, Filey, North Yorkshire
Printed in Great Britain on acid-free paper by
Bookcraft Ltd,
Midsomer Norton, Somerset

For Stephanie Hope and John Casimir

Acknowledgements

With no pun intended, this book has been a labour of love for six years. The first legitimate history of Mills & Boon, Ltd. could not have been attempted without the support and enthusiasm of two men: Alan Boon and his younger brother, John, the sons of Charles Boon, the co-founder of the publishing house. Alan Boon, Editor Emeritus, is the genius behind the modern romantic novel. John Boon (who died in 1996) was Chairman of Mills & Boon, Ltd. (now known as Harlequin Mills & Boon, Ltd.), and past president of the International Publishers Association. Both men provided unfettered access to a long-lost archive of 50,000 letters which has proven to be a treasure trove. John Boon, reflecting his Cambridge training as an historian, placed no restrictions on this work nor asked for editorial approval. Both brothers also displayed an extraordinary generosity of time and the legendary Mills & Boon hospitality which made years of research a joy.

I am also grateful to the many employees at Harlequin Mills & Boon, Ltd. in Richmond who welcomed me and answered innumerable questions throughout the course of this project. In particular, Gillian Griffiths provided expert assistance in her unofficial role as 'Keeper of the Archive'. Her successor, Eva White, has held up the tradition with style. Paul Bulos patiently endured countless requests (usually by transatlantic fax) for information about Mills & Boon authors, living and deceased, and guided me through the complex permission process.

One great advantage of writing the history of a firm founded in this century is the opportunity to interview people who once worked for, or still work for, Mills & Boon, Ltd. Among family members, employees, and associates, I am indebted to Alan Boon, John Boon, Dinah Norman (née Boon), Gillian Clements, Lawrence Heisey, Brian Hickey, Gordon Wixley, Dr Peter Mann, and David Boorman. At D. C. Thomson & Sons Ltd., I spoke with former editors Maurice Paterson and David Doig. H. J. Haden shared his research findings on the Gerald Mills family.

Among authors who wrote, and in some cases still write, for Mills & Boon, Ltd. (now known as Harlequin Mills & Boon, Ltd.), I am grateful for the chance to interview, or exchange letters with, Betty Beaty, Jay Blakeney ('Anne Weale'), Ida Cook ('Mary Burchell'), Ethel Connell ('Katrina Britt'), Joyce Dingwell, Jane Donnelly, Essie Flett ('Essie Summers'), Kay Green ('Roumelia Lane'), Sheila Holland ('Charlotte Lamb'), Marjorie Lewty, Wynne May, Betty Meijer ('Betty Neels'), Rosamunde Pilcher ('Jane Fraser'), Dr Margaret Sands, Dr David Waddington, Jean Walton ('Jean MacLeod'), Kay Thorpe, Anne Vinton, and Gwen Westwood. Betty Richards shared information of her great aunt, Sophie Cole.

I am indebted to Harlequin Mills & Boon, Ltd., for permission to quote from correspondence and documents in the archive; to quote from published novels; and to reproduce book covers, advertisements, photographs, and other archival material. Every attempt has been made to contact authors represented in the Mills & Boon archive or their respective estates for permission to quote from correspondence. In particular, Jennifer B. Gooch has given permission to quote from the letters of her mother, Alex Stuart; Marilyn Rutherford, for her mother-in-law, Grace Rutherford ('Eleanor Farnes'); and Rupert Crew, Ltd., for Lilian Chisholm. Dinah Norman and her daughter, Gillian Clements, have generously given permission to reproduce family photographs.

Finally, I wish to acknowledge the significant contributions of several individuals. Alexander Heald, fresh from reading History at Balliol College, Oxford, was invaluable at the outset in sorting and cataloguing the Mills & Boon archive, providing insightful comments along the way. Dr Ross McKibbin (who, as supervisor of my Oxford D.Phil. thesis a decade ago, introduced me to Mills & Boon and its historical significance) and Rosemary Giedroyć generously gave of their time to read the manuscript and offer astute criticism. At Oxford University Press, I would like to thank, in particular, Dr Anthony Morris and his successor as History Editor, Ruth Parr; Anne Gelling; and Dorothy McLean. Heather Watson was an exceptional copy editor. Bryan Page performed miracles with his camera. Lastly, my insight into British life and letters was enhanced by two dear friends, Gwendoline Williams and Walter Tyson.

My family in America has endured the trials and tribulations of a part-time historian. I am grateful for their patience and support. To inspire a new generation of historians—and readers—this book is dedicated to two special young people, my niece and my godson. Among the many life lessons ahead of them, may they learn from this history the value of decency and professionalism, and believe that a happy ending can be just a short read away.

Joseph McAleer
Stamford, Connecticut
January 1999

Contents

Plates

Figures

Author's Note

One measure of the popularity of Mills & Boon is that its name has taken many forms over the past ninety years. The original name of the firm, Mills & Boon, Limited (now known as Harlequin Mills & Boon, Limited), has often been shortened to 'Mills & Boon' or expressed as 'Mills and Boon'. These usages have not been changed in this book. Furthermore, 'Mills & Boon' has been used as a noun to describe an individual novel or series of novels published by the firm; for example, 'a Mills & Boon' or 'Mills & Boons'.

Similarly, Harlequin Books, Limited has been referred to as 'Harlequin'; its novels, 'a Harlequin' or 'Harlequins'.

'Mills & Boon' is today a registered trade mark owned by Harlequin Mills & Boon, Limited, UK. 'Harlequin' is a registered trade mark owned by Harlequin Enterprises Limited, Canada.

Introduction
Look Back in Amusement

Publishing is how you relate to authors.

Alan Boon

Mills & Boon is a trademark that is so imbued in the British psyche. It's like Blackpool Rock. It is a tremendous pull. If anyone says Mills & Boon, you know immediately what they mean.

Jane Donnelly

IN a dusty corner of the Mills & Boon archive at the firm's headquarters in Richmond, outside London (the address, fittingly enough, is Paradise Road), lies a tattered notebook called *Boon Mots*. Subtitled 'An Anthology of Artless Extracts culled from the writings of Mills & Boon's Authors', the book was compiled over several years by the firm's editors, who copied and pasted in memorable entries as they read manuscripts—and before they applied the blue pencil. The collection was intended for amusement, and it certainly is amusing. Of the hero in one novel, for example, it is said, 'He looked like a two-egg man,' and, 'Lucky man, Magnus, not only a leading stud but a profitable banana farm.' The heroine's curiosity 'seemed to leap forward on its own violation'. About her Mother, 'It was easy dishwashing and she did have a conscience about Mummy, who was frequently under the doctor for something or other.' The heroine in one of Mills & Boon's famous Doctor-Nurse novels hears the surgeon whisper during the operation, 'Careful—a small prick coming.' Seduction scenes, which were intended to be serious and romantic, sometimes had the opposite effect:

> 'My darling, help me to grope back to your white ways,' he said, his voice hoarse with emotion.
> 'You won't have to grope. You got there last night.'

In another manuscript, the hero pledges his eternal love: 'Anything you desire—I'm ready, willing, and able, as the hose pipe said to the fire.'

Mills & Boon, Ltd., as the leading publisher of romantic fiction in Britain for sixty years, has always been the butt of jokes (even among its own employees), suffering as much for the storylines of its novels as for the unprecedented success of its 'product'. But behind the sniggering lies a unique chapter in the history of British publishing, as well as of British exports. Ninety years after its founding, Mills & Boon is one of only two British publishers to have become a household name in Britain and throughout the Commonwealth (the other is Penguin). The Mills & Boon imprint is better known than the firm's authors, and is asked for in bookshops rather than specific titles or names. 'Mills & Boon is a trademark that is so imbued in the British psyche,' said Jane Donnelly, one of the firm's authors, who joined the list in 1968 with *A Man Apart* ('an attractive novel of a girl's forbidden love'). 'It's like Blackpool Rock. It is a tremendous pull. If anyone says Mills & Boon, you know immediately what they mean.' In 1982, to mark the sixtieth anniversary of the British Broadcasting Corporation, a time capsule was buried in the grounds of Castle Howard in Yorkshire, containing 'vital clues of life in 1982 for generations to come'. Along with music, cosmetics, and contraceptives were buried three Mills & Boon novels, 'since Mills & Boon books are read by an enormous section of the British public'. In 1997 the *Oxford English Dictionary*, as if to crown the firm's achievements, added 'Mills & Boon' to the canon, meaning 'romantic, story-book'.

The Mills & Boon imprint, like any successful commodity in a mass market, stands for a quality product, a kind of guarantee of an easy, thrilling, and satisfying read with an obligatory happy ending. This flavourful confection, wrapped in a brightly coloured paperback cover with a dreamy scene, is to many addictive in its escapist nature. Alan Boon, the acknowledged genius behind the stylized Mills & Boon romance, admitted the restorative quality of the novels which he edited for some forty years: 'It has been said that our books could take the place of valium, so that women who take these drugs would get an equal effect from reading our novels.' The firm today confirms this important point in guidelines prepared for aspiring Mills & Boon authors:

> We're in the business of providing entertainment, a short foray into the emotions. Our readers don't expect to read about the sort of petty worries they can encounter any day of their lives, such as an overdue library book, or the sort of serious problems which cause too much heartache or anguish. We're talking about escapism. But escapism must be based on reality.

The question everyone asks about Mills & Boon is, simply: How did they do it? How did Mills & Boon, from the humblest of beginnings in 1908 as a general publishing house, build a worldwide publishing empire, which in 1998 sold in excess of 200 million paperback novels in 100 overseas markets and translated into 24 languages? In the United Kingdom alone, Mills & Boon claims 11 million loyal readers, representing 4 out of every 10 women, and a novel is sold every two seconds. The firm has cornered 54 per cent of the UK paperback romantic fiction market, a sub-market which comprises 32 per cent of all mass market paperback sales.

According to John Boon, former Chairman of Mills & Boon, Ltd., and son of the co-founder, Charles Boon, the answer to the question is twofold: hard work and respect:

> You see, we never despised our product. I think this was highly important. A lot of people who publish romantic novels call them 'funny little books' that make a bit of profit. We never did that. We never said this was the greatest form of literature, but we did say that of this form of literature, we were going to publish the best. In any field, if you despise what you're making, you're in for trouble.

Mills & Boon's specialization in a single genre of fiction supported by a loyal and steady market was the key to the firm's longevity in a century when small publishing houses folded or were absorbed into giant multinational conglomerates. Mills & Boon identified a distinct readership, nurtured the demand, and won a fierce loyalty from women readers drawn mainly from the middle and working classes. For the Boon family, the results were financially rewarding, if intellectually somewhat inferior. In 1967 Alan Boon turned down an offer of a manuscript from a literary agent, as it did not meet Mills & Boon's strict specifications. 'We have an extremely specialised list,' he explained, 'and would, indeed, have to turn down Shakespeare if he sent one along.'

Times had indeed changed by the late 1960s, since Mills & Boon in its early years published Shakespeare, along with school textbooks, travel guides, socialist tracts, art books, humour, politics, child care, memoirs, plays, and a host of other categories of books. Founders Gerald Mills and Charles Boon were committed to general publishing, including fiction of a 'popular' and a 'quality' vein. The latter included the great and the near-great, some of whom were given their first big 'break' by Mills & Boon: P. G. Wodehouse, Hugh Walpole, Victor Bridges, Jack London, E. F. Benson, Georgette Heyer, Denise Robins, and Constance Holme were all published by the firm. It is Mills & Boon's success in these early years which makes the firm's transformation in the 1930s into a 'library house', catering to the patrons of Boots Booklovers Library and the tuppenny lending libraries with 'light' (and distinctly unliterary) fiction, all the more interesting.

The story of Mills & Boon is almost a romance in itself, the tale of a handful of men and hundreds of dedicated women. In its personal attention to authors, eschewing literary agents for a more direct approach, the firm won a loyalty and a writing production level that was unprecedented. 'Publishing is how you relate to authors,' Alan Boon explained. 'We became good friends with the author.' Hundreds of women, some writing as many as twelve novels a year, flourished under the Mills & Boon system which was, for its day, one of the rare opportunities for a woman to earn a considerable amount of money. No one, in fact, knows precisely how many women (and several men, with female pen-names) wrote for the firm since its founding in 1908, nor how many titles were published, or how many were sold. One thing is certain, however: the number was considerable. Between 1937 and 1953, for example, 1,067 new romances were published, an average of 67 per year, or five each month. Twice that many novels were reprinted and sold each month in cheaper editions, and the stock list held as many as 500 back titles.

The keys to Mills & Boon's success, as we will reveal in this study, were a steady volume of new titles by popular authors; clever publicity; a dependable market with good distribution outlets; and vigorous research of the readership. The latter is the reason why Mills & Boon's novels can be a valuable source for the social historian of the twentieth century. The firm has never been afraid to change with the times and tailor the portrayal of the heroine in particular to current tastes and attitudes. In terms of romantic fiction, this has translated into greater degrees of permissiveness, in line with the changing views and roles of women in society, and as regards relationships, marriage, and sex. 'I have never got out of my mind that romantic fiction has more influence than anything to do with its literary worth, because it is read by unsophisticated people,' said Mary Burchell, who wrote over 130 novels for Mills & Boon in fifty years and appreciated the responsibility she had towards her readers. Unsophisticated they were, perhaps, but no less demanding as 'consumers' of the product. 'Readers know exactly what they want,' said Sheila Holland ('Charlotte Lamb'), one of Mills & Boon's top-selling authors (and top-earners, having made millions from sales of paperbacks). 'They're like dogs and children. I'm talking to an audience which feels about things as I do.' Hence editorial policy was organic, a reflection of the expanding (and changing) middle and working classes in Britain.

C. S. Lewis, in *An Experiment in Criticism* (1961), described the tastes of the section of the reading public, which lacked the experience of reading all kinds of books as 'unliterary'. His conclusions could be applied to the typical Mills & Boon reader: 'The woman reader does not believe that all eyes follow her, as they follow the heroine of the book, but she wants to feel that, given more money, and therefore better dresses, jewels, cosmetics, and opportunities, they might.' Clearly such escapism is at the root of the popularity of Mills & Boon romances. But this quality has also been heavily criticized. Some critics, for example, have condemned romantic fiction as representing a product of monopoly capitalism and its leisure industry. These books, they claim, conceal the truth about a reader's life-situation, encouraging her to dream, rather than face reality. The status quo, therefore, is preserved. The fact that the majority of publishers in Britain (all of whom, like Mills & Boon, served the demand for light fiction) were controlled by Conservative-minded men only enhanced this belief. Feminist critics, moreover, regard popular fiction as a form of social control. By learning to equate the happy ending with marriage and motherhood, women readers (primarily of the 'unsophisticated' lower-middle and working classes) have their world-views restricted, and their aspirations dimmed.

As such, Mills & Boon novels have been an easy target. In 1993 the Archbishop of York, Dr John Hapgood, caused a sensation when he blamed the 'high romantic expectations' created by pop songs and Mills & Boon novels for Britain's rising divorce rate. The reaction in the press was swift but dismissive. 'One could as well blame the Lassie films for the incidence of abandoned dogs', wrote one critic, while another marvelled, 'The astonishing thing is that the Mothers' Union did not hurl eggs at him.' The irony of Hapgood's remarks was lost on the public: in the early 1960s Mills & Boon gave a rising young cleric named John Hapgood a leg-up by publishing his book, *Religion and Society*, in Mills & Boon's non-fiction list.

※

Clearly, passions run high when people discuss Mills & Boon and the impact of popular fiction on its readers. But under closer scrutiny there are several 'myths' about the firm and romantic fiction that we will examine, and largely refute, in the course of this book. Among these are:

The Orwellian Agenda.   Since George Orwell published his landmark essay on 'Boys' Weeklies' in 1940, popular fiction has often been associated with a sinister agenda, part of a conspiracy of the ruling classes to control and influence its subjects. Orwell suspected that, since publishers of popular magazines (and novels) were conservative, and since storylines promoted God, King, and Country as well as the status quo, fiction was fundamentally designed to promote a certain conservative vision of the future. The reality, however, was more complex. While it is true that Mills & Boon acknowledged its influence over its readers, and took pains over the years to rein in its authors within a socially acceptable 'moral' code, it avoided 'hot button' topics such as religion and politics, venturing into public affairs only during the Second World War (when heroines, fiercely patriotic, joined the fight). The firm, moreover, was not static in its views, changing its policy towards sex and personal relationships in order to maintain the appeal of the novels. Mills & Boon was, first and foremost, a commercial enterprise dependent on a certain class of reader. Nor could it, in practice, determine or even predict the rate and manner of social change. Not, therefore, to change as its readership's attitudes changed (especially after the Second World War and during the 1960s) would simply have been bad business. 'Everyone would say we're just in it for commerce. Well, to some extent we are, and, why not?' John Boon said. None the less, the firm did, and does, draw a moral line. 'We don't like bad language. We don't like abortion in the books, or brutality, or sadism,' Boon noted. 'But, I think that is a reflection of the morals of the company', not to mention contemporary society.

'Regressive' Storylines.   Some feminist literary critics have condemned the emphasis on the happy ending, translated as either a proposal of marriage or the wedding itself. As such, romantic fiction has been labelled 'old-fashioned' and 'regressive' for its age, and certainly out of place in the 1990s. When novels are placed in their original context, however, nothing could be further from the truth. The heroine's evolution as a strong character, especially after the Second World War (reflecting the improved social standing of women), displays a kind of feminism promoted by the authors, who were working women themselves. If we examine popular titles in their social context they rarely seem 'out of date'.

The Formula.   Mills & Boon's success since the Second World War and its ever-expanding list of titles has always been associated with talk of a 'formula', a strict list of specifications which authors had to follow to the letter before a manuscript was accepted for publication. It is true that, today, there are 'tip sheets' providing guidelines to new authors. In 1986 Mills & Boon distributed 9,000 copies of a cassette tape, '*And then he kissed her . . .* ', which contained a dramatized version of editorial guidelines. But between 1930, when Charles Boon identified romantic fiction as the firm's specialty, and the 1970s, it is difficult to speak of a rigid editorial policy and a precise formula, so to speak, evolved. The firm did have guidelines which reflected a commonly held, but not unchanging, conception of morality and its acceptable limits. But within the basic framework—heroine meets hero in an interesting setting, falls in love, and marries—there was considerable room for growth. We can trace the evolution of the 'formula' as Mills & Boon itself matured as a publishing house, and as the social assumptions of women readers also matured. Mills & Boon novels since the 1970s, for example, have featured premarital sex scenes, once a taboo but now considered natural by a large segment of the readership. 'In our books now there is an awareness of sex, and I'm afraid they sometimes get into bed without the benefit of a priest,' Alan Boon said. 'But they should marry each other in the end.'

The Dominating Imprint.   In studying the history of Mills & Boon, we can trace the evolution of the firm's greatest achievement and the source of its financial success—the imprint, a recognizable brand name that has given Mills & Boon a distinct advantage in sales. 'At your library you can always ask for "a Mills & Boon novel" in the confidence that you will get an enjoyable story', the firm assured readers in the 1950s. But while Mills & Boon did promote its imprint more aggressively than it did individual authors, exceptions abounded, and certain 'stars' have often received more attention than others. And they did play an important role. These authors, such as Denise Robins in the 1930s, Lilian Warren ('Rosalind Brett') in the 1950s, and Violet Winspear in the 1960s, set new standards for the Mills & Boon novel, and in their success inspired—and elevated—the rest of the 'team' of writers. 'Authors really take in each other's washing, if you like, and learn by reading each other's books,' Alan Boon said. 'This would help to lift them higher in the Mills & Boon operation.'

Publishers' archives are notoriously limited and, in most cases, extremely rare. Much was lost when Paternoster Square in London, the heart of the publishing industry, was bombed during the Second World War. The high cost of storage space in and around the capital, moreover, militated against retaining records and documents before the computer age.

The happy exception is Mills & Boon. The firm's archive was retained but 'lost', languishing in a warehouse in Kent before its rediscovery in 1992. As publishers' archives go, it is a treasure trove, containing 50,000 letters between Mills & Boon and its authors, literary agents, and women's magazine editors from 1930 well into the 1970s. Since Mills & Boon was always a small firm, the correspondence is personal, warm, detailed, and informative. Mills & Boon was deliberately paternalistic with its authors, partly in order to persuade them to be as prolific as possible (as the lending libraries possessed an almost insatiable demand for these books). Thanks to this correspondence we can trace for the first time the evolution of editorial policy, and consider how Mills & Boon influenced its authors in terms of style and content. This evidence confirms that these novels were managed, carefully, with an eye on commercial success as much as on 'morality'. 'There is one aspect of the new story (which we liked),' Alan Boon informed an author in 1951, in a good sample of the correspondence. 'It concerns an incident where, as things stand at present, it appears that Rachel spent the night at the flat of either Toby or the hero. I do not know what your ultimate intentions are, but we think it advisable that it should be made clear that Rachel did not, in fact, spend a night in a man's flat. This is a precaution we have to take, bearing in mind the views of certain sections of our public.'

In many cases in this study, the archival material is enhanced and supplemented by interviews conducted with major and minor figures associated with Mills & Boon, Ltd., throughout the past ninety years. In addition to brothers Alan and John Boon, several authors have described their experiences, some of whom—such as Mary Burchell and Jean MacLeod—started their Mills &

Boon careers in the 1930s, and continued to write for half a century. We can learn as much about the relationship between publisher and author, and the challenges of writing popular fiction, from the careers of the successful novelists, as we can from the lesser (and now forgotten) figures. 'I always feel Mills & Boon with dear Alan in charge of us all is like a family,' one author wrote to Boon in 1971. 'I am sure you must be the finest publisher in the world for you have the wonderful art of encouragement and the ability to teach both wisely and so subtly that one is hardly aware that one is being helped.' The history of Mills & Boon is a story of personalities, and these interviews offer a glimpse into the private life of the firm.

But Mills & Boon does pose unique challenges to the historian. It is difficult to identify some authors, for example, as pen-names were used on contracts before the Second World War. A novel could be published in one version (and title) as, say, a serial in *Woman's Own*, and in another version (and title) for book readers. Given the vast number of authors and titles, a history of this nature has had to be selective. Fortunately, since Mills & Boon's success was built on consistency and quality, we can identify the successful novels and the successful authors who exemplified the major trends in the firm's policies.

This study is organized in two sections, with much overlap between the two. Part I is a chronological history of Mills & Boon, Ltd., from its founding in 1908 until the end of the family-owned business in 1972, when it was acquired by its partner, Harlequin Enterprises of Canada. We can trace Mills & Boon's evolution from general publisher to specialized library house to major paperback publisher, witnessing the effect of changes in the readership, markets, and distribution along the way. We also reveal Mills & Boon's innovations in book design and promotion, reader research, and author relations, and view the firm's dependence, and ultimate dismissal, of a similar growth industry, the women's weekly magazines.

Part II mines the riches of the Mills & Boon archive in an examination of editorial policy, and its evolution from the 1930s (when we can first speak of 'a Mills & Boon romance') until 1972. The impact of the market, readers, the cinema, and the Second World War are all considered, as well as changes in the roles and responsibilities of women in British society. After the Second World War, authors were under greater pressure to conform to the 'formula' as the mass market matured, and the 'product' (as it was increasingly known) became more standardized. Here we can glimpse the genius of Alan Boon and the idiosyncrasies of the lady authors from all walks of life in his 'harem'. Boon's personal attention to his authors is likened to the Hollywood star system: he had an eye for talent, and for authors who could write frequently, and he moulded them such so that they could produce fiction of a consistent quality to feed an expanding, and seemingly insatiable, readership.

Part I

Establishing the Imprint
The History

Chapter 1
Mr Mills and Mr Boon, 1908–1913

It was an adventure, this starting a new firm of publishers, eighteen months ago, when trade was bad and political controversy the order of the day. Everybody whom we met was full of doubts and warnings. Yes, it was an adventure, but it has been so far successful beyond expectation. We have not only enjoyed the excitement of it, but we have found the results financially excellent.

Mills & Boon, Ltd., press statement, 1910

Gentlemen . . . as I have written to Mr. Massie more than once, you have done splendidly by me in making me popular in England. I haven't a word of complaint to make; but I do have many hearty words of thanks.

Jack London to Mills & Boon, Ltd., 1914

WHEN Gerald Mills and Charles Boon decided to launch a new publishing house in 1908, they were two among many young entrepreneurs. The decades before the First World War witnessed a significant expansion in the number of publishers in Britain, and consequently the number of books published. This proliferation was applauded by the country's literary magazines, not to mention aspiring authors. A critic in the *Sphere* in 1912 was pleased to record that 'several publishing houses that have arisen within the last decades have published admirable books and are building up for themselves a sure and certain success . . . They magnify the chances of getting one's books published on reasonable terms. Only in the abundant production of books can the real masterpiece in many cases see the light.' Among these new, smaller publishing houses were T. Fisher Unwin (founded 1882), Gerald Duckworth & Co., Ltd. (1898), George G. Harrap & Co., Ltd. (1901), Eveleigh Nash (1902), T. Werner Laurie, Ltd. (1904), Stanley Paul & Co., Ltd. (1906), Sidgwick & Jackson, Ltd. (1908), Mills & Boon, Ltd. (1908), Martin Secker (1910), and Herbert Jenkins, Ltd. (1912).

The newcomers entered an industry dominated by a few large firms which published both fiction and non-fiction. The principal players were William

Collins, Ltd. (1789), Hodder & Stoughton, Ltd. (1868), Hutchinson & Co., Ltd. (1887), Methuen & Co., Ltd. (1889), and William Heinemann, Ltd. (1890). Not surprisingly, some of the new publishers were spawned from the larger houses: Mills & Boon from Methuen, and Stanley Paul from Hutchinson.

Why was there such publishing activity? It was an opportune time to be a publisher. For thirty years the market for reading had been steadily growing, reflecting in part the increase in literacy encouraged by compulsory element-ary education. Books, like weekly magazines and daily newspapers, were pub-lished in increasing numbers and promoted with greater marketing flair. The number of book titles published increased from 7,000 in 1900 to 10,914 in 1911. By 1914 there were 335 publishing houses in Britain. With a maturing market and an increasingly sophisticated system of book selling, wholesale distribution, and lending libraries, a publishing house could be founded on a small investment, and with a small staff, so keeping overheads low. The Net Book Agreement (1900), which allowed publishers to fix the price at which their books were sold to the public, permitted a level playing field of sorts. Large editions of single-volume books, both cloth-bound and paper-covered, could be produced quickly and relatively cheaply for sale within Britain and overseas.

Needless to say, the publishing of fiction was predominant at a time when the term 'best-seller' was first used for publicity purposes. In 1911 the *Westminster Gazette*, in its 'Forecast of the Autumn Publishing', cited the publication of a large number of works of history and biography, as well as 'the growing importance of the novel as it emerges through the work of known and well-tried writers and closes upon many problems and aspects of modern social life.' Amid the nods to the larger firms, the Gazette high-lighted three smaller houses: Alston Rivers, the Bodley Head, and Mills & Boon. These, the journal claimed, promised an 'abundance of fiction' from which 'we may look for enlightening discoveries of that dark horse, the "first novelist" '.

It is not surprising that the founders of Mills & Boon were aware of the favourable publishing situation. By 1908 Gerald Mills and Charles Boon, both aged 31, were experienced publishing men who knew how to edit and sell books. Although their backgrounds and personalities could not have been more different, the two men shared an interest in publishing and an ambition to strike out on their own. Mills was refined and intellectual, inter-ested in non-fiction and book production. He was also the chief financial supporter. Boon was a scrapper and charmer, an indefatigable man who took charge of sales and advertising, as well as the development of the fiction list, attracting established and first-time authors.

Mills came from a well-to-do family in Stourbridge, West Midlands. His mother, Jane, was the daughter of Isaac Nash, a wealthy industrialist and the largest manufacturer of scythes in the country. His uncle, Frederic, and his grandfather, Richard, were partners in prosperous glassworks factories. In 1908 Gerald Mills was executor of his uncle's estate, which was valued at over £50,000. It is possible that Mills came into some of this money, to invest in his new business venture.

Mills attended King Edward VI Grammar School in Stourbridge, and Caius College Cambridge (1895–8). After university he worked as a teacher before entering the publishing world at the firm of Whitaker & Co., educational publishers (not, apparently, J. Whitaker & Sons, Ltd., publishers of *Whitaker's Book List*). In 1903 he joined Methuen, and put his Whitaker experience to good use as Educational Manager.

Unfortunately, little else is known about Mills. In 1912 he married Rose Sharwood Anderson, daughter of John Graham Anderson of Hong Kong. They had no children. Some insight into Mills's character can be gleaned from an obituary notice in 1928, which spoke of his 'love of books and of the making of them' which 'gave him great joy'. Also included was a memoir written by 'a correspondent', quite possibly Charles Boon:

> His death is a very great loss to a host of friends, who admired his ster-ling character and who will always treasure the memory of his unselfish-ness and his tactful kindness. His genial and quiet personality endeared him to all who knew him, and among them must be counted especially the loyal staff of his firm. . . . As the business which he founded with Mr Boon gradually matured, it was his increasing joy to father a good book, especially if it were one of the educational works which were his partic-ular care.

Charles Boon came from Ramsholt, Suffolk. His father, Charles Boon sen., was a farmer. Married to a local woman, Boon sen. had six children: William, Charles, Robert, Alfred, Margaret, and Frank. When the agricultural depres-sion affected East Anglia in the 1880s, the family moved to London.

Unlike Gerald Mills, the junior Charles Boon grew up poor in Seven Dials, a tough area of central London. The family lived above a brewery, where Boon sen. worked. On his father's death, Charles, then 12, left school and took a series of odd jobs, including working in the brewery, a boot fac-tory, a bookshop, and for Mudie's Circulating Library. 'Father had a rough childhood,' Charles Boon's daughter, Dinah, recalled. 'He was the original wide boy.'

Boon joined Methuen in 1893, when he was 16 and Gerald Mills was still at school. Presumably he served first as an office boy or warehouse clerk, eventually rising through the ranks to become Sales Manager and General Manager.

Charles Boon and Gerald Mills spent five years working together at Methuen. They were contemporaries and, presumably, friends. 'Mills was a rather easy going, nice guy. I never heard of Mills and my Father having a row or anything like that,' Alan Boon recalled. But they were as different as chalk and cheese. 'My Father had no private means, so he was not relaxed like Mills,' John Boon said. 'Perhaps because of his early history he was not an easy man.' In fact, these early struggles may have forged Boon's ambitious nature. He was a self-made man who overcame his poor background through sheer hard work. This drive, combined with Mills's income, proved a recipe for success.

Neither Gerald Mills nor Charles Boon could have asked for a better training ground in publishing than working at Methuen. In Methuen, we can see the origin of future Mills & Boon policies and trademarks. The founder, Sir Algernon Methuen (1856–1924), published a wide-ranging list of titles including popular fiction and educational textbooks. He was also a pioneer in cheap editions, launching an innovative series of sixpenny paper-covered novels, featuring titles by H. G. Wells, Henry James, Mrs Oliphant, Bret Harte, and Joseph Conrad. Methuen books were sold at bookstalls, to schools, for export, and to the large circulating libraries run by Mudie's (founded 1842), W. H. Smith Stationers (1860), and Boots Chemists (1899). The firm's best-selling—and worst reviewed—author was the pulp novelist Marie Corelli. Her 1895 novel, *The Sorrows of Satan*, had an initial sale greater than any previous novel (20,000 copies), bestowing upon it the title of the first 'best-seller' in English history. This was at a time when, if a novel sold one thousand copies, it was doing extremely well. Corelli remained Methuen's leading female novelist (and major seller) until her death in 1924. 'It might be mentioned,' the firm admitted in 1925, 'that but for the novels of the late Miss Corelli, [Methuen's] prosperity must have been far less notable.'[1]

Charles Boon was joined at Methuen by his younger brother Alfred, who worked as a sales representative in the London area. Both Boons would have worked closely on selling and promoting Corelli's books, witnessing first-hand her popularity. They also would have learned some valuable lessons in acquiring a thick skin. After publishing Corelli's *Barabbas* in 1893, Sir Algernon himself observed, 'Few books in late years have received such savage and merciless treatment from the critics as Miss Corelli's latest romance. . . . Meanwhile the public, indifferent to the voice of the critic, and to charges of blasphemy, crowds to the sale.'[2] The point here is an important one. Methuen did not mind enduring such attacks if these books made money for the firm. Charles Boon paid attention, and learned this lesson well.

Methuen was also a committed editor and prospector. 'He was ceaselessly vigilant in the search for new books, himself frequently devising the lines on which the author could best work. His instinct was so right as often to appear almost uncanny,' noted one employee. Added another 'editor/writer': 'One always felt that his judgement was as nearly unerring as a man's can be, and his wide sympathies endeared him to all who knew him.'[3] These same qualities were attributed later to Charles Boon.

Boon also picked up tips on sales strategy from Methuen, who 'pushed' sales of cheaper editions (priced at 1*s.* or 6*d.*) as a bread-and-butter line through vigorous advertising. The fiction list, with both new and reprinted titles, was vast. In 1911, for example, Methuen published 170 authors of fiction, including W. W. Jacobs, Arnold Bennett, George Gissing, Arthur Conan Doyle, H. G. Wells, and A. E. W. Mason. Some authors were marketed in cheap 'Fiction Sellers' editions, including Corelli, Robert Hichens, Hope, and Eden Philpotts.

Not surprisingly, a number of popular fiction authors who were published by Methuen during the time Charles Boon and Gerald Mills worked there were later published by Mills & Boon. These included Robert Barr, Harold Begbie, E. F. Benson, Mrs B. M. Croker, William Le Queux, Jack London, Max Pemberton, and Marie Van Vorst. Since Charles Boon would have worked with these authors and sold their books, he undoubtedly nurtured these contacts and carried them with him when he left Methuen. Later, Mills & Boon also acquired reprint rights for cheap editions of many successful Methuen titles, which demonstrated sound business sense.

Methuen was also a successful educational publisher, with Gerald Mills managing the extensive list. The subject headings in its 2*s.* series included Classical, School Education, Commercial (career preparation), Science and Mathematics, Technology, German, and Historical. As was the case with the fiction list, several Methuen textbook authors were later published by Mills & Boon.

In 1908, after years of service, Gerald Mills and Charles Boon decided to strike out on their own. The story goes that they were restless and ambitious. They had watched Methuen expand and had contributed to its success, but felt they had not been fairly rewarded. Mills was then earning £500 per year; Boon, £400. 'That was a lot of money in those days,' John Boon admitted. 'My Father had a house, and a maid. But he felt he was worth much more.'

Mills put up the bulk of the £1,000 initial investment in the new company (£500 more than William Heinemann invested to launch his new firm in 1890). Other investors included a mutual friend, C. C. Longley (who would become the chief manuscript reader), and Mills's brother Kenneth, who worked in Rangoon with the Bombay Burmah Trading Corporation. 'My Father had no money,' John Boon explained. 'The main bank came from the Mills family. Kenneth Mills could always ante up a bit of cash, and when the firm was strapped for cash, he'd slip over a few hundred pounds, which was a lot of money then.' No wonder that the new company was christened 'Mills & Boon' rather than 'Boon & Mills'.

Mills & Boon, Limited, was registered on 28 November 1908. In the Certificate of Incorporation, Mills was listed as Publisher and Chairman, and Boon and David Stanley Hodge, Barrister-at-Law, as Directors. Hodge was also appointed Secretary. The 5,512 outstanding £1 shares in the new company were divided up among the principal shareholders: Mills (1,750 shares), Hodge (1,500), Boon (1,250), and Kenneth Mills (150).

In a tattered scrapbook of newspaper cuttings in the Mills & Boon archive, one is labelled, 'First notice of the firm'. It was printed in the London *Daily News* on 2 December 1908, under the heading 'BOOKS AND BOOKSELLERS':

> Early in January a new firm will open its offices in Covent Garden under the name of Messrs. Mills and Boon, Limited. Both the gentlemen mentioned have for many years worked in the house of Methuen, Mr G. R. Mills having managed the education department for some years and Mr Charles Boon having a record of fifteen years' service. The firm will publish both educational works, novels, and general literature. We are promised some interesting announcements later.

The *Bookseller* was also optimistic: 'The two partners have had ten years' experience with Messrs. Methuen and Co., and propose to throw their publishing net widely.'

What happened at Methuen after the departure of Messrs Mills and Boon should be noted. In 1910 Sir Algernon decided the time was right for Methuen to become a public company. George Webster, managing director, and E. V. Lucas, chief reader, joined Sir Algernon as company Directors. Sir Algernon also offered some of his own shares to members of staff, who earned dividends instead of Christmas bonuses. Many staff were recruited from the same Church of England school, St Augustine's in Kilburn. The overall effect was to engender loyalty among employees: a strategy he learned from the now departed Mills and Boon.[4]

Mills & Boon's first offices were at 49 Whitcomb Street in Covent Garden. The staff was small, and included a number of Boons: Charles recruited his brother Frank and sister Margaret to work for him. 'My Father wanted everybody in the firm,' John Boon explained. 'He was an insecure man, and it made him feel safe.' Indeed, in the 1930s Charles Boon would draft his three sons—Charles ('Carol'), Alan, and John—to work for him. Frank Boon was one of two sales representatives who covered the London area (where undoubtedly he competed against his brother Alfred at Methuen) as well as the provinces, and also handled exports ('Colonial Editions').[5] Margaret Boon, who had worked for Mudie's Library, joined as office manager, and also acted as a proofreader, presumably bringing to bear the first-hand knowledge of popular fiction and authors she had learned at Mudie's.

Two fellow Methuen employees also joined Mills & Boon. John Dale, a long-time sales representative for Methuen, turned down an offer from Mowbray & Co., Ltd., to 'collect orders' for Mills & Boon instead. Also leaving Methuen was Joseph W. Henley, who had worked there for six years. He joined Mills & Boon as the general office boy. Mr H. Brooks joined the new firm from Edward Arnold publishers, where he was a sales rep. Both Brooks and Henley put in more than fifty years' service with the firm, with Henley eventually succeeding Charles Boon as Chairman.

From the beginning Mills & Boon published in a form and at a price that was within the reach of a wide readership. As the newcomer in the crowded publishing world, Mills & Boon seemingly published anything it could lay its hands on—fiction, politics, humour, health, child care, cooking, travel. The accent was on 'quality' and variety, and not on the romantic fiction we know today; though the very first Mills & Boon title was a six-shilling romantic novel, *Arrows from the Dark* by Sophie Cole, her second novel (her first, *Rachel Chalfont*, was published by Duckworth). The book was published on 25 March 1909. Reviews were glowing: the *Morning Post* called *Arrows* 'an original story' with 'the history of a group such as Jane Austen has made immortal'.

The choice of Cole's novel to launch the Mills & Boon list is a curious one. To the modern reader, it is completely unreadable, despite obvious (if clumsy) attempts at romance ('The next moment she was caught in his arms, her lukewarm sentiment fused by the fire of his passion, her scruples and doubts forgotten, while the barrier of his presence came between her and the unfortunate past.'). 'She was a boring writer, and was never going to set the Thames on fire,' Alan Boon admitted. 'Her books usually featured the heroine, a pie-eyed little girl, going down to Brighton and being seduced.' Still, Cole must have had a following and a name by 1909. *Arrows* turned in a respectable performance, selling 1,394 of its 1,500 copies by 1914.[6] Cole remained with the firm for over 30 years, writing 65 novels for Mills & Boon, usually two a year. By way of comparison, William Heinemann printed 3,000 copies of his first title, *The Bondman* by Hall Caine—and the novel, a blockbuster, sold 450,000 copies!

During 1909, the firm's first full year of operations, 123 contracts were signed. Advances ranged from £25 to authors such as Sophie Cole and newcomer E. S. Stevens to as high as £200 for established authors such as Robert Barr and £300 for E. F. Benson and Gaston Leroux (*Phantom of the Opera*).[7] Edition sizes were usually 1,000–1,500 copies for a 6s. first edition novel, more for cheaper editions.

Mills & Boon spared no expense in signing up big names, most of whom were contracted through their agents, which included Curtis Brown, Hughes Massie, and A. P. Watt. The fact that agents would place their clients' work in a new firm is a testimony to Mills & Boon's competitiveness and powers of persuasion. Among these 'names' were Robert Lynd, Cosmo Hamilton, Barry Pain, Maurice Baring, Max Pemberton, Oliver Onions, E. F. Benson, Marie Van Vorst, and Eustace Mills. The strategy here is worth noting. Along the lines of Sir Algernon's policy towards Marie Corelli, Mills & Boon paid handsomely for proven sellers whose books (new or reprinted) would attract attention and boost the list. We should bear in mind that Mills & Boon, like other small publishers, faced some intense competition in the fiction market in 1909. Two of the fiction best-sellers of the year were *The Rosary* by Florence Barclay (published by G. P. Putnam's Sons, and selling over one million copies) and another Hall Caine blockbuster for Heinemann, *The White Prophet*. Mills & Boon's expected financial rewards could be used on expanding the rest of the list.

But to sign up big stars, Mills & Boon had to pay—or exceed—the going rates. In 1909, for example, an offer was extended to a former Methuen author, Mrs B. M. Croker, via her agent, A. P. Watt, of a £500 advance for a novel by her for publication in 1910. It would appear that the 'novel' in question was a reprint of her old Methuen title, *Fame*, still a big seller. Croker's royalty was a substantial 25 per cent. Six months later, the firm offered another £500 for a spring 1911 novel, 'on the same terms as the author's "Fame" '. Similarly, in December 1909 Mills & Boon approached Horace W. C. Newte with an offer for his next three novels after *Calico Jack* (his Mills & Boon debut), including a £250 advance for the first novel, rising to £300 for the subsequent titles.

In these cases, the investments paid off. *Fame*, published in 1910, sold out its 7,500-copy, six-shilling edition. In 1913 a new sixpenny, paper-covered edition sold 8,762 of 10,000 copies. Mills & Boon published several editions of Newte's *Calico Jack* (1910) and *Sparrows* (1910, but first published by Alston Rivers in 1909), and a new novel, *The Lonely Lovers* (1911). All performed extremely well: *Calico Jack* sold 34,288 copies of 43,000 printed; *Sparrows* ran through 11 one-shilling editions between June 1910 and March 1915, and sold all 90,000 copies. Small wonder that an early advertisement of 'Mills & Boon Gossip' revealed that *Sparrows* had attracted three million readers (although no mention was made of the previous publisher's edition). Among fan letters received was one from New Zealand in 1911, which attested to the wide distribution of Mills & Boon's 'Colonial Editions':

> Having read the book Sparrows, I like it very much. I think it is a smartly
> written story and very interesting reading. There is one thing however I
> would like to know. How did you get the picture of the girl cover who I

presume is Mavis Keeves. Did you get it from a photo or was it taken from the living original. I am very curious to know as I have never seen a more beautifull [*sic*] picture and I should like to know if it was once a flesh and blood original. I am sending a stamped and addressed envelope for reply if you would kindly let me know who and what the girl is, trusting it will not put you to any trouble you will oblige.

While it is not known whether Mills & Boon replied, in later years the firm would place great stock by colourful dust jackets as an important sales tool.

❧

Gerald Mills, in charge of the educational and non-fiction lists, pursued a similar policy regarding 'names'. He often commissioned academic teachers to write textbooks on mathematics or chemistry, thereby ensuring that the published works would become set texts and reach large markets. An early advertisement named Eton, Harrow, and Sandhurst in a 'List of Schools and Colleges in which Mills & Boon's books are used'. One such prominent teacher was F. C. Boon, Principal Mathematical Master at Dulwich College. Boon (no relation) was previously published by Methuen, who issued his *A Commercial Geography of Foreign Nations* in 1901. Among his 1*s*. books for Mills & Boon were *Preparatory Arithmetic, Arithmetic for Schools and Colleges*, and *A Public School Arithmetic*. Books were offered for sale with or without answers and, oddly, often included a catalogue of Mills & Boon novels at the back. The educational list generally had larger print runs, and higher sales. *Practical Mathematics and Drawing* by W. E. Harrison, for example, ran through eight editions between 1910 and 1914. Of 12,700 copies printed, 9,363 were sold.

Building upon Gerald Mills's expertise—and contacts—Mills & Boon in 1909 purchased the rights to forty-four educational books from Mills's old employers, Whitaker & Co. 'I don't think many of their books were much good,' John Boon noted. 'But as so often seems to happen in publishing, some of the first books you do are very successful.' These included *Nerves and the Nervous* and *Mental Self-Help* by Edwin L. Ash, who was described as 'a specialist on the problem of nervous breakdown'. In a catalogue entry, Mills & Boon hailed the latter as an important book, noting, 'Want of nerve-tone, leading in many cases to serious nervous exhaustion—neurasthenia—is an important factor in reducing the nation's "driving-force" at the present time.' The *Daily Express* called *Nerves* 'One of the most refreshing books published for some time. Dr Ash not only probes into exactly what one feels when one is nervous or worried, but the treatment is so free from fads that it does even an unnervy person good.'[8] *Nerves* sold out its first edition of 1,000 copies in 1911, and was reprinted nearly every year.

'I think Mills looked after the Educational list side sensibly,' Alan Boon said. 'If he had been more successful, it could have altered the firm's history. Educational list books tend to sell like that, go on forever. But there wasn't much there. The old man had much more initiative than Mills.'

That initiative can be seen in the lively and extensive catalogues which Mills & Boon have used from the start to advertise its publication list. Reprinted at the back of its books, the catalogue made a direct, personal appeal to the reader. One of the first, published in June 1909, opened with the following message:

> Messrs. Mills & Boon are publishing novels by the most popular writers of the day. They will be glad to send their lists, giving full particulars of their new books, post free to any address. They have many new ventures in preparation, including a number of books in General Literature.
>
> Colonial Editions are issued of all Messrs. Mills & Boon's Novels, and of most of their books in General Literature.

The fourteen-page catalogue was dominated by fiction, with twenty-six *6s.* novels listed, including *Orpheus in Mayfair* by Maurice Baring and *The Adventures of Captain Jack* by Max Pemberton. Robert Barr's *Cardillac*—another Methuen reprint—dominated an entire page, and included the reader's report: 'A work of which I have read every word for the sheer pleasure of reading'.

Judging from the sales statistics, this hype was effective. *Orpheus in Mayfair* sold out its 1,500-copy run. *The Adventures of Captain Jack* sold 3,186 of 3,500 copies over three editions, backed by the distribution of 7,500 prospectuses. Five *6s.* editions of *Cardillac* were printed in 1909, totalling 6,000 copies, of which more than half were sold.

The catalogue also highlighted the first of the Mills & Boon 'Library' series, which, in their success, served to promote the Mills & Boon name and imprint, and offer useful lessons in series publishing. The 'Mills & Boon's Laughter Library' featured the one-shilling titles *Proofs before Pulping* and *The Diary of a Baby* by Barry Pain, another Methuen author. 'All readers who like wit and laughter should make a point of purchasing this splendid selection,' Mills & Boon recommended. Praise was generous from the *Bookseller*:

> A decidedly happy idea is that of the 'Laughter Library' of which the young and enterprising firm of Mills & Boon is just issuing the earliest volumes. In times of financial and meteorological gloom, like those we have recently experienced, it will be a fine thing to have a row or two of bookshelves allotted to a uniform series of tested and approved laughtermakers. . . . the 'Laughter Library' should come as a boon and a blessing to all sufferers from doleful dumps.

The *Sphere* agreed, calling the series 'ideal books for railway travellers and should prove a great success'. It was: *Draw in Your Stool* by Oliver Onions (1909), for example, sold out its 1,500-copy edition. *The Bolster Book: A Book for the Bedside (Compiled from the Occasional Writings of Reginald Drake Biffin)* by 'Captain' Harry Graham, ran through four editions from 1910 to 1912, with sales of 5,290 copies, out of 6,000 printed—including some bound for sale in the United States.

Another successful Mills & Boon series—and one with a clever gimmick—was the 'June 15 Novel'. This particular title, published each year on 15 June (a date selected for no apparent reason), was heralded as a major discovery of a new, first-time author. The first June 15 Novel was *The Veil: A Romance of Tunisia* by Ethel Stevana (E. S.) Stevens, brought to Mills & Boon by her agent, Hughes Massie. *The Veil* featured a fancy decorated cover with sheiks and an African street scene. Seven editions of *The Veil* sold out, totaling 7,000 copies. In 1910 a one-shilling paper-covered edition also sold out its 10,000-copy run. In 1913 Charles Boon, looking back on the firm's success, praised Stevens and her debut novel, which 'came to us through quite the usual channels' and 'achieved an unusual success'.

By most accounts, these early years of Mills & Boon were successful and prosperous ones for the new firm. Although statistics for this period are incomplete, the trends are upward (see Fig. 1.1). Turnover in Mills & Boon's first full year, 1909–10, amounted to £16,650, which generated a small profit of £125. By way of comparison, the trading profit of Hodder & Stoughton in 1912, after meeting all expenses, was £13,446, after a record turnover of £179,636. No wonder: in 1912 Hodder published *The Scarlet Pimpernel* by Baroness Orczy and *Peter Pan and Wendy* by J. M. Barrie. At Mills & Boon's annual general meeting in 1910, the Board approved salary increases for all employees, and a dividend of 2.5 per cent was paid to all shareholders. Bonuses were also paid as a percentage of annual profits. Although the available statistics for the number of books sold are incomplete, they none the less correlate with the profit picture (see Fig. 1.2). In this case, sales of first, 6s. edition fiction display a healthy growth through 1912, with a modest decline by the outbreak of the First World War.

Before long, Mills & Boon moved offices. 'Compelled by the growth of their business', reported the *Newsagent*, Mills & Boon rented larger premises at 49 Rupert Street, just north of their first location. They would remain here for twenty years. The number of shareholders also increased. In February 1911 the future Mrs Charles Boon, Mary Alice Cowpe of Burnley, Lancashire, applied for 300 shares. Since Boon had still not paid for 230 of his original 1,250 shares, these were transferred to Miss Cowpe, an apparently

Figure 1.1
Annual Net Profit of Mills & Boon, Ltd., 1910–1914

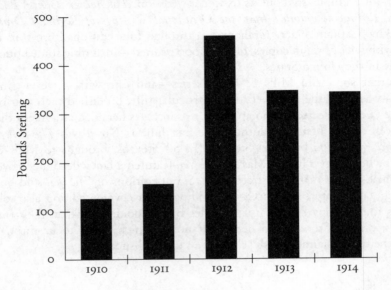

Figure 1.2
Annual First Edition Fiction Sales of Mills & Boon, Ltd., 1909–1914

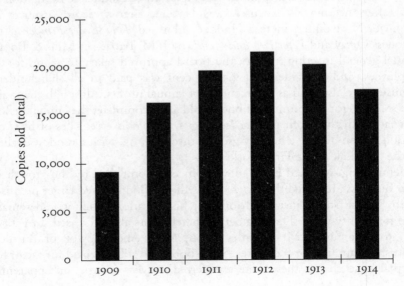

well-to-do woman. They were married on 1 June 1911. By October, Boon transferred another 250 shares to the now 'Mrs M. A. Boon'. Bailing her future husband out of trouble in this way was, in some respects, a romantic gesture by Mrs Boon worthy of a Mills & Boon romance. Not to be outdone, Mrs Gerald Mills bought 250 shares herself in 1919.

Their father's early success amazed the Boon sons, who would assume control of the prosperous firm in the 1940s. 'My Father had no intellectual interest in books, which was perhaps an asset,' Alan Boon said. 'He stuck to entertainment. He had a natural talent for this business.' Added John Boon, 'They started up together, with great heart-searching, everybody telling them they were going to fail.' The firm admitted as much in a 1910 press statement:

> It was an adventure, this starting a new firm of publishers, eighteen months ago, when trade was bad and political controversy the order of the day. Everybody whom we met was full of doubts and warnings. Yes, it was an adventure, but it has been so far successful beyond expectation. We have not only enjoyed the excitement of it, but we have found the results financially excellent.

⚜

Throughout Mills & Boon's first decade, notices of the firm and reviews of its first books and publication list in the press were generally favourable, and in some cases positively ecstatic. During his sales career at Methuen, Charles Boon undoubtedly had made many friends in the media, and might even have called in a favour or two to generate some positive publicity. 'Many new publishing houses are springing into existence, and among the more promising are Messrs. Mills and Boon,' wrote the critic in *Black & White* in 1909. 'They have made up their mind to please the great reading public, and are going about it in the right way.' The house was gaining a reputation. 'No firm has come so boldly to the front in such a short time as that of Mills and Boon,' a critic in the *Sphere* wrote in 1910:

> At first I thought that they were only going to 'tackle' fiction. This would have distressed me greatly as any publisher can issue fiction but not every publisher can judiciously select books of another character. Such a book as Mr E. S. Graw's *The Court of William III*, is the kind of book that really fills a gap, and I trust that Messrs. Mills and Boon will issue many more such books. This firm also has an eye on the kind of book which is said to make publishers rich in an unostentatious manner—*The Poultrykeeper's Companion*, for example, and even *The Aviator's Companion*.

But the critic in the *Croydon Chronicle* singled out novels: 'Those who desire to ensure good reading can adopt no better device than that of procuring one

of Messrs. Mills and Boon's new lists, and of sending it to their bookseller or
library with instructions to supply them in the order of rotation marked.' No
publisher could ask for higher praise.

Good publicity did not come by accident. Selling books was what Charles
Boon knew and did best. While Mills kept an eye on the finances and contracts, Boon displayed his innate genius for marketing and promotion, lay-
ing the foundations for what were later recognized as Mills & Boon
trademarks. To generate interest, Mills & Boon (like other publishers) distributed prospectuses and sample chapters as teasers. When E. S. Stevens's
follow-up novel to *The Veil, The Mountain of God*, was published in 1911,
Mills & Boon offered to send 'a souvenir chapter' post-free to any address.
That title sold 10,172 of 12,000 copies in three editions. In 1910 the
Newsagent singled out a Mills & Boon innovation:

> For so young a firm Messrs. Mills & Boon have made rapid strides. They
> have, as we said last week, issued some most successful novels, and their
> shilling series is going remarkably well. Among the many up-to-date
> methods of helping sales is the system they have established of sending
> to retailers for window-dressing purposes reproductions of the covers
> of their books. They also make up a special cash parcel of the shilling
> books, and we would advise retailers to write to them for particulars.

Window displays of book covers are common marketing practice today, but
Mills & Boon may have pioneered this. The 'attractive picture covers', the
Newsagent added, 'readily attract attention'. The covers of Horace Newte's
novels, for example, featured renditions of ladies with full, pouting lips and
penetrating gazes. The cover of *The German Spy System in France* by M. Paul
Lanoir (1910) was equally dramatic, with lines radiating outwards on a map
of Europe, stretching from Berlin across points in France. On publication
day, the *Daily Mirror* issued a long, news-type review of the book, which
claimed that up to 25,000 spies were at the disposal of German secret police,
15,000 stationed at fixed posts in France, and wrote of 'the enormous advantages such practices confer on a nation contemplating offensive war'. Sensational, perhaps, but effective: the first, 5s. edition sold 656 of 1,000 copies,
but the next two, 6d. paper-covered editions sold out all 8,150 copies.

The firm's so-called 'personal touch', a direct approach to the reader made
in statements in catalogues and advertisements, was always at the forefront.
This attention to readers, and insistence that books were carefully chosen
(almost guaranteed), may not have been unique among publishing houses,
but Mills & Boon used it to great marketing advantage to distinguish its titles
among the (increasingly vast) sea of publishers' offerings. In Mills & Boon's
1911 catalogue, for example, in a display for Gilbert Watson's *Toddie* (the
story of a caddie and his dog), the reader was told, 'TODDIE as a humorous
novel is the real thing; charming, tender, pathetic, romantic. MILLS & BOON'S

reader reported that he had read TODDIE at one sitting and then turned back and read it all over again.' Here then, reader, was a book you were bound to enjoy. *Toddie* sold 2,265 of 3,000 copies, an above-average performance.

※

Series publishing remained the major growth area of the Mills & Boon list. This experience in promoting series—and, indirectly, the Mills & Boon imprint—would prove vital later in Charles Boon's career, when Mills & Boon would make the transition from a general to a specialized publishing house in the 1930s.

Mills & Boon's new branded book series attracted much attention in the trade. Different series covered careers, thrillers, plays, travel, and children. The 'Companion Series', for example, comprised inexpensive (2s. 6d.) volumes which dispensed advice and instruction on a variety of professions and roles of appeal to both urban and country readers, including the chauffeur, gardener, six-handicap golfer, mother, lady motorist, dramatic author, and rifleman. Designed as a 'series of practical handbooks', each written by an expert in the field and in 'simple and untechnical language', Mills & Boon were 'confident that they will—in fact, those published already *do*—appeal to that large class who want an easily read and instructive book written by a person who thoroughly understands the subject he or she is writing about.' Sales were good, if not outstanding. *The Bee-Keeper's Companion* by Stephen Abbott (1911), for example, sold 917 of 1,500 copies.

On the heels of the successful 'Laughter Library' was the 'Thrilling Adventure Library'. Not surprisingly, Mills & Boon sought to tap into a large and growing market for detective and adventure fiction, always the most popular of genres. In the catalogue, the firm explained the venture in another direct, friendly appeal to readers, pledging to resist 'the writers of "shilling Shockers" ':

> Whilst entirely avoiding this most objectionable class, Messrs. Mills & Boon have decided to produce a special Library containing only really good thrilling adventure novels, whether written by deservedly popular authors or by those who await an opportunity to become so.

Among the first six-shilling titles 'of the highest possible excellence' were *The Phantom of the Opera* by Gaston Leroux, *The Lady Calpurnia Royal* by Albert Dorrington and A. G. Stephens ('the noted Australian Authors'), and *The Kingdom of Earth* by Anthony Partridge. The enterprise paid off handsomely: *Phantom*, for example, sold out its 2,000-copy edition, thanks in part to 5,000 prospectuses distributed.

It is no surprise that Mills & Boon published a popular series of 'Novels of the Plays', for one of Charles and Mary Boon's favourite pastimes was the theatre. 'Father liked the Haymarket comedies,' Alan Boon said. 'They had no great literary merit but a popular appeal.' In a 1911 catalogue Mills & Boon said it was 'gratified that their Novels of the Plays series has been received with remarkable favour':

> Their idea in initiating this venture was to give readers who prefer to read the story of a popular play before seeing it a chance of doing this at a very cheap price of 1s. net. Lovers of the theatre who are so unfortunate as to live in remote parts can now read many of the popular plays in novel form, and are therefore put on an equality with the ordinary theatregoer. Thousands of invalids who never have a chance of going to the theatre can now read by their fireside many of the most successful plays of recent years. Mills & Boon are making arrangements to issue simultaneously with the London production many forthcoming plays in novel form.

The appeal to invalids is one Mills & Boon will make again in the 1950s in pitching its popular romances to bedridden hospital patients desirous of an 'escape'. Among the first 'Novels of the Plays' published were *Arsène Lupin: The Duke and the Burglar* by Edgar Jepson and Maurice LeBlanc, *Peter Pan, Retold In Story Form From J. M. Barrie's Dramatic Fantasy*, by G. D. Drennan,[9] and George Edwardes's *The Quaker Girl*, 'which is playing to crowded houses at the Adelphi Theatre, London'. Of *Arsène Lupin*, 'now thrilling audiences at the Duke of York's', *Black and White* praised, 'I defy anyone who starts reading it to put it by until he has reached page 344, and then he will stop because that is the last page.' Sales were outstanding. *Arsène Lupin*, for example, ran through seven editions between 1909 and 1914. For the first, 2,000-strong, 6s. edition, 1,600 copies were sold—with Mills & Boon printing 8,000 prospectuses and 10,000 postcards. The publicity paid off. Of the six cheaper, 1s. editions, all 21,000 copies sold out: 11,000 in January and February 1910 alone.

※

One of Charles Boon's passions was finding new talent, and his knack for literary discoveries, particularly women authors, continued to generate publicity. The principal show window remained the 'June 15 Novels' series. The second year brought a major discovery: Ida Alexa Ray Wylie, sent to Mills & Boon by her agent, Hughes Massie. Her debut, *The Rajah's People* (1910), was a big seller and instantly established Wylie as a popular author. The *Bystander* praised:

> A finer Indian novel than I. A. R. Wylie's *The Rajah's People* . . . it has never been my lot to read. And it is a first novel—further proof, if any were needed, of the good service Messrs. Mills and Boon are doing in giving

new authors a chance of making a name . . . There is love, pathos, and excitement admirably blended, and interest is sustained throughout.

The *Sunday School Chronicle* agreed (even if it mistook the title): 'That energetic firm Mills and Boon, whose novel *The Veil* was one of the successes of last spring, appear to have made another hit with *The Rajah's Daughter* [*sic*], which was published only a few weeks ago and is already in a fourth edition.'

In her memoirs, Australian-born Wylie recalled the experience of her first novel: 'I had no literary connections. I wouldn't have recognized an editor or a publisher if I'd seen one. On my first appearance in a publisher's office . . . I shook hands with an office boy by mistake,' presumably Henley.[10] Fortunately for Mills & Boon, *The Rajah's People* was the sort of title publishers dream about: it sold out all 14,000 copies printed over ten editions in two years, thanks, no doubt, to Mills & Boon's publicity boost of 10,000 postcards and 4,000 souvenir chapters. By her third novel, *The Red Mirage* (1913), Wylie had become a darling of the media. The *Books Of To-morrow* even composed a poem about it, called, appropriately, 'Everybody's Reading It'. Among the (many) couplets were these, which targeted holiday-makers and lovers of light fiction:

> For energetic souls who long
> To read adventure hot and strong,
> And loathe the tale that tends to soothe
> The course of love that runs too smooth
>
> .   .   .   .   .   .
>
> We know a book by Mrs. Wylie
> And recommend it very hylie
>
> .   .   .   .   .   .
>
> You'll want upon your holiday
> At Brighton, Cromer, Douglas, Bray,
> Ostend, St. Malo, Paris, Plage,
> Southend-on-Sea—*The Red Mirage*.
> So buy it now and read it soon
> You'll find it is a (Mills and) Boon.

Subsequent June 15 Novels included *When the Red Gods Call* by the Irish novelist Beatrice Grimshaw (1911, sent by Curtis Brown); a second novel by Wylie (breaking the format), *The Daughter of Brahma* (1912); and, in 1913, *The Man from Nowhere*, the first novel by Victor Bridges. Of the latter, Boon admitted that this 'unknown male author' was a departure for a series dominated by female authors, but Bridges's success, he predicted, would make 1913 'a man's year'. Indeed it was: the title sold out its first two editions, over 8,000 copies, in just three months. The third, 1s. edition, published in 1914, sold another 4,441 copies.

Building upon the June 15 Novels gimmick, Mills & Boon promoted itself as the promised land for new writers. All publishers welcomed new writers, but Mills & Boon put the request in writing, both in print advertisements and in the back of its books at the beginning of the catalogue. This worked: the *Daily Citizen* in 1913 called Mills & Boon 'a publishing house which from its inception has made the discovery of new authors a *sine qua non* of its existence'.

In 1912, for example, the firm received 1,000 manuscripts for review, 75 per cent of them from women, and 95 per cent from unknown authors. The predominance of women authors was noted. True to its promise, the editors claimed to have read every one. 'Of the whole number, no more than six books were actually published by us,' Charles Boon revealed in an interview. 'You can therefore imagine the tremendous competition which authorship of the six-shilling novel is undergoing at the present time.'[11] Six out of 1,000 was probably an underestimate, but it made good advertisement copy.

Charles Boon paid close attention to the readers who purchased or borrowed his books. Mills & Boon's impressive performance in these early years attracted attention, and Boon, a showman of sorts, seemed to enjoy the opportunity to 'talk shop'. In 1913 the *Daily Citizen* profiled three of the young publishing houses: Mills & Boon, T. Werner Laurie, and Stanley Paul. The newspaper, noting that 'We have reached the age of the new author', wondered where he could be found. Mills & Boon, profiled first, was cited as a discoverer of new talent. 'It is the new author who makes the publisher's life so exciting and interesting,' Charles Boon said. 'The Stock Exchange can boast of no greater gamble.' Boon proceeded:

> It is, by the way, the author whose name reaches the public first through the medium of the magazines who stands an excellent chance of obtaining publicity for more ambitious work. Many novelists have commenced in quite a small way by first contributing to the magazines, a type of work in which strength, style, and execution are essential qualities.

Similarly, after the Second World War, Boon's son Alan would ground the firm's recovery on authors of romantic fiction who were published first in popular women's magazines such as *Woman's Weekly*, and therefore already had a considerable public following. It is significant that, at an Extraordinary General Meeting of the firm in 1916, it was resolved that Boon 'be empowered to act as agent for the purpose of selling the serial rights of novels by Mills & Boon's authors on the understanding that all payments for the sale of these serials be made direct to the firm, and that Mr Boon shall pay the firm a commission of 5% of the amount he receives for his services in selling these serials.' This was a milestone, given Mills & Boon's future dependence on the revenue from serial rights as well as the publicity from serial publication, and shows how mutually beneficial the magazine and book publishing industries were at this time, as they have been throughout the twentieth century.

Charles Boon also recognized that his future success was dependent on catering to the tastes of female readers. In 1913 he echoed the opinions of Hall Caine (whose Manx-themed adventure novels rivalled Marie Corelli's work in popularity). In a speech to the Associated Booksellers, Caine had said, 'If you want to know what a great, wide public is going to say about a book, try it on a woman.' Boon entirely agreed:

> 'So far as woman's criticism of novels is concerned,' he said yesterday to a representative of *The Daily Citizen*, 'I am certain that to-day the bulk of novels published are devoured by women before they reach the men.
>
> 'The great majority of the circulating libraries' readers are women, and these are quick to know a good book from a poor one, and do not fail to advise their friends accordingly. Men are not so much readers of novels as they used to be, and when they take one up it is generally because one of their women-folk has spoken highly of it. Of course, the sale of a novel is always influenced somewhat by newspaper criticisms; but I believe it is still more assured by its women readers.'
>
> 'Men,' added Mr. Boon, 'are not writing so much fiction as in past years, while the woman writer is immensely on the increase. Woman is doing really distinguished work in the realm of fiction, and there can be no doubt that, as time goes on, the number of women's names on our roll of honoured novelists will be very considerable. Men are running away from novel-writing. Perhaps they are not to be blamed, since the majority of them do not look upon it as sufficiently remunerative work. But publishers ought to be very grateful to women for taking their place with such excellent results.[12]

We have seen Mills & Boon's success with Sophie Cole, E. S. Stevens, I. A. R. Wylie, and other female authors, and have noted Boon's remarks on the female complexion of the firm's 'slush' pile of unsolicited manuscripts. Given the fact that Mills & Boon's future success depended on the work of women novelists, Boon's remarks here could not have been more prophetic.

But it was Boon's contemporary—and rival—Stanley Paul who spoke with robust enthusiasm for this new generation of publishers, 'enterprising firms' who 'have thrown open a wide door to the unpublished genius':

> Before our time publishers were too conservative to admit many new names to their lists; one a year was probably the limit. They looked upon him with suspicion, realising that he represented a possible loss. But different ages, different methods. We realise that the discovery of a new author is essential to the welfare of a publishing house. Consequently, we welcome him, and, when we have found him, use up-to-date methods to give him the publicity his work needs.

Paul added that the woman writer was 'far ahead of her male rivals' in this field; 'She is more enterprising and much more devoted to detail.' Stanley Paul was a top salesman (like Boon) at Hutchinson before he left to start his own firm in 1906.[13]

This attention to women authors may explain a curious publishing experiment by Mills & Boon in 1912, a first novel which attracted much attention, but which was not part of the June 15 Series. This was *Golden Vanity* by the so-called 'Shopgirl Novelist', Maisie Bennett (real name: Edith May Mayer-Nixson). Bennett, 21, worked as the librarian in a circulating library in a large store. She wrote her novel in her spare time, and an agent sold it to Mills & Boon. It was an instant hit with critics, and Mills & Boon subsequently announced it would grant Bennett one year's 'freedom' to write a second novel. This was just the sort of publicity stunt that the press loved. The *Daily News and Leader* noted that, in light of the recent suicide of a prominent poet and story writer who despaired finding conditions in which to work, 'it is worth recording that one courageous firm of publishers, because they think they have discovered a new writer, have taken her away from the office drudgery amid which her first novel was produced, and have given her leisure and security for future work.' The *Nottingham Guardian* called *Golden Vanity* a novel of 'very exceptional power'.

Golden Vanity is of additional interest given its structure and storyline, a precursor of the 1920s Mills & Boon romance. Small wonder Charles Boon published this title: its author, as a library worker, knew what her readers expected in a romance: high drama and throbbing passion, in the style of Elinor Glyn or E. M. Hull. In this novel, the 7-year-old heroine, Jeanette Pierce, meets the hero, Donald Brennan Scott, also 7, in an orphanage. They escape, part company, and grow up. Jeanette becomes an actress; Donald is a writer whose books become, not surprisingly, staples in the libraries (in one scene, the Princess of Wales opens one of his books on display at a charity bazaar).[14] Needless to say, Jeanette and Donald share a great romance. A future trademark of the Mills & Boon romance, which Alan Boon would call 'the punishing kiss', is apparent when the lovers embrace:

> He took a step forward before she could realise his intention, and caught her and held her so closely that she felt the beating of his heart and the strong vibration of his voice.... Her will vanished the rising blush, but the strong effort turned her giddy.
>
> 'I am going to kiss you,' he said, in a voice she hardly recognised.
>
> He might have said that he was going to kill her in the same tone. And again the blood in her veins turned to flame and scorched her, as he kissed her full and closely on the mouth.

Golden Vanity performed well for a first novel, selling all 1,500 copies printed in the first edition, earning the author a 10 per cent royalty. But it was not reprinted, and there is no evidence that Bennett wrote or published the much-anticipated second novel, despite the sum of £78 earmarked for Bennett's 'freedom', payable in installments of £6 10*s*. None the less, such public displays of generosity to authors of talent would become a hallmark of Mills & Boon.

✌

Mills & Boon continued to pay, sometimes dearly, for established popular authors for their fiction list. Among the stars whose novels were published by the firm before the First World War were E. F. Benson (*The Room in the Tower and Other Stories*), H. DeVere Stacpoole (*The Order of Release*), William Le Queux (*The Czar's Spy*), Marie Van Vorst (*The Two Faces*), and Hugh Walpole (*Mr. Perrin and Mr. Traill*). In 1911 the *Newsagent* praised this strategy: 'The bookseller who likes to give his customers sound reading would do well to look through Messrs. Mills and Boon's list.' The *Planet* agreed, on reviewing Walpole's novel: 'It is an admirable work, observant and restrained, and will constitute another "success" for Messrs. Mills & Boon, who produce "successes" with a regularity that becomes almost monotonous.'

In a somewhat daring strike, Mills & Boon signed up P. G. Wodehouse, through an agent, for a single novel in 1911. Contract terms were fairly standard: Wodehouse earned a £25 advance and 10 per cent on the first 1,500 copies sold. The book, *The Prince and Betty*, was a hit with the public, selling out a single edition of 1,000 copies in 1912. Although Wodehouse's tenure with Mills & Boon was brief, it was historic: *The Prince and Betty* was the only one of Wodehouse's many novels to appear in two completely different versions by the author that shared the same title. The first version, about gangsters in Manhattan, was published in March 1912 in the United States by W. J. Watt & Co., while in May, Mills & Boon's version appeared—as a love story. Wodehouse's next publisher was Herbert Jenkins.

Perhaps Mills & Boon's greatest coup as a young publishing house was in signing up Jack London, the 'American Kipling', author of the best-sellers *Call of the Wild* and *White Fang*. London was the first in a long line of popular and prolific Mills & Boon authors who sold well and allowed the firm the financial security to continue to publish widely and to experiment with the rest of its list.

Just how Jack London extended an exclusive contract to Mills & Boon to publish his books in Britain, Australia, and New Zealand is a story in itself. Methuen published *White Fang* in 1907. Charles Boon would have worked on this title, brought to Methuen by London's agent, A. P. Watt. But the experience was not a happy one. Methuen issued a colonial edition, for sale in Canada, Australia, and New Zealand, without London's permission, and to the consternation of his American publisher, Macmillan, which held these rights. Whether Charles Boon was involved in this mishap is uncertain, and Methuen paid London a large sum for damages. London, in turn, arranged for Macmillan to relinquish Australian and New Zealand rights so as to make selling his books easier to a London publisher.

The matter was settled, but Methuen decided to drop Jack London, apparently because Sir Algernon only wanted to publish London's 'animal' books such as *Call of the Wild*, and not his next effort, the 'socialist' title *The Iron Heel*. Apparently the Methuen experience was so distasteful that London let his agent know that he would shop around for a new publisher. In July 1909 he wrote to A. P. Watt, 'Regarding my books, I intend to settle down with one publisher, and under a general contract with him handle the book-publication of all my books.'[15] Later that year he enlisted Hughes Massie as his new agent.

But London's experience with his next publisher, Heinemann, was just as poor. By the time London's contract was torn up in anger in April 1911, Heinemann was accused of theft, incompetence, and greed. 'There is a whole string of my books recently published in the United States which you somehow are not managing to bring out in England,' London complained in December 1910. 'I don't see how you are ever going to keep up with me at the present rate of your going.' Apparently Heinemann was ten titles behind schedule. When the firm refused to sanction the sale of cheap editions to Thomas Nelson and Sons ('This means a good fistful of money to me,' London complained), London tore up his contract, told Massie to retrieve his manuscripts, and resumed his search for a publisher.

In the end, Mills & Boon's personal attention and vigorous publishing schedule suited London perfectly. 'Let me deal with a man,' a furious London wrote in January 1911. 'Let me deal with somebody who has enough decency to tell me what is being done with my stuff, what books are being published, what books are proposed to be published, etc., etc.' Hughes Massie knew Mills & Boon well, as he represented a number of its authors, including E. S. Stevens, I. A. R. Wylie, and Massie's stepson, Sinclair Gluck. A deal was struck, and in September 1911 Mills & Boon offered its first of many contracts to London, for *When God Laughs*. Terms were more than generous: a £100 advance, with a 20 per cent royalty on all copies to 5,000, and 25 per cent thereafter, with the promise of a 1*s*. edition within two years, and a 6*d*. edition within three years. London's contract terms steadily increased. For *The Valley of the Moon*, his advance increased to £200; for *John Barleycorn, or, Alcoholic Memoirs*, £250.

'I do get the impression that we had very good relations with Jack London,' Alan Boon said. Apparently Jack London himself was pleased, given the fan letter and autographed photo kept in the Mills & Boon archives. Dated 31 October 1914 and posted from Glen Ellen, his estate in California, London wrote:

Gentlemen: In reply to yours of Sept. 26, 1914, which finds me cruising on my yacht and hammering away at the closing chapters of my latest novel, THE LITTLE LADY OF THE BIG HOUSE. Indeed, as I have written to Mr. Massie more than once, you have done splendidly by me in making me popular in England. I haven't a word of complaint to make; but I do have many hearty words of thanks. Too bad this war has come along and knocked everything into disorder.

In March 1914 London wrote to Massie regarding bids he had received from other English publishers: 'I shall of course forward to [you] any propositions from other English publishers concerning my work. I cannot but feel heartily convinced that Mills & Boon are doing splendidly by me, and that they should reap, by later books, what they are now sowing.'[16]

Small wonder London was so pleased: unlike Methuen, Mills & Boon took everything, seemingly without question as to subject matter or likely profit. Of London's 49 published works, Mills & Boon published 36 for sale in Britain, Australia, and New Zealand. 'Mills & Boon publish exclusively for Jack London, whose books need no praise or advertising, for they sell in thousands wherever the English language is spoken,' the firm boasted in a 1914 advertisement. Within two years, Mills & Boon already had nine London titles in print in two editions: 6s. and 1s. They also picked up reprint rights to all previously published London titles, except for the 'animal' stories; they never published *White Fang* or *Call of the Wild* (possibly London's biggest sellers worldwide). In a gesture of friendship, the firm even accepted Mrs Jack (Charmain) London's books, including *Voyaging in the Wild Seas*, *A Woman Among the Headhunters*, and *The New Hawaii*.

There is little doubt that London's books were popular, earning good money and much attention for Mills & Boon. The *Observer* called *The Valley of the Moon* 'one of the finest novels in its own way', and the *Daily Express* said *The House of Pride* 'grips the heart and stirs the imagination'. Demand was heavy for London titles, and Mills & Boon published at least three editions of every work, at several prices. *When God Laughs*, for example, ran to seven editions in two years. Cumulative sales totals were impressive: *God* sold out its 27,000 copies, as did the 15,500 copies of *The Cruise of the Snark* (1913) and 32,000 copies of *Valley of the Moon* (1913).

By the outbreak of the First World War, Mills & Boon's good fortune was evident. Sales, to the general public and to libraries, were good, reviews were better, profits were rising—and the industry was beginning to take notice. This publisher—and its imprint—was gaining a reputation. Indeed, the goal of any publisher is to have his imprint recognized by the public and respected as a kind of guarantee of good reading. The seeds of Mills & Boon's future success as an imprint were planted in these early days, thanks in part to the prominence of the firm's name on its dust jackets, and the promotion of branded book series. As early as 1911, the *Publishers' Circular*, in a glowing review of *The Sea-Lion* by Patrick Rushden, wrote:

> Messrs. Mills & Boon are rapidly coming to the front as the publishers of much of the best fiction of the day. It is a great thing for the publisher's imprint to come to mean 'first-class'; it has happened for some periods in the histories of some publishing houses. What a fortune if it could last![7]

The firm's obvious confidence in its list and its publishing prowess must have been strengthened by the mail it received from the great and the near great. 'Though I have never had the honour of any dealings with you,' G. K. Chesterton wrote in 1912, 'I am, of course, well acquainted with your position in the good opinion of the literary public.' Chesterton proceeded, somewhat meekly, to inquire whether Mills & Boon would consider publishing a friend's poems and articles, 'all of which have that essential quality that ought to sell or be made to sell'. Another admirer (and also an invalid) was Edwin Greene, a composer of popular songs, and a fan of Wylie's novels. 'I would like to tell you that I have for a long time known that when the name of "Mills & Boon" appears as publishers of a book, one is sure and certain of a pleasure in store,' Greene wrote in 1913. 'I have been recommending books from your list for 2 years now. . . . One is so often disillusioned after reading the reviews in Dailies - Never once have I been with any book published by your firm.'

Chapter 2
The Bubble Nearly Bursts, 1914–1928

That authors and publishers cannot be friends
Is an adage as old as the hills,
I can only remark it's a lie in the case
Of V. Bridges Charles Boon and G. Mills!

Victor Bridges in 1922, just before he left for Hodder & Stoughton

I remember old Charles Boon, my publisher, visiting me in Sussex one Sunday. I opened a cupboard in my study to show him a pile of manuscripts. He gave them one glance, then said: 'I'll give you a good cheque now this moment for the rights of the whole lot.' (He mentioned a tempting sum.) But my business sense had developed with the years and I laughingly refused his offer.

'You are right, you know!' said Charles with a twinkle.

I was. I've since made a lot more money with those stories than he offered then.

Denise Robins, on meeting Charles Boon in 1927

THE story of Mills & Boon's next fifteen years is not nearly as rosy as that of the firm's first five years. While it is true that Mills & Boon's early success bolstered its position, enabling it to survive the First World War relatively unscathed, the 1920s would bring a rapid decline in Mills & Boon's fortunes, sending the partners to the brink of bankruptcy.

That the firm's success should unravel so quickly after the war is surprising, considering the fact that the 1920s was a good decade for publishers in Britain. Following the rapid expansion of other leisure activities such as the cinema and radio, publishing was increasingly commercialized, cheaper (and larger) editions proliferated, and advertising was used as never before to promote books as if they were commodities. As sales of cheaper editions increased, orders rose from the expanding libraries, particularly the smaller, 'pay-as-you-read' operations in shops and newsagents, which relied on 'light' fiction. While Mills & Boon exploited the new markets by expanding its fiction list and 'positioning' authors and their books as 'stars', the firm was too small to compete with the bigger houses, which could cushion the financial impact of the decade's industrial disputes with a larger publication list. The firm's very existence was threatened when a wave of consolidation swept the industry, and Hutchinson sought to add Mills & Boon to its list of acquisitions. Even though Mills & Boon still published, and promoted, 'important' books and novels, the trend in the 1920s was towards the commercial sellers, particularly romantic fiction. At the end of the decade, Charles Boon would face the future alone—and have a whole new outlook on the publishing business.

The First World War may have changed trading conditions, but like most publishers, Mills & Boon performed well. As during the Second World War, wartime stimulated reading and the desire to 'escape' with a good book, and demand was up, mainly from the libraries. *The Times*, surveying public libraries across the country in 1917, attributed the reading 'boom' to 'the fact that people seek distraction from the worry of the times in the reading of works of imagination', as well as to restrictions on other leisure activities, such as outdoor sport. Indeed, there is no evidence that the war had a negative impact on Mills & Boon and, for the most part, it was business as usual (see Fig. 2.1). Profits were steady from 1914 to 1917, and hit a record level in 1918. Mills & Boon emerged from the First World War strong, robust, even a little cocky. Its first decade had been, with few exceptions, a resounding success.

Wartime publishing featured more of what the public wanted—namely, novels. A full-page advertisement in the *Evening Standard and St. James's Gazette* in July 1914 targeted holiday-makers: 'There is always a new MILLS & BOON Novel; "You'll want them on your holidays!"' Among the 6s. offerings: Bealah Marie Dix, *Little Faithful*, Constance Holme, *The Lonely Plough*,[1] Mrs George De Horne Vaizey, *Grizel Married*, and Arthur Applin, *Shop Girls*. *Shop Girls*, subtitled 'A Novel with a Purpose', sold extremely well, running through four editions by 1915, and selling out 18,250 copies. Also prominently displayed were Mills & Boon's 'Shilling Cloth Library' ('Thousands selling weekly') and 'Sixpenny Novels', including titles by Jack London, Horace W. C. Newte, Max Pemberton, and Cosmo Hamilton.

The Mills & Boon catalogue in 1915 is an impressive sight, and it is interesting to see how the catalogue had evolved, with books carefully grouped into series and categories. The stock list was vast: 226 novels, some issued at several prices, and 125 works of non-fiction, divided into categories such as, 'For Politicians and Other Readers' (*Captive of the Kaiser in Belgium* by Georges La Barre), 'For the Contemplative Mind' (*The Enclosed Nun* by Anonymous), 'On Matters Theatrical' (*An Actor's Hamlet* by Louis Calvert),

Figure 2.1

Annual Net Profit (Loss) of Mills & Boon, Ltd., 1914–1928

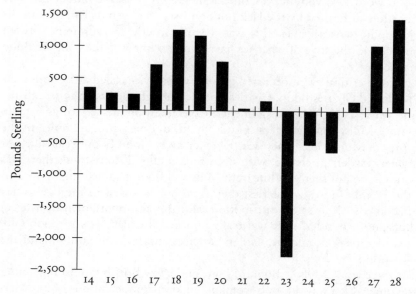

'Romantic History' (*The Petticoat Commando: or, Boer Women in Secret Service* by Johanna Brandt), 'For Everyday Life' (*Household Accounts* by Rupert Deakin and P. J. Humphreys), and 'Sports and Pastimes' (*England v. Australia* by P. F. Warner). Heads of schools were invited to write for specimen copies of 67 educational books, including textbooks on English, French, Geography, Mathematics, Chemistry, and Scripture. Jack London's novels headed up Mills & Boon's export list, heralded as 'The Most Popular Shilling Novels in the World'. These 'shilling' novels, however, were offered at 'a special war price' of 1s. 6d., reflecting current trading conditions.

Within one year, however, problems appeared. The roots of Mills & Boon's decline can be traced to 1916 and two events. First, Jack London died, unexpectedly, aged 40. Such was his impact on the young firm that we can only wonder what might have happened had he lived longer. 'Jack London could have changed our future,' Alan Boon said. 'We would have gone on alone publishing his books.' Given his suspicious nature and distrust of publishers, London probably would have remained with Mills & Boon, where he was apparently quite happy.

Upon London's death, Mills & Boon (taking advantage, no doubt, of public sympathy) reissued all of London's titles. In 1920 Jack London was cited by W. H. Smith's wholesale book department as one of the company's top-selling authors, ranking alongside Kathryn Rhodes, Freeman Mills Young, and Zane Grey. Charles Boon maintained close contact with London's widow, Charmain, and in 1921 Mills & Boon published her massive, 250,000-word, two-volume, 36s. official biography of Jack London, 'the only publication authorised by the Jack London Estate'. Given its length, and the hagiographic writing style, this was a work strictly for admirers, written (ironically) in the style of what we have come to know as the Mills & Boon romance.

A second critical event occurred in 1916: war service called away both Gerald Mills and Charles Boon. Charles Boon, although aged 39 in 1916, enlisted in the Royal Navy, with assignment to the hydrophone service as a radio operator.[2] Mills, apparently less physically fit, did his national service in the Ministry of Munitions. 'They were all taken away,' John Boon recalled. 'Aunt Margaret was left in charge, with disastrous results. I don't think there was anyone else to put there.' While both Mills and Boon retained their positions on the Board, and their salaries, they were not involved in the day-to-day transactions such as sales, distribution, and the all-important nurturing of authors and new titles. 'The war really knocked the firm for six,' Boon said. 'It lacked direction, and my father lost his contacts with authors and the book world.'

For three years, Mills & Boon was one of the few British publishing houses at the time which was run by a woman—if an incompetent one. 'Aunt Margaret was gutsy,' John Boon recalled. 'She was very kind to us. She had a really sharp tongue, but a warm heart and a generous spirit.' But, Boon added, it was difficult to know what she did, or what her specific talents were. 'She was a sort of general manager. She did do some proofreading, and she would handle anything in the office, people coming in.'

Clearly, Margaret Boon was an unimaginative leader, a caretaker publisher who maintained the status quo, which was, presumably, her mandate from the Board. Judging from a full-page advertisement in the *Bookseller* in May 1919, nothing much had changed at the firm. Amid 'Mills & Boon's Summer Fiction' and its 'powerful List of Novels', there was no dearth of superlatives: Newte's novels were described as having 'sold in hundreds of thousands'; the Mills & Boon Cheap Popular Reprints were 'Selling in Millions' at three prices: 2s., 1s. 6d., and 1s. 3d. Of Louise Gerard, whose latest novel was *The Mystery of the Golden Lotus*, Mills & Boon wrote, 'A new long novel by an author who is a "best-seller". Everyone reads this popular author's novels, and her cheap popular editions sell in thousands and thousands.' The Jack London collection had grown to an impressive twenty-seven titles. 'It is sheer muscular "chestiness" that wins him his popularity,' noted the *Manchester Guardian*.

But behind these so-called sales of hundreds of thousands of copies lay a major problem. It is true that when the war ended and the Directors returned to full-time service they found a firm with a robust balance sheet and a good performance record. But on closer inspection, they also discovered one million unsold books in storage, a stock whose valuation would have a severe impact on future profits. In her zeal to maintain the status quo Margaret Boon had taken production matters to extremes. Her inexperience led to the accumulation of large stores of reprinted titles, and the firm grew complacent about nurturing talent, losing touch with the literary market. This did not bode well for the future, and a post-war reading public hungry for new titles. Among the items in storage: 250,000 copies of Jack London's *Valley of the Moon* (530 pages, at a cost of just 1s.). John Boon noted that Mills & Boon during the First World War exposed the vicissitudes of small publishers: while larger firms could have compensated for the loss of managerial talent, a firm with a small staff like Mills & Boon could not have continued to perform well without Mr Mills and Mr Boon.

Clearly, Margaret Boon was a competent day-to-day caretaker, but did not have a grasp of publishing and future planning. Quite possibly she was distracted by the affair she was then having with a married man, Frederick Maule, who happened to be the brother-in-law of Sophie Cole. The scandal precipitated Cole's departure from Mills & Boon. Margaret met Maule and his wife, Daisy, through Cole's other sister, Gladys, who typed Cole's manuscripts and delivered them to Mills & Boon for proofreading by Margaret. 'Maule had several clandestine affairs with various people, usually with spinsters who were well off. Margaret probably was,' Betty Richards, Cole's grand-niece, recalled. The affair continued until 1939, when Margaret Boon moved in with Maule, and nursed him for two years, while Daisy lived elsewhere. Richards noted that clues to the affair are scattered throughout Cole's books. In one, for example, a character is called 'Madge'. In another, the hero sports a red Jaeger dressing gown, similar to one that Margaret gave Maule.

Five years before she died in 1947, Sophie Cole left Mills & Boon, and sold the fifty shares in the firm she had bought in 1928. Why? 'Maybe it was because of Margaret Boon and Grandfather,' Richards said. 'Sophie may have been upset. She was very fond of Daisy. Madge had come between her and her husband.'

Certainly there were no hints of concern over Margaret's performance at the 1919 Annual Meeting. Due to the record net profit in 1918 (£1,272, a 60 per cent improvement over the previous year), the Managing Directors awarded themselves a £100 bonus (15 per cent of their salaries), while raising the dividend from six per cent paid in 1918, to 10 per cent, the highest ever. Moreover, the Directors split another £500 bonus between them. There is no record of special compensation given to Margaret Boon.

But analysis of Mills & Boon's balance sheet for the period 1914–28 shows the firm's rapid descent (*see Fig. 2.1*). Progress was steady at the beginning of the First World War, given the initial restrictions imposed by paper rationing, and reached a peak in 1918. The immediate post-war years were a boom time as paper rationing ended in 1919 and business was strong, if production costs had risen. But the bubble started to burst in 1920, with a drastic drop in profits, which fell further in 1921 to just £40, the lowest since 1911. Mills & Boon's first net loss, a gigantic (for them) £2,270, occurred in 1923. Mills & Boon's fortunes would not start to recover until 1926, and the firm would not show a dividend again until 1929.

What happened? Judging from the available statistics, book sales were distinctly lacklustre (*see Figs 2.2 and 2.3*). Sales of first edition fiction peaked in 1919, and then declined at various degrees until 1926. Fiction sales in 1927, 31,518, nearly matched the 1921 figure, 32,064. Educational sales were solid and steady, but a general publisher of Mills & Boon's size could not be supported by non-fiction alone. During a time when publishing was accelerating and industry observers were complaining of the 'overproduction' of books, Mills & Boon was obviously not growing, nor meeting the public demand for new titles, especially fiction. In 1921 Mills & Boon's sales fell by 22 per cent—in a year that Hodder & Stoughton sold 100,000 first edition copies of *If Winter Comes* by A. S. M. Hutchinson. In 1922 sales fell another 17 per cent, and would continue to fall until 1927. At the Annual General

Figure 2.2

Annual First Edition Fiction Sales of Mills & Boon, Ltd., 1914–1928

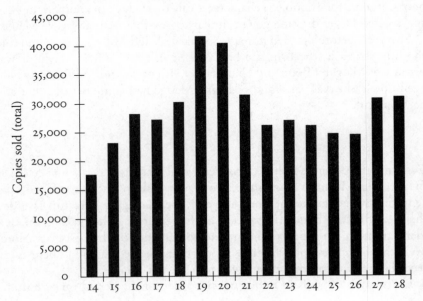

Figure 2.3

Annual Educational Title Sales of Mills & Boon, Ltd., 1922–1928

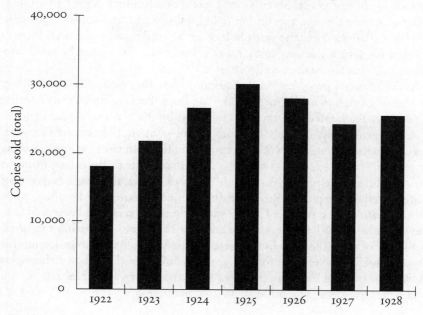

Meeting in March 1925, Mills reported that 'general business' during 1924 had improved, compared to 1923. However, he proceeded:

> owing to the collapse of the two shilling novel (war produced stock) it had been necessary still further to write down the value to such a price as could be obtainable for it. He stated that during the first six months of the year a very considerable loss was made owing to such writing down, but that during the last six months of the year the business had been run on a paying basis. He regretted, however, that the profit made during this period was not sufficient to wipe out the first six months' loss, though it had considerably reduced the deficit. The Net Loss on the year was £530. 2. 0.

A key point should be noted here: by 1924 Mills & Boon was still saddled with war inventory, a legacy of Margaret Boon. 'The valuation of stock had a large impact on annual profit,' noted Gordon Wixley, who worked for Mills & Boon's accountants, Alliott Makepeace, for over forty years. 'Stocks were quite large in those days. Some books were there for years and years.' Alan Boon recalled a lavishly produced (and expensive) hunting diary, which languished for years in the warehouse. 'We'd sell one copy every Christmas,' he said.

Apart from poor sales, there were other problems. For one, the cost of book production had risen after the war. By 1921 the cost of printing and paper had more than doubled since 1914, while binding costs had tripled. Whereas before the war a publisher could sell 500 of 1,000 copies of a single title to break even, after the war 1,800 of 2,000 copies had to be sold. Hence, to offset higher production costs, more books had to be sold. The retail cost of first editions also increased, from 6s. to 7s. 6d.

Amid financial pressures, Mills & Boon, like other publishers, were beset by a series of strikes in the mid-1920s. The Book Packers' and Porters' Strike in October 1925 lasted five months, followed by the General Strike in 1926. In an advertisement in the Christmas Number of the *National Newsagent, Bookseller and Stationer* in November 1925, the firm offered reassurances to its customers: 'MILLS & BOON—BUSINESS AS USUAL. Mills & Boon beg to point out that during the present dispute in the Book Trade, they are in a position to supply all orders promptly.' But at the Annual Meeting in May 1926, Mills did not paint a good picture. Of the 'very serious' Packers' and Porters' Strike, 'the whole of the Wholesalers in the country, the chief Circulating Libraries, and many of the Colonial Houses were unable to purchase books during this long period. The Net Loss for the year as shown by the balance sheet was £628. 0. 8, making with the previous loss carried forward viz. £1135. 16. 5 a total of £1763. 17. 1.' The outlook for 1927 was bleak.

❧

Behind this poor performance lay what was perhaps Mills & Boon's biggest handicap in the 1920s: its size. For other general publishers in Mills & Boon's industry, business was good, if difficult. The economic circumstances of the 1920s allowed a more dense exploitation of the publishing market, due in part to rising living standards. Real wages were growing and spending was up, while the average work week was declining, allowing more leisure time. The social and demographic changes created by the war revealed for publishers a vast, untapped market: the female reader. The age of the women's magazine and the light, largely romantic novel was born.

Throughout the 1920s Mills & Boon faced increasing competition from larger and more established publishers such as Methuen, Macmillan, Collins, and Hodder & Stoughton, who were all expanding their fiction lists. This commercialization of publishing, we have seen, stemmed from a need by all publishers to increase their revenues, to meet spiralling production costs. The target for new fiction was the middle and upper working classes, who patronized the biggest growth market, the circulating libraries. The demand was prodigious in the 1920s for what became known as 'light' fiction, much to the dismay of the literary elite. The cinema intensified the demand for this escapist fiction, often tied in as the 'novel of the film'. 'The largest buyers of bad novels are the libraries,' McMahon Trevor wrote in the *Publishers' Circular* in 1921. Noting that the person with shillings to spend to buy a book was more exacting than one with a few pence to borrow a title, Trevor proposed that 'borrowers "consume" far more novels than buyers; some of them want a fresh book every day, and to meet their exorbitant demand it is necessary to fall back from the good on to the bad, and from the bad to the worse'.

Publishers fed this expanding market with books that were increasingly promoted like any other mass-market commodity, with splashy advertising and much publicity. Methuen's fiction list expanded particularly into the genres of science fiction and Westerns. In 1920 Hutchinson and Hurst & Blackett sold over one million copies of their new 3*s.* 6*d.* fiction series, featuring Ethel M. Dell, Arnold Bennett, and a Mills & Boon author, Dolf Wyllarde. Hodder & Stoughton pushed its 'big 5' novelists—A. S. M. Hutchinson, A. E. W. Mason, John Buchan, 'Sapper', and 'O. Douglas'— while publishing over 100 novels each year in its immensely popular 9*d.* 'Yellow Jackets' series. Launched in 1923, this series produced more than 600 titles before the Second World War, by popular authors such as Edgar Wallace, Ruby M. Ayres, William Le Queux, E. Phillips Oppenheim, Rex Beach, Annie S. Swan, and Margaret Pedlar. Two Mills & Boon defectors in the 1920s, Hugh Walpole and Joan Sutherland, were also on the list, as was a future Mills & Boon star, Berta Ruck. Fuelled by the Yellow Jackets success, Hodder reached its zenith in 1928 with sales of £637,770. Collins also expanded its series of popular detective novels, publishing its first (of many) Agatha Christie title, *The Murder of Roger Ackroyd*, in 1926. In its Autumn 1926 catalogue Collins promoted its list in a very Mills-&-Boonish fashion: 'We have accordingly set a very high standard. Only the best will do. That is why we have today the finest list of Detective Novels in existence.'

Because of Mills & Boon's size, and therefore limited resources, it could not compete with the larger houses, nor afford to hold on to its 'star' authors. The big names gathered during the first decade, such as E. F. Benson and P. G. Wodehouse, were limited to single titles. In 1923 Mills & Boon published Georgette Heyer's third novel, *The Transformation of Philip Jettan*, under the pen-name Stella Martin. This was reprinted in 1929 by her next publisher, Heinemann, under the new title *Powder and Patch*, and with a different ending (Heyer's debut with Heinemann, *These Old Shades* (1926), sold 100,000 copies). Hugh Walpole, who founded the Society of Bookmen in 1921 (of which John Boon was later President), was poached by Macmillan after the war, taking his copyrights with him. Macmillan soon brought out new 3*s.* 6*d.* editions of two Mills & Boon successes, *Mr. Perrin and Mr. Traill* and *The Prelude to Adventure*. 'We put money up for Hugh Walpole to write,' Alan Boon said. 'When he'd been established, he left us.'

Another rising star, I. A. R. Wylie, also left Mills & Boon. When she wrote her first 'adult novel' (as she called it), *Towards Morning*, in 1918, Mills &

Boon apparently objected to its wartime setting, and the effort, she said, to 'explain and excuse Germany'. Wylie wrote about the experience with her 'first publishers' in her memoirs:

> My first publishers were very unsympathetic. Nobody wanted to read about decent, misled Germans. Besides, what they called 'my public' would be disappointed. They liked my adolescent fairy-stories about Sahibs, Mem-Sahibs, ayahs and Bo-trees. On no account was I to write about anything about which I knew anything.

It is interesting to note the strong editorial control that Charles Boon imposed on his authors at this early date, in order to remain focused on 'the public' and what it apparently wanted. To be fair, Boon did allow Wylie to spread her wings in non-fiction travel books, such as *My German Year* and *Rambles in the Black Forest*, both of which were not controversial. Wylie claimed that 'another publisher friend', Newman Flower of Cassells, told her to leave, and she did. 'He'd take a chance with me. But I'd have gone ahead anyhow,' she wrote. Since Mills & Boon 'discovered' Wylie, it could exert a degree of control, unlike, say, with a 'star' author such as Jack London.[3]

Another 'June 15' discovery, Victor Bridges, also left Mills & Boon. His departure was heralded in an advertisement, 'The inevitable has happened! Victor Bridges has moved to Hodder and Stoughton!' Bridges's last title for Mills & Boon was *Greensea Island: A Mystery of the Essex Coast* (1922). 'It's very sad about Victor Bridges,' Alan Boon said. 'They thought he was the new Edgar Wallace.' Ironically, just before his departure, Bridges lauded his publishers and the good relationship, autographing a caricature of himself as follows: 'That authors and publishers cannot be friends | Is an adage as old as the hills, | I can only remark it's a lie in the case | Of V. Bridges Charles Boon and G. Mills!'

Interestingly, the same fate befell even the 'quality' houses such as Hodder & Stoughton. Some authors, for example, did not like to be labelled 'popular' and disliked the uniformity of the Yellow Jackets series, leaving to find other publishers. These included Rose Macaulay, Sinclair Lewis, and Margery Allingham. But Hodder, by its size, could survive these departures; Mills & Boon could not. The firm would learn this lesson the hard way, and find its future success in quantity as much as quality.

We must not imply that, given the firm's poor performance in the 1920s, Mills & Boon lost its nerve and ceased to grow. Quite the contrary: the firm followed the major publishing trends of cheaper editions, targeted markets, and stronger advertising. It also matured. While Mills & Boon still prided itself in promoting and publishing 'important' books, more and more the firm was promoting fiction, and romantic fiction at that, in full-page, bold ads with flashy language. It relied heavily on advertising in all of the daily and Sunday newspapers, from the London *Sunday Times* to the *Glasgow Herald*, as well as the trade journals. Headlines were laden with superlatives. A big seller of 1923, for example, was *The Scarlet Tanager* by J. Aubrey Tyson, which, Mills & Boon proclaimed, had sold 'over 10,000 copies within a very short period' and 'was one of the most popular Mystery novels of 1923'. In 1928 Alice Grant Rosman's *The Window*, 'a delightful romance of England to-day', had, Mills & Boon claimed, 'taken America by storm, 20,000 copies having been sold in six weeks'. In *The Commercial Side of Literature* by Michael Joseph (1925), an intriguing analysis of the burgeoning publishing industry, Mills & Boon was listed along with all of the other principal publishers, large and small. 'We are interested in fiction, general literature of a popular nature, and educational books', the company described itself in the chapter, 'What Publishers Want'. 'We are particularly keen on new authors.'

Early on, Mills & Boon was aiming at the circulating libraries, a market which would become the firm's lifeblood. In the 1922 catalogue, 'MILLS & BOON's Special 3/6 net Novels With Jackets' were billed as 'especially suited to Circulating Libraries'. Most of the titles listed were by Anthony Carlyle, Sophie Cole, Horace Newte, Marie Van Vorst, and Ben Ames Williams. A May 1925 ad in *Menzies' Monthly List* touted 'MILLS & BOON's NEW FICTION', and listed titles at a variety of prices, including 7s. 6d., 6s., 3s. 6d., and 2s. 6d., urging agents and librarians to 'Send for full lists of these popular Series.' A full-page ad in the February 1927 *National Newsagent* boldly proclaimed, 'SELLING IN TENS OF THOUSANDS! But you know how they sell! Large Size, Picture Wrappers.'

These picture wrappers were emerging as a major selling point, and, increasingly, books were sold by their covers, with advertisements featuring reproductions of dust jackets. The jacket of Joan Sutherland's *The Dawn*, for example, featured an Arab sheik on a galloping horse, with the heroine draped over the horse's side. Denise Robins's *Women Who Seek* portrayed a glamorous flapper checking her make-up. For Louise Gerard's *Jungle Love*, the swooning heroine is depicted as about to be attacked by a menacing Negro, arms outstretched, clad in only a loincloth. Alice Eustace's *Flame of the Forest* showed a gypsy-dressed woman worshipping a large statue of the Buddha. Obviously jacket designs varied, and there were no rules apart from a certain element of sensation and titillation. The Mills & Boon name, however, was always displayed prominently across the bottom edge.

Like many publishers large and small, Mills & Boon looked overseas for sales growth and profits. This so-called 'imperial publishing' of 'colonial editions' was accomplished by smaller publishers through licensed agents rather than overseas branches. Accordingly, English-language sales (mostly of fiction) were prominent throughout the Empire, via representatives in Australia,

New Zealand, South Africa, Singapore, and Canada. Foreign translation rights were also sold to publishers in Norway, Germany, and Holland. For foreign markets, Mills & Boon issued special brochures addressed, 'To the Colonial Trade'. Terms for the Australian market, for example, were 250 assorted novels at a unit price of 1*s.* 6*d.* Australian merchants were enticed by the now-famous Mills & Boon 'guarantee':

> Wherever the English language is spoken, this remarkable Series meets with extraordinary success. The reasons are not surprising, for the titles are carefully chosen, and none but tales with a big popular appeal are included, whether they be by well-known authors or new writers with a reputation to make. The production is excellent, large size, best quality paper, bound in cloth boards with picture wrappers. Thus the books are eminently suitable for Circulating Libraries, just as much as for private individuals with Libraries of their own. Unlike most other Series, each title is a guarantee of good reading and first rate Fiction. It is therefore not surprising that the volumes are selling in hundreds of thousands, and in increasing numbers all the year round.

Mills & Boon publications seemingly travelled wherever the English language was spoken. A crudely written 'fan letter', in 1922, from an import-export book and stationers firm in Singapore called The Foo Rai & Company, is a good indication of how widely Mills & Boon's fame was spreading:

> There have been no fresh arrivals here of the latest published. . . . How shall we be the very glad if you can allow us send your catalogue? . . . We wish you to open an imports many kind of these from your civilized countries . . . You can given us cheapest prices we fell disposed to make a traial [*sic*] of your goods at Singapore. And also; we dare to say that we are able to deal the ideal business transaction with you herafter [*sic*].

There is no evidence Mills & Boon took up this intriguing offer.

If Mills & Boon's general fiction list was unpredictable and inconsistent in the 1920s, one genre was thriving: romantic fiction. 'At this time we didn't see a specifically romance market,' Alan Boon noted. 'In the lists in the back of some of the books, we have Jack London's *The Iron Heel* being advertised alongside one of Denise Robins's novels. It was ridiculous. It gradually happened.'

The authors who stand out in the 1920s lists were all writing what has been classified as 'romantic' fiction: Joan Sutherland, Louise Gerard, Elizabeth Carfrae, and Denise Robins. These authors were 'pushed' often and the publicity surrounding them was never modest. This strategy demonstrates that

Charles Boon recognized the emerging market, and the money to be earned by large sales of cheaper, half-crown (2s. 6d.) editions.

Romantic fiction had always been a staple of Mills & Boon's list, whether trumpeted as a June 15 Novel, a Shopgirl's Romance, or Sophie Cole's gentle love stories. But a distinctive list started to develop on the success of two authors, Louise Gerard and Joan Sutherland. They had much in common. Both were represented by A. P. Watt, and both had been previously published, Gerard by Methuen (but after Mills and Boon had departed), and Sutherland by Cassell and Hodder & Stoughton. Both captured the public eye (and library users), and were promoted aggressively in a style that would become common at Mills & Boon. Both combined the current fashions of lavish romance, exotic background, and high adventure dictated by popular authors of the day such as Elinor Glyn (*Three Weeks*, 1907), Ethel M. Dell (*The Way of an Eagle*, 1911), and E. M. Hull (*The Sheik*, 1921). Both were marketed as series: 'The Louise Gerard Novels' and 'The Joan Sutherland Novels'. And both stayed in print for years amid multiple editions. As such, Gerard and Sutherland set a kind of company standard for the romantic novel which cast a long shadow in the firm (although their exotic settings and adventure plots were not long-lasting).

Gerard joined the Mills & Boon list in 1911 with *A Tropical Tangle*, an adventure set in the jungles of darkest Africa. The *Daily Chronicle* called it a 'cause for rejoicing' and an exception to the 'general rule of lassitude' which has befallen most publishing houses of late. Gerard, the newspaper added, 'is capable of making a summer afternoon pass pleasantly, and that is recommendation enough for any novel'. *Tangle* was a popular success, too, selling out two editions of 2,000 copies. She was also one of the first authors for whom Charles Boon negotiated serial rights in magazines and newspapers, including an exclusive arrangement with the *People*.

'Louise Gerard was not a great writer, but she had a punch in her way,' Alan Boon recalled. 'Her style was very old fashioned. Although she was a lady, she wrote quite sexy sorts of books.' *The Virgin's Treasure: A Romance of the Tropics* (1915) was typical of Gerard's florid style. Dashing Dr Keith Harding, 36, heads to West Africa to treat tropical diseases. 'This was not England,' readers were told, 'but the tropics, where blood runs hotter, and where incredible things happen with amazing swiftness.' Indeed: before long Harding treats the exotic Heon de Lousada, who hides a secret: she is the daughter of the uncrowned king of West Africa. Harding cannot resist her charms, and seduces her:

> To the child it was as if a great warm flood had burst upon her, carrying her into some strange, new, happy world, such as she had always wanted and never known. . . . All she knew, lips, eyes, hands, hair and throat, she gave up freely for him to caress and fondle. . . . The whole world seemed halved with the white flame of a pure passion.

Though Harding is terribly guilty about his actions—'He, who up till now had deemed himself a man of honour!'—Heon was delighted: 'Surely this is my king. And he can do no wrong.'

Born in France, Sutherland joined Mills & Boon with *The Hidden Road* (1913). Her contract terms and advances (£100) were more generous than Gerard's, perhaps since she had been more widely published. She was one of the first Mills & Boon authors, along with Gerard, Cole, and Wylie, who signed lucrative, multi-book contracts, usually for 'three long novels'. She was also a consistent seller. *The Hidden Road* (1913) sold 3,222 copies in its 6s. edition, and 3,562 copies in the 1s. edition. *Cophetua's Son* (1913) sold 2,209 of a 3,000-strong first edition.

Sutherland's 1917 novel, *The Locust*, is a good example of her style of romantic adventure. Anthony Colin Goring, 37, the hero explorer of 'the wilds of Central Africa' and author of the 'best-selling book' *The Unknown Tropics*, cut a dashing figure, even in the dark:

> Seen in the light from the club within, it was only possible for a passer-by to note that he was just over middle height, with lean hips and powerful shoulders—it was too dark to observe the line of hard jaw and chin, the bronzed skin and the brilliant grey eyes so beautifully shaped and set. Yet even so in the indistinctiveness of the night and the rain there was something so arresting about the motionless figure, something virile and exceedingly male.

The heroine, Damaris Wyndham, 26, is, Colin notes, 'extraordinarily attractive', although, 'according to all the canons of loveliness, quite plain, except for the *svelte* beauty of her figure'. She also 'walked well'; because Colin is 'such an out-of-doors man himself he always noticed the way his fellow creatures moved'. Colin is a man of strong opinions, especially about love:

> He had, too, a vein of romance running through his nature, and he believed almost passionately in the power and glory of a great love. But it must be great—and there he found his complaint. Marriage to him was only possible as the crown of rare passion and tenderness. He knew himself unable to understand the wedded lives about him—how those concerned endured the daily destroying of ideals, the intimacies, the sordid disagreements and mechanical caresses.

In short, Colin prefers the company of men, and is a confirmed bachelor. Colin specializes in the study of sleeping sickness; although he's 'no sentimentalist over the nigger', he wants to save lives—to the dismay of his friends and relatives. Needless to say, Damaris and Colin fall in love, journey back to Africa, survive countless adventures — including Damaris shooting her own lion—and marry. Here is another example of the so-called 'punishing kiss':

There was a violence in his low voice and in the grip of his hand on hers that she had not seen in him before, and all the passion in her leapt to meet it.

'I will stay,' she said almost in a whisper, and with a smothered exclamation he bent and kissed her, a hard lingering kiss that seemed to draw her very life through her lips.

She knew the meaning of those last muttered words, and something wild and lawless in her nature that she had not known existed save in rage, when she had met Anthony Goring, rose in full force to meet the intensity of his passion.

Gerard and Sutherland—and their successes—were emphasized often in trade advertisements. In 1925, the *National Newsagent, Bookseller and Stationer* pitched Gerard's latest, *A Sultan's Slave*, as 'One of the greatest Popular Successes of recent years. . . . The "First National" Film is now appearing everywhere.' The dust jacket featured the hero and heroine, in Arab garb, in an embrace, framed by a Moorish arch. Similarly, in 1926, an ad in the W. H. Smith *Trade Circular* hailed Sutherland as 'Author of "CHALLENGE" one of the greatest successes of 1925' and Gerard as 'Author of "THE SHADOW OF THE PALM," one of the greatest successes of 1925'. In 1928 Gerard merited a full-page ad in *Eason's Monthly Bulletin*, heralded as 'The Novelist with Millions of Readers—THE LOUISE GERARD NOVELS SELLING IN TENS OF THOUSANDS.'

As with other popular authors on the Mills & Boon list, the firm encouraged readers to write in for a post-free copy of the author's biography, such as, 'Louise Gerard By Herself'. This practice would become more common as the list was increasingly specialized. 'The "Louise Gerard" readers know their author is never hackneyed, that they are sure of an original and enthralling story that will carry them along, absorbed, to the end', promised Mills & Boon. Of Sutherland, the firm enthused, 'For years this writer has been one of our foremost novelists, and there can be no question whatever that her latest romances have added tens of thousands of readers to her already vast public.'

No doubt inspired by the success of Gerard and Sutherland, Mills & Boon promoted grandly two other authors of romantic fiction in the 1920s: Elizabeth Carfrae and Denise Robins. Both were prolific writers, and their sales would serve to consolidate the Mills & Boon romantic fiction list begun by Sutherland and Gerard.

Carfrae, who was matron of one of the houses at Rugby School, was brought to Mills & Boon by an agent. Her first contract, in 1924, was for three novels, for which she received a £30 advance, and the usual 10 per cent terms. The first novel, *Barbed Wire*, featured what would become a Carfrae trademark: a high-spirited, independent, and somewhat daring heroine. Joy

Beresford, just 16, is the daughter of a university professor. She asks her new governess, 'All the men in books kiss the heroines passionately, and I want to know what it's like. Do tell me, Robin.' She is determined to marry a 'very handsome six-footer', and she does: Stephen Barclay, an artist with 'colossal shoulders' who rents the neighbouring house.

By the time she moved on to Hutchinson in 1942, Carfrae had written 23 novels for Mills & Boon in 17 years. Early on, she was evidently very pleased by her success, and with her publishers. In 1928 she understandably dedicated her latest novel, *The Distant Stars*, 'To CHARLES BOON, Whose kindness and help has enabled me to add a new clause to my profession of faith and to say with truth and heartfelt gratitude: "I believe in the great humanity of publishers."' No wonder: Mills & Boon positioned Carfrae as a star. 'Within three years Elizabeth Carfrae has become one of the most widely read novelists,' ran one advertisement in October 1927. 'ELIZABETH CARFRAE (A Mills & Boon discovery) is a novelist full of action and resource, and many thousands of readers are clamouring for her novels.'

Unlike Carfrae, Denise Robins was an established author and a big seller, having published novels for ten years before meeting Charles Boon in 1927. In her autobiography, *Stranger than Fiction*, Robins recalled that first meeting:

> I remember old Charles Boon, my publisher, visiting me in Sussex one Sunday. I opened a cupboard in my study to show him a pile of manuscripts. He gave them one glance, then said: 'I'll give you a good cheque now this moment for the rights of the whole lot.' (He mentioned a tempting sum.) But my business sense had developed with the years and I laughingly refused his offer.
>
> 'You are right, you know!' said Charles with a twinkle.
>
> I was. I've since made a lot more money with those stories than he offered then.[4]

Robins was represented by Curtis Brown. Her first contract with Mills & Boon in 1927 contained terms similar to Carfrae's: three novels, for which she received a £30 advance, and 10 per cent terms. Once Robins's novels started selling, however, her terms improved dramatically. The next two contracts, covering six novels, earned advances of £25 for each book, but the third contract, for four novels, raised the advance to £100, with terms rising to 12.5 per cent.

Women Who Seek (1928), Robins's second novel for Mills & Boon, is typical of her provocative style which was in the vein of Gerard and Dell. Eve Walton-Evans, 'a young, beautiful girl of ultra-modern type', is raised by old-fashioned parents. She marries Dr Michael Graham, who is decent but dull. Eve lusts for Michael's new partner, Dr Nicholas Rayne, and the feeling is mutual. Robins presents Eve as the 'eternal Eve' who is irresistible to men:

A man might look long at Eve's mouth and lose his strength of will. It was a fascinating mouth, rather large but perfectly shaped, the lower lip full, the upper lip attractively short. An impulsive, passionate young mouth. Certainly the child had depths in her—and very passionate depths, too.

Although Eve 'was by no means a woman of the world yet. She was very young and inexperienced', she is desperately in love with Nick, whose kisses provoke 'all that was primitive and fierce in her'. Eve pleads with Nick for 'one hour of real love'. He demurs: 'It's a sin, Eve. You're not the sort of woman to do wrong and be callous about it. You'd regret it, terribly.' But Eve disagrees, and amid a violent thunderstorm, they make love:

> The consulting room was plunged in shadow. In the dim light he saw Eve, arms stretched out above her head, ecstatic young face tilted back, eyes shut. He thought she was like some pagan priestess, offering herself to the gods. He walked back to her and took her in his arms.

Afterwards, Eve has tinges of guilt about her adultery but no real regrets: 'It was a frightful problem. She was one of thousands of married women in similar circumstances.' She and Nick regretfully agree to part, for kindly Michael's sake. But when Nick contracts 'general blood poisoning' and dies, Eve confesses all. Michael forgives her, even blames himself for her infidelity, since he was not a good enough husband. She pledges to try to reform herself, as her 'seeking' has only lead to disaster.

In her nine years and thirty-three novels with Mills & Boon, Robins dominated the publication list and was the firm's top fiction seller. Her success, at the end of a difficult decade, must have been heartening to Gerald Mills and Charles Boon. By 1929 Mills & Boon already had ten Robins novels in print.

It is interesting to see how Robins and Carfrae were used by Mills & Boon to establish its two popular fiction lists: first edition and cheaper editions. New titles by these authors were sometimes offered at full price (7s. 6d.), but sometimes at the cheaper price (2s. 6d.), to bolster the low end of the market. The firm's strategy was shared with readers and booksellers in a 1928 advertisement, entitled, 'MILLS & BOON's Popular 2/6 Novels':

> [The 2/6 Novels] are selling in tens of thousands, but booksellers know how they sell. Last year Mills & Boon introduced ELIZABETH CARFRAE's Novels to Half-Crown readers, and they have sold in thousands, and are sell-ing better every day. This year MILLS & BOON introduce the novels of DENISE ROBINS in this extraordinarily successful Library, and the first three volumes will be
>
> | | | |
> |---|---|---|
> | THE INEVITABLE END | (April) | 2/6 Net |
> | THE PASSIONATE FLAME | (May) | 2/6 Net |
> | WHITE JADE | (July) | 2/6 Net |

to be followed by others during the Autumn. THE INEVITABLE END has enjoyed remarkable success in 7/6 form, and is certain to appeal to tens of thousands of readers in Half-Crown form. THE PASSIONATE FLAME and WHITE JADE are entirely new long novels—never before published—and issued in the first place at 2/6 net. MILLS & BOON are confident that the DENISE ROBINS Novels will repeat the remarkable successes of the other novelists in this superb series, such as Louise Gerard, Joan Sutherland, Elizabeth Carfrae, Sinclair Gluck, Victor Bridges, etc., etc.

In the *Menzies List* for April 1929, a large ad entitled 'A MILLS & BOON PAGE' advertised 'THE ELIZABETH CARFRAE NOVELS' (6, including the latest, *Guarded Heights*), and 'THE DENISE ROBINS NOVELS' (9, including the latest, *Heavy Clay*). Seemingly on the strength of these two women alone, Mills & Boon was restored to prosperity by the end of the 1920s.

❧

Romantic fiction may have dominated the publication list in the 1920s, but Mills & Boon did not neglect its non-fiction list, including its traditional bread-and-butter line, educational textbooks. Sales of textbooks continued strong and steady during the decade. Some titles sold did extremely well— Ethel M. Goddard's *A First School Botany*, for example, went through nine editions by October 1928. Goddard was the botany mistress at the County School for Girls in Colchester. Sharing the list was *A First Year Experimental Chemistry* by W. H. Crabb, senior chemistry master at the County School for Boys in Altrincham (Crabb also wrote texts for the *Second Year* and *Third Year*), and *Outlines of the Calculus for Science and Engineering Students* by Terry Thomas, headmaster of Leeds Grammar School. Readers were urged to write for Mills & Boon's 'complete Educational Catalogue'.

In 1926 Mills & Boon spotlighted four non-fiction books 'which LIVE Booksellers should SELL LIKE HOT CAKES'. The diverse subjects covered by these titles reveals how widely Mills & Boon cast its net to attract readers. They were: *Broken Lights: A Short Study in the Varieties of Christian Opinion* by Harold Begbie, *Where Did I Come From, Mother? The Story of Birth written for children* by Millicent Gordon, *Cornwall and a Light Car* by Filson Young (author of *The Complete Motorist*), and *London in Seven Days: A Guide for People in a Hurry*, by Arthur Milton. Begbie's serious book, readers were told, 'is devoted to the ethic of Christianity and argues that without the religious consecration of that ethic the social, industrial, and political life of a nation must of necessity drift towards the confusion and destruction of materialism.' Young's title, said the critic in *Eve*, was 'A most useful little book' for the current motoring craze which 'contains most of that information which a driver-motorist would want to know were he not already acquainted with the London–Cornwall road'. The one-shilling paperback by Gordon included a

'Private Letter To Mother' in a special inside pocket, urging her to read this book aloud to children by the age of 9–10:

> You can make them understand better than I the sacredness of this subject and all the parts of the body connected with it. That to speak lightly of these things instead of seriously, is like the difference between a white lily that is dragged in the mud, and the same lily growing in all its purity on its stalk.

Begbie, a former Methuen author and social critic who also wrote under the pen-name 'A Gentleman with a Duster', was a big seller. *The Mirrors of Downing Street—Some Political Reflections*, for example, reached seventeen editions between October 1920 and February 1922. There is little doubt that Begbie's esteem brought Mills & Boon good publicity and enhanced its reputation in the industry. G. K. Chesterton hailed Begbie as 'That valuable public servant', and in 1922 Mills & Boon received a glowing, handwritten letter from none other than Marie Corelli:

> I take the quite unconventional liberty of writing to <u>congratulate</u> your firm on the courage, patriotism and energy you show in publishing those three admirable books by 'A Gentleman with a Duster'—i.e. 'The Mirrors of Downing Street'—'The Glass of Fashion'—and last though not least 'Painted Windows'. These books contain truths, <u>necessary to be told</u> to our 'running amok' people of the present day and though I do not wonder at the author's eloquence (for every right minded person must be <u>burning</u> with indignant zeal at this moment) I <u>do</u> wonder at and admire the publisher's fearlessness! For scarcely a house of mere 'trade' would venture on such a 'dash for liberty', ruled as the mob is by a bound and servile press! You are evidently above 'mere trade'—and nevertheless success attends your venture, as it <u>invariably</u> does in the long run when one matters for the <u>right</u>.

Since Charles Boon and Gerald Mills undoubtedly knew Corelli personally, her familiarity in this letter is not surprising.

Begbie may have gathered good reviews and acclaim, especially for the 'Gentleman with a Duster' series, but he was not a moneymaker for Mills & Boon. His relationship with Mills & Boon presents an interesting case of 'hidden' costs. Begbie was a popular author, and his novels and commentaries sold well for several publishers, including Hodder & Stoughton, Hutchinson, and Constable. *Broken Earthenware* (1909), for example, sold over one million copies for Hodder & Stoughton.

However, as revealed upon Begbie's death in 1929, Mills & Boon had to assume large fees to keep an author like Begbie, and often the author's advance was not earned, leaving the firm in financial difficulty. In 1929 solicitors for Begbie's estate contacted Mills & Boon to inquire about royalties due or expected to the author. 'It is with much regret that we cannot help feeling that the Estate cannot hope to benefit for a long time,' Charles Boon wrote in reply. The £300 advance paid on *The Picture Book*, for example, published in June 1917, still had over £139 unearned by September 1929. Begbie collected a £1,000 advance in December 1928 for two novels he negotiated directly with Mills & Boon, *The Lazlett Affair* and *Black Rent*. By September 1929, over £344 remained unearned. A special clause in Begbie's contract allowed Mills & Boon to divert any earnings from his other published works to pay down this advance, but Begbie died too soon. His last book, *Plain Sailing*, appeared in August 1929. The advance of £500 was paid in twelve monthly instalments; the first nine months had been paid before Begbie died in September. The earnings on the novel on his death: just £363.[5]

Small wonder, then, that Mills & Boon took special care when publishing other books whose financial returns appeared uncertain. For example, *Dutch and Flemish Flower and Fruit Painters of the XVIIth and XVIIIth Centuries* by Ralph Warner, an oversized, lavishly illustrated book with 280 illustrations, was issued in 1928. By an elaborate arrangement, the first edition of 1,000 copies was published on subscription (an old-fashioned concept), thereby ensuring a return on investment. Mills & Boon only put up £160, plus £50 for publicity, with the author himself paying £400. Perhaps the only way this title could be safely published was by sharing costs.

❧

Mills & Boon's recovery, beginning in 1926, can be tied to the end of industrial action, and improved sales of the reinvigorated popular fiction list. At the Annual General Meeting in March 1927, the Board minutes recorded that strikes 'resulted in three wasted months out of 6 months with very serious results. There was a loss in these 6 months of £782. 7. 0.' However, 1926 was not a total loss, according to Gerald Mills:

> Business improved very considerably during the July to December period. Mr. Mills pointed out that it was most gratifying to know that not only had the first six months loss of £782. 7. 0. been made good, but that over and above this there was a profit of £160. 13. 5 on the year. It was resolved to carry this amount forward thus reducing the deficit to £1603. 3. 8.

This corresponded with improved sales of both fiction and educational books. Moreover, 'Mr. Mills pointed out that the Managing Directors had owing to bad trade in the early part of 1926 decided not to draw their full salaries during July to December but that they would do so in the event of 1927 being a satisfactory year draw the undrawn balance of £37. 10. 0 each during 1927.' Strikes, moreover, 'practically prevented trade being done for five months'.

Indeed, 1927 was a 'most satisfactory' year of trading. 'The profit was £1048. 15. 4', Mills proudly reported:

> The year, unlike the previous two years, had been free of labour troubles, with the result that the Company had been able to increase the turnover and while he regretted that it was not possible to clear off the whole deficit of £1603. 3. 8, the profit had reduced this amount to £554. 8. 4, and he hoped that during 1928 the remaining adverse balance would be wiped out.

Perhaps cautiously, and without tempting fate, the Directors awarded themselves bonuses of just £50 each, their first since 1924.

Towards the end of the 1920s, Mills & Boon's recovery seemed assured. The little firm was so profitable, in fact, that Walter Hutchinson, who succeeded his founder father George as head of Hutchinson & Co., Ltd., in 1925, attempted to purchase the company to add to his list of publishing acquisitions. Among the smaller publishers bought by Hutchinson were Hurst & Blackett, Stanley Paul, and Jarrolds. These acquisitions not only reduced the competition but enhanced Hutchinson's list of popular fiction for sale to the public and the commercial libraries. But Mills & Boon were not interested in Hutchinson's offer, John Boon noted. 'My father was very independent, and he wasn't going to work for anybody else, and he very much disliked Walter Hutchinson. He was an absolute bastard, really, and my father could not see himself working for him. Hutchinson would have probably screwed it up. They would have parted in five minutes.'

As 1928 approached, however, Mills & Boon's run of good fortune seemed in jeopardy. In December 1927 C. C. Longley, one of the firm's original directors, died, and it was agreed not to appoint a new Director for the time being. Less than a year later, in September 1928, Gerald Mills died suddenly, after surgery for prostate cancer. He was only 51, and a considerable portion of the company rested in his estate.

Mills's will, witnessed just nine days before he died (an indication he may have known that his time was short), dictated that upon his death all his shares in the firm were to be offered for sale, or converted into preference shares and held for one year by the Public Trustee. As such, according to John Boon, Mills's death caught the firm off guard, and the company nearly foundered. 'The capital problems were extraordinary,' Boon said. 'My father had no money. The main bank came from the Mills family. When Mills died, that all collapsed. It's understandable that my father panicked.' The alternative—a merger with or takeover by another publishing house such as Hutchinson—was unpalatable.

So Charles Boon worked quickly to find a new partner—and discovered one in house: Joseph W. Henley. Henley, the former office boy from Methuen who worked in book production, apparently came into wealth from his father, a successful builder. Henley was elected company secretary in October 1927, on Longley's illness, and, only three days after Mills's death, was named Director, upon his purchase of 750 shares from Gerald Mills's estate. At the same Extraordinary General Meeting, 'It was resolved that Mr. Charles Boon be appointed Chairman of the Company in place of the late Mr. Gerald R. Mills'. Boon also received a rise; his salary was now £1,000 per year.

'It was not easy in 1928 to get someone to put up money in a small publishing firm', especially one with an uneven record in the 1920s, John Boon admitted. Henley persuaded his father to put up the cash for him. 'Henley wasn't a publisher,' John Boon said. 'He had no feel for books whatsoever. He was a meticulous bookkeeper. He kept all production schedules immaculately. He was a great man for routine. He did essentially office jobs. Mills was absolutely hopeless at that side of the business. Undoubtedly, when Henley took over, there was a big increase in profit.'

So why choose Henley? 'Mills & Boon was a very small firm in 1928, and not very valuable,' John Boon recalled:

> My father had worked with Henley for a long time. Henley couldn't stand up to him. They were chalk and cheese. I don't think he wanted anyone to dispute his reign. The fact that this man happened to have some money through his father was advantageous. Henley was there, he had money, it was an easy deal. My father probably could have raised the money himself, or have found someone else, but he didn't.

Henley was also a safe choice, as he lacked ambition, and would not interfere with Charles Boon's running of the business. As Boon apparently dominated Mills, so Boon would keep Henley in check. Since Mills's executors were anxious to cash in and recalled the shares, Henley's cash provided an end to Charles Boon's financial worries.

Gerald Mills left a wife, one brother, and two sisters, but no children. Control of Mills & Boon, therefore, rested in the Boon family after 1928. Kenneth Mills began to divest his shares in 1929, selling 250 of 500 shares. Boon bought 50; Henley, 150; and Sophie Cole purchased 50 shares.

Did Mills's death provoke a crisis? 'At the time, I think it was Auntie Margaret, a pretty shrewd old girl, who said it was nonsense, really,' John Boon recalled. 'Father needn't have brought Henley in. Not everybody makes the best logical decisions in a crisis.' Given Henley's future clash with the Boon sons, they would rue their father's decision in 1928.

For now, Charles Boon consolidated his position in the firm in 1928, and the future course of Mills & Boon was left to him. He was the dominant force before Mills's death, and would remain so long afterwards. With the storms of the 1920s at his back, Boon was determined to remake his company in the 1930s, so as to secure a more profitable and stable future. In his decisions, Boon would set his firm on a new and irreversible course which would lay the foundations for the company we know today.

Chapter 3
A Boon Without Mills, 1929–1945

... There will come a day when no one will any more think of buying a book without first inquiring the publisher's name, than he would now of buying a motor car without knowing the name of its maker. It should be just as much in a publisher's interest to educate the reading public to look for his imprint, and for him to make it easily recognizable by means of the format and typography of the books that he publishes, as it should be an author's right to get good production as well as fair royalties.

Richard de la Mare, *A Publisher on Book Production* (1936)

Old Charles Boon used to say to me, 'Never pass a Boots shop in Eastbourne, anywhere you are, without going in and making yourself known.' The personal touch. I can't say I always did it, but I did sometimes. And they'll say, 'Oh, yes, I've heard of you.' I remember I said once to a woman at the bookstall in Victoria, she was looking at one of my books. I said, 'Buy it. I wrote it.' She looked up, and put it down, and thought, 'She's one of those who ought to be locked up!'

Mary Burchell, on being a Mills & Boon author in the 1930s

MILLS & BOON'S first twenty years were marked by extremes: a brilliant launch, ten years of prosperity, and then a rapid decline, culminating in Gerald Mills's death in 1928, just two months shy of the firm's twentieth anniversary. This, however, would be the last decline for Mills & Boon. Like the hero in one of his romantic novels, Charles Boon was determined to avoid all future adversity, and provide a safe haven for his firm and its growing readership of middle- and upper-working-class women. Boon's radical redirection of his firm in the 1930s as a specialized romantic fiction publishing house would set Mills & Boon on a course which would bring its greatest financial success, if little critical acclaim.

We could argue that Mills & Boon had been heading in this direction for some time. Since the First World War the firm's publication lists had become increasingly dominated by fiction, especially by women authors, and usually of a 'popular' vein, namely romance and adventure novels. By 1929 the firm's best-selling authors were all writing romantic fiction: Denise Robins, Elizabeth Carfrae, Louise Gerard, and Sophie Cole. With commercial libraries opening across the country, particularly during the early 1930s, there was money to be made as a 'library house'. In the 1930s we can begin to speak confidently of the modern Mills & Boon imprint, and of a certain 'look' of the books: bold and colourful jackets, brown bindings, expressive blurbs, flashy advertising. This decade heralds a boom for Mills & Boon, a golden age for the company.

An analysis of the firm's balance sheet during this period illustrates the extent of Mills & Boon's financial recovery before the Second World War (see Fig. 3.1). The company Board minutes throughout the 1930s are filled with good cheer, as the firm continued to set new sales records. In July 1934 the company attained an all-time sales record, with 'just over £6000 worth of books having been sold'. Beginning in 1929, the firm resumed investing its new-found profits outside of the business; each year £1,000 was placed on reserve. By November 1934, Boon reported that, 'since the Bank Balance had considerably increased', investments in holdings outside the business now totalled £4,159. 5s. 0d. By 1935, sales and profits were double those of 1929, and by

Figure 3.1

Annual Net Profit of Mills & Boon, Ltd., 1929–1945

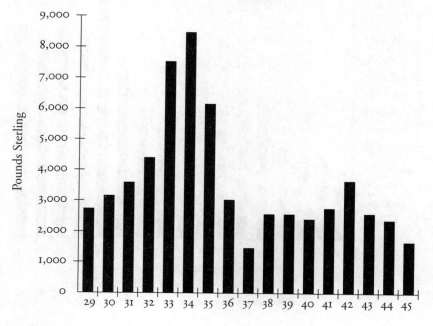

1939, turnover reached £70,000. The decline in net profit from 1935 until 1938 reflected the increased investments outside of the business, higher taxation (including defence taxes) and reinvestment of monies within the expanding firm.

A look at sales statistics reveals the reasons for such prosperity (see Figs. 3.2 and 3.3). Although the statistics are incomplete, they do illustrate important trends, and are, moreover, a vindication of Charles Boon's new strategy. Although sales of educational titles declined before the Second World War (along with the number of titles published by the firm, reflecting the firm's change in direction), sales of first edition fiction (at full, 7s. 6d. price) remained steady. The major development, however, was the growth of cheaper editions of new and reprinted fiction. Sales of the Mills & Boon Half-Crown Library soared, from 162,266 in 1929 to a high of 499,662 in 1935. This library, which contained 'all-new' and reprinted titles by Robins, Carfrae, and others, was pitched especially to the smaller commercial libraries. Although the profit margin on these titles was lower than for first editions, the volume sold would have translated into good cash flow for the

Figure 3.2

Annual Fiction Sales of Mills & Boon, Ltd., 1929–1945

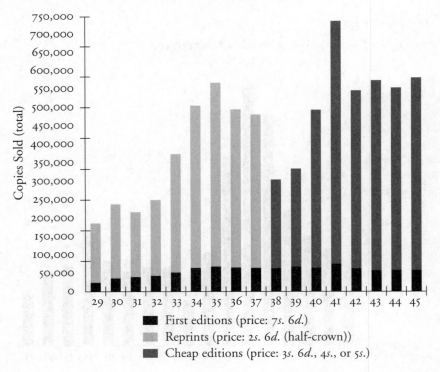

First editions (price: 7s. 6d.)
Reprints (price: 2s. 6d. (half-crown))
Cheap editions (price: 3s. 6d., 4s., or 5s.)

Figure 3.3

Annual Education Title Sales of Mills & Boon, Ltd., 1929–1945

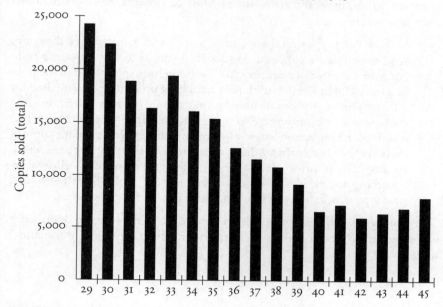

firm. Moreover, at the same time, Mills & Boon was increasing the number of new titles published each month. The publication list for January–June 1938, for example, contained 47 new novels (by 36 authors) and 37 reprints: a total of 84 publications, or 14 per month—and all of them romances.

The prosperity which accompanied these statistics in the 1930s encouraged Charles Boon to expand his firm and prepare for the future. In June 1931 Mills & Boon moved offices north from Rupert Street, behind Leicester Square, to smarter Fitzroy Square, and larger premises at 50 Grafton Way. In 1934 and 1935, the best pre-war years, the firm added warehouse stock space, leasing the basement of 52 Grafton Way, and 25 Fitzroy Square. There were four packers on the payroll, which numbered 21 by 1939, including Boon's three sons: Charles jun. (Carol), Alan, and John. Carol and Alan Boon joined the firm in 1931, when 19 and 18 years old, respectively. Both started as clerks: Alan reading manuscripts and processing invoices, and Carol assisting Henley on the production side. 'I remember my father saying, "Since you can't get jobs elsewhere, you might as well join the firm,"' Alan Boon recalled. 'I worked in editorial. There I picked up any knowledge I have of romances.' In 1934 Carol and Alan were elected Directors.

John Boon joined in 1938, aged 21, and fresh from a Double First at Cambridge University. 'It was absolutely bloody awful,' he recalled. 'I sat at a desk. My father wanted me to develop a direct mail operation. And the way to do that was to look through the London telephone directory and pick out a name and send a card and catalogues. It wasted my time.' Perhaps, but this attention to readers was a hallmark of Mills & Boon. One of John Boon's form letters survives:

> Mills & Boon present their compliments, and ask whether they may send their Fiction catalogue regularly to you or to any of your friends. For over a quarter of a century, Mills & Boon have specialised in the publication of Light Fiction, until they have built up a library unequalled for quality. They carry on an unremitting search for new talent, reading every manuscript submitted to them, but they only include in their lists novels of the highest merit. For this reason, though you may like some of their authors better than others, every book in their catalogue is worth reading. The imprint 'Mills & Boon' is the guarantee of a well-written, absorbing and wholesome story. If you will fill in the form below and post it to them, they will send you their Fiction List regularly, post free.

The promotion of the 'imprint' here is significant, as the Mills & Boon name was now firmly established and identified with light (specifically romantic) fiction.

Although the crises of the 1920s had been overcome, and Mills & Boon was restored to prosperity, the difficult struggles, John Boon suggested, had a profound psychological effect on his father. Charles Boon was determined to remake his company in order to cushion the impact from future crises. For one, the costs of production were still rising, and archaic arrangements made with printers by Gerald Mills had to be renegotiated. Publishing, moreover, had to be more selective and consistent, and relations with authors and agents nurtured, to prevent misfortunes such as Hugh Walpole's departure. The list should be large and varied, and not dependent on a single star such as Jack London, who could vanish overnight. 'The firm needed to stand off and pick the right book,' John Boon said. Charles Boon knew he had found a 'rich ball' in romantic fiction, and how to follow it. In this respect, he may in fact have heeded the advice of his publishing peers. At the height of the Depression, with his sales in flux, Ernest Hodder-Williams of Hodder & Stoughton told an audience of booksellers of the four guidelines for a successful publisher: 'Hard work; publish what interests the public; study the newspapers; "travel" books yourself.'

For a publisher of Mills & Boon's size, what interested the public in the 1930s was light fiction, and Mills & Boon's future lay as a library supplier. The 1930s witnessed the continued expansion of the commercial circulating libraries. Given the Depression, and the frequency of novel reading, borrowing books was preferred over buying, and many subscribers read two books each week. '[In] practically every town in England there is now a well run commercial library', the Commercial Libraries' Association observed in 1938. Q. D. Leavis, in her landmark study *Fiction and the Reading Public* (1932), illustrated how dependent 'ordinary' readers were on these circulating libraries. The process of book selection, she found, was increasingly consistent, and usually ruled by the librarian. 'The assistant is generally consulted in some such formula as "Another book like this one, please," or "Can you recommend me a nice book?"' Leavis wrote. 'The assistant glances at the novel held out and produces another novel which is accepted without question.' No wonder Charles Boon paid so much attention to his library clients.

Mills & Boon supplied the larger libraries, including Boots and W. H. Smith, as well as the myriad of smaller libraries in shops and attached to newsagents. The operations, and demand, were vast. By 1935 Boots was purchasing from publishers over one million books a year, with its headquarters handling over 700,000 volumes per month for 400 branches. The 'tuppenny' libraries, which tended to stock only the 'lighter' fare, were maintained by chains or wholesalers. Among these were the Argosy & Sundial Libraries Ltd. of London and Liverpool (2,217 branches and 1.3 million books in circulation by 1934), Army & Navy Stores of London, and Ray Smith Libraries of London. Foyle's Libraries, Ltd., founded in London in 1930, supplied 747 libraries, with an average of over 200 books each per week, in 1934. Foyle's purchased the books in bulk and rented them to retailers, newsagents, clubs, and institutions at a rate of 10 shillings a week for 250 volumes, which cost Foyle's £30 to buy, or about 2s. 6d. each. These volumes, in turn, were loaned to the public at 2d. or 3d. per volume per week.

With the expansion of circulating libraries, sales of Mills & Boon novels were prodigious. On average, in the 1930s between 6,000 and 8,000 copies of each title were printed. Of these, as many as 3,000 would be kept and sold later as a cheap edition. Each of the library chains had standing orders. Boots purchased between 300 and 500 copies of each title, and Argosy & Sundial Libraries, up to 700 copies. Public libraries, if they ordered at all (prejudice against spending public money on 'trash' books was common), took 150 copies. By the middle of the 1930s, Mills & Boon promised to issue two to four new books every fortnight. The numbers Mills & Boon dangled before the public in newspaper advertisements were impressive. In February 1935 Denise Robins, with 35 novels to her credit, had sold 506,000 copies, an average of 14,500 copies per title. A distant second was Elizabeth Carfrae (264,000; 17 titles), followed by Helena Grose (133,000; 13 titles), Deirdre O'Brien (108,000; 14 titles), and Marjorie M. Price (86,000; 10 titles).

Mills & Boon's penetration of the library market is evident in the writings and surveys of the period. When in 1935 F. R. Richardson wrote in defence of the 'Circulating Library', he noted indirectly the popularity of Mills &

Boon among borrowers, 'a new reading public which is being reached for the first time by salesmanship adapted to their mentality and circumstances':

> In the long run anything which makes more people read more books is for the good of the readers themselves and of the book trade as a whole, and it is just this service which the circulating libraries perform: they extend the reading public. . . . In every section, however, the life of the individual book is becoming shorter, again a result of over-production. There are some exceptions. The works of such a writer as Hugh Walpole go on for ever; and so, too, do some pleasant novels (those of Elizabeth Carfrae, for instance) which have never been trumpeted in any quarter, but have the most effective and persistent of all advertisements— friendly recommendation from one to another of that great majority of readers who are seeking only good recreation, and care nothing about being au fait with 'the book of the moment'.[2]

Carfrae was, as we have seen, one of Mills & Boon's top sellers (as, ironically, Walpole once was). Similarly, in 1935 the *Bookseller* analysed the stock of 'one of the largest and newest' of the commercial libraries in a quest to reveal 'What the Public Likes'.[3] Among the Mills & Boon authors listed in 'the "best-seller" class' (alongside Edgar Wallace) were Denise Robins, Joan Sutherland, Sophie Cole, Louise Gerard, Elizabeth Carfrae, Deirdre O'Brien, and Marjorie M. Price.

❧

When John Menzies published *A Selected List of Popular Fiction Suitable for Lending Libraries* in 1935 and 1937 (identifying titles priced between 3*s*. 6*d*. and 1*s*.), Mills & Boon was prominently listed as, 'The Popular Fiction Publishers'. The firm, however, faced much competition. T. Werner Laurie's '3/6 Library', for example, included *Desert Lover* by Joan Conquest. Wright & Brown published Annie S. Swan and Paul Trent, while G. Putnam's rather old-fashioned 'Romance Library' offered Florence Barclay and Flora Klickmann. Philip Allan & Co. purchased the rights to the novels of Denise Robins (a recent Mills & Boon defector) and Pamela Wynne. Finally, Collins's romance list featured Renee Shann and Reita Lambert. Collins was perhaps Mills & Boon's biggest competitor in the romantic fiction market.

With competition from other publishers, Charles Boon brought all of his sales and marketing talents to bear to promote Mills & Boon as the pre-eminent source for romantic fiction. For one, he discarded the traditional method of advertising each book and author individually. 'They were still promoting hardback books in the way they promoted Walpole in 1915, like the precious life of a master,' John Boon said. 'We started doing the list as a block. We published fortnightly. We produced catalogues to tie in to that. Ladies could pester libraries.'

Building upon examples prepared in the 1920s for Denise Robins and Elizabeth Carfrae, publication lists were slickly labelled and packaged, and advertisements laden with superlatives were placed in all the major newspapers and trade journals. 'Every WIFE and SPINSTER should read Helena Grose's MARRIAGE AT MIDNIGHT. A worthy successor to BACHELOR'S WIFE', ran a *Sunday Times* ad in May 1931. Grose was a favourite of 1930s advertisements. When *Painted Lady* was published in 1933, Mills & Boon boasted in the *Observer*, 'SOLD OUT AGAIN! within seven days of publication. First and Second Large Editions.' There was no doubt of the audience that Mills & Boon was targeting: in a February 1935 advertisement in the *Sunday Times*, Mills & Boon announced two new authors: Elizabeth Phillips and Dorothy B. Upson. 'MILLS & BOON confidently recommend these two New Novelists and will be glad if Library Subscribers will ask for them. They represent Authors likely to be extremely popular in the near future and can be read by everyone interested in first rate popular romance.'[4]

Packaging and production was standardized, in an effort to control costs and promote the imprint. Brown bindings with brightly coloured jackets which would leap off the library shelves became trademarks.[5] Jackets were alternatively daring and provocative, or lush and romantic, the latter following the style of Hollywood film posters. By the mid-1930s Mills & Boon advertised its Half-Crown Library with reproductions of covers ('JACKETS THAT PULL'), and, as we have seen, books were advertised, not by their name and reviews, but by their jackets. Since the commercial libraries (unlike the public libraries) usually kept the jackets on their books, the cover was the 'loss-leader' to persuade women to pick up the title. *Young Bride* by Helena Grose (1936), for example, featured a full-length portrait of the bride and groom in a tender embrace, and *Stolen Eden* by Annabel Lee (1936) presented an aviator hero, in goggles, scarf, and bomber jacket, clutching the well-coiffed heroine. *Frail Amazon* by Juliet Armstrong (1941) did not include the hero, but a dramatic double view of the heroine, in business dress, and as the dramatic stylish fashion model she would become. *Little Brown Girl* by Jan Tempest (1940) offered a cosy domestic scene, with the hero seated before his typewriter, smoking a pipe, and the heroine fetchingly perched beside him.

All this attention to production values had one aim: branding. The Mills & Boon imprint was acquiring a reputation, like any other commodity in a mass market, for a particular type of book demanded by a particular class of reader. The publishing industry was not unaware of this phenomenon. In 1936 Richard de la Mare, long-time production manager for Faber & Faber, delivered the Sixth Dent Memorial Lecture, entitled, 'A Publisher on Book Production'. De la Mare may have had Mills & Boon in mind when he spoke of standardization and imprints:

I am sadly aware that the number of those book buyers and readers, who look for the publisher's name as a matter of course and remember it, is still small; but I believe that their number is growing and that there will come a day when no one will any more think of buying a book without first inquiring the *publisher's* name, than he would now of buying a motor car without knowing the name of its maker. It should be just as much in a publisher's interest to educate the reading public to look for his imprint, and for him to make it easily recognizable by means of the format and typography of the books that he publishes, as it should be an author's *right* to get good production as well as fair royalties. [6]

De la Mare added that more and more publishers were adopting a 'house style', making the appearance of books 'recognizable as members of one family'. In addition to Mills & Boon's emerging style, Hodder & Stoughton's Yellow Jackets were prominent on library (and retail) shelves, as was Victor Gollancz's crime series (founded in 1928) with its bright yellow and magenta wrappers. Gollancz apparently surveyed railway bookstalls and determined that yellow was the colour which would stand out best on a dust jacket.

Two future hallmarks of the Mills & Boon house style, an obsessive attention to book titles and to character names, originated with Charles Boon. Then as now, the fear of libel was foremost in a publisher's mind when selecting the names of characters and places in a novel. In 1939, for example, Boon wrote to one of his more popular new authors, Cecilia Lacey ('Margaret Lovell', who also wrote as 'Valerie K. Nelson'). While he liked *The Girl from the Beauty Shop*, Boon asked for specific changes:

> We think the names of the characters are quite satisfactory, except KAY FENNER, because there are many of this name in the London Directory, and also there are Hairdressers shops, etc. with the names of Duval, where this young lady worked. Will you kindly send us an alternative for FENNER?

Lacey was agreeable, substituting Fendrile and Montclare. Boon proceeded to review all of the character names. 'Colonel Critchlowe' was acceptable, as were Rex Largate, the hero; Miss Otterburne, school headmistress; Sir Godfrey Tralish; and Mrs Coster who ran the beauty parlour. Similarly, in 1948, when Alan Boon asked Joan Blair to change character names in her latest manuscript, he recalled his father's problems with Blair's debut novel, *Sister of Nelson Ward* (1937), a romance set in a London hospital:

> This business of names has always been difficult. We do not have names altered if we can help it, but when we do, we incline to the school of opinion which favours unlikely names. In the past—touch wood—this has worked satisfactorily for us. Your letter has brought back to my mind the gentleman who wrote to us before the war and said, indignantly, if I rightly remember, that his name was Nelson Ward.

Book titles were chosen with the same care as the dust jacket, and also checked for problems. In 1932 Charles Boon exchanged letters with E. F. Boyman, director of J. M. Dent & Sons. Boon objected to a title announced in Dent's Autumn List: *Beauty for Ashes*. This was the same as that of a Joan Sutherland novel published by Mills & Boon in 1922. Boyman arranged, on Boon's suggestion, to change the title. One wonders whether, after ten years, Sutherland's novel was still in print, or whether this was simply a matter of principle.

&

The Mills & Boon List in 1930 was a very different-looking one from 1920, and reflects the changes in the company and the market-place. As early as 1930, the list was squeezing out all titles except fiction. In fact, the 1930 Mills & Boon catalogue was composed entirely of novels, filled with promotions for specific authors (the 'Elizabeth Carfrae's Novels' or the 'Denise Robins' Novels', price 7s. 6d.), as well as for series, such as Mills & Boon's 'Three-and-Sixpenny Novels' and 'Half-Crown Novels'. There were 110 different titles offered, by 31 authors. Of the cheaper editions, some were 'Entirely New', so as to spur interest in the list. By 1933 Mills & Boon's catalogue had swelled to 200 titles, over half of which were offered at 2s. 6d., by 36 authors.

Clearly, in order to sustain this growing publication list (and the libraries' appetite), Charles Boon had to nurture his existing authors, and find new ones. Discoveries and first novelists continued unabated, but with an emphasis on romantic fiction. Fortunately, as we have seen, Boon had a gift for picking talented and prolific authors. Most of his highly touted discoveries lived up to expectations, and a few went on to publish 'best-sellers' (of the Mills & Boon variety) for forty or more years. But a distinct change from the past was a lack of 'names' among the newer authors. Perhaps Charles Boon had had his fill of prima donnas, desiring 'team players' over divas. It was a winning strategy.[7]

Since Mills & Boon kept to its published promise to read every manuscript received, either from an author herself, or via an agent, the firm was inundated with manuscripts. According to company records, in 1935, for example, the firm received 531 manuscripts, and accepted 37, or 7 per cent. Of these, four were the first novels of future Mills & Boon stars: Eleanor Farnes, Jan Tempest, Sylvia Sark, and Valerie K. Nelson. Hughes Massie represented Sark; A. P. Watt, Nelson. These ladies came from very different backgrounds and income levels. Nelson (Cecilia Lacey) was a schoolmistress from Nottinghamshire. Farnes (Mrs G. W. Rutherford), a Londoner, was a housewife and mother living in Sussex. Sark (Lady Flora Cochrane) lived in Richmond. Tempest (Irene Swatridge) was a mysterious recluse who ran a sheep farm in Devon.

When Charles Boon spotted talent in a writer, he encouraged her to be as prolific as possible, and some authors published as many as seven novels in a single year. Since the larger libraries, notably Boots and W. H. Smith, would normally not take more than two books from any one author in a given year, pen-names were used often. Readers were unaware of the subterfuge, and each pen-name was treated as a separate author. For example, two star authors made their debuts in 1932: Constance M. Evans (*The Pattern of a Star*) and Maureen Heeley (*Favourites Sometimes Win*). Evans, born in Canada, came from Darlington, and worked as a schoolteacher and a secretary for London North East Railroads. Heeley (Marguerite Hills) had published a novel before joining Mills & Boon, and was represented by A. P. Watt. But in 1933 Mills & Boon lauded two 'new' authors, Nina Bradshaw and Mairi O'Nair, although they were the pen-names for Heeley and Evans, respectively. *The House with the Orange Curtains* by Mairi O'Nair was described as, 'A story of thrills and charm, by a new novelist'. The *Morning Post* called Bradshaw's debut, *Wild Sanctuary*, 'finely told, which will make an appeal . . . Most promising'. She certainly was a promising 'new' author: Bradshaw's *The Net Love Spread* was cited by W. H. Smith as one of its bestselling titles in 1935, outselling Agatha Christie and E. Phillips Oppenheim.

Hills and Evans were the prototype Mills & Boon authors of the new generation. Like the works of Denise Robins, the Heeley/Bradshaw and Evans/O'Nair novels were consistently good. These authors were also prolific. Hills eventually wrote 61 novels: 33 Heeleys and 28 Bradshaws. From 1934 until 1938, she published four titles a year. Evans wrote over 120 novels for the firm, six in 1935 alone: three by Evans (*Sandra Goes Downstairs, Secret Daughter*, and *Green Satin Girl*), and three by O'Nair (*The Girl With the X-Ray Eyes, Jennifer Disappears*, and *Peggy Paradine, House Agent*). She repeated the performance in 1937 and in 1938, and from 1939 to 1941 wrote five novels a year.

Clearly, behind the promotion and aggressive growth which surrounded new authors lay an important strategy. Charles Boon was determined to build up a large list—and backlist—of titles to weather any publishing crisis. Never again would his firm become so dependent on the fortunes of a single author, such as Jack London. This policy was justified in 1935 when the firm lost its star author: Denise Robins. Robins was at the top of her form, a major seller with thirty-four titles in print, and a one-woman publicity engine, akin to her future rival, Barbara Cartland. In August 1933, for example, Mills & Boon trumpeted in an advertisement in the *Sunday Times*, 'ALL ENGLAND is reading DENISE ROBINS' lovely story SHATTER THE SKY. FOURTH EDITION PRINTING.' The critic James Agate wrote in the *Daily Express*, 'Half the world does not know how the other half lives. Still less does it know what it reads. Miss Robins' sales in this country approach 500,000 copies.'

Not only was Robins the most prolific author on the Mills & Boon list, but she had the most lucrative contracts in the firm's history. In 1932 an eight-book contract, covering publications from July 1933 (*Shatter the Sky*) until June 1935 (her last Mills & Boon novel, *How Great the Price*), paid Robins £100 each month up to £2,400, or £300 for each title. Her agent, Curtis Brown, presumably took a percentage. But this was not sufficient. As so often happened to Mills & Boon in its early days, Robins was poached by a new publishing house, Nicholson & Watson. In her autobiography Robins told her side of the story:

> For eight or nine years now, Mills & Boon had been my publishers. Suddenly a young man named Ivor Nicholson came along—a clever, charming journalist who, with the wealth of Bernard Watson to back his venture, launched a new publishing house—Ivor Nicholson & Watson. They wanted my name on their list. They tempted me with what was the biggest offer I had ever received from any literary quarter. A cheque for *one thousand pounds*, free, gratis, and for which I need do no work. It was merely for signing the contract!
>
> I did not go behind Charles Boon's back. I told him the facts. Unfortunately he was so annoyed by this offer from Ivor Nicholson that he refused to compete and at once released me from my contract with his firm. Somewhat reluctantly I left my old publishers and became the new Nicholson & Watson 'star' author.[8]

'Denise Robins, one of our greatest authors, knew she could sell on her name more than other authors could,' explained Alan Boon. 'She was a superstar, and she knew it. Our problem was to find a way to satisfy the superstar. What could Mills & Boon offer a superstar? Superstars weren't grateful. We went on publishing all the authors all the same.'

Robins's first book with Nicholson & Watson, *Life and Love* (1935), was launched with an unprecedented publicity campaign, which featured the slogan 'Robins for Romance' emblazoned on London buses. Significantly, one of her first duties for her new publisher was a personal appearance in Liverpool to open a commercial lending library, no doubt thanking the public which had made her fortune. Mills & Boon made no public comment on Robins's defection, but capitalized on her fame. In March 1935, in the *Sunday Times*, under the dramatic headline '26,546', an advertisement ran, 'MILLS & BOON have sold since January 1 (8 weeks) the above number of the DENISE ROBINS Novels and they are confident that Fiction readers will read with alacrity ALL THIS FOR LOVE 7s. 6d. net which will be published on March 22. It is the finest novel DENISE ROBINS has yet written.'

Significantly, Robins was the last 'big' Mills & Boon author to leave the firm. There are many reasons why. For one, the list was expanded and broadened with many quality authors, which bolstered the imprint and lessened the dependence on a single star of the Robins mould. Also, a concerted effort was made to nurture authors, and sign them to lucrative multi-book contracts. Mills & Boon's future prosperity, therefore, was achieved through quantity as much as 'quality'. Eventually the Mills & Boon imprint became better known than the authors themselves, which offered a distinct advantage in promotion and sales.

It is not surprising to discover that in the wake of Denise Robins's departure Mills & Boon spent heavily on promoting its existing authors and prominent new ones, and looked to poach authors from other houses. At the end of 1935, perhaps to offset the Nicholson & Watson promotion of Robins, Mills & Boon embarked on a large-scale advertising campaign for a 'New British Novelist' hailed as a 'Mills & Boon brilliant discovery': Jan Tempest, who was discovered in the 'slush' pile. The *Sunday Times* advertisement placed in December 1935 (which cost £24) was unique for a Mills & Boon novelist, even for Robins:

> JAN TEMPEST: A NEW BRITISH NOVELIST. Do you wish to be one of the earliest readers of a Popular Novelist who within a short time is certain to be a 'Best-Selling' writer of Romances of remarkable human interest, and who will be read wherever the English language is spoken? 'Best Sellers' are not published every day, but now and again there comes into the Fiction market a writer who, by sheer imaginative skill and superb treatment of the difficulties and trials of human existence, enters that very limited circle of writers possessing great story-telling qualities, and soon is read by everybody.... When the following novels are published they will be read with alacrity by millions of readers everywhere.

The first four 7s. 6d. novels were: *Be Still, My Heart!*, *All This I Give*, *Stepmother of Five*, and *Someone New to Love*. Fortunately for Mills & Boon, Tempest was a gifted storyteller, and her success must have seemed providential: *Be Still, My Heart!* sold out eight editions in its first year. She was also prolific: between 1936 and 1945 Tempest averaged seven novels per year, divided among two pen-names: Tempest and Fay Chandos, launched in 1937. Thus in the *Daily Telegraph* in September 1936, Mills & Boon could boast, 'MILLS & BOON'S 1936 Fiction has enjoyed a record success. More copies have been sold than ever before. The reason is not far to seek—every novel MILLS & BOON issue is worth reading—and thus the popular fiction reader insists on reading them all.' The volume strategy was working.

But Tempest was only the beginning. Between 1936 and 1939 Mills & Boon added twenty new authors to its list, at least thirteen of whom were both popular and prolific: Juliet Armstrong, Joan Blair, Frances Braybrooke, Mary

Burchell, Cicely Colpitts, Ann Deering, Elizabeth Hoy, Vicky Lancaster, Jean MacLeod, Valerie K. Nelson, Philippa Preston, Sara Seale and Susan Taylor. On the whole, authors were from solidly middle- or lower-middle-class backgrounds, and worked for a living. Hoy, for example, was born in Dublin, and worked as a nurse, and journalist with the London *Daily News*, selling her first story at the age of 14. Ann Deering (Nancy Collier) and Susan Taylor (K. P. Collier) were sisters from Birmingham. Mary Burchell (Ida Cook) was from Northumberland, and Jean MacLeod (Jean Walton) from Scotland. Frances Braybrooke and Cicely Colpitts were pen-names of Frances Wellesley-Smith of London, who eventually wrote eighty-nine novels.

Mills & Boon was not averse to publishing authors poached from other firms, if their talent and success were proven—and if they did not mind being part of a larger list. In 1937 Joan Blair (the pen-name of two authors, Anne Pedlar and Helen Rees) arrived from Wright & Brown, and her Mills & Boon debut, *Sister of Nelson Ward*, was one of the first of a new genre: the Doctor-Nurse romance. In 1939 Berta Ruck and Barbara Stanton joined the list, presented by Mills & Boon, somewhat defensively, as 'well known as writers of fiction. It is their ability to write compelling stories of a popular appeal which makes their work harmonise with the rest of MILLS & BOON's list.' Berta Ruck was a fixture on Hodder & Stoughton's Yellow Jackets list, and was married to a former Mills & Boon author, Oliver Onions. Barbara Stanton, the pen-name for a male–female writing team, had been published by Hurst & Blackett.[9]

Two new authors, Mary Burchell and Jean MacLeod, merit a closer look, as each emerged from this decade to give fifty years' service to Mills & Boon, writing over 130 novels apiece. Like most of this new generation of Mills & Boon authors, both were in their late twenties when they signed their first, three-book contracts. Both came from the North, had solidly lower-middle-class roots, and worked as journalists. Trained as serial writers for women's weekly magazines, both settled easily into writing three or four novels a year for Mills & Boon.

Burchell had worked as a sub-editor on *Mab's Fashions* in Fleet Street, and wrote short stories, followed by her first stab at a romantic serial. 'I am I think by nature a tale-spinner, and passionately interested in people,' Burchell recalled. 'The thing that I found I was capable of doing was romancing—rather strongly for my period.' She also needed the money, to finance an extraordinary operation in which Burchell and her sister, Dorothy Cook, travelled often to pre-war Germany, helping to smuggle twenty-nine Jews to freedom in England. The story of the sisters' efforts is told in Burchell's autobiography (as Ida Cook), *We Followed Our Stars* (1956). The sisters never married, living together all their lives.

When Charles Boon handed Burchell her first, three-book contract, she was eager to sign on the spot:

'No, no!' he said firmly. 'You must never sign anything like that. You take that contract home and show it to your father, and if he says you can sign it, you can.'

How's that for the wicked old world of publishing? No wonder I knew from that moment I was in safe hands.'[10]

Her debut, *Wife to Christopher* (1936), was a lively tale of two sisters, one of whom is compromised into marriage, which in the end is transformed into love. Burchell regarded romance novels as an excellent escape from reality, which certainly was true for readers during the Second World War. 'Of course we all like make-believe, particularly when things are not going awfully well, naturally,' she said. 'Charles Boon, certainly, and Alan I think as well, were prepared to publish whatever I wrote. And so they must have believed in me. And then of course I was completely spoiled.' During her first ten years with the firm, Burchell wrote thirty-six novels.

MacLeod, born in Glasgow, was one of Mills & Boon's first Scottish novelists, and promoted as such in the *Scotsman* and other Northern newspapers. She began as a writer of short stories and serials for popular Scottish magazines such as the *People's Friend*, published by D. C. Thomson. 'I didn't know [the ropes] when I started,' MacLeod recalled:

> I just picked up the first directory and looked for publishers' names. I found the Nonesuch Press and I thought, 'Well, that sounded like me, nonesuch.' And I had a lovely letter back from them that said, 'Dear Madam, We're so sorry but we only publish definitive editions of Kipling and George Bernard Shaw.' So I thought, well, I'm on the wrong track there. And then I looked again and found Mills & Boon, and that's the end of the story.

MacLeod's first manuscript, *Summer Rain*, was rejected by Charles Boon. 'I sent Mills & Boon a summary and they thought it had a very unhappy ending and they don't deal in that,' she recalled. 'So they said, "Well, could you let us see your next one?" And they bought *Life For Two*. You have to realise that novelists can have the power to change a life a little bit, and for the type of thing that I was writing, they expect a happy ending.' MacLeod eventually revised *Summer Rain*, and it was published as her third novel.

From 1938 to 1945, MacLeod averaged four titles a year. 'I was the only one doing a real Scottish background,' she said. 'I love Scotland, come from three generations of farming people, and could describe it apparently. You're local to start with, and then you suddenly spread your wings a bit. Once you get experience you can write wider.'

Both Burchell and MacLeod agreed that writing for Mills & Boon was a lucrative way of earning a living, especially for a woman in this period. 'If you were making a thousand [pounds] a year then, that was very big money,' Burchell said. 'In my days of middle-classery, I was madly interested in getting the money.' Both women echoed the opinions of a rival best-selling author of popular romance, Ruby M. Ayres. 'If you want to make money writing, you must write about love,' Ayres told the *Trade Circular* in 1933. 'I never could understand why it should be thought a disgrace to write five books a year and sell them.' And sell books they did—encouraged by Charles Boon, both Burchell and MacLeod made personal appearances when necessary, and courted their fans. Burchell gave speeches to Women's Institutes and other groups around the country, which she considered the best advertisements for her books, as they encouraged people to talk about them. 'There's nothing like the personal touch,' Burchell added:

> Old Charles Boon used to say to me, 'Never pass a Boots shop in Eastbourne, anywhere you are, without going in and making yourself known.' The personal touch. I can't say I always did it, but I did sometimes. And they'll say, 'Oh, yes, I've heard of you.' I remember I said once to a woman at the bookstall in Victoria, she was looking at one of my books. I said, 'Buy it. I wrote it.' She looked up, and put it down, and thought, 'She's one of those who ought to be locked up.' She didn't believe it a bit!

MacLeod noted that women from all classes and backgrounds wrote to her on how much they enjoyed her books. 'A friend of mine was a bit of a cynic,' she recalled. 'She went into Harrod's and said, "Now *who* reads Jean S. MacLeod's books anyway?" "Oh," the girl said, "Young girls, happily married young women, *and* the dowagers." She came away with her tail between her teeth!'

🌿

'In the 1930s we used to go to library conferences, and there were about ten publishers there, all publishing romances, and we were not so well known,' Alan Boon recalled. 'The people who ran the libraries knew us, but the public at large did not. They used to call them the "Books in Brown", which I suppose gradually helped in the end. I think we were probably first among equals—we were dominating with the Books in Brown.'

The important point here is that by the outbreak of the Second World War romantic fiction or 'romances' had emerged as a genre, a distinct market recognized by the industry and the media, and reinforced by the cinema. In 1934 W. H. Smith surveyed 'Romance Authors and their Publishers' and listed thirteen publishing houses. All of the larger firms were present, including Collins (who published Phyllis Austin), Hodder & Stoughton (Annie S. Swan), Hutchinson (Isabel C. Clarke), and Ward, Lock (E. Maria Albanesi). Mills & Boon (listing only, for whatever reason, Sophie Cole) joined other smaller houses, including Wright & Brown (Nora K. Strange) and Rich & Cowan (Elinor Glyn). In addition to full price, 7s. 6d. editions, all of the publishers were publishing 'cheap editions' of price 3s. 6d. and lower. Similarly, in 1938, Ronald F. Batty, author of *How to Run a Twopenny Library* (whose publication attests to the popularity and financial rewards offered by commercial libraries), listed 'The Most Popular Twopenny Library Authors'. Under the category 'Love and Romance', sixty-eight authors were listed. Of these, eight were Mills & Boon regulars, including Elizabeth Carfrae, Sophie Cole, Louise Gerard, Helena Grose, Marjorie M. Price, and Marjorie Warby. Denise Robins and Joan Sutherland also made the list, as did Ruby M. Ayres, Maysie Greig, Baroness Orczy, Ethel M. Dell, and Rafael Sabatini.

Of all the publishers, Collins offered the strongest competition in the romance market. Collins had a large list in 1939, featuring Betty Trask, Pamela Wynne, Renee Shann, Carol Gaye, F. E. Baily, and a former Mills & Boon star, Helena Grose. Not surprisingly, Collins's marketing methods resembled Mills & Boon's. Advertisements for Collins's Romances, for example, featured the tag-lines 'Keep The Blues At Bay'. Beside a write-up of her latest book, *Shes and Skis*, Carol Gaye merited a Mills & Boon-style biography:

> Carol Gaye has quickly come to the front as one of the most delightful of all writers of romance fiction. Her light and human touch, with the undercurrent of drama which strengthens her novels, makes them welcome to a wide public. One of her ambitions is to go to Hollywood.

Collins, like Mills & Boon, invited readers to write: 'May we send you news of our books?'

'Romance was synonymous with Mills & Boon, but we had some strong competitors publishing considerable amounts of romance, but as just a section of very big lists,' John Boon said. 'We were unique in having so extensive a programme. I think they aimed to publish a few a month, as they happened to be available, whereas we started off with the aim to publish so many books each fortnight. It fitted in with our marketing strategy.' As such, Mills & Boon was a good training ground for authors, many of whom left to support competitors' lists. Helena Grose, as mentioned, left for Collins in 1938, as did Marjorie Warby in 1941, and Marjorie M. Price and Deirdre O'Brien in 1942. Elizabeth Carfrae departed for Hutchinson in 1942, as did Guy Trent in 1944. Sophie Cole moved to Ward, Lock in 1942. Ray Dorien went to Herbert Jenkins in 1941, and Sylvia Sark to Rich & Cowan in 1947.

What further distinguished Mills & Boon from the competition during this decade was its emerging marketing strategy. In the 1930s Charles Boon brought to fullest fruition the 'personal touch', a device which promoted sales by encouraging close contact, even a sense of kinship, with readers, first used in 1909. The endpages of each Mills & Boon romance, which usually featured the current publication list, opened with a full-page notice headed 'To Fiction Readers: Why you should choose a Mills & Boon novel':

The Fiction Market to-day is overburdened with new novels, and the ordinary reader finds it most difficult to choose the right type of story either to buy or to borrow. There are always the big names, which, by the way, do not always give satisfaction, but here at any rate in the main there should be no difficulty in making a choice. Best sellers are not published often enough to keep the ordinary reader going, and the average person has to pick and choose from hundreds of titles, many of which would have been better never to have seen the light of publication. Really the only way to choose is to limit your reading to those publishers whose lists are very carefully selected, and whose Fiction imprint is a sure guarantee of good reading.

Indeed, the Mills & Boon reader was no 'average' lady who had to browse endlessly through titles. Rather, she was 'special', with Mills & Boon, her own personal librarian, at her disposal:

The reason, therefore, why you should choose a Mills & Boon novel is because, without exception, only the best type of Fiction is accepted by them, and they make a point of reading every MS. that is sent them, whether it is by a known or an unknown author. In this way Mills & Boon have introduced to the public many of the most popular authors of the day.

Mills & Boon issue a strictly limited Fiction List, and the novels they publish all possess real story-telling qualities of an enduring nature. It is not necessary for Fiction readers to make a choice from a Mills & Boon new Fiction List. They can rest assured that each novel has been carefully chosen, and is worth reading.

Therefore ask your bookseller or librarian to put on your list every novel published by Mills & Boon.

Mills & Boon's Fiction List will be sent regularly, post free, to any address.

Clearly, the personal touch was a kind of money-back guarantee of fine reading, not dissimilar to the quality guarantees attached to any number of consumer products in the increasingly mass market.

Production values were also geared to be pleasing to the reader. Dust jacket art, for example, became 'dreamier', more sensual, and thereby more escapist, with heroines resembling Hollywood starlets. Special attention was also paid to the dust jacket blurbs, summarizing the novel within. The blurb for *The Girl from the Beauty Shop* (1939), the 'first novel' by Margaret Lovell ('Valerie K. Nelson'), is a good example of how tightly Mills & Boon held the potential reader's hand:

When Kay Fendrile left her job as an assistant in a Beauty Shop to live at High Ways Hall with her newly-discovered grandfather, she believed that she was starting the most exciting adventure of her life. Excitement, indeed, was not lacking, right from the beginning. It was a curious experience to be taken into her grandfather's home in the arms of a perfectly strange young man and to hear herself referred to as a bride being carried across the threshold. There were many other surprises for Kay in her new life, many adventures, too, much storm and a little heartbreak. The clash of temperament between a city girl, bred in the artificialities of modern life and a man, very near to the soil, very human, very elemental, is cleverly brought out in this novel of incident and emotion. The love of Kay and of Drew Enderly surmounts every obstacle, however, and we leave them in the end happy in that love.

Clearly, nothing was left to chance and the blurb reminded readers of the guaranteed happy ending.

※

On the eve of the Second World War, Mills & Boon's transformation into a 'Library House' was complete. The firm was confident, even boastful, in describing its authors in 1939—on its thirtieth anniversary:

> Thirty years ago Sophie Cole wrote the first book MILLS & BOON ever published. Since then her mastery has only increased . . . Marjorie Moore has fulfilled her early promise and stands second-to-none as a writer of powerful romance . . . Is Francis Braybrooke another Charles Garvice? A prominent newspaper has suggested the comparison. Certainly, this new writer possesses many of the characteristics of her famous predecessor, but readers will also recognise in her work an individuality and originality that is entirely her own.

'In the thirties we made a good profit for a firm of our size,' John Boon noted. 'There were not many employees. We controlled costs. We were doing extremely well in a period when most publishers were not doing well. It was a very profitable small firm then.' Having fought off overtures by Hutchinson, Mills & Boon now considered purchasing another publisher or library house themselves, and negotiated for a time with Wright & Brown. 'We had a look at them,' John Boon said. 'We were very short of romances then. Our list was expanding; it was difficult to get books very often. We looked through their list and it wasn't worth it. The literary standard and the editorial standard weren't high enough.'

But the build-up to the Second World War, and wartime itself, effectively stopped Mills & Boon's growth (see Fig. 3.1). The first payment of National Defence Contribution (1937), amounting to over £500, depressed profits. At a Board meeting in November 1938, Boon reported that business was unsettled due to the international crisis. While 'the 7s. 6d. novel market had suffered considerably with all the leading Publishers,' Boon noted that 'in a general way, this loss had been made up by the Company by the very substantial sales of their cheaper issues', a list that had been growing through the decade.

Unlike the First World War, Charles Boon, then aged 62, was not called away in 1939, and continued to oversee his firm, with Henley by his side. All three Boon sons, however, were called up. Carol was in the fire service, stationed in London and southern England. Alan followed his father into the Royal Navy, and John joined the Army, serving with the Royal Norfolk Regiment and South Wales Borderers. In 1941 Captain John Boon was appointed a Director, *in absentia*.

The declaration of war in September 1939 had a definite impact, as revealed at the November 1939 Board meeting:

> Sales of the cheap editions of the Company during 1939 had been most satisfactory, but in regard to 7s. 6d. editions of novels, most of the big Libraries had suffered a very considerable reduction in Library Subscribers' yearly subscriptions by reason of A.R.P. Work etc. The Directors hoped and believed that during 1940, there would be a return to something like a normal state with the Libraries.

Although sales in the first six months of 1940 matched the same levels as in 1939, Mills & Boon braced for the worst. 'During the last fortnight—owing to the War—trade had dropped, and at the moment there were very little signs of improvement,' Charles Boon announced in June 1940. 'The Booksellers and Libraries have not been ordering with any confidence during the last 14 days.' Among other worries, Boon noted that the firm faced potentially crippling added costs, including higher taxes and insurance premiums, and a rise in the price of printing, binding, and advertising. The price of paper, Boon reported, 'is practically 100% more than last year . . . we are not getting big supplies, and understand that we shall only receive 60% of our pre-war consumption'. Indeed, paper rationing was based on 1939 consumption, which was not the best of Mills & Boon's previous ten years. 'Publishing will certainly be considerably handicapped in the future, owing to the strictly limited supplies of paper available,' Boon reported in August 1940. 'This will mean fewer books being published, and will result in a definitely decreased turnover until such time as the world is at peace.'

But wartime also created an unusual market situation. Since paper rationing limited edition sizes, books sold out quickly, returns disappeared, as did the backlist, and publishers earned a modest profit. In Mills & Boon's case, no more than 4,000 copies of each title could be printed during the war, 50 per cent fewer than usual. 'Undoubtedly the war encouraged readership,' John Boon said. 'If we had paper we would have sold probably ten times as many. There wasn't a lot to do during the war. Every book was sold, and publishing was limited. We made money during the war, but then there was the excess profits tax.' Mills & Boon titles went out of print as soon as they were published. The same story was told at other publishing houses. John Attenborough of Hodder & Stoughton recalled that men and women read 'voraciously' and 'anything they could get' during the war:

> The publisher's perennial problem of selling all the books he prints no longer existed. So Hodder & Stoughton sold out its pre-war stock, including all that was left of the Yellow Jackets, at three-and-sixpence, half-a-crown, two shillings, and ninepence. Authors and agents loyally accepted the firm's assurance that their books would be brought back into print as the first priority when peace and paper rationing permitted.[11]

But for most publishers, that time would not arrive until 1949, when paper rationing restrictions were fully lifted.

✌

With Charles Boon's health deteriorating at the outset of the war, Joseph Henley assumed most of the responsibility for running the firm. While he appears to have done a better job managing Mills & Boon than Margaret Boon did during the First World War, he was, like her, more of a caretaker than a publisher, and his forte was production, not editorial. None the less, Mills & Boon did expand its stable of authors during the war. Lilian Chisholm, a nurse and member of the Bromley Writing Circle, joined the list in 1941 with *Dancing Feet*, her first of 73 novels. 'She finds there is a constant war between the urge to write and the desire to keep the family clean, comfortable and well-fed,' Mills & Boon informed its (no doubt sympathetic) readers. Phyllis Matthewman, a girls' story writer from Surrey, made her debut in 1944 with *Set to Partners*, her first of 43 novels. From Scotland came two prolific authors: Margaret Malcolm, a nurse (*Loving Heart*, 1940), and Nan Sharpe (*Just a Wife*, 1942).

Certainly Mills & Boon anticipated a major publishing boom after the war, once paper supplies were released. From 1944 Henley signed a number of new contracts with several authors, including the most prolific ones: Evans, Colpitts, Nelson, Burchell, and Tempest. Tempest's 1944 contract, for example, covered 12 books, to be published between July 1944 and June 1947, with a quarterly payment of £50 paid as her advance. Burchell's 12-book contract had even better terms: £90 paid per quarter. Colpitts's six-book contract earned her advances of £100 per title; Nelson's, £150.

While Henley did his best to keep his authors writing and thereby maintain production levels during the war, he did not hesitate to alert readers and the trade of shortages. In 1940 the firm told subscribers that, 'owing to the necessity for reduced paper consumption', they were unable to send out their annual summer catalogue of new fiction. Instead, for most of the war the firm relied on crudely typed and mimeographed lists of coming novels. 'It is suggested that you give your marked list to your Librarian in good time,' readers were advised. Between July and October 1940, Mills & Boon's list of 'New Library Novels' (as they were now known) totalled 38 at 7*s*. 6*d*., and 31 at 3*s*. 6*d*., of which 12 were 'entirely new'—significantly below pre-war levels. Not surprisingly, cheaper editions sparked the biggest sales. 'I would point out that our 3s. 6d. and 2s. 6d. editions have been in great demand, and <u>orders now are exceeding all previous sales</u>,' sales representative Frank Boon warned his customers in November 1940. 'At the moment, owing to shortage of paper and increasing costs, 83 titles of our 2s. 6d. Library are unobtainable.'

In a January 1941 letter to its shareholders, Mills & Boon was blunt about the difficult trade situation. The devastating raid on 29 December 1940 on Paternoster Row destroyed or partly damaged the offices and warehouses of many publishers, including Collins, Ward, Lock, Hutchinson, and Hodder & Stoughton. Six million books in storage at the wholesale distributors Simpkin, Marshall were also lost—which included, presumably, thousands of Mills & Boon novels. The offices of Mills & Boon's chartered accountants, Alliott Makepeace, had been bombed, forcing the postponement of the firm's annual meeting. Mills & Boon admitted, in the letter, that the timing could not have been worse: 'We have, during 1940, done very good business, and the last three months—October, November and December—was a record for this period since we started publishing.' But the London bombings, coupled with another raid on Southampton, forced a setback. 'We are insured under the Government scheme for the actual cost of the books, paper, etc.,' Henley reported, 'but unfortunately the insurance under this scheme does not provide for replacement value. Our catalogue will be short of roughly one hundred titles until we can reprint them.' That did not happen, and the popular Half Crown Library (raised to 3*s*. 6*d*. in 1941) was discontinued in 1944. In 1941 a price increase to 8*s*. 6*d* was implemented, the first rise in twenty years. From this date, the firm's publication list was a shadow of its former self. For July–December 1941, 18 titles at 8*s*. 6*d*. were offered, and 47 4*s*. novels were listed in stock, including three by Jean MacLeod; four by Valerie K. Nelson; six by Philippa Preston; and nine by Jan Tempest. The firm valiantly continued to advertise, whether in newspapers or via typewritten flyers for distribution to librarians and readers. 'There is ALWAYS a new MILLS & BOON NOVEL' blared ads in the *Woolston List*, *Birmingham Gazette*, *Menzies List*, and the *Scotsman*. On these crude, seat-of-the-pants lists, the author's name and a simple statement, 'A NEW LONG NOVEL', were deemed sufficient, as indeed they probably were for most regular library users.

In 1943, fifteen years after the unexpected death of Gerald Mills, Mills & Boon faced another potential crisis. On 2 December, at the age of 66, Charles Boon died. Unlike Mills, Boon had been ailing for some time, following a heart attack early in the war. 'He had been drinking an awful lot,' recalled Dinah Boon, who had just started her nursing course. 'He had had his coronary, and he had gotten over that. The doctor said to him, "If you have a whiskey each evening, that will help you." So Father said, "If I have one whiskey, that will help me. If I have several whiskies, that will help me even more so." That's what happened.' Boon died following a second heart attack.

At a hastily called meeting on 3 December, Henley formally expressed 'the deep regret that all present felt at the loss of Mr. Charles Boon who would be greatly missed, and it was resolved that this expression of appreciation be recorded on the Minutes'. Tributes were made in several trade papers. The *Bookseller*, in a nod to Mills & Boon's recent successes, reported that Charles Boon 'had a flair for the light romantic novel, and a fair number of writers who have since gained fame and fortune in that field of literature were Mr. Boon's discoveries'. A testimonial in the *National Newsagent* agreed, adding:

> Mr. Boon's business-like and genial nature endeared him to all who had the pleasure of knowing him. My own personal acquaintance goes back many years and I have always felt how brilliantly he gauged public taste and how successful he was in meeting it. Mills & Boon novels, as my library readers well know, are always in the biggest possible demand.

What now? The three Boon sons, all Directors, proposed that Henley be elected Chairman 'until further notice'. Control of the firm, at least until the Boon brothers returned from the war, remained in the hands of Henley, whom John Boon described as 'hard-pressed, elderly, and with no thoughts on future policy'. In 1944 Charles Boon's widow, Mary, was also appointed a Director, ostensibly until Carol, Alan, and John returned from active duty. Although Mary Boon had, up to this point, taken no interest in the running of the firm, her entry now was significant. She was undoubtedly pressed into service by her younger sons to keep an eye on Henley.

Charles Boon's death left a major vacuum in Mills & Boon, one that would not be filled until after the war and the return of his sons (who were hardly experienced publishers themselves). Henley, like Margaret Boon (who was still working in the office), kept the daily business going, maintained a healthy balance sheet, and sold all the stock in the unusual wartime market conditions. He acted as caretaker until the end of the war, assisted by Carol Boon, when he was stationed in London. But while the firm maintained its market position and profit, it did not look to the future. 'Henley had no vision,' John Boon recalled. 'He was presented with a firm. He and Carol were very cosy, very comfortable. They didn't want to risk anything. I'm afraid business isn't like that.' The firm, Boon added, was 'dominated by the production department: how to produce books, not what books to produce. They knew nothing about publicity, design, or sales.'

Somewhat surprisingly, John Boon, with little direct publishing experience (but possessing keen analytical and leadership skills, on famous display when, as Major Boon, commander of the Second South Wales Borderers, he led his men on D-Day), did. In October 1945 Boon wrote a spirited defence of 'popular books' and the contribution of popular publishers such as Mills & Boon. Entitled, 'A plague o' both your houses!', this was the first of many articles by the youngest Boon son, and provides a glimpse into the philosophy of the future Chairman of Mills & Boon:

> The dealers in popular books do a service to the trade. They are the missionaries who preach the reading habit. The readers of quality books form a fairly constant group; they are less set in their tastes, and less inclined to be distracted by cheap modern entertainments. The popular reader more often than not represents what is called in politics the 'floating vote'. He has to be won from football pools, the dogs, the cinema, the wireless and kindred temptations. In fact, the popular trade bears the brunt of the competition with those forces which tend to make people read less.[12]

Boon added that if this demand was not met, readers would not turn to quality books, but would cease to read altogether. 'The trade is the servant of the public; a trusted, skilled servant perhaps, who can give advice and point the way, but the public is the final arbiter,' he wrote. As a result, most publishers need a 'cheap' list to follow this market. 'Every new reader of Edgar Wallace does not mean one less of Proust,' Boon concluded. His defence was both sound and timely, as Mills & Boon and other 'popular' publishers feared an even greater reduction in their paper allowances, should those allowances be judged on the 'worthiness' of their titles.

※

Authors had a mixed experience with the rather charmless Henley, who was no Charles Boon, nor did he pretend to be. In 1945 Constance M. Evans wrote to Henley from her Darlington home of her special visit to London. 'What a tremendous thrill at the Author's Tea when the Queen came in!' she said. 'I had hoped it would be Winston Churchill when you said nobody knew the guest of honour but the Committee; but this was a bigger pleasure still' (It is not certain whether Queen Elizabeth or Winston Churchill were fans of Mills & Boon novels, nor whether this Author's Tea was an annual affair.) In the same year, Jan Tempest thanked Henley for her latest royalty cheque. 'The accounts make very good reading,' she wrote. 'I would like to thank you for the wonderful way in which you have kept my books going during these dreadful war years. From the sales figures it looks as though your support of me was not misplaced.'

But Henley was not a social person, and during the war it would appear that relations with authors somewhat soured. 'Henley had no tact at all,' John Boon said. 'He would take an author out to lunch and say, "You're our favourite author. You never give us any trouble."' In 1946 David Higham, a director of the literary agency Pearn, Pollinger & Higham, Ltd., wrote to Alan Boon of a problem regarding Elizabeth Hoy:

> I am sure you would find it in your interests to make personal friends with this author—indeed with the several other authors of ours already on your list. More than one of them has the feeling that they really know no one at Mills & Boon: and of course there was excellent reason for this, since all you lads were away and Henley obviously couldn't cope with it all and go on doing his admirable job of keeping the business moving.

Higham added that Hoy 'in particular is, I warn you, restive' and that new author Betty Stafford Robinson 'has much the same feeling'. In his reply, Boon offered thanks and lunch at one of his favourite London restaurants, L'Etoile (the scene of countless future lunches with authors). 'We much appreciate your openness in a matter in which, to be perfectly candid, we are sometimes encouraged to be hesitant,' Boon wrote.

Evans's fondness of Henley was not long-lasting. In 1947 she complained to Alan Boon about a memorable exchange she and her sister had had with the Chairman. Her letter reveals Henley's tactlessness:

> He nearly broke my heart and my very pleasant connection with you about two years ago, when I was up in London and took Cicely to see him. He was talking about your wonderful connection and the hold you had upon the public, and he said to Cicely, 'I can tell you this, quite frankly, that if you, as a new author, sent us in a book now, we could sell as many of them, and it would be as popular as any of our authors who have been with us longer.' . . .
>
> For a long time after I had returned home, I felt as though I had no further interest in writing for the firm! I said to Cicely, when we got out, 'Well, if that's all you get for writing for years and trying to improve as you go on, trying to make each book a little better than the rest, and then to be told that a little new untried author can have sales quite as large as yours, then it doesn't seem to me worth while trying.' Especially as I saw, on the bookshelves, a book by an author who joined you at the same time as I did, but changed over, later, that her latest book had reached the 67th thousand! . . .

I can't imagine Mr. Boon greeting any of his old writers with such a statement! It had the most terrific effect both upon Cicely and myself.

Boon replied swiftly and with his usual charm, praising Evans (first published in 1932) and assuring her of the firm's high regard. In response to those 67,000 copies of a novel sold by a rival publisher, Boon expressed his scepticism:

> When in these past years of acute paper shortage and production difficulty I have seen great sales advertised for some contemporary writers, I have honestly believed that some publishing firms employ copywriters of imagination to make these claims. We do not fear comparison with any other publishing house, and we believe that when production grows easier many of our competitors will be very envious of our sales.

Evans was appeased, and went on writing romances for Mills & Boon for another 25 years, with ultimately 112 novels to her credit.

By the end of the Second World War, as Mills & Boon passed its thirty-fifth anniversary, the firm's transformation as a romantic fiction publishing house was complete. Charles Boon's fifteen-year campaign to remake his firm was a success, and the Mills & Boon imprint, backed by a large publication list and a growing number of talented authors, was well known. The Second World War, while a financial setback to Mills & Boon and other publishers, none the less served to consolidate the business of publishing and the popularity of reading.

But the post-war world would bring new pressures on Mills & Boon, which required dynamic leadership. Henley was not equipped to cope with soaring production costs, nor with the ruthless publishing climate which emerged once paper rationing restrictions were lifted. Fortunately for him (and the firm), the Boon sons returning from war were naturals as publishers, and Mills & Boon was set for another golden age in the 1950s.

Chapter 4
Regrouping and Restructuring, 1946–1956

Rosalind Brett is quite correct in sensing that Mills & Boon's stomach is not 100 per cent cast iron. We have to take into account reactions of certain sections of the community, as for instance the Irish market. Nevertheless, it seems to be that we can digest stronger meat than can the serial stomach.

Alan Boon to Curtis Brown, Lillian Warren's agent, 1950

People who say they are 'too busy to bother with a library' do not realise what they are missing. . . . In December, 1953, I bought a copy of 'All This I Gave', by Jan Tempest, a 7s. od. edition costing me 5s. This particular book made 9s. 2d. in loans and fines before being sold secondhand a year later at 10d., showing a profit of 100 per cent on cost. The firm's novels can invariably be relied upon to show equally good figures.

Roland G. Bigg, commercial librarian, 1955

WHEN Alan Boon and his brother John returned from the war in 1945 and settled into running their father's business, they found a healthy balance sheet and good team of prolific authors, and had every reason to be optimistic about the future. Joseph Henley, for all his faults, had kept the firm intact during the unusual wartime market conditions, which in fact reinforced Mills & Boon's standing as a romantic fiction publisher. The Second World War, however, may have ended in 1945, but for publishers, wartime conditions lingered for many years. Paper rationing, for instance, was not fully lifted until 1949, and the costs of production had risen dramatically. The once-resilient commercial libraries slipped into a decline, as inexpensive 'disposable' weekly magazines and paperback books became increasingly popular. The public read anything it could get its hands on during the war, but readers were not as undiscriminating in peacetime. Soon there were new temptations, including television.

For Mills & Boon, the post-war decade was a critical period when the firm's strengths were challenged and its weaknesses exposed. In the end, it was a time of restructuring, experimentation, and renewal, marked by an injection of youthful vitality. Like his father, Alan Boon, aged 33 in 1946, was an editorial genius, and during the 1950s the modern Mills & Boon romance, written to strict editorial specifications, was born, emerging even more as a commodity that bound itself more tightly to its loyal readership. John Boon, aged 30 in 1946, reorganized the financial operations, and restored some lustre to the firm by re-establishing general publishing. Advertising was also renewed, and an editorial alliance with the mass-market women's weekly magazines was mutually beneficial. Finally, the 1950s saw a return to low-cost, low-priced editions, which would prepare readers for the next big step: the launch of paperback novels.

An analysis of the balance sheet and book sales statistics for this period illustrates, after a slow start, the dramatic improvement in Mills & Boon's fortunes once the younger Boons established themselves in the firm (see Figs. 4.1, 4.2, and 4.3). The slow easing of paper rationing, beginning in 1947 and ending in 1949, had a big impact on the profit margins, as edition sizes were increased along with the number of titles published. In 1948 Mills & Boon exceeded its previous record profit, £8,477, set in 1934, by nearly 150 per cent.

Figure 4.1

Annual Net Profit of Mills & Boon, Ltd., 1945–1956

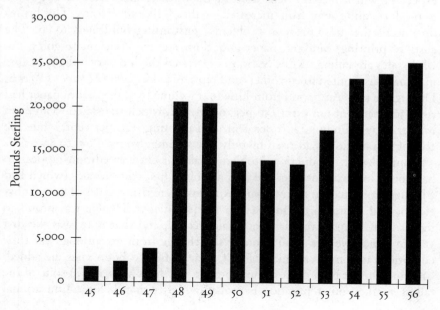

Figure 4.2

Annual Fiction Sales of Mills & Boon, Ltd., 1945–1951

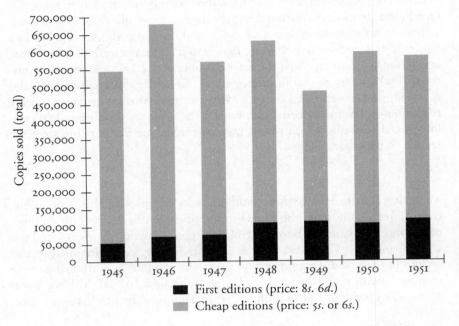

First editions (price: 8s. 6d.)
Cheap editions (price: 5s. or 6s.)

Still, Henley told the Board of Directors, profits were not rising as fast as expected, 'which means briefly that the books themselves were costing more to produce, quite apart from increased overheads like advertising. This brings up one of the most pressing problems confronting publishers today. The costs of printing, binding, paper and cloth etc. are continually going up, while sales are falling.' Mills & Boon illustrated the industry's plight in 1951 in a chart distributed to customers and reproduced in *John O'London's Weekly.* During the ten-year period from June 1941 to June 1951, the cost of paper had risen 300 per cent (an extra £30 per ton in 1951, which translated to an extra 1d. per copy), binding, 200 per cent, and printing, 100 per cent, while the cost of first editions had risen by only one shilling, from 7s. 6d. to 8s. 6d.

Coupled with production problems, sales of cheaper editions appear to have been inconsistent after the war, although first edition sales (which had a higher profit margin than cheaper editions) were rising. Sales of 8s. 6d. novels doubled, from 59,356 in 1945, to 121,288 in 1951. Henley was proud to report that, in 1948, the firm set a sales record, and that 1949 'was the first year in which we felt at all strongly the change from exceptional war time conditions to a more normal state of trade'. Mills & Boon sales, he added, 'are much better than those of our competitors. In some ways, in spite of the falling market, our reputation is probably higher than before.' Educational

Figure 4.3

Annual Educational Title Sales of Mills & Boon, Ltd., 1945–1951

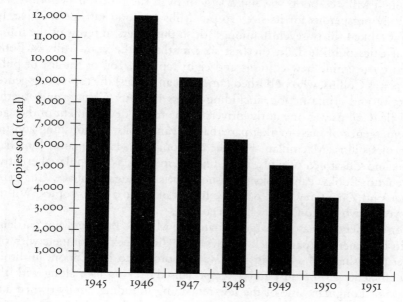

sales also received a temporary boost after the war, peaking at 11,916 in 1946, the highest level since 1936.

But Mills & Boon entered the 1950s with falling profits and uncertain sales. In 1951 the firm was compelled to increase the price of first edition fiction to 9s. 6d., due to rising production costs. 'This had the effect of reducing sales, and I am afraid that if we had to increase our price further, there would be a further fall in sales. We are not anxious to do this at all, but it may be compelled upon us,' Alan Boon told Joan Blair. Print runs were reduced from 8,000 copies to 7,000 or 6,000, just enough to recoup costs and earn some money for both publisher and author.

'It was pretty clear to some of us that the circulating library bonanza was not here to stay,' John Boon noted, given the expansion of public libraries, and the growth of television and other forms of entertainment. 'We realized that the short-term solution was to increase the number of books we published.' By reducing print runs but increasing the number of titles, Mills & Boon managed to survive. From 1950 Mills & Boon offered up to ten titles per month, published fortnightly, mostly new editions, but an increasing number of reprints. The results are evident from the statistics: profits grew rapidly from 1953, and throughout the decade Mills & Boon issued an annual dividend of 50 per cent. There would be no turning back.

Although Mills & Boon was not a large firm in the post-war period, it was relatively prosperous for its size. To put Mills & Boon into perspective, in 1949 it ranked thirty-seventh among British publishers in terms of the number of titles published. In the first six months of the year, Mills & Boon issued twenty-nine new editions and eight reprints. Top of the list of publishers was Collins, who published (among many types) the top-selling genre, detective and crime fiction, including works by Peter Cheney and Agatha Christie. Collins was one of the drivers of the major development of the age, the emergence of mass-market paperbacks. Pan Books, a publishing consortium of Collins, Macmillan, Hodder & Stoughton, Heinemann, Jonathan Cape, and Chatto & Windus, was launched in 1944, as a popular alternative to Penguin Books. Pan Books published Christie, Edgar Wallace, Georgette Heyer, and Zane Grey at 1s. 6d., in editions of up to 25,000 copies. Within two years, two million copies had been sold.

For a variety of reasons (largely financial), Mills & Boon did not participate in the emerging paperback business, nor did it seek to compete with the larger publishers. The firm in 1946 was, according to John Boon, 'in limits very efficient, prosperous, and very specialised'. It was also, along with the House of Longman, one of the few remaining founding family-owned and run publishing firms in Britain. But the legacy of Charles Boon was strong. 'We were brought up on the difficult times Mills & Boon had when it was a general publisher,' Boon said. 'My father managed most effectively to undermine all of our self-confidence. To branch out, do anything new, that we had not been doing for 20 years, was like we were risking the end of the world. We had such a bad time publishing educational and general books, and a good time on fiction, that no one would change anything. My father's influence was so firm.'

All that would soon change. After the war, roles and titles were clarified. Henley, for example, was signed to a new contract. Although his title was changed to Chairman and General Manager (as held by Charles Boon), his salary was reduced from £5,300 per year to £4,000, the same as each of the three Boon sons (all Directors). Carol Boon was named Manager of the Production Department; Alan, Manager of the Literary Department; and John, Manager of the Sales Department. Although John and Alan Boon lacked experience as publishers, they displayed a remarkable confidence and ability. Their energy overshadowed their older brother Carol, who fast disappeared into the shadows, as did Henley. Before long, Mills & Boon resembled its former self, a two-man operation.

In a sense, Mills & Boon did not have a strong incentive to compete or change much, as the war strengthened its pre-eminent position as a library supplier. In 1948 Boots Booklovers Library (perhaps Mills & Boon's biggest customer) instructed its librarians about 'Light romances and Family Stories' in one of its Literary Courses for employees. 'Most women find so much to do these days and are entitled, if they wish, to spend an hour enjoying a book which provides them with a chance to sit down and relax, both physically and mentally', Boots noted of these readers of light fiction. The leading publishers, according to Boots, were Mills & Boon, Collins, Hutchinson, and Ward, Lock. Boots pointed out the use of 'a distinctive binding which helps both librarians and the public' as 'there are far too many titles to attempt to memorise'. Mills & Boon, as we know, used brown or red bindings; Ward, Lock's Blue Panel Romances and Westerns were also distinctive. In 1949 Miss F. L. Belton, a Boots employee in Walsall, told the company magazine *The Bee* of her exasperation when an elderly lady requested a particular romance, and all she could remember was that it had a brown binding:

> Desperately I clung to my only clue—a brown book—and prayed to heaven for inspiration. I hadn't realised before just how many brown books there were in the Library, and silently I cursed Mills and Boon for choosing the colour for their publications. 'Was it "Meant for Each Other" or "Teach me to Love?"' I asked hopefully.

The book was *Forever Amber*—and had a green binding.

Boots further advised its librarians to 'be familiar with the names of these authors, so that when the books are rebound we can find them easily'. In Boots's supplied list of 81 popular authors of romantic fiction, 40 were published by Mills & Boon, from Jane Arbor and Mary Burchell to Sara Seale and Jan Tempest. Among those on the list who were not published by Mills & Boon were Ruby M. Ayres, Barbara Cartland, Charles Herbert, and Denise Robins.

As we have noted, the most immediate problem facing Mills & Boon after the war was the rise in production costs. The effects of this were mixed. On the one hand, higher costs depressed profits for the firm. But there were advantages. For one, closer attention was paid (as it was during the war) to the length of novels, and shorter manuscripts were preferred. Alan Boon was also able to rein in authors who experimented in their writing, warning them to stick to romance. The long-term impact of these decisions was a further standardization of the 'product', the romantic novel. When Lilian Chisholm offered her latest manuscript, *I Shall Be There*, to Alan Boon in 1948, warning that it was 'different', Boon's response was swift—and negative:

> In recent years, your faithful readers have come to look forward to a special type of romantic story from you. (Your most recent published novel has earned you over £400, and this has been achieved by the fact that

readers know when they choose one of your novels that they can rely on reading a special type of story.) We do feel that readers who choose 'I SHALL BE THERE' in expectation of enjoying a typical Lilian Chisholm novel would be disappointed, and in these days when sales are not so easily obtained we must always be careful about the future.

Similarly, Boon had to stand firm when a veteran author started to fade. In 1951 Errol Fitzgerald (Lady Josephine Clarke), published by Mills & Boon since 1929, quit, after her latest manuscript, *Unwanted Bride*, was returned. 'Over the passage of the years,' Boon was forced to admit, 'our respective ways as author and publisher have tended to diverge.' The brusqueness of Boon's letter may have been necessary, since given the difficult publishing climate, Mills & Boon could no longer afford to be charitable to an author of long standing. Lady Josephine was hurt that she had not been told sooner. 'I cannot imagine your father, who was always so kind and helpful in his criticisms, treating an author . . . with so much lack of consideration, and I regret that you should not have acted in his tradition,' she wrote. After fifty-one novels, she left the firm, and with her exited a distinct class of author, educated and well-bred, that we would not meet again.

A similar situation occurred when Louise Gerard resurfaced in 1957, some twenty years after her last novel had been published by Mills & Boon. New manuscript in hand ('a love story, pure and simple, with suspense enough to keep the reader wondering what is going to happen next'), Gerard wrote to Alan Boon:

> I do not know what sort of novels are likely to be popular these days, but I do know the reading public is getting somewhat tired of the sort of stuff that is put on the market nowadays, that seems to have neither beginning nor end and finally leaves the reader all up in the air. The novel I am in the act of finishing, in the very rough, is just a straightforward story, not high-brow. In length it is about 60,000 words, which is not entirely a drawback in these days when production costs are at least three times what they were before this last war.

Mills & Boon did not publish the novel. As Boon recalled, 'It was awful and boring. It was hopeless for the new product. Louise Gerard had lost her kick. She'd lost the punch. We must deliver the punch. If the Mills & Boon punch is lowered, the public must fall over.'

Hard times also provided the firm with a good excuse to review its contracts and royalty rates. Alan Boon's concerns probably led him to compile a list of his top twenty-seven authors in 1948, detailing their contract provisions. The list is revealing. All of the authors were well over the age of 30 (not a good sign), and a majority, eighteen, used an agent. The more popular (or prolific) the author, the better the contract terms. Eighteen authors earned advances of £100 or more per title, with Lilian Chisholm (represented by

Rupert Crew) earning £150 per book. The most prolific authors on the list were Jan Tempest (an eight-book contract; £100 advance per title); Phyllis Matthewman (seven novels; £75); Mary Burchell (six novels; £90 per quarter); Nina Bradshaw/Maureen Heeley (six novels; £125); and Jean MacLeod and Margaret Malcolm (five novels; £125).[1]

Although new to the business, Alan Boon did not hesitate to contact authors and agents to discuss terms, and share details of the firm's financial difficulties. In 1948, for example, Boon opened negotiations with A. P. Watt on revising the royalties scale in the contracts of several of his authors, including Frances Wellesley-Smith (Frances Braybrooke and Cicely Colpitts), Marguerite Hills (Nina Bradshaw and Maureen Heeley), and Cecilia Lacey (Valerie K. Nelson and Margaret Lovell). The reason: the 'considerable increase' in the cost of production of books which Mills & Boon had borne itself, without resorting to a retail price increase. 'Without entering into any moral or patriotic motives for keeping the price of our novels down, we seriously believe that any increase in price would have an effect on our sales,' Boon said. Sales were good, he added, but 'these higher sales have now brought us into a position of difficulty and embarrassment on account of their effect on royalties'. The reason: royalty rates in contracts had not changed since before the war, and increased on a sliding scale tied to sales, so that too much cash was being paid to authors. Mills & Boon had to pay Hills and Wellesley-Smith, for example, royalties set at 20 per cent, a rate 'impossible for us in conjunction with the increased costs', Boon said. He proposed reducing the rate to 15 per cent on the first 3,600 copies, and 20 per cent thereafter. These authors, Boon maintained, would not earn less money with this arrangement, but 'considerably more' through higher sales:

> To put it succinctly, 'what they lose on the swings, they will gain on the roundabouts,' and help us as well as themselves in so doing. These are our rough estimates as to how the changes would affect the various authors. We should plan 7,000 printings of the 8/6d editions of Francis Braybrooke's AS HANDSOME DOES and Cicely Colpitts' THY SWEET IS BITTER respectively; each one of which should earn about £400. We are planning to publish 6,000 of Valerie K. Nelson's DEAR MR. RIGHT shortly, which should bring her between £350 and £400. We would go on to 7,000 for ADVENTURE FOR FLORA, which should earn more than £400. For Maureen Heeley's THE SPLENDID GIFT and Nina Bradshaw's DARK BLOSSOMS we would plan printings of 8,000, which should earn about £500 in royalties. These figures are all irrespective of any later cheap edition.

Boon concluded with an appeal for loyalty and goodwill, pledging these sales were 'within our compass', and that these authors, who had 'long and honourable associations with our firm', could trust Mills & Boon 'to do our honourable best'.

Boon's strategy was not without risk, for these popular authors could have packed their bags and headed for another publisher. But the goodwill established between the firm and its authors over twenty years prevailed. The response from authors was swift and positive, and all agreed. Lacey, for example, gave her acceptance in a letter to A. P. Watt:

> Mr. Boon puts his case very clearly and I have every sympathy with the position in which he finds himself. Indeed the situation of most business men, faced with shortage of labour, shortage of and high prices of raw materials and new wage claims, is unenviable. I am, therefore, quite willing to agree to the amended royalty scale proposed by Mr. Boon. May I add my endorsement of his remarks about my long and pleasant association with his firm. I have always felt that I was getting very fair treatment from them.

Mills & Boon was not alone among publishers struggling with post-war conditions and unreasonable contracts. In 1949 Heinemann contacted John Masefield, lamenting how the costs of production had risen by 300 per cent over pre-war levels. Heinemann's solution was to raise book prices from 8s. 6d. to 10s. 6d., with a caveat: 'If we accept the price of 10s. 6d. as the only one in the circumstances, we must face a reduction in our own returns and that, I am afraid, is why I have had to make this proposal of a reduced royalty to you.' Masefield accepted.[2]

Upon sorting out the contract situation, the Boon brothers moved to capitalize on improved sales after the war, with a vigorous publicity campaign based on the legacy established by their father: the Mills & Boon imprint. Little was left to the imagination in promoting the brand to readers and distributors alike. Here the composition of Mills & Boon's readership was a distinct advantage. Richard Hoggart has observed how working-class readers in particular, in their selection of popular fiction, tended towards uniformity rather than anonymity, and the same type of novels.[3] This characteristic could be applied to Mills & Boon readers, who increasingly asked for 'a Mills & Boon novel' or 'a book in brown', rather than a particular author, confident of the consistent 'quality' of the 'product' they were obtaining.

By 1951 Mills & Boon 'Romantic Novels' were presented as 'Library Novels', 'Profitable Books', and 'Romances That Fill The Till' with an 'average profit' of £2 per book. Behind this campaign was a concern that the firm, and publishers of popular fiction in general, faced increasing competition from the expansion of public libraries, magazines, the cinema, and television. 'There is no doubt in my opinion that the libraries will feel increasing competition from television,' Alan Boon told Jan Tempest in 1954. 'I was in a library a little time ago and the owner of the library told me of one lady who had recently purchased a television set. Previously this customer used to borrow 12 books a week, but had now reduced the number of borrowed books to 3.' By promoting its own success as a library supplier, Mills & Boon hoped to expand its market share and build support for the libraries themselves.

Seemingly at every point in the post-war period, Mills & Boon advertisements appeared, articles on the firm were published, and authors made personal appearances or granted interviews. In 1948, as paper rationing was eased, a large advertisement in the W. H. Smith *Trade Circular* headed 'MILLS & BOON ROMANTIC FICTION' seemed designed to refresh the trade's memory and notify dealers of new volume:

> Years of experience and careful searching have produced the consistent quality which makes Mills & Boon's list of romantic novels the best that is published. ... Mills & Boon plan to publish two to four books each fortnight steadily throughout the year. Every book is well written and well produced. It is this quality of consistency which means you can safely go to your wholesaler and PLACE A STANDING ORDER.

Every book, furthermore, contained advertisements of its own to entice readers. In addition to the usual catalogue of current titles, a full-page ad spotlighted the author's next title: 'If you liked *The Golden Peaks*, then you'll love Eleanor Farnes's next, *The Dream and the Dancer*. Ask for it at your library.' Another full-page ad, which included an illustration or photograph of an attractive Mills & Boon 'reader', asked, 'Are You Taking Full Advantage?':

> If this book gave you pleasure, you will certainly enjoy our other Romantic novels, but are you taking full advantage of the service we provide?
>
> At your library you can always ask for 'a Mills & Boon novel' in the confidence that you will get an enjoyable story, but unless you know what we are publishing, you may miss a book by a favourite author.
>
> Do you know that there is a new Mills & Boon novel for every week of the year? That every six months we publish a free catalogue giving the titles and authors of the books we shall be producing, as well as the date of publication?
>
> Our catalogue is a complete guide to our novels, and you ought to have it. Just post a card with your name and address and make sure of many hours of pleasant reading.

Similarly, on the back flap of dust jackets, an attractive, middle-class woman smiled broadly from behind a tall pile of books. 'I always look for the "MILLS & BOON" when I want a pleasant book!' she says. Underneath is a similarly cheerful, persuasive message: 'Your troubles are at an end when you choose a Mills & Boon novel. No more doubts! No more disappointments! A Mills &

Boon novel will give you hours of happy reading. Next time, just say to your librarian, "A Mills & Boon, please!"'

Given the difficult trading conditions, Mills & Boon was not reticent in its advertisements, fond of blaring headlines and frequent quotes from 'experts' or 'readers'. There was extraordinary co-operation between Mills & Boon and the libraries. A 1949 advertisement, placed in several trade papers, was headed 'Mills and Boon, of course!':

> This novel has been out more than two hundred times. It has earned at least £2 10s.— nothing very exceptional for a Mills & Boon Romance, although with such a demand it would have been better policy for the Librarian to have bought two copies and made his profit in half the time. With our books in your Library you can make similar profits. If you do not stock them, you are losing trade to those who do.

Accompanying the ad was a photograph of the tattered book, with the inside front cover plastered with library date stamps. Similarly, librarians themselves acted as spokespersons for Mills & Boon's novels, which were the lifeblood of many circulating libraries. A frequent supporter was Thomas Joy, chairman of the London Branch of the Booksellers Association, as well as Librarian of the Army & Navy Stores, and author of *The Right Way to Run a Library Business*. 'Any experienced Librarian will tell you Mills & Boon's Romances are the backbone of his library,' Joy wrote. An unnamed colleague was quoted in a full-page ad in *Simpkin's Catalogue of Popular Fiction* in 1949:

> MILLS & BOON: A YORKSHIRE LIBRARIAN WRITES: 'I started my library fourteen years ago; since then I have had almost every romance published by you. They are by far the most popular romances; some have been lent up to two hundred times and many over a hundred.'

Longevity was a popular theme. Another 1949 ad illustrated Mary Burchell's staying power:

> 406,473 copies of Mary Burchell's books have been sold, mostly to the Library Trade. On average each book is lent 100 times at 3d. a time, thus earning 25s. 25s. × 406,473 — £508,091 5s., not a bad figure for one author.

By 1949 Burchell had published 41 novels; according to this information, each could have sold (with reprintings) an average of 10,000 copies, and so (at 100 lendings per copy) could have been read by as many as one million people. According to John Boon these statistics were not exceptional for a Mills & Boon author during this period: Burchell was a popular but not a top author, and anyone writing for as many years as Burchell had been (since 1936), would have achieved comparable figures by 1949, given frequent reprintings. 'I think where we scored was that so many of our authors achieved these sort of figures,' Boon said. 'We had a very high general level, because the imprint was very well known.'[4]

Sometimes the best publicity fell out of the sky. Mills & Boon received an unexpected Christmas gift in 1952, when one title made the *Sunday Times*'s annual Books-of-the-Year list. The supporter was none other than the Poet Laureate, John Masefield, a Heinemann author. His testimony: 'I have not been able to read many new books this year, but I have had much pleasure from two novels: *The Chequered Flag* by Bethea Creese (Mills & Boon) and *The Queerfella*, by Sir David Bone (Duckworth). I have felt both these to be outstanding stories.'

The Chequered Flag was Creese's third of twenty-five novels for Mills & Boon. A journalist, magazine editor, and short story writer, Creese may have known Masefield personally. In any event, Masefield's choice is puzzling, as *Chequered Flag* is a thoroughly unexceptional story set against the world of race cars and dealerships. Rosel Vermont, the heroine, is a receptionist for Flick Distributors, the West End agents for Hazzard Cars. 'A job at reception was what you dreamed of when you were twenty and longed to meet interesting people and feel yourself in the swim of life,' she mused. The hero, Fort Hazzard, well-known motorist and head of Hazzard Motors, is a misunderstood playboy, with 'a sinewy strength in every line of his alert, upright figure'. Needless to say, poor girl and rich boy fall in love. When Fort proposes, he promises 'everything that goes with love—a home, fulfillment, always being together, closely together'. Racing metaphors are commonplace in this novel:

> 'Rosel,' said Fort, in a low, pleading voice. 'I used to think that I could not ask a girl to share a life that might not run clear through until—until the flag dropped. But I know enough of you to be sure already that you can take the bends as well as the straight. Will you risk it with me, beautiful? I love you.'

Rosel accepts, picks a diamond ring, and ponders her future: 'Did it matter what lay at the turn of the road, so long as you went up to it hand in hand, with courage and hope and the love that endures?'

Masefield's recommendation brought the firm some welcome publicity, as well as a temporary boost in sales. Mills & Boon told the *Bookseller* that, thanks to Masefield, Creese had broken the mould, since usually 'an author of light fiction must write 10 or 12 novels before he is known in the libraries unless he has exceptional good fortune'. *Chequered Flag*, published in June 1952, had sold 174 retail copies before the *Sunday Times* article appeared (notwithstanding the pre-publication subscription sales of 5,000–6,000). From then onwards, Mills & Boon had estimated average retail sales of ten copies or so a month. Instead, between January and March 1953, Mills & Boon sold 140 copies, thanks to 'this brief mention in, what is for us, an unsuitable medium . . . It is not uninteresting.'

While targeting the librarians and book-buyers in advertisements, Mills &

Boon renewed efforts to establish a direct mail catalogue operation. Twice a year, the 'Happy Reading' catalogue was published and sent to an ever-expanding mailing list of loyal Mills & Boon readers. 'We scheduled very, very carefully,' John Boon explained. 'We used to list these monthly. The ladies used to go into the libraries and demand these books, which is a marvellous way of advertising.' The 'Happy Reading' series evolved over the years into 'New Books', 'Pleasant Books', 'Pleasant Reading', and 'Books that Please', all perpetuating the customer 'guarantee'.

The catalogue operation begun in the 1950s is the precursor to the firm's successful direct mail operation, which dominates the business today. An interesting article in the *Bookseller* in 1955, written by John Boon, described the effectiveness of catalogues and their role in market research. Of 16,000 catalogues mailed monthly to Mills & Boon readers, Boon noted, 2,700, or 14 per cent, responded to a questionnaire. The responses illustrate Mills & Boon's market penetration in the British Isles, as well as its continuing dependence upon libraries. Of the home market, the most replies (2,254) came from England, followed by Scotland (131), Wales (101), and Ireland (79). Replies from overseas ('this section of our mailing list is much smaller than the home section') came from Australia, New Zealand, South Africa, and Canada. Most readers (1,152) obtained their novels from Boots or W. H. Smith (still the firm's biggest customers), followed by 'small, single-unit libraries' (639), public libraries (465, an encouraging number), and 'multiple libraries' (309) such as Red Circle Libraries of Sheffield. Readers in England and Wales favoured Boots and W. H. Smith; Scotland and Ireland (where Boots and W. H. Smith shops were less common), single-unit libraries. The highest public library usage, moreover, was found among readers in Lancashire, Yorkshire, and Staffordshire.[6]

As Editor of the fiction list, Alan Boon followed in his father's large footsteps. Fortunately he inherited his father's charm and stamina, engendering a loyalty and affection from his authors which served the firm well over Boon's forty years of service. It is impossible to underestimate Alan Boon's impact, on building a stable of popular and prolific authors, as well as fine-tuning the 'product' and editorial policy. 'Mills & Boon were different from most publishers,' Alan Boon said. 'We paid a great deal of attention to author relations. We became good friends with the author.' Jay Blakeney, who joined Mills & Boon as 'Anne Weale' in 1955, recalled that several of the older authors were 'deeply smitten' with Boon, and suspected he was amused by the attention:

> Everyone on his list liked and admired him, sometimes to the point of idolatry. With good reason. He gave us long vinous lunches at the Ritz

and other elegant restaurants. He was lavish with praise and tactful with criticism. He sent flowers to our hotels and homes, telegrams of congratulation at every opportunity and always rang up on Christmas Eve. Our letters were answered by return. Every possible help and encouragement was given. It was a golden era, and those of us who experienced it realise now how lucky we were to have enjoyed those happy times.

In her first year, Blakeney noted she received thirty letters from Boon. Given the amount of correspondence in the Mills & Boon archive, that was a low figure; most authors wrote twice a week to Boon. He answered every letter.

One of the biggest decisions Boon made, which would affect the firm's future direction, was to establish an alliance with the women's weekly magazines. While Mills & Boon had had a close relationship with the magazines since the 1920s, it was in the 1950s that contact intensified, and the magazines themselves become a kind of extension of the editorial department. By 1948, pre-publication serializations of Mills & Boon novels were fixtures in the top three women's magazines, which together were selling over three million copies per week: *Woman, Woman's Own,* and *Woman's Weekly* (see Chapter 9). This association with the weekly magazines served more than an editorial purpose. Mills & Boon reaped extra publicity when a serial 'sold' well, encouraging readers to seek out the complete novel in the libraries, or other titles by the author. Moreover, selling serial rights—for as much as £1,000—helped Mills & Boon's cash flow. The firm usually retained between 15 and 25 per cent of the serial fee.

Increasingly, new authors came to Mills & Boon after achieving some prominence in the women's magazines or with other publishers, rather than directly from literary agents, or via the slush pile. In 1949, for example, Jean Herbert (Dr Mary Isabel Leslie) joined Mills & Boon. An English lecturer from Dublin, Herbert was first published by Hodder & Stoughton. She was, however, hardly prolific, writing fewer than a dozen novels for Mills & Boon. But waiting in the wings was a true star who would not only set sales records but would establish a new style for the Mills & Boon novel in the 1950s. Her name was Lilian Warren.

Warren wrote under three pen-names—Rosalind Brett, Kathryn Blair, and Celine Conway—and contributed 59 novels to Mills & Boon. Born in London, Warren was 19 and working as a secretary when her first magazine story was accepted. She married and moved to South Africa, and travelled widely throughout the African continent. Her first novel was published in 1940. Warren's prominence in the women's magazines (notably, *Woman's Weekly*) and her lush, romantic, and somewhat violent and erotic style captured the imagination of British readers. The foreign settings appealed to readers weary of wartime deprivation, and the independent heroine, making her way in a foreign land and conquering the hero, set a new style. 'She had an immense influence on the romance novel, by the way she portrayed these handsome heroes, the sunshine backgrounds, and her skill in dialogue,' Alan Boon said.

Warren was a considerable star when her agent, Juliet O'Hea of Curtis Brown, approached Alan Boon in 1950, with the news that Warren wished to leave her current publishers, Rich & Cowan, over their 'dilatory methods' and 'the small editions they print'. Writing from South Africa, Warren said she wanted to sign with Mills & Boon, if the firm would publish her novels in complete form, not in the tamer versions required by Winifred Johnson, editor of *Woman's Weekly*:

> The Rosalind Brett novels are what Miss Johnson calls 'strong meat' — they have to be toned down for the serial market. I find them a relief to write between the stereotyped Kathryn Blair stories, and I believe they help me to get more work done. I have the impression that Mills & Boon novels consistently avoid 'sexy' situations; for instance, the girl is never seduced by the hero before she is married, which is laudable, but restricting to the writer. If the Rosalind Brett novels were not slightly daring they might become indistinguishable from the Kathryn Blair ones.

Warren suggested that Boon read her latest Brett novel, *They Came to Valeira*. He did, and responded at once to O'Hea:

> Rosalind Brett is quite correct in sensing that Mills & Boon's stomach is not 100 per cent cast iron. We have to take into account reactions of certain sections of the community, as for instance the Irish market. Nevertheless, it seems to be that we can digest stronger meat than can the serial stomach. We have read bits of BRITTLE BONDAGE and THE NEW OWNER in the magazines, and believe that as they stand we could achieve a good success with these stories. Of course, we do not know to what extent they have been toned down.

As for *Valeira*, Boon added that he was 'much impressed by the sheer power of this author's writing. I have not the slightest doubt that we could do big things for her. . . . We should like, naturally, to get cracking as soon as possible, and, if the situation offers, take over Rosalind Brett's outstanding novels.'

They Came to Valeira (which Mills & Boon published in 1954) is a lushly romantic tale of Julian Carwell, 35, cacau plantation manager on Valeira, a tropical island. On his estate lives a lone white girl, Philippa Crane, 18 and newly-orphaned, who refuses to leave her cottage, even though her life has been threatened. Needless to say, love blossoms between the two. This was not the typical Mills & Boon romance, but something more erotic, closer to Ethel M. Dell than to Mary Burchell. For instance, when Philippa wanders off and is lost in the jungle, Julian rescues her. She is hot and sweaty ('Her pink silk dress was plastered flat to her back and hips') but defiant, resisting Julian's demands to return with him. It is the last straw:

'Before we leave here I'll compel you to admit you love me.'

She was becoming frightened: a heaviness gathered in her chest. 'And how will you set about it?' she challenged. 'With another tainted kiss?'

Like a smouldering fire splashed with oil, he blazed. With a wrench of her wrist he had her back and was pinning his shoulders into the crushed leaves. She saw his jaw angular against the arching spears of the palms, heard the violent shuddering of his breath in his lungs before he pulled her into a furious, ruthless embrace.

Philippa awakes in the next scene. 'Her mouth felt bruised, her throat parched and behind her eyes stabbed scorching pain. She wished she were dead.' Significantly, Julian begs her forgiveness, as 'nothing of that kind ever happened to me before in my life'. Philippa accepts, while Julian reasons, 'We'll live it down because we love each other.'

Admittedly, Warren's novels written as Rosalind Brett were sexier than her titles written as Kathryn Blair and Celine Conway. Mills & Boon treated each pen-name as a separate author, and all three became best-sellers. Celine Conway's debut in 1953, *Return of Simon*, was promoted as, 'Even though this story is set in England, we think we can say that if you enjoy Kathryn Blair's writing, you will enjoy Celine Conway.'

The fact that Alan Boon introduced this new, racier brand of fiction into the Mills & Boon list is significant in many ways. First, although Warren wrote in a more sensual style, she was not explicit. Second, since she had a growing following in the women's magazines, Boon sensibly signed her up to follow the popular taste. Like his father before him in signing Jack London, Boon was willing to be flexible when the opportunity arose to acquire a proven seller, someone who would lift the entire publication list to new heights, and inspire other Mills & Boon authors. In a similar (but less racy) fashion, the older authors on the list, such as Mary Burchell and Constance M. Evans, inspired the newcomers with their prolific talents and healthy returns. Jay Blakeney recalled being inspired by Brett's novels when she started writing, as 'Anne Weale'. 'Brett bought something terribly exciting into the dull and familiar,' she said. 'She had wonderful heroes. She was the inventor of the "punishing kiss". You spent the whole book waiting for the punishing kiss. I loved Brett's foreign backgrounds. I always longed to travel. The English people did not travel much after the war.' Sheila Holland, who would become Mills & Boon's top author as 'Charlotte Lamb' in the 1970s, cited Brett as her favourite author, whom she read as a teenager. Brett's novels, she explained, had 'a hesitant, frightfully sensitive, not to say neurotic English girl and a hero who is an Empire building Englishman with a pipe in his mouth and a belief that the little woman should be protected and stay in the kitchen. He was the autocratic father figure, of course.'

Another star author with a large following among magazine readers was Mary Lutyens, daughter of Edwin Lutyens, who wrote as 'Esther Wyndham'. She offered nine novels to Mills & Boon via her agent, Curtis Brown. Such was Wyndham's popularity—and the quality of her novels—that she was closely identified with the Mills & Boon imprint in a 1953 advertisement:

> *Author* + *imprint* = *profit.* An imprint that your readers know, like 'Mills & Boon', brings you profit, so does a leading author like Esther Wyndham. Put the two together and you get something you should buy.

Wyndham was indeed a money-spinner: her first novel for Mills & Boon, *Black Charles* (1952), was a best-seller. Mills & Boon spent £140 on advertising this title in the *Sunday Times* and *Woman's Weekly* ('Black Charles awaits your order to bring readers to your library and profit to you'), and in 31,000 special inserts in North Country editions (given the novel's Northumberland setting) of *Home and Country*, the magazine of the National Federation of Women's Institutes. The fuss for this title was deserved, as readers had contacted Mills & Boon (assuming they were Wyndham's publisher) for copies after the serial was published in *Woman's Weekly* in 1948. Published by Mills & Boon in March 1952, *Black Charles* sold out its initial print run of 4,700 copies by July, when Alan Boon informed Lutyens, 'It has not made a duck in any week since publication. Under the very difficult conditions which obtain today for the selling of novels, we think you may be perfectly satisfied with these figures. I expect this edition to sell steadily until early 1954, when we shall plan a cheap reprint.' On 1 April Boon could confidently tell Lutyens that, according to W. H. Smith, *Black Charles* was selling better in Leeds than the latest Agatha Christie novel and in Hull, the book was more popular than *The Cruel Sea* by Nicholas Monserrat.

Black Charles contains one of the best hero characterizations in the canon: Charles Pendelton, 40, known as 'Black' Charles due to his dark features and temperament. The heroine, Audrey Lawrence, 25, who works for an antiques firm in London, has no trouble spotting him at a crowded drinks party:

> There was no mistaking him. He stood out like a full grown oak in a grove of saplings. There was boredom and contempt written in every line of his strong dark face, and a sort of fury that took possession of her. He had no right to look like that, he had no right to think himself so superior. . . . He was just the kind of man who had brought down the prestige of the aristocracy in England—proud, arrogant, conceited. She hated him with her whole heart.

But soon Audrey is a guest at the Pendleton castle in Northumberland, and she falls for Charles—literally. On a fox hunt, Audrey is thrown from her mount and sprains her ankle. In a dramatic scene, she lies down close beside Charles to watch the stars and 'listen to the night' until help arrives:

> She was lying on her face again now, and Charles, also lying on his face with his hands under his chin, was not more than a foot away from her. She did not know at what moment it was that she became conscious of his nearness, his magnetism, but suddenly all at once it was present with her like an overwhelming electrical force drawing her towards him. She did not stir a muscle but her whole being yearned to move closer to him, to touch him, to lie against his side and encounter the living warmth of his body.

Soon thereafter, Charles proposes, pledging, 'You will be my queen.' Wyndham continued to be a top author and seller, and had a ready series of titles on hand for Mills & Boon to publish. For her next novel, *Man of Steel* (which had nothing to do with the Superman myth), 30,000 dust jacket copies were inserted in major trade magazines.

Warren and Wyndham were only the beginning. Between 1946 and 1956 Mills & Boon added thirty-five new authors of note to its ever-expanding publication list. If the best-selling authors came via the women's magazines, the majority had read Mills & Boon novels before, and decided to try their hand at writing, submitting their manuscripts themselves. Some, moreover, became very successful: Roberta Leigh (first published in 1952), Alex Stuart (1953), Nan Asquith (1954), Anne Weale (1955), Joyce Dingwell (1955), Anne Vinton (1956), and Elizabeth Gilzean (1956) are a few examples. Each would acknowledge her debt to current best-sellers (notably Brett, Blair, and Conway) while seeking to emulate the prolific veterans and their large bank balances (Burchell, MacLeod, Tempest, Seale).

Where did these new authors come from? There are some common characteristics. First, fewer writers were from London, and tended to come from the Midlands, Northern England, and Scotland (all popular Mills & Boon sales areas). Many were members of local or regional writers' circles where aspiring and successful authors traded stories and reviewed each other's manuscripts: Alex Stuart and Anne Weale belonged to the York Writers Circle, while Elizabeth Gilzean, a nurse, was a member of the Birmingham Writers Group, which spawned several Mills & Boon authors. Most authors were either married and raising children, or single working women. Nan Asquith, a Midlands journalist, was a copywriter for Lewis's department stores in Liverpool and Birmingham (another big client of Mills & Boon's).

Given their future success and productivity, three new authors deserve a closer look here. Jay Blakeney (Anne Weale) wrote her first novel for Mills & Boon in 1955, when she was 24 and working as a reporter for the *Yorkshire*

Evening Press. She recalled reading several Mills & Boon novels, most notably those by Rosalind Brett, at the urging of her landlady in Bristol, a Mills & Boon 'addict' who read a dozen novels a week. 'I had always intended to become a novelist but, at 23, felt it was too soon to attempt a big "serious" novel. Light romance seemed within my reach,' she said. So she drew on her personal experience—two years living on a rubber estate in Malaya—for her first novel, *Winter Is Past*, which Alan Boon accepted, and which was sold immediately as a serial (unusual for a new author). 'Alan said *Woman's Own* had made an offer for first British serial rights and he would pay an advance of £150. Together the payments represented about two-thirds of my newspaper salary for a year,' she recalled. On publication day, Boon wrote to congratulate her, with the personal touch for which he was famous: 'Tomorrow is the great day when WINTER IS PAST makes its bow to the world, and we would like to take this opportunity of wishing it a big success.'

Soon afterwards, Blakeney met Boon in London. 'I was considerably in awe of him,' She recalled. 'Alan asked, "Is this a flash in the pan, or do you intend to write romances?" As I was still amazed at having earned so much money in such an enjoyable way, my answer was an enthusiastic, "Yes."' Blakeney has written over seventy novels for Mills & Boon in forty years. In 1958 Anne Weale was cited by Mills & Boon as the firm's most popular author, alongside Eleanor Farnes.

Anne Vinton also drew upon personal experience overseas in writing her first novel, *The Time of Enchantment* (1956), set in Africa. Married to an intelligence officer, Vinton had lived in Nigeria for several years. A member of a local writers' circle, Vinton met a literary agent, Irene Josephy, who sent her manuscript to Mills & Boon. 'As I had been offered a bursary to Lady Margaret Hall in Oxford, in my late teens, and turned it down because I was already earning my living as a music teacher, you will gather that the height of my ambition as an English scholar was <u>not</u> to write for M&B, which was just money in the bank as far as I was concerned. I was sometimes ashamed to admit that I did write for them,' Vinton recalled. But write she did: Vinton eventually produced fifty-two novels for Mills & Boon, some under another pen-name, 'Juliet Shore'. 'I found love stories after my more serious efforts were like sausage machine material,' she said. 'They poured out of me.'

The arrival of Joyce Dingwell, Mills & Boon's first native Australian author, attests to Mills & Boon's sales success in Commonwealth nations.[7] A third-generation Australian, Dingwell was inspired by her Welsh mother, who was an avid reader of Mills & Boon novels, borrowing ten books at a time from the library. In 1955 Dingwell, then 47, tried her hand. 'I found it very pleasant,' she recalled. 'I thought out a system of sitting down and telling myself a story. It worked. Mills & Boon did the rest.' Her debut was *Australian Hospital*. In 1957 Alan Boon praised Dingwell for her 'consistent high standard' and 'good progress with the public':

Over here there is an ever increasing interest in Australia. A daily news-paper yesterday reported that 41 per cent of us would emigrate if we could. Of course a large number of these would emigrate to Australia, and novels with Australian backgrounds are of special interest to these would-be emigrants.

Indeed, when Dingwell's *The Girl From Snowy River* (1959) was published, a tale of an English woman emigrating to Australia, Boon sent a copy to the Hon. A. R. Downer, MP (then Australian Minister of Immigration), at Australia House, with the message, 'We feel it is good propaganda for immi-gration.' Dingwell proceeded to write eighty-three novels for Mills & Boon, including five in one year. Boon eventually encouraged her to take a pen-name, 'Kate Starr', a combination of her mother-in-law's name, and Dingwell's maiden name. 'No one ever commented,' Dingwell said. 'The only thing that was said to me was, "Did you know that now you have a rival?"'

Both Vinton (herself a nurse) and Dingwell set their first novels in hos-pitals, with their heroes as doctors and their heroines as nurses. In the 1950s the Doctor-Nurse romance was gaining in popularity, and Alan Boon encouraged many authors to specialize in this category. Here television was an ally, since medical dramas such as *Emergency Ward 10* and *Medic* were very popular. The arrival of the National Health Service, moreover, increased interest in all things and situations medical, as well as in the nursing profes-sion. Boon also followed the lead of the women's magazines, which usually featured one hospital-set serial story. By 1955 the Mills & Boon catalogue included a section on 'Doctor Stories', billed as, 'Everyone likes books about doctors and hospitals and nurses.'

Certainly for new authors, 'nurse books' provided an opportunity to gain attention on a crowded list. The medical profession could not ask for better endorsements than these novels, which consistently upheld the achievements and sacrifices of doctors and nurses. In Vinton's debut, *The Time of Enchant-ment*, nurse Triss Wayne, 23, heads to the Gold Coast of Africa with her patient. In the bush Triss is called to deliver an Ashanti baby: 'This was a job, her job, delivered by providence right into her hands. Here, in a remote rest-house, deep in the bush country, the story of creation was being told in all its wonderful intricate detail; a new life was surging into the world, and she—Beatrice Wayne—was privileged to see it happen.' The first novel by Elizabeth Gilzean, *On Call, Sister* (1956), was based on the author's own experiences as a nurse. Sister Elizabeth Sheldon, assisting in the operating theatre of St Hilary's Hospital, enjoys her work: 'Elizabeth felt the familiar thrill of assisting, of matching her skill to the greater skill of a good surgeon.'

Not surprisingly, Mills & Boon attracted a large readership in hospitals for its Doctor-Nurse titles. In 1957 Lilian Chisholm asked Alan Boon for his annual Christmas donation of books for her hospital library. Chisholm worked on the committee of the St John & British Red Cross Hospital Library Department, which gave away that year over 11,500 books, 'a large percentage' of which were Mills & Boons. 'It beats me how long-term patients can bear to read about hospitals, however glamourised, whilst they are enduring the actual background in grim reality—but there, one can never fully account for human nature, can one?' Chisholm wrote. Boon was delighted, noting that the popularity 'is a sound indication that we are all working on the right lines'. He proceeded, a bit cheekily:

> I must say however that I feel that the situation is a little tantalising. With such a demand, how nice it would be if the Government were to give the hospitals a grant so that they could buy our books; but then perhaps I am prejudiced, being on the sales side of the business.

Some authors attributed a restorative quality to Mills & Boon novels. In 1957, for example, Joan Blair told Boon of a 'miracle':

> I took one of Joan's books, it was THE DOMINIE'S LODGING, to one of my Red Cross welfare people who had just lost her husband and was inconsolable. She didn't care for TV, couldn't be bothered with the sound wireless, but did just murmur that she 'liked a love story'. So on Easter Sunday I popped the book through the letter box, with her name and Joan's autograph, and when I went to see her next she said that it had made all the difference. She looked alive again. And she said it was the first thing that had meant anything to her. I must say that just about made the book worth writing, as far as I was concerned. So many people seem just to want 'a really good love story' as a means of forgetting their troubles.

Ironically, although Mills & Boon as a firm did not attract much respect from the general public nor from other publishers in the 1950s (a victim, as today, of literary snobbery), it does deserve credit for offering women an opportunity to achieve financial success and security. Alan Boon often sympathized with the plight of many of his authors in finding time to write, amid family and job responsibilities. 'I suppose the really perfect publisher would have a mobile domestic help on his staff and when authors were in difficulties, the publisher would dispatch this member of their staff to the author's aid forthwith,' Boon told Dorothy Rivers in 1953. 'I think it would pay the publisher in saving the author's time for writing.' In fact, one of the first big expenses a newly-enriched author undertook was to find domestic help.

How much money were authors earning at this time? Although financial records are sketchy (and confidential), Sara Seale provides an interesting case study. Seale was a popular Mills & Boon author during the 1940s and 1950s, and consistently sold well, in both serial and book form. But since she was not a prolific author (34 novels in as many years), other Mills & Boon novelists, including Burchell, MacLeod, and certainly Lilian Warren, would have earned much more. In 1949 Seale earned £2,370, comprised of book royalties, serial rights for *These Delights* and *The Gentle Prisoner* (together drawing nearly £1,000), and £170 for the film option of *The Reluctant Orphan*. At a time when, if an author earned £1,000 a year she was considered a big success, Seale was clearly doing well. By 1952 Seale's earnings were £3,105, thanks to £1,000 in serial rights for two novels, £1,500 in royalties, and the sale of twelve foreign translation rights to publishers in Germany, Holland, and Switzerland. New author Alex Stuart earned £2,003 in 1957, while Constance M. Evans, who was showing her age (having first published in 1932), earned just £605 in 1956.

Apart from British magazine serial rights, which generated income for Mills & Boon and the author, Mills & Boon also hawked its novels around Europe. Although foreign translation rights fees were minimal—£15 in Holland, for example—the exposure was none the less important. One of the largest post-war markets for Mills & Boon romances was, ironically, Germany, where women enjoyed the tales of English roses and domineering Englishmen. For these rights, Mills & Boon enlisted an agent, Mrs Passow-Kernen, who worked from Switzerland. 'Right after the war, she started to translate our books into German,' Alan Boon recalled. 'We took 15 per cent of that. She showed it could be done.'

The foreign translations took many forms. In 1951, for example, Mortagen Verlag, based in Zurich, published several Mills & Boon novels in a hardback series called *Die Blaue Reihe* (The Blue Series), for distribution in Switzerland and Germany. These included *Das Haus Im Moor* ('The House on the Moor', or *The Gentle Prisoner*) by Sara Seale; *Und hatte der Liebe nicht* ('And he did not have love') by Mary Burchell; and *Herzen in Not* ('Hearts in Distress') by Marjorie Moore. The same series featured a golden oldie, *Der Rosenkrantz* (*The Rosary*) by Florence L. Barclay. In France, Éditions Gautier-Langereau offered a paperbound series '*Bibliothèque de ma fille: Choix de Romans pour les Jeunes Filles et la Famille*'. Here Seale seemed to hold her own among largely French authors. *Sous le ciel d'Irlande* (*The English Tutor*) was published in 1951, with the English names Brian, Eileen, and Kevin sprinkled throughout the French text.

The small amounts garnered from the foreign rights, however, could add up to a nice-sized income. Jean MacLeod, for example, agreed to publication of her novels in German, Dutch, Swedish, and Italian after the war. In 1946 Alan Boon reported that First German Rights of *The Tranquil Haven* had been sold for 400 Swiss Francs, or £20. In 1951 Dutch serial rights for *The Silent Valley* sold for 125 florins, or £12, and MacLeod also earned £36 from Sweden and £29 from Holland. In 1956 her foreign sales totalled £250. 8*s*. 3*d*., a respectable sum.

Standardization of the Mills & Boon 'product' continued throughout the 1950s. In addition to agreeing on a set length—188 to 192 pages—and maintaining the brown bindings (although red was also used), the firm paid careful attention to dust jackets, titles, and blurbs. 'Readers tell us they always look for a Mills & Boon jacket when they go to their libraries,' the firm informed readers in the 1954 'Happy Reading' catalogue. 'It's a guarantee, they say, of a pleasant book. They know that inside they'll find hours of happy reading.'

Jackets retained a 'dreamy' quality, although increasingly the heroine was positioned more prominently, with the hero in the background or, indeed, absent altogether. Mills & Boon often purchased the illustrations used in the magazine serial, which was cost-effective and promoted reader identification. Since the smaller commercial libraries (unlike Boots, W. H. Smith, and the public libraries) kept the jackets on the books, the motivation in designing a dust jacket was 'a strong commercial appeal' while maintaining 'the characteristic appearance which enables library customers to spot a Mills & Boon at a distance of ten yards'. As Mills & Boon told W. H. Smith readers in 1954, the literal approach was best:

> When we receive from abroad copies of our novels that have been translated into foreign languages, we are impressed by the jackets—Grave conferences take place and numerous styles are reviewed—But the end is always the same—We go back to our nice young couple, neatly (and always fully) dressed with a bit of background, every object clearly recognisable for what it is.

Mills & Boon continued to be very specific in its instructions to artists, including Jack Faulks and Philip Simmons, who also worked for the magazines. For *They Met in Zanzibar* by Kathryn Blair (1962), Alan Boon outlined all of the details on the hero and heroine for the artist, Edwin Phillips: 'The hero is dark and has a strong mouth . . . good looking . . . and extremely well groomed.' Boon suggested a white dinner jacket and black tie; 'If Phillips would like any further dope about the man's rig, I suggest he could telephone Mr. Barrett at Gieves (Hyde Park 2276) and mention my name.' The heroine, Boon proceeded, should have 'short and curly corn coloured hair. . . . We should like the heroine to be "sweet" rather than sophisticated and hard.' The couple, moreover, 'could be posed—but not in a clinch'. The end result was certainly attractive, even eye-catching: the hero resembling James Bond (the blurb described Steve Cortland as 'a man of immense attraction'), the heroine slender, long-limbed, gazing intently into his eyes. The attraction between them is palpable.

Alan Boon, wisely, did not give his authors the power to approve their dust jackets, knowing full well how opinionated and indecisive they could be.

Consequently, he often heard from authors who were disappointed with their covers. Alex Stuart and Jean MacLeod frequently complained when artists drew the incorrect kilt on the hero or Scottish dress on the heroine. For *Island for Sale* (1954), Stuart supplied samples of the Macrae and MacDonald tartans, and sketched precisely how the hero's sporran should look. Even readers complained. In 1954 Miss C. Elleray of Manchester wrote of errors on the jacket of Jan Tempest's *Leave It To Nancy*, a book she 'quite enjoyed':

> I thought I would point out that your cover artist does not appear to have read the book — surely the picture is of Nancy being shown the daffodils by Wayne! Where are her glasses (which she appears to wear all the time!)? Surely she was dressed in her uniform 'she smoothed down her crumpled apron' (page 119) and her eyes were brown (page 8/9) not blue as depicted by your artist. Do these inaccuracies mean you have a few standard covers to suit all books?

Certainly not, Alan Boon replied, as this cover was 'specially designed for this particular book'. Similarly, while Jan Tempest liked the cover of *Stranger to Love* (1960), she complained to Boon, 'What a pity the artist didn't read the story! The heroine's vividly blue eyes were one of the important features, and who could visualise a refugee with painted finger nails?' However, the fetching and stylish Minna Braun, hair upswept, who has escaped 'from behind the Iron Curtain and reached England in search of her unknown English grandparents', lived up to her description as 'young, beautiful and spirited — not people's idea of a refugee'.

Finding just the right title was a long and arduous task. Alan Boon claimed that a novel with 'wedding' in its title, or a 'hospital flavour', practically guaranteed increased sales. In 1953 Boon told Marjorie Moore, 'You have never let us have a hospital flavour in the title, and I know it is something rather difficult to achieve. If you can achieve this, however, it is a definite asset to sales.' On the other hand, Mills & Boon tried to avoid 'obviously romantic' titles. In 1955 Alan Boon suggested to Valerie K. Nelson that she not call her next novel *Bid Me Love You*:

> There is a section of readers who do not like to ask at the libraries for purely romantic titles, and there are also readers who do not like to be seen reading a story which has a very romantic title. There are, of course, many other readers who are not affected in this way, but we consider it the best policy to appeal to the greatest number of readers possible.

Surprised but compliant, Nelson offered four alternatives, all rather unromantic: *The Stolen Years*, *The Years Between*, *Sister to Lisa*, and (Boon's choice) *Green Harvest*.

Other titles were rejected for obvious reasons. In 1946 Alan Boon asked

Jan Tempest to consider another title for her latest novel, *Not So Dumb Blonde*. 'The one you have selected does not, in our opinion, seem very attractive,' he said. Similarly, Boon wrote to Tempest in 1948, 'We are not too keen on the suggested long Fay Chandos title, "WEEK-END TOGETHER" and wonder whether in due course you could think of an alternative title to this.' They settled on *Since First We Met*.

All of these efforts to shape and consolidate the Mills & Boon 'product' enhanced the firm's greatest asset, the imprint. In 1953 Christina Foyle, in an address to the Royal Society of Arts on 'The Novel, the Bookseller, and the Public', noted that with few exceptions a publisher's name meant nothing to readers. 'The only firms who are really familiar to the public are Messrs. Batsford, Messrs. Mills & Boon and, of course, the incomparable Penguins,' she said. 'People always ask for a "Mills & Boon novel".' In the same year, John Piper, a librarian and bookseller, wrote in the W. H. Smith *Trade Circular*:

> There is one publishing house which I always recommend rather than the authors in its list — MILLS & BOON. Without ever having read a MILLS & BOON romance I know I can quite safely say to the vague customer in search of 'a nice romance' — 'Try a MILLS & BOON romance!' No one has ever come back to throw the book at me — or to make a less spirited complaint. I have a growing number of customers who ask me for MILLS & BOON romances.

It's not surprising that Mills & Boon attempted to expand and diversify its publication list in the 1950s, beyond first and cheap editions of romantic novels. There was a certain safety in numbers, John Boon explained. 'It was a rather hairy time,' he recalled. 'We did what everybody does in these circumstances. We increased our output of titles to make up for turnover.'

Coupled with selling serial rights to British magazines, and foreign translation rights to Europe, Mills & Boon extended its international book sales during this decade, and featured its success in trade advertisements. In the back of novels in the 1950s, Mills & Boon reminded overseas readers (who also borrowed their books from lending libraries) to send for their catalogue: 'Are you reading this book in some place far away from London — in New Zealand or Australia, in South Africa or Canada or in Singapore? — for these novels go everywhere.' Foreign sales brochures advertised 'Books that pay', praising their 'popular stories', 'bright jackets', 'strong bindings', and, most of all, consistency. 'You want consistency in a list, to know that you are not buying any duds, and that is our policy, too. Every book in our list will show you a profit.' Supporting all this, Mills & Boon promised, 'is an organisation geared to library needs, such as the regular publication of a suitable number of books each fortnight, prompt attention to orders, careful packing and all the things that make business a pleasure'. Indeed, in 1951 a South African reader testified, 'The familiar brown cover is one of the recognised articles lying by every girl's (there are 250) desk in this office; the lending library here does an enormous trade.'[8]

To increase output (and feed the newer international markets), Mills & Boon resurrected old titles, 'recycling' them as 'new' books or old favourites. The practice continues today. In 1952 Mills & Boon informed its clients of the launch of the 7s. 'Favourite Library' series, 'the pick of our back list, chosen for their popularity and at our readers' request. Most have been out of print for ten years or more, but they do not date. They will be published during 1952 and will bring you profit.' The oldest titles among the first fifteen were *Sally in the Sunshine* by Elizabeth Hoy and *Kiss and Forget* by Jan Tempest (both fourteen years since the last edition appeared). The most recent title was *But Not for Me* by Mary Burchell (seven years). Clearly, the younger Mills & Boon readers would not have been familiar with these titles, and could easily have accepted them as brand new.

These older novels, however, were rarely reprinted verbatim, and special care was taken to avoid dated references. In 1953, for example, Joan Blair was asked to update *Sister of Nelson Ward* (first published 1937) for a new edition. Mills & Boon's reader carefully noted phrases and names that were considered passé and offered alternatives. 'Mufti', for example, was considered 'out of date slang. Nobody talks of mufti nowadays, as far as we know.' Similarly, gas lighting was changed to neon; penicillin, 'discovered since book was written', had to be mentioned; and the 'latest menace' to world destruction was not nerve gas (as Blair would have thought in 1937), but the 'hydrogen bomb'.

Romances were not the only 'new' features in the Mills & Boon list in the 1950s. The firm's diversification in two other directions were throwbacks to an earlier time: Westerns and general and educational (G&E) publishing. Sixteen years after letting their (small) Western list lapse, Mills & Boon revived the genre in 1953. The industry must have found the action puzzling, given Mills & Boon's specialization of late in romantic fiction. John Boon offered a lengthy explanation in the *Bookseller*. 'After producing 1,892 romances (1,067 new books and 825 reprints) in a row, we all felt like a change,' Boon wrote. He added, however, 'we were trying to make our business less vulnerable'.[9] Westerns were 'simple, easy publishing', Boon recalled, and offered a 'modest' profit. Indeed, library surveys in the 1950s often showed that the Western was the second most popular genre after detective stories; romances were third.

Selling Mills & Boon 'Diamond W' Westerns to the same library market also made perfect sense. The female reader of Mills & Boon romances was encouraged to pick up a hearty Western at the library, for the man in her life. 'Westerns—for the men', the new line was advertised in the 'Happy

Reading' catalogue: 'Just the thing for your husbands, brothers, sons and sweethearts! Please tell your menfolk.' An anecdote from a reader bolstered this plea: 'Why don't you publish some Western stories? My brother reads nothing else. As he works late, I have to get his books from the library. I always forget what he has read and he is furious if I bring back one he had read before. Won't you publish some and put the titles in your catalogue?'

While we cannot say that Westerns made much of an impact (although, as they were cheap to produce, they had a high profit margin), the renewed G&E list brought profits, publicity, and a certain prestige. Clearly, John Boon was the driving force here, hoping to test his publishing skills beyond the rather automatic, straightforward publishing of romances and Westerns. But Boon admitted that the idea was met with firm resistance by Henley and Carol Boon:

> The folk memory was that general and educational publishing was the way to lose money. But we had all our eggs in one basket, and believed we would not go on publishing romances all one's life. We were sort of casting around. There's a lot of luck involved in publishing. You try this and try that. You follow up anything that does well.

The ultimate goal, Boon noted, was to restore the backlist and the security which it offered—namely, a degree of freedom from the libraries, and a new foothold in retail sales. Admitting that general fiction was 'too speculative' a road to take, Boon announced in 1955 that Mills & Boon would enter a publishing sector which was expanding in popularity: 'the semi-technical, semi-educational how-to-do-it books. Better education standards, shorter hours of work, rising costs and so on are all on its side. The new forms of entertainment like television which compete with fiction actually give it a boost.' Cookery programmes were one example.

Hence, Mills & Boon's initial foray into general and educational publishing, like Westerns, made perfect sense: a series of 'practical' books on subjects of interest to women, the same women who were borrowing Mills & Boon romances. Health, cookery, and embroidery were the first subject areas. 'The idea behind this whole project is that the two types of books shall be complementary and helpful to each other rather than competitive,' Boon assured the trade. 'We are hoping that our success in the romantic field will give our practical books a good send-off among women readers.' Adding to Mills & Boon's advantage was a first-class mailing list of at least 16,000 women who could be targets of publicity, as could the readers of the women's magazines. Since Mills & Boon estimated that at least 50 women read each romance they published, and that at least 100,000 copies were distributed each year, up to 5 million women could see the advertisements for these books in the back of romance novels. 'We probably have the best mailing list of women's names of any book publishing house,' Boon maintained.

Thus began the G&E list, symbolized not by the Rose of Romance but by the Owl of Athene, the guardian spirit who cared for handicrafts and women. The books were published under the Mills & Boon imprint, since their subject matter was regarded as complementary, not threatening. They were advertised as, 'Practical Books for the Practical Sex' in the 'Happy Reading' catalogue:

> You've relied for years on our romances to give you pleasant reading, so believe us now when we say that our PRACTICAL BOOKS (as they will be called) have a little extra something that lifts them above being 'just another' book on the subject.

Initially two to six books were published, at prices as high as 21 shillings. Most were written by schoolteachers for the housewife, student, or reference library audiences. The books generated much attention in the women's magazines, on the BBC's 'Woman's Hour', and in the 'women's pages' of daily and Sunday newspapers. The series' initial success even made publishing history of a kind: 'Mills & Boon, by providing practical books for those who read their romances, encouraged the practice of owning books amongst people who had not formerly felt the need for a bookshelf.'[10]

Discovering Embroidery by Winsome Douglass (1955) was the first G&E title. Described as 'an authority on her subject', Douglass enlisted the help of pupils in the Needlework Development Scheme in Glasgow in illustrating and testing her lessons. Nearly 2,500 copies were sold before publication. 'That was quite a good number for a new book, as we were not known in the area,' John Boon said. 'We were looking for niche publishing. Batsford was quite strong in it.' Certainly reviews for the debut title were good: 'What a perfect gift for a young bride! Plenty of how-to-make-it instructions for the belts, bags, cloths, boxes, caps, plus the how-to-embroider-them instructions, too,' said *She*. *Discovering Embroidery* was an unqualified hit, running through six editions with sales of 60,000 copies.

The other star G&E title at this time was *Better Cookery* by Aileen King (1956), the Principal of Radbrook Domestic Science College, Shropshire, where her students helped check and recheck all 1,000 recipes. Because of this, 'it will almost certainly become their official text book and we hope be recommended by similar institutions throughout the country,' John Boon predicted in 1955. Indeed, *Home Economics* called it the 'publishing event of the year so far as the domestic science world is concerned . . . it is among the best up-to-date professionally written books on cooking principles on the English market . . . It is certainly a *must* for every college and school library'. With sales totalling 80,000 copies, Boon admitted that King's work 'broke the ice'. King herself was shocked by her royalty cheque in 1957: 'We just cannot believe our eyes and it has taken me almost a week to realise that I can pay it into my slender and almost emaciated account. I feel the cashier who accepted it this morning looked at me with positive respect instead of the usual detached manner—obviously reserved for the poor.'[11]

The handicraft and home economics lists expanded, and clearly reflected the times. *Halving Your Housework* by Phyllis Lovell (1958) was, the *Oxford Times* noted, 'a book for beginners, brides who have never learned the ABC of domestic chores at home, or for older women who have lost touch with current trends in labour-saving devices and cleaning preparations'. The value of *What Shall I Say?* by Lola Mulcaster (1956) was not lost on the reviewer of the *Cumberland and Evening News*:

> More and more are women coming to the fore in public life and it may well fall to the lot of us to open a bazaar or give a talk on chicken farming or some other subject of which we have specialised knowledge. Lola Mulcaster has written a book that will be of immense help to the shy and uncertain, to all who have to introduce a speaker at their local W. I. or deal with any other social contact from neighbours to bores and borrowers.

See What I Mean by Amy Landreth (1957) was a combination phrase and flash-card book for the inexperienced traveller, who might find herself in a strange foreign country, not unlike the typical Mills & Boon heroine of the decade. The *Manchester Guardian* said it 'enables the stranded Briton to ask for almost anything from a breakfast cereal and globe artichokes to upper cylinder lubricant and zip fasteners without uttering a word'.

By the middle of the 1950s Mills & Boon had good reason to smile, even crow. The firm, headed by its new young leaders, had weathered most of the post-war storms and was enjoying a new degree of prosperity. 'Light romance', the *News Chronicle* reported in January 1955, was the only 'niche' in the publishing industry that was performing consistently well. Indeed, in 1955 Mills & Boon expanded its office and warehouse space in Grafton Way and Charlotte Street, and in 1956 purchased two company cars: a green Standard Vanguard III van and a Daimler.

As if to seal the success of the Boon family, Rose Sharwood Mills died in 1958, severing the last connection with the Mills family. Mills & Boon seemed settled and secure, confident in the romantic fiction market, and pleased with its new publishing ventures. All that would soon change as the 1960s grew closer, and Mills & Boon would face yet another transformation, precipitated by the arrival of the mass-market paperback.

Chapter 5
The Paperback Revolution, 1957–1972

Is there any future for us as publishers (as well as for our Authors) when so many commercial libraries have closed? The answer is that we are confident there is such a future, by increasing our sales to the public libraries and extending our participation in the field of paperbacks. We are doing both. Our sales to the public libraries (Dublin is a very good customer!) are increasing steadily and our series of paperbacks is proving outstandingly successful.

Alan Boon to Henrietta Reid, 1966

Steady sales like this come from reader loyalty, and over the years we've built up something like a personal relationship with our readers. They come from that large group of people who are bored with tales of sex, violence and sadism and just want a pleasant book. Once they came to the libraries each fortnight and asked for 'the new Mills & Boon's,' now they come each month and buy the new paperbacks. With this backing it's extraordinary how sales have snowballed, largely by word of mouth, without much advertising or ballyhoo.

Mills & Boon advertisement, 1968

IN their 1960 book, *Romantic Fiction: The New Writers' Guide*, Anne Britton and Marion Collin advised potential authors that popular romance was synonymous with only one publisher in Great Britain:

> The best publisher for romances in England is Mills and Boon, because they deal with little else and cover a very wide market. Read as many of their books as possible, for although they vary considerably the standard is always high. There are slight gentle romances, romances with strong backgrounds, family stories and romances that border on mysteries. Some sell as serials, some do not, but in their own way all are successful and can teach a beginner a great deal.[1]

Britton certainly would have known this, as fiction editor of *Woman's Own*, and a Mills & Boon author herself (as 'Jan Anderson'). Such acclaim illustrates how established Mills & Boon had become in its first fifty years as a publisher, and, indeed, how successful the Boon sons had been in the 1950s in consolidating the firm's position in the industry. Replying to Joyce Dingwell, one of many authors who sent in congratulations on Mills & Boon's golden anniversary in 1959, Alan Boon wrote, 'We will now have to see what we can do about the second half of the century.'

However, Boon's company was on the verge of an even greater transformation. The 1960s was an exciting decade for Mills & Boon, a period of sweeping change, not just to the 'product' (as romantic novels were increasingly known) but to the structure of the company, its markets, and distribution outlets. The eventual closure of the commercial libraries forced Mills & Boon to take the first steps towards a mass-market retail operation. Its ally was a small Canadian printer, Harlequin Books. Harlequin's experiment with paperback publishing in North America would expand into a full-fledged, worldwide operation, and precipitate a merger of the two companies in 1972.

≈

Mills & Boon's financial performance in the 1960s was nothing short of spectacular (see Fig. 5.1). At the outset profits remained good, if flat, following the recovery of the 1950s. During the years from 1958 until 1964, the commercial libraries were winding down, and the transition to paperbacks was under way, but not yet complete. In 1964 Mills & Boon started printing paperback novels in Britain (as opposed to importing a limited number of novels printed in Canada), allowing a fuller saturation of the home market. Readers responded—and profits rose annually. By 1966 paperbacks represented 50 per cent of Mills & Boon's turnover, and were the most profitable half of the business. During each year from 1963 until 1967, turnover increased between 20 and 30 per cent.

By 1969 Mills & Boon was publishing 144 hardback titles a year at 13s. 6d., and 72 paperback titles at 3s. 6d.. English-language sales totalled 15 million per year, of which 10 million were considered exports or foreign sales, which alone brought in £350,000 per year. Mills & Boon had indeed come a long way in fifty years, posting a £134,500 profit in 1969, a lifetime away from the £125 net profit recorded in 1910.

≈

The Boon brothers were the first to admit that Mills & Boon arrived late to the paperback business. Alan Boon discussed the idea as early as 1949, when Phyllis Matthewman and her husband, Sydney, raised it. 'There is at present

Figure 5.1

Annual Net Profit of Mills & Boon, Ltd., 1957–1971

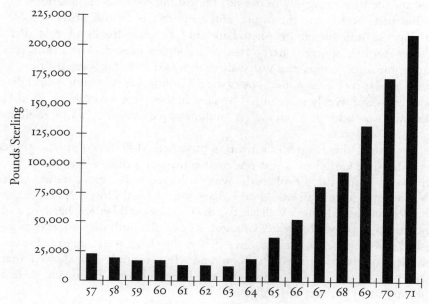

quite a large demand for fiction in a cheap format, and at present this is being fed largely by either highbrow novels (Penguin, Pan etc.) or thrillers (the same plus most of the other reprint publishers). But no one is doing romance in any cheap form,' they claimed. The Matthewmans often dispensed publishing advice:

> Our own belief is that if you put out some of your older titles in paper backs at 2/- or even 2/6, they would sell very readily—readily enough, in fact, to justify the large editions which would be necessary to bring the price down. I don't think that there is any need to drop as low as eighteen pence—Pans go quite well at 2/- & 2/6 and certainly [there is] no need to follow Cherry Tree & others down to 1/-: they mostly do reprints of cheap American stuff—and do it very badly—which nobody wants anyhow. Jenkins have put out a 2/- line in cloth. In any case costs wouldn't allow a 2/- book in cloth today.

Alan Boon thanked the Matthewmans, but replied firmly, 'For the present we have no plans to put out any [cheaper editions] in paper backs.' Behind the scenes, the Boon brothers and Henley did debate the logistics of paperback publishing, but were not convinced that their cadre of loyal readers would be willing to spend 2s. 6d. to purchase a Mills & Boon romance when they could borrow it for two or three pence, especially in the difficult post-war years. Furthermore, start-up costs for paperback publishing and retail distribution—not Mills & Boon's forte—were prohibitive. Mills & Boon's safety net, for the time being, lay in the still-flourishing commercial libraries.

But paperbacks were the future, and a number of British firms were following the trail blazed by Allen Lane and Penguin Books in 1935. Pan, Corgi, Panther, Sphere, Cherry Tree, and Fontana paperback imprints, featuring romance, crime, and war stories, appeared after the war. At prices of between sixpence and 3s. 6d., books were becoming as accessible—and disposable—as a weekly magazine. The sales figures were astonishing. By 1955 Penguin was achieving sales of 11 million copies a year; Pan, 8 million; Corgi, 4 million.

But few of these paperback firms approached Mills & Boon, and those who did (like Corgi) took just one or two titles at a time. 'They didn't like the books,' John Boon explained. 'We've achieved rather more status, while they've gone down. Pan would never have touched us.' This, despite the fact that Pan published Edgar Wallace, Agatha Christie, and Leslie Charteris, and picked up most of Hodder & Stoughton's popular authors who were published in the old Yellow Jackets series. 'There may have been a degree of snobbishness on Pan's part,' Alan Boon said. 'But I think Pan showed that paperbacks could be sold at three-and-six. They had James Bond, and we had the equivalent perhaps of James Bond.'[2]

Mills & Boon did negotiate paperback editions of some novels before Harlequin's offer in 1957, but these were limited and infrequent. In 1954, for example, the firm agreed to license 25,000 paperback copies of a Diamond Western title, for sale in Australia and New Zealand. In 1956 Alan Boon asked Jan Tempest if she would agree to a paperback edition for 30 guineas, representing a leasing of the 'volume rights'. Tempest was thrilled: 'Every stationer—and even my grocer!—seems to be flooded with cheap paper-backs from 1/6 to 2/6. Yes, I would like to have a few titles done in paper-backs. The fee is certainly low, but it might be an advantage in attracting new readers.' Similarly, Corgi Books picked up Mills & Boon's Doctor-Nurse titles for its 2s. 'Corgi Romance' series, billed as 'reprints of best-selling books originally published at higher prices, and now made available to a wider public at the minimum cost'. Among 1958 'best-selling' titles were *On Call, Sister!* by Elizabeth Gilzean (first published by Mills & Boon in 1956) and *Sister Brookes at Byng's* by Kate Norway (Olive Norton, 1957).

But Mills & Boon's formal entry into paperback publishing began in a modest way, with the arrival of a letter in May 1957, postmarked from Winnipeg, Canada. It was sent by Ruth Palmour, secretary of Harlequin Books Limited, a small printer, packager, and book distributor. 'We are looking for light romances dealing with doctors and nurses for publication in our Harlequin line of paper-covered pocket-type books,' she wrote, 'and wonder if the Canadian reprint rights for any of your books of this type might be available to us.' Harlequin offered editions of 25,000 copies, for sale at 35 cents in Canada and parts of the United States. Five days after Palmour posted this letter, Alan Boon replied in the affirmative.

Harlequin Books was founded in 1949 by Richard Bonnycastle, a maverick entrepreneur and veteran of the Hudson's Bay Company. Bonnycastle, his wife, Mary (who chose the books), and Palmour (who followed Bonnycastle from Hudson's Bay) ran the small firm, publishing books of a wide variety, including fiction. The fiction list was a thoroughly undistinguished mix of paperback thrillers, Westerns, and mysteries, but did include reprints of novels by Agatha Christie, James Hadley Chase, and Sir Arthur Conan Doyle. By 1957 Harlequin had published 400 titles.

Legend has it that Mary Bonnycastle noticed the popularity of Mills & Boon novels among Canadian women, 'these nice little books with happy endings', and wondered why Harlequin could not add these to its publications list. She had a particular fondness for the Doctor-Nurse books, and, for several years, these were the only type of romances accepted by Harlequin. 'Harlequin asked if we could supply more "nurse books" every month,' Alan Boon recalled. 'They were not publishers at all. But we saw the opportunity to put the Mills & Boon book into the mainstream. That's how they suddenly took off.'

The first two contracts with Harlequin were signed in July 1957. Terms were identical for editions of *Hospital in Buwambo* by Anne Vinton (set in West Africa) and *Hospital Corridors* by Mary Burchell (set in a large Montreal hospital). Harlequin paid $200 on account of a royalty of 1.4 cents, to be paid on publication. *Hospital in Buwambo*, Harlequin number 407, was published first, under the Harlequin name, and with a Canadian-produced cover. When the initial 1,000 trial print run sold out quickly, Harlequin set up a publishing schedule, printing 7,500 copies of each of four Mills & Boon romances every few months. In 1958 Harlequin published sixteen Mills & Boon titles, all Doctor-Nurse romances, including four by Alex Stuart, and two each by Burchell and Jean MacLeod.

⚮

Although the Boon brothers insist that the beginning of paperbacks and the winding-up of the commercial libraries were coincidental, the timing could not have been more fortuitous for the firm. 'I think the libraries collapsed because of the change in trading conditions,' John Boon said. 'There was not much spare cash for spending in the 1930s, therefore shops and chains welcomed anything which would give them extra profit and bring customers into their shops. After the war, that changed. There was less incentive to open libraries.' Gordon Wixley, Mills & Boon's auditor for some forty years, agreed. 'There was a period when danger was seen in the demise of libraries on the corner,' he recalled. 'The books you were publishing were not going to be taken up in a big way by the public libraries. That's when the paperback proved to be the means for achieving success.'

But Mills & Boon did not achieve paperback success overnight. Upon the closure of W. H. Smith's library in 1961, and Boots library in 1965, Mills & Boon was forced to engage the public libraries more directly, in an appeal to increase their purchases. Although public libraries were expanding, many were still reluctant to spend money to stock 'light' fiction. In 1964 Alan Boon informed Margaret Malcolm that hardback editions of Mills & Boon novels were now limited to 3,500 copies (down from 7,000–8,000), given the deterioration of library orders. 'The sales situation is something about which you know as well as I—W. H. Smith and All That, the continuing closing down of Boots' libraries—and is in no way a reflection on the popularity of your writing,' Boon wrote. Malcolm's royalties, moreover, were reduced from 15 to 10 per cent, like other authors.

But once again, timing was on Mills & Boon's side. The refugees from the commercial libraries found a new, and free, home in their local public library. Public library expenditure was rising in Britain, from £15 million in 1957, to £24 million in 1962, and £45 million in 1968, at which point most of the population in the UK was served by a public library. Here was a new market for Mills & Boon, and the firm did not hesitate to ask its readers—now public library users—for help. 'You must, and we know that you will be firm but polite, speak to your librarian and persuade him or her to change the policy,' Mills & Boon asked readers in its October 1964 catalogue. 'Please let us know if you have any difficulties; we might be able to reinforce your arguments, supply useful lists and generally help.'[3]

Alan Boon also enlisted the support of the new Romantic Novelists Association (RNA), an organization founded in 1960 by four top novelists: Denise Robins, Barbara Cartland, Netta Muskett, and Alex Stuart. The expressed aim of the RNA was 'to use all means in its power, individually or collectively, to raise the standard and prestige of Romantic Authorship'. While it is doubtful that the RNA achieved anything for authors apart from being a social centre,[4] it did initially rally its membership to survey public library shelves and demand interviews with librarians. Boon was sympathetic and recognized a vocal ally. In 1962, for example, he supported Alex Stuart in her personal crusade against criticism and snobbery. 'All writers cannot be Shakespeares—or, in their field, Shutes,' Stuart told Boon. 'I shall be quite happy to be represented, as exponents of the romantic novel, by those leading romantic authors of today (whose names you know as well as I) who have helped establish the enormous world-wide popularity of the romantic novel.' Boon could not agree more:

> There are a great many popular misconceptions about many romantic novels today, as though they are soppy, and rubbish. They are not. Is any

category of English literature so much translated abroad today, and why is this so? ... The continental countries come to England for the romantic novel—not to America or Europe, because our romantic novel is outstanding. (It is, incidentally, interesting to consider the great influence such reading must have abroad—remembering the influence of American television and films over here.)

The strategy worked, thanks to the patrons of the newly expanded public libraries who requested their favourite light fiction. 'Is there any future for us as publishers (as well as for our Authors) when so many commercial libraries have closed?' Alan Boon posed to Henrietta Reid, an Irish author, in 1966. 'The answer is that we are confident there is such a future, by increasing our sales to the public libraries and extending our participation in the field of paperbacks. We are doing both. Our sales to the public libraries (Dublin is a very good customer!) are increasing steadily and our series of paperbacks is proving outstandingly successful.' Boon concluded by promising Reid that she was 'potential paperback material'.

Finally, as if to hedge against another decline in library orders, in 1965 Mills & Boon offered readers the chance to order books directly. This was a departure from past practice, whereby readers would obtain a catalogue from Mills & Boon by post, to carry to their library to place an order. Now, if readers experienced trouble getting books, they could contact Jane Lovell, a direct mail bookseller based in Croydon, and purchase them. This was the beginning of the successful Reader Service operation. By 1968, 17 per cent of readers surveyed obtained their novels this way. In recent years, Reader Service has displaced retail sales as the chief distribution outlet for Mills & Boon romances.

In 1960, to test the British waters, Mills & Boon decided to import some Harlequin-produced paperbacks for sale locally. At the time, romance paperbacks were not unique in Britain. 'The difference was, they had not the volume, nor the seriousness, of Mills & Boon,' John Boon recalled. 'Volume talks. But we didn't feel that we could finance, or take the risk of financing, a big venture ourselves. When we had the opportunity of buying the Canadian edition at run-on cost, without incurring any production cost, that made a big difference.' Mills & Boon imported 4,000 copies of each title at a rate of four titles every month. 'We could experiment in the market without too much risk,' Boon said. 'After one or two hiccups, it began to go.' But not before persuading W. H. Smith and other retailers to display the books. 'W. H. Smith didn't believe it was possible,' Alan Boon recalled. 'They said, "We'll give you a chance on Waterloo station." We put four of our books in for two months, to see how they'd sell. They were appallingly produced by

Harlequin. They did sell, with some of us going around, buying the books ourselves. But it was considered a success, something people wanted.'

This was the beginning of a deluge. With commercial libraries closing and personal incomes rising, paperback purchases were becoming more accessible to readers of all classes. In these early years Mills & Boon paperbacks were reprints of popular titles; original novels continued to be published first in hardback. 'We are publishing these editions in response to the requests of readers,' Mills & Boon told its readers in the Summer 1960 catalogue, which advertised 'Mills & Boon's Paperback Romances', price half a crown (2s. 6d.). 'In the past we have received many letters from readers who tell us they have no library near at hand and are unable to get our books.' By May 1961 Mills & Boon announced that paperbacks would be available 'throughout most of the Commonwealth' at newsagents and booksellers. 'These romances of hospital and nursing life are tremendous favourites,' a Mills & Boon trade advertisement ran in Australia in 1961. 'In this new attractive format [they] will find a tremendously extended market.' The firm also explained to readers when the paperback title differed from the hardcover novel, since these early paperbacks were printed in Canada to Canadian specifications. *Sister all at Sea* by Juliet Shore (Anne Vinton), for example, was retitled *Nurse at Sea*. By 1962 Woolworth's was stocking Mills & Boon paperbacks, along with Boots and W. H. Smith. Safeway supermarkets and other non-traditional bookselling businesses were not far behind.'

As Harlequin's purchases of rights to Mills & Boon novels accelerated, so did Mills & Boon's profits, and authors' earnings. In 1959, of the 54 novels Harlequin published, 34 were by Mills & Boon authors, largely those who specialized in 'hospital stories': Burchell, MacLeod, Stuart, Vinton, Gilzean, Marjorie Moore, Elizabeth Hoy, Kate Norway, and Caroline Trench (other authors in the list included Edgar Wallace, with five titles, and A. E. W. Mason). Harlequin bought English-language rights, as well as translation rights for smaller French-language editions to sell in Quebec. In 1960, 53 of 60 titles were by Mills & Boon authors; in 1961, 54 of 57; and in 1962, a bumper year, 64 of 70. In 1963 Harlequin published a non-Mills & Boon author for the last time. Between 1964 and 1972 Harlequin published 860 Mills & Boon titles, or an average of nearly 100 per year. By 1968 sales in Canada ran between 30,000 and 40,000 copies of every book published. 'I didn't realise at first how well I was selling abroad,' Betty Beaty recalled, 'until I got a cheque for over £9,000' for a single North American edition. 'This was a large amount at that time, and I rang Mills & Boon saying I thought they'd made a mistake.'

In 1964, when Canada suffered a currency crisis, Mills & Boon contracted to print paperbacks in Britain. Two sales representatives were now devoted to paperback sales, with hardback sales mainly to the public libraries on subscription—as they are today. Mills & Boon had made the transition.

It is no wonder that paperbacks superseded magazine serials as a primary source of earnings and profits. In 1959, for example, Jean MacLeod's Harlequin best-sellers were *Dear Dr. Everett* (36,000 copies); *Air Ambulance* (33,000); and *The Silent Valley* (17,000). Mills & Boon had never seen sales like this before. To keep Harlequin happy, Mills & Boon 'overbalanced' its list with 'mediocre' Doctor-Nurse titles, Alan Boon said: 'We were very concerned that another publisher would get into our list.' The titles published in paperback were hardly the most popular among readers in Britain, who were devouring Rosalind Bretts and Kathryn Blairs. But this way, Mills & Boon could maintain a (small) presence on the paperback shelves in the UK market, until it could expand on its own.

🙚

It is not surprising to discover that a good number of new Mills & Boon authors in the 1960s specialized in Doctor-Nurse romances. Ivy Ferrari, for example, arrived in 1963 with *Sister at Ryeminster*. She came from Alnwick, lived in Norfolk, and belonged to the Norwich Writers' Circle. New Zealander Nora Sanderson was a nurse; her first novel was *Hospital in New Zealand* (1961). Before her election to Parliament for Halifax, Shirley Summerskill, a Londoner, doctor, and daughter of Edith Summerskill, wrote *A Surgical Affair* (1963). Margaret Chapman's debut was *Good Morning Doctor* (1966). Born in Newcastle, she was a geriatric nurse who was happy to boast that writing was profitable: one book bought her a new kitchen range, another a bedroom carpet, and a third provided a new extension to her home. These authors were proud of the renewed appreciation for the nursing profession which was generated by their popular books. 'At all events, there is a certain poetic irony in the fact that what was for generations a notoriously underprivileged profession—nursing—is now, best-sellers apart, about the most lucrative line in fiction,' wrote Olive Norton, herself (as 'Kate Norway' and 'Erica Bain') an author of Doctor-Nurse novels, and a registered nurse. 'In a sixpenny library a few days ago I heard a child say: "Three more nurse-books for Mum, please." No titles. No authors. Just "nurse-books". So long as the dust-jackets depicted a uniformed nurse and a clear-cut doctor-type, Mum was obviously going to be quite happy.'

The star Doctor-Nurse author who arrived on the scene in the 1960s was Betty Neels, whose debut was the Dutch-set *Sister Peters in Amsterdam* (1968). Neels, who started writing at the age of 58 after a career in nursing, was a storyteller of the old school, clearly cut from the Burchell and MacLeod cloths. In 30 years, she has written over 120 novels (but not all Doctor-Nurse romances) for Mills & Boon and (unlike most ageing authors) has increased in popularity. Her daughter encouraged her to write when she overheard a library patron exclaim, 'I'm sick of all this pornography.' Neels typed her manuscript on a borrowed children's typewriter, basing the story in Holland, where she met her husband during the war, and lived for eleven years.

'I'll never forget the delight at seeing it in print, nor the pleasure at getting my first royalties cheque,' Neels said. After *Sister Peters In Amsterdam* was published, Neels granted a full-page interview to the local Dorset newspaper. She expounded on her reasons for writing. 'There are lots of older women like me who don't want to be shocked or horrified in their reading,' she said. 'I admire Mills and Boon for sticking to their principles and not allowing sordid details. Some of the books I object to are awfully clever and well written, but I think there should be a self-imposed limit on pornography. After all, life is rather romantic.'

To Neels, hospitals were the best settings for romance. 'The hospital world is a bit of mystery to most people—dramatic and exciting,' she wrote. 'Members of the medical profession are indispensable and for the most part are splendid men and women, modest about their skill, and working for and with them, a nurse realises that, although she may not feel romantic about it, others do.'

As the 1960s proceeded, Mills & Boon's relationship with Harlequin grew closer, but more complex. On the one hand, personal relations between the Boon and Bonnycastle families were excellent. They liked each other, and found the business arrangement mutually beneficial. Harlequin could not have expanded without Mills & Boon's source of titles, nor could Mills & Boon have grown without the financial independence offered by the lifeline to Harlequin.

Although Mills & Boon eventually entered paperback publishing in its own right, for now the ever-expanding North American sales were the real money-spinners. For this reason, the Boons had to pay close attention to Harlequin's requirements—and objections. Slowly Harlequin agreed to accept romantic novels that were less 'traditional', not based solely on upright doctors and nurses, but which reflected changing times and progressive attitudes, particularly in regard to sex. Ruling the roost in Canada, however, was Richard Bonnycastle's wife, Mary. As chief reader and editor, she had final say over whether Harlequin would publish a particular Mills & Boon title. Needless to say, every Mills & Boon author wanted to be published in Canada, given the financial rewards, but Alan Boon often had to explain to his anxious authors why their novels—successfully sold in Britain and elsewhere—were rejected by Harlequin. Canadian editors, Boon informed Nora Sanderson in 1966, wanted straightforward love stories that could be read by young Canadian girls in their teens. 'They do not like heroines to be in love with married men, or married heroines in love with other men, or unhappy married situations, and no touching on differences of colour,' he said.

'This is sometimes where we disagree with Canadians,' John Boon explained. 'I think they sometimes feel that the job of the editorial department is to keep Canada pure.' He proceeded:

> We don't feel that it's our job to keep Britain pure, but to satisfy as large a percentage of the population as we can. We wouldn't offend or shock. First of all, commercially, it would be a bad decision. Everyone would say we're just in it for commerce. Well, to some extent we are, and, why not? We have certain moral principles, I think. We don't like bad language. We don't like abortion in the books, or brutality. Sadism. But, I think that is a reflection of the morals of the company.

But Mary Bonnycastle and her daughter Judy continually turned down Mills & Boon's recommendations for Harlequin paperbacks, despite the fact that these were books which had already been published in Britain, and had sold well. The top authors, including Violet Winspear and Roberta Leigh, were not published by Harlequin until the late 1960s. The Bonnycastle verdict was usually succinct and severe. Of *Doctors Don't Cry* by Elizabeth Gilzean, for example, the word was: 'Boring, too much hospital detail, not enough romance.' Of Wynne May's *The Tide at Full*: 'Tasteless, unattractive characters.' On *Circles in the Sand* by Marjorie Moore (ironically, first published in 1935): 'No—marital troubles and nasty people.'

'The feeling was, Harlequin couldn't publish those books because of the "sex" in them,' Alan Boon said. 'Sex', of course, referred to intense lovemaking of the Mills & Boon variety, not actual intercourse. 'So, we were really sitting on the top of a volcano. There were other publishers, I'm sure, who would have been delighted to publish these books. But, we couldn't, because of Mrs. Bonnycastle. We couldn't offer them to another publisher.'

The divergence of editorial opinion at Harlequin and Mills & Boon in the 1960s reflects just how ready the latter had become to meet the changing tastes and attitudes of the times. The 1960s was a time of great social change, particularly in the status of women, and in attitudes towards love, romance, and marriage. Fiction serialized in the women's magazines became more realistic, even explicit, and the legacy of *Peyton Place* was evident in the racy novels of Harold Robbins and Jacqueline Susann, not to mention the publication victory of *Lady Chatterley's Lover* in 1960. Editorial had to grow, to build on its strengths, and seek out newer, younger, fresher talent. Mills & Boon's accent was on excitement, but of a 'wholesome' nature. 'Not everyone likes stories of sex, violence, and sadism; a substantial body of folk in every nation still looks for something more wholesome in its reading,' ran a 1966 Mills & Boon advertisement, pitching its 'Paperbacks that please. Clean, wholesome and big selling romances.'

Not surprisingly, the new authors signed up by Mills & Boon in the 1960s were influenced by the current style of popular romance established by Lilian Warren (Rosalind Brett *et al.*) and carried on by Anne Weale, Roberta Leigh, and others. Warren specialized in the foreign background and a strong degree of sexual tension between hero and heroine. Unfortunately, her time was cut tragically short. She was at the top of her form in 1961 and Mills & Boon's best-selling author when she was killed in a car accident in South Africa. We can only wonder how Warren would have changed the course of Mills & Boon in the 1960s had she lived. Like Jack London fifty years earlier, Mills & Boon reissued Warren's novels (now more popular than ever) for several years, and she remained a top seller.

Fortunately for Alan Boon, several popular authors made their debuts in the 1960s and would go on to publish for decades, to great acclaim. The majority arrived without an agent in tow, but via the unsolicited slush pile. Among these was Violet Winspear, whose first novel, *Lucifer's Angel*, was published in 1961. Born in Hackney, Winspear worked in a variety of jobs from the age of 14, including as a clerk in a W. H. Smith shop, a dishwasher in a pie shop, and a packer in a cake mix factory. An avid reader of Mills & Boon novels, Winspear continued with odd jobs until royalties allowed her to quit and write full-time.

As a writer, Winspear was the mistress of titillation and a mild form of eroticism which explains her lack of popularity in Canada. She never crossed the moral line in her novels, but often came perilously close. *Lucifer's Angel*, for example, contained what would become Winspear trademarks: a glamorous setting (the Hollywood film industry), a darkly handsome, brooding hero (famous director Lew Marsh), and a young heroine (Fay) tortured by circumstances. Fay and Lew are married, but for convenience, not love. Eventually they will find happiness together, but not before a whirlwind of dramatic events, including a train wreck, talk of divorce, and a miscarriage. Winspear's description of the hero leaving his bath (watched vicariously by Fay) illustrates her passionate style of writing:

> As she passed him, she put out her own hand and drew her fingertips across his bare back. When he was like this, so boyishly fresh and clean from his bath, his brown skin gleaming, the muscles of his back and his arms rippling with health, he seemed incapable of any despicableness. He seemed like a brown god, come up out of some deep, clean pool of enchantment. He shone with a cleanliness that seemed of the spirit as well as of the body.

By the end of the decade, Winspear had become Mills & Boon's top-selling author. In twenty years she wrote thirty-seven books. Although most of her novels were set overseas, particularly in Spain, Africa, and Greece— destinations of many an English holidaymaker—Winspear herself had never been abroad. 'Her knowledge of life came from Metro-Goldwyn-Mayer films,' Alan Boon recalled. 'Her style was flamboyant. That was very successful, financially. But you wouldn't have expected her to be able to write as she did. She was a Cockney girl, obviously highly sexed, but not experienced at all. She was getting her knowledge of it second hand.'[6]

Like Winspear, Ethel Connell was a fan of Mills & Boon novels, especially those by Rosalind Brett, and set her novels in foreign lands, although she also never travelled abroad. From her native Blackpool, Connell, a cashier and shop assistant, wrote to Mills & Boon in 1968 with her manuscript:

> Enclosed is my first attempt at writing a light romance. My mother, who during her lifetime was more or less an invalid, derived great pleasure from reading your books. I felt I wanted to contribute to giving that pleasure to others who, like mother, are never happier than when they are reading another light romance of Mills and Boons.

Connell's debut as 'Katrina Britt' ('I chose Katrina because I thought that it was romantic. The Britt part was part of Britain. I am English and Church of England') was *A Kiss in a Gondola*. 'I set it in Venice because Shakespeare had made it a very romantic setting for romance and I loved Shakespeare at school,' Connell said. 'I went to the library and got all the books on Venice. I got the pictures. You have to use foreign phrases to lend a little realism.'

The novel was a success, and Connell thanked Alan Boon for her first royalties cheque: 'I am very pleased with the result for I know that there is a certain amount of risk when launching a new author. The book is still on the waiting list at the library and quite a number of people who live locally have told me how much they have enjoyed it and are eagerly awaiting my next. I have also received several letters from readers who like it and want to know when my next one will be published.'

Connell, whose success (and talent) was far inferior to Winspear's, eventually wrote thirty novels for Mills & Boon. 'It's the most wonderful career,' she said. 'I never thought about the money. I never thought I'd make money. I went in for it to give people the pleasure that my mother got from it. I thought, "How wonderful. I can bring pleasure to thousands of people like they did to my mother." And I did.' In 1970 Boon wrote, 'I think you can be well satisfied with the progress of Katrina. One of our aficionadas from Brazil asked whether she was the daughter of Kathryn Blair!'

In his search for the next Kathryn Blair (or Joyce Dingwell), Alan Boon prospected the slush pile for foreign-born authors, and discovered a good number of talented writers, many of whom were fans of the Mills & Boon novels exported to their homelands. One of the most popular Mills & Boon authors in the 1960s, Essie Summers, was born in Christchurch, New Zealand. Married to a Presbyterian minister, Summers was promoted by Mills & Boon with the same enthusiasm as her friend, Dingwell, who encouraged her. 'Summers rather initiated the strong New Zealand back-woods man,' Boon said. 'In the end she was another like Mary Burchell who was very successful. The strong hero–heroine relationship made her most popular. Slightly old-fashioned. Strong hero, little girl. Exotic locations. Sheep farms.' Summers went on to write thirty-five novels.

Other foreign-born authors were more aggressive, even Brett-like, in their writing styles. From South Africa came several Brett hopefuls, including Wynne May, who joined the list in 1966. A member of the Durban Writers Circle and reader of romantic novels, May wrote her first novel, *The Highest Peak*, which after a rejection from Hodder & Stoughton, she sent to Mills & Boon, since she was a fan of Rosalind Brett. 'I received a letter from Alan Boon saying that they liked the writing but that the book was not quite on their wavelength (Divorced hero, for one thing!),' May wrote. 'If, he went on, I was prepared to change the novel they would commission me to do so.' She did, and Boon sent a contract for six books. 'Alan used to write that I had my own particular brand of dynamite. Often a holiday will set my mind going,' she said. Mills & Boon told its readers of Wynne May 'may remind readers of the writings of Rosalind Brett.' She recalled the excitement of seeing her first of thirty books for Mills & Boon:

> My biggest thrill concerning THE HIGHEST PEAK was going to a motel, whilst on holiday, for the night. It was, then, and still is today a well above average kind of motel. It was snowing (up country) and we went to book in and there, in the attractive reception area with its arrange-ments of proteas and African artwork was a rotating book stand to one side. Above it were the words: BEST SELLERS. THE HIGHEST PEAK was one of the books—along with really best selling authors—well known names!

Similarly, Wynne May's friend (and fellow writers circle member), Gwen Westwood, joined the Mills & Boon list in 1968 with *Keeper of the Heart*. An author of children's books, Westwood was looking for a change of pace. 'I wrote to Alan Boon asking for Mills & Boon requirements,' she recalled. 'He immediately sent eight books by airmail. I wrote a first chapter and synopsis and was offered a contract.'[7] Westwood credited her engineer husband for her exotic backgrounds. 'My husband had a very great rapport with Africans, had spoken their languages from childhood, and was keen to show me the wild places of Africa,' she said. 'My books owe a great deal in their background to his influence.'

Westwood claimed she was not popular in her native South Africa where, in fact, *Keeper of the Heart* and several of her novels were initially banned. But gradually her books found favour, and Westwood was delighted by the recognition. She recalled an incident when arriving for an interview with South African Radio, book in hand. 'The receptionist said, "Oh, you have that book. I bought it yesterday and I couldn't put it down. My husband

The Paperback Revolution, 1957–1972   127

grumbled at me because I wouldn't come to bed until I'd finished it."' She also related a story of her husband's: 'There had been a bad storm and some Indian houses were very badly flooded. He had to go to inspect the damage and he met a very pregnant little Indian lady sitting in her garage surrounded by damaged furniture and electrical equipment completely ruined, and she was sitting there with a pile of Mills & Boon books beside her, avidly reading.'

By 1971 Mills & Boon had a record 109 authors under contract. An analysis of these authors reveals that Alan Boon's strategy of building a large stable of dependable authors had been achieved. Of these, 21 wrote one book a year; 36, two; and 32, four. Only 10 authors exceeded five books a year. Together the 109 authors contributed 315 new titles a year, or 25 a month. The stable had grown considerably.

⚶

In tandem with the growth of paperback publishing, Mills & Boon continued to expand its General and Educational list, in new directions. 'The small firm has large problems and the first of these is to get *volume*,' John Boon wrote in the *Publisher* in December 1967. 'A back list must be rapidly built up or acquired to generate capital for reinvestment in new books ... contributors should be approached and persuaded to write books on the subjects in which they specialise.'

Clearly, John Boon spoke from experience. Mills & Boon's backlist was bolstered in 1961 when the firm purchased Allman & Sons, Ltd., one of the oldest publishing firms in England, founded in 1800. Allman had a small staff but an enduring, established list strong in domestic science, revision notes, and English grammar texts. 'Allman's turnover, when we bought them, was only £20,000,' John Boon recalled. 'They had several interesting books, including a Victorian grammar that sold in Nigeria in the thousands. They had a network of retired schoolmasters to sell books in their schools.' But they did bring a certain expertise in the science and textbook publishing fields that Boon decided to enter.

Building upon the handicrafts and home economics series, Mills & Boon took serious steps to re-enter the educational textbook market so enamoured by Gerald Mills. The firm turned to textbooks in the early 1960s and, on the forecast that the number of science students would double in ten years, the first subject chosen was chemistry at the secondary school (11–18) level, followed by biology, technical books on woodwork, metalwork, and technical drawing, and technical and scientific monographs. 'When you start teaching you will want: The best textbooks for your pupils, The best library books for them and yourself,' ran a 1969 Mills & Boon ad in the *Gloucester College of Education Guild Chronicle*. 'Fortunately, this isn't too difficult to manage. You

can get off to a good start by writing for our free general and educational catalogue. Remember the name: MILLS & BOON.'

Mills & Boon's chief competitors were Heinemann, John Murray, and
Longman. 'The Mills & Boon list was not known at all,' noted Dr Margaret
Sands, who edited the biology list for Mills & Boon from 1974. Sands joined
the firm from McGraw-Hill, as she knew Dr David Waddington, who edited
the Mills & Boon chemistry list. 'The Mills & Boon science books earned
respect because of the quality of each text, not because it was from a
good/bad list or well known/obscure science publisher,' she said. Sands
recruited authors for her biology series from successful schoolteachers, as
John Boon called on his Cambridge teachers for advice on science authors.
After dining with Boon, Waddington found himself with an agreement to
write a textbook, which turned into a successful series of chemistry texts. 'I
asked him later why he had not commissioned me to submit a proposal, a
work plan, a sample chapter and so on,' Waddington recalled. '"Real publishing is not about work plans; it is about people and one's own feelings" was
his answer. He and Alan, his brother, may be among the last breed of publishers and what fun they gave authors, and with what skill they chose and
promoted them.'

But John Boon sensibly passed on the books that would not earn a return.
One such proposal was made by Dr A. M. Taylor of the British Food
Manufacturing Industries Research Association, and author of *Basic Physics
for Food Technologists* (1961). 'I do not like you to think that we are entirely
obsessed by the commercial aspect of publishing, but it is difficult to divorce
it from the educational,' Boon wrote in his reply. 'It costs so much to produce a book today, quite apart from the cost of marketing, that publishers
can only do it if they see a fairly substantial and well defined market. Your
own book would have cost at least £1,500 to print and bind and, as it was
aimed at a fairly small group of people, we did not think that sales would give
us anything like this in return.' Better luck was had with science textbooks
that would become set texts in schools—as Gerald Mills had discovered forty
years earlier. Similarly, although Mills & Boon's series on home beer making
was very successful, a companion series on wine making—including how to
grow your own vineyard—did not appeal to British readers, for obvious reasons. In 1966 Margaret Gore-Browne, a vineyard owner, promoted her book,
Let's Plant a Vineyard, to John Boon, convinced that droves would purchase
the title:

> You asked who would be likely to buy the book. One can't guarantee,
> naturally, but last night I rang Anton Massel about another matter and
> mentioned <u>Let's Plant A Vineyard</u>. He said he was extending his book
> department and would of course stock it. So I said, 'Well, who would
> you sell it to?' and he said, 'Everyone of my 2,200 wine merchants will

want one'. Also his students, growers, etc. Edward Montagu, who has over half a million visitors, will sell it at one of his Motor Museum kiosks. I think I will ask him if I might have a vitrine for the book. We would 'doll' it up with artificial grapes, etc.

Somewhat concerned, Boon offered advice on the manuscript: 'Your own vineyard is so large and efficient it may possibly discourage some people who are interested. Could you perhaps give a little more encouraging advice to those who want to grow only a dozen or so vines?' Boon later recalled that Gore-Browne could not be swayed in her conviction that every wine merchant would want a copy: 'They didn't want one. It was not a successful book. She rather insisted they would take them. I mean, who has enough land or time to have a vineyard?'

Mills & Boon's experiment with 'Books for Women' continued with some success, and plenty of free publicity. The titles certainly complemented the values and concerns associated with the Mills & Boon readership. Among the more popular books were *The Young Girl's Guide to Intelligent Dressing* by Dora Shackell (1960), *Pennies into Pounds* by Esme Booker (1962), *Dating Without Tears* by Joan Biggar (1963), and *Manners for Moderns* by Gilda Lund (1965). The latter, noted *she*, 'will cause no social revolutions but makes reasonable sense', thanks to a list of old and now incorrect words and their modern equivalents, such as 'underclothes' for 'lingerie' and 'lavatory' for 'toilet'. *The Young Homemaker* by Angela Creese (1965) was praised by the *Ulster Teachers' Union News*: 'The publishers believe that this book constitutes a break-through in writing for the girl who, though she may be classified as of "average or below average ability" is probably going to grow up to the most responsible job in the world—that of wife and mother.' Finally, *Cooking for Prizes* by Alice Richardson (1963) merited a disappointing review in the *Spectator* by Elizabeth David, who disliked the association of food with competition. 'Mrs. Richardson goes into detail about how to win prizes for jam tarts. (I cannot help calling to mind a saucy Edwardian postcard I once possessed, which bore the caption, "Tarts are Nicest when they are Warm.").' she wrote. Still, a review by Elizabeth David, good or bad, was something of which Mills & Boon could be proud.

☙

By mid-decade, with Mills & Boon clearly enjoying a golden age, the firm was ready for reorganization and expansion. In 1966 Joseph Henley, approaching 80 years old and semi-retired for years, tendered his resignation, clearly to the delight of Alan and John Boon. At a meeting, the Board (including newly appointed Managing Editor, John Boon) granted Henley an ex gratia pension, in recognition of his 'valuable service as a Director of the Company from 1909 to July 1966'. In the 1968 Honours List, John

Boon was made a Commander of the British Empire, for his services to the publishing industry. As President of the Publishers' Association from 1961 to 1963 (nice recognition of both Boon's talents and his firm's prominence in the industry), Boon mounted a successful defence of the Net Book Agreement.

By 1968 Mills & Boon was publishing 130 hardback and 72 paperback romances a year, and 30 titles in the General and Educational list. 'Mills & Boon romances have become one of the fastest selling paperback lines in the world over the last seven years and are particularly popular in Canada and the United States,' the firm announced. 'Steady sales like this come from reader loyalty,' Mills & Boon explained to *Paperbacks in Print* in 1968:

> Over the years we've built up something like a personal relationship with our readers. They come from that large group of people who are bored with tales of sex, violence and sadism and just want a pleasant book. Once they came to the libraries each fortnight and asked for 'the new Mills & Boon's', now they come each month and buy the new paperbacks. With this backing it's extraordinary how sales have snowballed, largely by word of mouth, without much advertising or ballyhoo.

Snowball indeed. By 1968 Olive Norton (a popular but not top author for Mills & Boon) had 26 Mills & Boon titles in print under her three pen-names. Her total sales had approached an astonishing 1.1 million copies. Considering that several authors, including Winspear and Leigh, would have outsold Norton at this time, we can only marvel at these numbers, and the profits generated for the firm.

Paperback publishing was the last step in the standardization of the look and length of Mills & Boon novels. By their nature, paperbacks encouraged a common appearance and size. During the 1960s the regulation book length was enforced—188 to 192 pages, whether hardback or paperback. Jacket design also evolved, with the same artwork used for the hardcover jacket as for the paperback cover. The biggest change, apart from increasingly trendy appearance of the heroes and heroines, was in the format. The artist's canvas was narrowed, as titles and authors were now printed on a broad band across the top. Generally, the heroine, who used to share billing with the hero, appeared more front and centre, dazzling, and confident. For example, for *Nurse at Ryeminster* by Ivy Ferrari (1964), artist Jack Faulks filled the canvas with a portrait of a full-lipped, red-haired nurse. 'It almost makes one want to go into hospital!' Alan Boon said. Perhaps Faulks's most dramatic cover, with a dominant heroine, was painted for *The Voice of My Love* by Pauline Ash (1964). In this novel the temporarily blinded hero falls in love with the voice of the girl who broadcasts talks. Boon requested a 'heavy' treatment, suggesting 'a large, dominating head-and-shoulders study of the girl' with 'full red lips' and the bandaged hero, facing the camera. 'Perhaps you could do a sort of serious, Maria-like study of her, as the poor girl has considerable domestic troubles, but she is of course a very nice girl.' The result was a powerful cover.

In 1970 Boon requested from Philip Simmonds a cover for *Isle of the Rainbows* by Anne Hampson, an author known for her 'strong situations'. 'The hero should be one of your dark types in a white tropical suit and the heroine has dark brown hair and should be wearing whatever women wear in a tropical island like Dominica,' Boon wrote. The result was somewhat startling: the hero, Max, looks like a tanned Londoner; the heroine, Penny, was unkempt and sloppy, in sunglasses, hat, and plain blouse. Although there was a beach in the background, the setting could have been Ramsgate or Blackpool. At least Max, pointing and looking stern, lives up to his description in the blurb: 'Max is by nature a very strong-willed man. Always he has expected to be obeyed . . . Here was one girl who was not going to comply.'

In 1970 Violet Winspear told Alan Boon, 'You know my feeling about covers; they're like a gay coat of paint that helps to sell a boat or a house.' But covers alone did not sell the novels. Just as important as a good 'product' was a superior distribution system. In 1968 John Boon decided to abandon Book-Centre, a co-operative venture among publishers to distribute books, to join a new company, Distribution & Management Services Ltd. (DMS), founded by David Boorman. DMS tailored its services to Mills & Boon's unusual, but precisely timed, publishing schedule. 'The books were really monthly periodicals, a January edition, February edition, etc.,' Boorman recalled. 'If booksellers got the June edition at the back end of July, they would send it back.' Boorman, who handled distribution for Heinemann, offered Mills & Boon an exclusive contract. He tied his system to Mills & Boon's deadlines, and worked to improve cash collection from dealers, which could take as long as three months. 'Our only innovation in the beginning was to work to deadlines. We offered simple systems that worked to deadline on both distribution and cash collection. All we needed were the systems to make sure the books were on the shelf at the right time, and in good time,' Boorman said. With DMS Mills & Boon saw profits increase, and its distribution costs cut in half.

Mills & Boon's success in romantic fiction publishing came at the expense of other publishing houses, which did not fare as well. In 1968 Ward, Lock announced that it would stop publishing fiction, which it had done for longer than Mills & Boon. In an address to the RNA, Alan Boon reassured authors that Mills & Boon's own future was sound, but offered safe haven to Ward, Lock's authors. 'We intend to increase our output (much of which, by the way, is exported) if we discover suitable novels, and remain confident of the future,' he said. 'A number of the Ward, Lock authors will be joining our list.' These included Jean Dunbar, Barbara Perkins, Dorothy Quentin, and Doris E. Smith. Quentin, first published by Ward, Lock in 1939, was rejected by Mills & Boon in 1936. A nurse raised in India, Quentin's sixty-sixth novel was published by Mills & Boon in 1969.

Although Mills & Boon was at the top of its form in 1968, it did not shrink from a fight when its interests were threatened. Such was the case when a celebrated incident of plagiarism arose in 1967, involving two veteran authors, Betty Beaty (first published in 1956) and Mary Burchell (1936). A Dublin man had copied serializations of Mills & Boon novels out of the *Irish Times*, given them a new title, and then sold them as 'original' manuscripts to an unsuspecting aspiring author in the US, Dr Delphine McCarthy. McCarthy had answered an advertisement in an Irish magazine which read: 'For sale: plots and unpublished stories.' For $60 she purchased an 80,000-word manuscript called *Beyond the Clouds*—which was, in reality, Beaty's *The Atlantic Sky*. After she was published by Crown Publishers Inc. of New York, McCarthy was hailed as 'the literary find of the month'. But when McCarthy's agent offered reprint rights of the novel to Mills & Boon, Alan Boon spotted the deception immediately, and launched an investigation.

'Unless you've read every book, it could happen,' Boon recalled. 'All our books are basically similar, aren't they?' The affair was exposed by Jonathan Aitken in the *Evening Standard*, just in time to prevent publication of McCarthy's next novel, *Holiday in Bayville*, which was really Burchell's *Cinderella After Midnight*. 'The morals of this tale are that authors should do their own work and that everyone in the book industry on both sides of the Atlantic should be very much more careful,' Aitken wrote. McCarthy had to repay all advances and royalties.

Beaty forgave McCarthy, and they became friends. 'There were extenuating circumstances for the plagiarism,' Beaty explained. 'The lady doctor in question was elderly. She had an invalid daughter, and she appeared to truly believe that novels were written in this way—that you bought them from a producer and put your name to them. In the end, we used to exchange Christmas cards.'

In 1968 Mills & Boon, now a powerful and successful publishing company, celebrated its Diamond Anniversary. It did so with a publicity coup: the publication of a report on its readership that challenged the old stereotypes— and made Mills & Boon even more attractive to potential buyers.

'It seemed to me that we had this readership identifiable through Reader Service,' John Boon recalled. 'Peter Mann had written an article in the *Bookseller* doing an analysis of readership. We pulled him aboard and asked him to do research. He was commissioned, yes, but he was carrying out a research job for us. We influenced him in no way whatsoever.'

Mann was senior lecturer in sociology at Sheffield University when invited by Mills & Boon to survey 9,300 readers on the catalogue mailing list. Nearly 3,000, or 30 per cent, replied, completing a 25-item questionnaire. The results were published by Mills & Boon in 1969. While Mann's report must be handled with care (some of the collection methods are unsubstantiated and unscientific), his survey is none the less significant, for several reasons. It stands as one of the first analyses of the readership of romantic novels in Britain. The report generated a great deal of publicity in the media, and undoubtedly encouraged further study of the subject. The Mann report also enhanced Mills & Boon's standing in the industry and financial circles, positioning the firm (as John Boon intended) as an attractive acquisition or merger partner.

In most respects, Mann's findings were a vindication of everything Mills & Boon believed in, and had worked hard to achieve. Romances, Mann determined, were read by women of all ages, from 15 to 80. Reading increased between the ages of 25 and 44, and when women were married. Interestingly, 42 per cent of respondents said they had been Mills & Boon readers for the past 10 years or less (the paperback years); 26 per cent had been readers for over 20 years. 'Mills & Boon are not dependent on an old readership as had been thought possible,' Mann concluded.

The social composition of Mills & Boon readers was also analysed, and the readership, Mann discovered, was 'not quite so homogeneous a group as might have been expected'. Over half the readers did not have children at home, while 38 per cent of respondents were housewives. Some 37 per cent were office or clerical workers in 'white collar' jobs, while only 9 per cent did 'factory or manual work'—shattering the stereotype that Mills & Boon romances were read by 'unsophisticated' women. As regards education, 44 per cent completed secondary modern or grammar school, and 17 per cent technical, art, or secretarial college—educational levels higher than average for society at the time. 'The readers contain a fair number of reasonably well educated women, with middle class occupations, and most occupations given are of the lower middle class office and clerical type,' Mann wrote. 'This fits in well with a picture of young women, and older ones too, who have the literary skills to cope with and enjoy a full length book, as against the mere magazine or cartoon strip type novelette.'[8]

How the respondents obtained their books was also encouraging. A majority (65 per cent) bought 'some or most' of their romances as paperbacks, a healthy audience. Points of purchase included bookshops (25 per cent), W. H. Smith (23), Boots (22), newsagents (11), or Woolworths (8). '3/6d. is a lot out of your wages', wrote one reader, an 'ex-hairdresser', aged 19–24, 'but I go without a pair of nylons to get the books'. Those who did not buy books borrowed from a public library, or from a friend. Mann noted the 'mild surprise' that 55 per cent of borrowers said they had 'no difficulty' in obtaining romances from libraries, but 21 per cent said there were too few in stock.

Most respondents praised the ease of reading and the 'wholesomeness' of the books. Some 33 per cent claimed that the books were 'well-written, interesting, good stories and plot', while 25 per cent cited 'pleasant light reading';14 per cent, 'relaxing, easy to read'; and 12 per cent, 'Clean, wholesome, not sordid'. The Mills & Boon guarantee seemed to register with readers, as well as the promise of escape. 'Your books are "pleasant books" and most other paperbacks appear rather sordid,' reported one housewife, aged 25–34. 'I read them when I am tired and wish to relax, so I must have something light and uncomplicated with enough story to help to keep me interested,' said another, aged 55–64. An office clerk, unmarried, aged 19–24, said that she chose Mills & Boon novels for 'Excitement and romance. I suppose I like to think something like that could happen to me.'

Interestingly enough, the most popular authors were old-timers. Essie Summers was first with 21 per cent, followed by Kathryn Blair/Rosalind Brett/Celine Conway (13 per cent), Violet Winspear (10), and Anne Weale (10). All of these authors, with the exception of Winspear (and Lilian Warren, who was dead), were well over the age of 30. The favourite type of story contained a 'foreign background', with 48 per cent, followed by the Doctor-Nurse storyline (21 per cent), and the 'Mystery Romance' (11). Winspear's *The Honey Is Bitter* (1967), set in Greece, was cited as 'Top of the Pops', the most popular title. In this typical Winspear novel, young Domini agrees to marry stern Paul Stephanos to save her family from its crippling debts. Once in Greece, her feelings begin to turn to affection, even love, for this 'devastatingly attractive man'. In the finale, they are drawn together as true man and wife:

> He gathered her close to him. 'Sun, moon and stars are dark right now, Domini, as in Samson's song,' he murmured. 'What if they stay dark for me?'
>
> 'Two people can see across mountains and oceans, Paul, if they're together and in need of each other.'
>
> 'For better or worse you're my husband,' she said to him. 'We can't break the marriage bond whatever else we destroy.'

'The report created quite a sensation,' John Boon admitted. 'Mann was part of my deliberate policy. By treating the genre seriously, by looking at it, analysing it, we should win much more acceptance for it. Which we have. You become interested in it. The mocking and sneering goes away.' And, Mills & Boon acquired more lustre. As Alan Boon told Phyllis Matthewman, part of Mills & Boon's motivation was to overcome any lingering public library prejudice. 'Our task has been in many cases to eradicate the mistaken comprehension that the novels are the favourite reading of Great-Aunt Maud, when in fact the range of readership is extremely wide and is in fact most preponderate among younger readers,' he wrote. Authors themselves knew as much, as Iris Danbury wrote to Alan Boon: 'I have many times seen all ages of women reading romantic novels in buses, trains and on one occasion between the acts at a theatre. (My husband using opera glasses identified the book as M.&.B. but tantalisingly could not read the author's name!) It is surely a fallacy to believe that only the middle-aged char reads our books.' Indeed, the *Observer* reported in December 1968 that one in two people in Britain did not read books, good or bad. But those who did read, read Mills & Boon novels, as light romantic fiction was the fastest-selling category in paperback publishing.

'The possibility, or perhaps, the necessity for a merger or takeover with someone was in our minds from perhaps the middle of the 1960s onwards,' John Boon said. 'The reason for this was, essentially, money. So, we were looking around for suitable partners. In fact, we were wooed by many large firms.' In the end, to the surprise of no one, Mills & Boon accepted an offer from Harlequin, and the two companies merged in 1971.

On paper, Mills & Boon certainly did not need to merge with anyone. The firm was prosperous, and the relationship with Harlequin was close and mutually beneficial. That bond was made even stronger when a formal contract was struck with Harlequin in 1969, just before the Canadian firm became a public company. In an 'Export Coup' heralded in the London press, Harlequin agreed to expand distribution of Mills & Boon romances throughout North America, with Curtis Books assisting in the United States. The agreement was struck between the Boon brothers and Richard Bonnycastle, Jr., who succeeded his father upon the elder Bonnycastle's death in 1968. The *Financial Times* noted, 'In this age of realism the Brothers Boon are proving the rest of the publishing world wrong by sticking to this age-old formula of romances that lack violence, profanity, illicit sex scenes and rarely print a harder word than "dash".'

The agreement accelerated sales around the world. By 1969 Mills & Boon's English-language sales totalled 15 million per year, of which 10 million represented exports, which brought in £350,000 per year. Sales in Canada alone amounted to 4 million per year, or £120,000. By 1971, Mills & Boon translations were offered in 14 languages: Afrikaans, Danish, Dutch, Finnish, French, German, Greek, Hebrew, Italian, Maltese, Norwegian, Portuguese, Spanish, and Swedish. Of all of the British book exports to the Philippines in 1971, 30 per cent were Mills & Boons. 'I am a housewife and a busy businesswoman with four children,' wrote one Filipina fan. 'Every day I work very hard. In my siesta hour I read only Mills & Boon pocketbooks to rest my nerves.'

Betty Neels was one of many authors delighted with the Canadian connection and its international benefits. 'It's nice to know that things are going satisfactorily in Canada, I hope they continue to be so for I am already delighted with my earnings,' she wrote in 1970. The 'magnificent' royalty cheque, Neels added, was 'the main talking point in the family since it arrived. I shall never get used to getting such a lot of money all at once and what a nice feeling it is.' By 1973 Neels's advances topped £1,000. Most Mills & Boon authors, Alan Boon noted, were earning between £5,000 and £10,000 per year, with the top novelists earning far more.

These were happy times for Mills & Boon. In 1970, due to 'the expansion of their business', Mills & Boon moved from Grafton Way to larger head-quarters in Foley Street. In reporting the move, the *Bookseller* announced Mills & Boon sales as 'running at 18 million copies a year'. By 1971 the fig-ure had risen to 25 million, described as 'the biggest selling romance series in the world with the highest sales in the Commonwealth, the U.S.A. and Canada'. The *Bookseller*, in analysing the top paperback publishers in Britain in 1971, ranked Mills & Boon, with 'an established supremacy' in romance and historical fiction, at No. 8 in terms of retail sales (4.5 million, represent-ing UK sales), behind Penguin (35 million), Fontana (20 million), Pan (18.5 million), Corgi (15 million), Mayflower/Panther (11.5 million), Coronet (8.75 million), New English Library (8 million), and Arrow (6.5 million). Consid-ering the low overheads at Mills & Boon (with just 30 employees on the pay-roll), it is not surprising that 1971 profits exceeded £212,000.

Clearly, Mills & Boon's success—and profits—made the industry take notice. 'Publishing was much more snobbish then,' John Boon recalled. 'As we expanded, we made money. Money talks.'

Ironically, the major publishing houses did not pose serious competition, nor did they take much interest in Mills & Boon. 'We did have competition, but not very aggressive competition,' Boon said. 'The big firms didn't realize what they had. They missed on it. They were literary snobs. Collins could have done it. Hutchinson. Hodder & Stoughton. They didn't take the job seriously. Alan did—and he was absolutely serious about it. He didn't say they were Jane Austen. They were simply the best books of the type or product.'

John Boon spoke frankly in giving his reasons for seeking a merger. 'I was under some pressure,' he confessed. 'Alan was desperate to do this, desperate for money. We had no pension.' As a small firm that had had its share of struggles over the years, Mills & Boon had not made provisions for its employees. The prospects for financial security and pension coverage offered by another company were attractive. Plus, the Boons were not getting any younger: in 1968 Alan was 55, Carol, 56, and John, 52; both Alan and John had wives and large families. The desire was to strike an equitable agreement with a sympathetic partner, which would preserve the strengths—and independence—of Mills & Boon.

It is thus not surprising that by 1970, Mills & Boon was engaged in merger talks with a number of firms, including Collins and Heinemann, and the American publishers Macmillan and Time-Life. 'We've been approached by potential purchasers so many times I've lost count,' John Boon confessed to *The Times* Diary. With publishing profits elsewhere 'generally in a parlous state', *The Times* commented, 'It's no wonder that Boon can say, "It's like being the only woman on a klondike."'

The Heinemann talks in July 1971 were recounted by Alan Hill in his history, *In Pursuit of Publishing*. Dwye Evans, group managing director, was a good friend of John Boon's, and opened negotiations for acquisition, 'foreseeing (correctly, as it turned out) great financial advantages thereby'. But the deal was cancelled abruptly on the verge of an agreement. Charles Pick, Heinemann's publisher, objected, and no one could challenge him. 'He felt that the M&B style of publishing would not fit the William Heinemann image. "What will J. B. Priestley say when he hears of this?" said Charles to me,' Hill recalled. Hill, none the less, mused on what might have been:

> I don't now believe that the eminently reputable firm of Mills & Boon would have had any effect on the Heinemann image. In fact it could have enhanced it. After all, our great best-seller Georgette Heyer (J. B. Priestley's neighbour in Albany!) started her career by writing M&B novels. More importantly, not only did M&B subsequently achieve enormous financial success, but their acquisition would have brought into the Group John Boon himself—one of the book trade's leading personalities.[9]

As John Boon noted, 'In those days leading publishers regarded themselves as not exactly royalty, but as aristocracy. The great name of Collins, for example, would not have been associated with anything romantic. They did a lot of romance themselves, but they never developed the line.'

꧁

'One of the difficulties doing a deal was that, although we were very profitable for a firm of our size in those days, about 60 per cent of the profits came from subsidiary rights, derived from sales to North America,' John Boon recalled. 'We had then the traditional British market, with all the exports, or 30–40 per cent of our editions. If they had been straight book sales, it would have been easier to sell the business.'

Harlequin, of course, recognized this, and struck early to court Mills & Boon as an acquisition. 'While the Boons and Bonnycastles have enjoyed a good personal relationship over the past several years, which I am certain will continue into the future, if someone other than yourself obtained control of Mills & Boon they might not recognize this relationship,' Richard Bonnycastle wrote from Toronto in August 1970. Clearly, Bonnycastle understood that, apart from the five-year distribution agreement signed in 1969, there was no iron-clad contract binding the two firms together, apart from a clause that Mills & Boon could not supply another romantic fiction publisher. 'If we had gone to X, Y, Z and cut out Harlequin, Harlequin would have been in real trouble,' John Boon recalled.

Bonnycastle, in a letter to John Boon, suggested a 'tie-up' of the two firms. 'A marriage between Mills & Boon and Harlequin would bring new strengths to both companies. (I suppose the word in vogue is synergy),' Bonnycastle wrote. He proposed, for example, applying Harlequin's direct mail/marketing experience to British and international markets, while expanding Mills & Boon's fiction and non-fiction publishing lists in North America.

John Boon maintained that Mills & Boon regarded the deal as a publishing one, and not purely as a financial settlement. 'By bringing the two firms together, we would produce a much more efficient, larger firm,' he replied to Bonnycastle. 'I had always previously thought of any tie-up between the two of us in financial terms, whereas it could be far more than that. With the distribution that Harlequin can give in Canada and the USA and that we can achieve elsewhere, we could have a world operation.'

But striking the deal was not easy, given Harlequin's new financial backers. 'Harlequin were absolutely terrified of the deal,' John Boon recalled. 'They had some printing works, but were publishing nothing really. It was very hard for Dick and myself to persuade them that this would be a good purchase. It turned out to be probably one of the best purchases in publishing for the last 30 years. There was an enormous good will element to it.' Apparently the idea of acquisitions had soured in Toronto, after a bad experience Harlequin had had with the purchase of Jack Hood School Supplies, a Canadian educational supply company.

Clearly Bonnycastle appreciated the benefits of a merger, but Harlequin did not. 'They were nervous of a small, unquoted company overseas. The only threat was that we might take our books away from them,' John Boon said. But she added, there was more to it than that; 'I don't know that they really liked the idea of going into romance. There's always a bit of intellectual snobbery in dealing with our books with their people. But, for whatever the reason, Dick Bonnycastle had a very hard time persuading them.' How did he succeed? 'I think he had a lot of friends in financial circles,' Boon explained. He was very persuasive. I think the meetings were conducted in an atmosphere of almost neurosis. We got one telex, which I unrolled in the corridor. It was 30 feet long. They were very difficult negotiations.' Boon remembered Harlequin's William F. Willson, vice-president for planning and corporate development, threatening to buy up all of Mills & Boon's authors if a deal wasn't struck. 'In negotiating with us, I said, "Well, you're not going to do awfully well without Mills & Boon books,"' Boon recalled. 'Bill Willson said, "Our information is that we could easily replace them." That was a load of codswollop.' Bonnycastle gave his assurance that negotiations would proceed. 'I personally believe we can iron out our differences on this subject without "losing our cool",' he wrote.

Lawrence Heisey joined Harlequin as President in 1971, after a successful tenure at the US consumer products giant Procter & Gamble. He plunged almost immediately into the merger talks. Heisey remembered the bank as being very unkind, requiring Harlequin to raise $1 million in equity.

'The two companies had to get together,' Heisey explained. 'If we hadn't been able to do the deal, Mills & Boon should have come back and bought us. They could have had the relationship end and gone into publishing in North America on their own account, because they had the editorial. That was the crucial thing.' It was good business sense to acquire Mills & Boon, Heisey said, to 'get a lock on editorial', and take the product around the world, not just to the eighteen or so countries to which Mills & Boon was then exporting.

In the end, the deal was struck. Effective from 1 October 1971, Harlequin acquired Mills & Boon Limited (although the deal was not made public until December). The purchase price was £1.2 million (C$3 million), an improvement over the original offer of £700,000. John and Alan Boon joined the Harlequin board of directors, with John becoming Deputy Chairman. Carol Boon resigned as Director of Mills & Boon, replaced by Willson.

Was £1.2 million (£15 million to £20 million today) a good price? 'I think it was not a bad price for the time, considering inflation,' John Boon said. 'On the pension side, it was enough money so we could live in reasonable comfort for the rest of our lives.' *The Times* Diary, on hearing the news, called it a '£1.2m Boonanza'.

Legally, the deal was not a 'merger', as the UK press release stated, but a 'takeover', as the Canadian release reported. 'They call it a merger, but it wasn't a merger—it was a takeover,' Heisey said. 'The Boons ended up with a lot of shares—they took cash and shares and 'kickers' and all that stuff. There was really no doubt about that. But they were very jealous of this idea that they were still independent, which they weren't—although sometimes it was very hard for them to believe that they had to follow some orders.' Gordon Wixley, still providing Mills & Boon with accounting services in 1971 (after 40 years), agreed. 'Harlequin was the better offer, but there was an attraction in having the holding company 3,000 miles away,' he recalled. 'I don't think John would have taken kindly with working with someone just around the corner, frankly. He was Managing Director. Having Canadians in Toronto was fair enough. They were, after all, the controlling company. To be a merger sounds better. But it was a takeover.'

In the 1971 Harlequin Annual Report, Mills & Boon was introduced by Chairman Bonnycastle to shareholders as 'the largest publisher of romantic fiction in the English-speaking world, with substantial international sales of books and rights. In addition to romantic fiction, Mills & Boon Limited publishes general and educational lists ... Since 1958, your company has been the licensed publisher for North America of romance books selected from the Mills & Boon Limited backlists.' The performance of the new acquisition was compared to the Harlequin Book Division, in thousands of Canadian dollars:

	1969		1970		1971	
	Sales ($000)	Profit ($000)	Sales ($000)	Profit ($000)	Sales ($000)	Profit ($000)
Mills & Boon	1,900	179	2,248	251	2,875	279
Harlequin	2,412	405	2,576	286	3,262	434

Clearly, the companies were not too dissimilar, although Harlequin's profit margin was higher. 'Total revenues of Mills & Boon Limited have increased from £582,000 ($1,513,000) in 1967 to £1,145,000 ($2,875,000) in 1971, or at an annual rate of 18%,' the analysis continued 'During this same period, pre-tax profits increased at an annual rate of 28%, to £212,000 ($532,000) in 1971.' Harlequin added that Mills & Boon romantic novels have 'international appeal' in 18 languages and 'returns are negligible by North American standards'. In 1971 Harlequin Romances represented 14 per cent of mass-market paperback book sales in Canada, and 3 per cent in the US, where Simon & Schuster handled distribution.

In the press release issued by Mills & Boon on 18 December 1971, the following statement is revealing:

> Although Harlequin's experience has been primarily with fiction, the two firms are fully committed to the growth of the general and educational list. Both small in terms of staff, their plan is to publish as before in a flexible, personal manner. They believe that by bringing together the financial and marketing skills of Harlequin with the publishing expertise of Mills & Boon the two will form a group stronger and more effective than if they remained independent.

This, then, was the vision of the two companies. In terms of romantic fiction—the product—this statement proved true. Upon hearing the news, Olive Norton thanked Alan Boon for 'your Harlequin love-affair (or was it rape?)', the result of which was that 'we do seem to have come to a point where we <u>matter</u>'. Violet Winspear was less enthusiastic, fearing intrusion by foreigners. 'Nothing must happen to you!' she wrote. 'I'd hate to think what would become of the "harem" if anything ever happened to the "sheik" who puts up with our tantrums with a charm that must feel very strained at times. It's one thing to write a romance; it's another to deal with the writers of them, all temperamental, and most of them with the female urge to be "harem" favourite!'

Nothing did happen to 'Sheik' Boon, as he was the acknowledged genius behind the Mills & Boon romance. Alan Boon maintained that Harlequin could not have expanded operations around the globe without a good product. 'You need to have the Derby winner before you can win the race,' he noted. Years later, Boon issued his famous paper, called 'A Rationale of Mills & Boon with Observations'. Here he compared Mills & Boon to an oil well, and Harlequin to a petrol pump. 'There can be no doubt as to which of the two is the more important to the publishing operation,' Boon wrote. 'Oil wells can always find petrol pumps but petrol pumps need to find oil before they can function. The Mills & Boon oil well is therefore vital to the filling of the Harlequin petrol pump. It is the foundation of all Harlequin's success.'

But in terms of the general and educational list, and the promised 'flexible, personal manner' of publishing, the Harlequin–Mills & Boon merger was not a success. It would have been impossible for the Boon sons to predict the future of the new company in 1972, and the direction it would take. Dramatic management changes would slowly erode the Mills & Boon influence, and eat away at its fundamental principles. Financial glory aside, John Boon would live to rue the day he signed the 1971 'takeover' agreement, effectively ending the family-owned firm after sixty-four years. 'If my father were alive today he would have been very upset, very sorry that it was merged with another company,' he recalled. 'He would have told me I should run the whole thing myself rather than throw away money. I think he would not have been very pleased.'

Part II

Romance and Responsibility
Editorial Policy

Chapter 6
The 1930s: A Genre is Born

'I suppose you have to spoil your pretty mouth with that sticky rubbish. When I was young, if a girl had gone to an engagement party made up like that ...'

Claire laughed:

'In your young days, it would have been a crime to do this.' She took a cigarette from the case lying on the dressing-table and lit it. 'But Time marches on, you know.'

Barbara Hedworth, *How Strong Is Your Love?* (1938)

'I was thinking how lovely it must be to write novels. You can make everything end just as it should.'

'I only write light stuff,' he said deprecatingly.

'That's the nicest kind of writing. I love books which make you feel all excited and happy because everything comes right for everyone. Doesn't it make you feel warm inside when you think of the people who get cheered up by your stories and tell themselves that perhaps their love stories will come right, too?'

Jan Tempest, *Little Brown Girl* (1940)

THE mature Mills & Boon paperback romance that was published in 1972, written to a standard length and with a plot increasingly tailored to specific editorial guidelines, bears little resemblance to the novels published by Charles Boon in the 1930s. In fact, it is difficult to speak of a specific Mills & Boon editorial policy before the Second World War. The reason is obvious: Charles Boon, although restructuring his firm to become a 'library house' in the 1930s, was still a general publisher at heart. The 1930s was still a time of experimentation, and novels were novels in their own right. Boon did not impose many restrictions on his authors and, to a large extent, relied on the authors for guidance on current tastes and attitudes. These authors were, increasingly, young women, who brought to their writing a fresh (and up-to-date) point of view. If a book or style sold well, it was copied. Denise Robins, Elizabeth Carfrae, and (to a lesser degree) Louise Gerard were all influential, as were the cinema, the wireless, and popular best-sellers such as *Rebecca* and *Gone with the Wind*.

None the less, there were 'limits'. Charles Boon, reflecting his personal tastes (like any publisher), preferred 'wholesome' and 'moral' books, novels that entertained and offered a happy ending. 'The books in those days were not nearly as stylized as they are today,' Alan Boon explained. 'They had a much broader canvas. But I think the old man would not have published a book that wasn't romantic. His legacy was not the strong moral line. Or marketing. I think it was a certain readability.' Added John Boon: 'A lot of people were doing romance—Collins were very considerable competitors, and Hurst & Blackett. I suppose this was father's gift, and certainly the gift that Alan had—we hit the right formula.' Amid the variety of romantic novels published, there did emerge certain ground rules which shaped the Mills & Boon romance we know today. To study these early novels is to reveal these lasting threads.

※

Charles Boon's views on romantic fiction were undoubtedly shaped by his personality. Dinah Boon remembered her father as a dyed-in-the-wool Tory: 'Father was a member of the Constitutional Club, the Conservative club in London. Absolutely King and Country. He used to say, "Right will prevail!" When there was the Coronation, we had a huge crown in electric lights outside the house, and anyone who didn't look at it was a Communist!' Charles Boon was also 'terribly protective' of his daughter. 'Father was always there to see whether I was talking to anyone at the bus stop. He was totally fearful of white slavery,' she recalled.

Popular fiction, and the escapism which it offered to readers from (primarily) the middle and some of the working classes, was usually overseen by right-wing publishers such as Charles Boon. Storylines, however fantastic, were designed to promote the status quo, as well as the institutions of marriage and motherhood. This escapism was bolstered by the Depression and the build-up to war in the 1930s, and complemented the popular films of the age. In 1927 Jermyn March, a Hurst & Blackett author (*The Man Behind the Face*), emphasized that a novel must have a 'strong human appeal', of 'a stirring ambition, a deep passion, or a moving renunciation'. What readers demand, he added, was a certain 'thrill': 'They like to feel that the least little turn of fortune's wheel might have involved themselves in just such a throbbing romance, have headed straightway on just such a reckless, joyous adventure, or high enterprise, as the hero and heroine embarks on.' A happy ending was just as important:

I am a great believer in the 'happy ending'. It need not be a *triumphant* ending, rising step on step to the final clash of joybells; it needs not even the old traditional fairy tale *denouement* ... like to close a book with a sigh of content and say, 'After all, that was the best thing that could have happened—the *right* thing. Nothing else would have seemed quite so satisfactory.'

Berta Ruck, who joined the Mills & Boon list in 1939 after twenty-five years of writing romances, also believed in escapism. Ruck made no apologies for the fact that 'the people in my books are young. Youth, Strength, and Shapeliness are gifts from the Gods. Why must they be "Indian gifts", inevitably taken back again?'[2] She was just as proud of being called by critics an 'incurable Happy-ender': 'Rather than the vitriol-and-vinegar-and-railway-station-waiting-room-smell in so much "real-life fiction", give me the sugariest Kitsch that ends optimistically and (Kipling again) "with a scent of old-world roses through the fog that ties you blind" ... Joy, adventure, fullness of living, satisfaction in human relations, are the right and the lasting things.'[3] Mary Burchell, one of Mills & Boon's rising stars in the 1930s, would have agreed. 'The girl's reactions are basically your own, unless you're doing it as a business,' she recalled. 'You cannot really, in my view, write a good romance where the girl, who is of course the person [through] whose eyes you see it, has reactions that are basically not your own. I think this is almost always the case.'

David Doig, who joined D. C. Thomson, the Scottish magazine publishers (the *People's Friend, My Weekly*) in 1927, made an important point about Mills & Boon romances and the pattern that developed in the 1930s:

In general I would say the Mills & Boon story could be rather slighter, perhaps with a little less drama. I don't mean violence—probably a less dramatic situation. You very often got the Mills & Boon story, rather a sort of follow-up to *Jane Eyre* and the Brontë stuff, where the girl was to be governess in some house, where the man is married to a dreadful wife, or where he's not married at all, or he's fed up about something and he doesn't speak to anybody. The Rochester character again. You've got people writing these things because it's a story that's written again and again in various ways.

The *Jane Eyre* storyline—a waif heroine and enigmatic, domineering hero— was just as popular in Hollywood, where Daphne du Maurier's *Rebecca*, for example, was translated into a successful film. But the cinema also provided stronger, more independent roles for women, such as Vivien Leigh as Scarlett O'Hara in the film version of Margaret Mitchell's *Gone with the Wind*. Alan Boon also cited as an influential film *It Happened One Night* (1934), in which Clark Gable and Claudette Colbert 'spend the night together' (their beds separated by a blanket).

It is interesting to study two Mills & Boon novels from these early years which featured main characters who themselves wrote romantic fiction. These 'novels within novels' are revealing as they were written by two authors who had achieved considerable success: Sophie Cole and Jan Tempest. We have already reviewed Maisie Bennett's novel, *Golden Vanity* (1912), with its hero, Donald Brennan Scott, a writer whose books become staples in the lending libraries. In Cole's *Secret Joy* (1934), the heroine's burning ambition is to write a romantic novel. Celia Halstead is married with three children. Her novel, *Anna Croone*, is published anonymously by the firm of Spender & Trant, whose imprint 'is a guarantee the novel's worth taking seriously'. The same could be said by this time of the Mills & Boon imprint. Celia speculated on the joys of writing:

> It had always been her instinct to hide the fact that she was romantic —
> 'romantic' was the word, there was no gainsaying it, much as she was
> ashamed of the weakness. But in those hidden pages she could let her-
> self go — could give the reins to sentiment without fear of being called
> 'sentimental' by her matter-of-fact family, and indulge in romance with-
> out incurring the risk of being labelled 'romantic'.

Then, as now, to be labelled 'romantic' or 'sentimental' was to attract a degree of snobbery from the literary establishment. Needless to say, *Anna Croone* is a hit and Celia finds a 'sudden accession to comparative wealth', something Sophie Cole knew a thing or two about.

Similarly, *Little Brown Girl* by Tempest (1940) told the story of a penniless but handsome novelist, Sebastian Chepney, who is kind to shy Drusilla Fakenham, a plain, brown-haired and dark-skinned heiress who reads romantic fiction. By force of circumstance, they are engaged. Sebastian, it turns out, is really romantic novelist 'Selina Saffron'. Drusilla, raised on romances, is thrilled and promises to keep his secret:

> He smiled, half-amused, half-touched that this queer child should be the
> one person who took his work seriously. The Chepneys refused to
> believe that he ever worked at all. Their attitude stung him, and he
> wouldn't attempt to undeceive them. Actually, he made a useful if mod-
> est income from his novels. He wrote four a year — light, romantic nov-
> els which were published under the pen-name 'Selina Saffron'. He had
> never divulged his pen-name to his friends or relations. He was secretly
> a little ashamed of writing such whole-heartedly romantic stories. He
> felt that writing thrillers would be a more masculine occupation, but he
> loathed thrillers. He never read them and he hadn't the faintest idea how
> to write one. It seemed to him to need a close acquaintance with such
> unpleasant subjects as corpses, courts, coroners, and clues.

One wonders whether Tempest, a notorious recluse, also felt this way about writing—and public sentiment.

Through her characters, Tempest also offered some advice on writing. Sebastian confesses that 'Heroines are more important than heroes. I always use myself for the hero.' A happy ending was essential: 'Selina Saffron's readers expected it.' Drusilla believes that people should write only gay and amusing and light-hearted books. 'She didn't like depressing books. She couldn't understand why people wrote them. After all, you didn't read books to be made miserable. Often, you buried yourself in a book when you were miserable, hoping that it would take your mind off your troubles.' She expressed this to the hero:

> 'I was thinking how lovely it must be to write novels. You can make everything end just as it should.'
>
> 'I only write light stuff,' he said deprecatingly.
>
> 'That's the nicest kind of writing. I love books which make you feel all excited and happy because everything comes right for everyone. Doesn't it make you feel warm inside when you think of the people who get cheered up by your stories and tell themselves that perhaps their love stories will come right, too?'

Drusilla adds, 'You kiss just like heroes do in books.' She loses her fortune but sticks with Sebastian, whose twenty-first novel is an enormous hit, selling 'in the thousands', with the film rights garnering £3,000. The book's title: *Little Brown Girl*.

※

Although the modern Mills & Boon romance, tied to a specific formula, did not yet exist in the 1930s, it is apparent that Charles Boon did set down a few ground rules for his authors. Some have survived, and were passed down through the years in the firm by two names: 'Lubbock's Law' and 'the Alphaman'. Both still have an impact today.

Lubbock's Law was derived from Percy Lubbock, critic and author, who published *The Craft of Fiction* in 1921. Lubbock maintained that the best fiction, such as Gustave Flaubert's *Madame Bovary*, succeeded in part because the author wrote from the heroine's point of view. 'To have lived with their creations is to have lived with them as well,' Lubbock maintained. Fiction, he added, must 'look true'. Flaubert's style was pictorial, which made Emma's existence 'as intelligible and visible as may be':

> We who read the book are to share in her sense of life, till no uncertainty is left in it; we are to see and understand her experience, and to see *her* while she enjoys or endures it; we are to be placed within her world, to get the immediate taste of it, and outside her world as well, to get the full

> effect, more of it than she herself could see. . . . If it is the experience and the actual taste of it that is to be imparted, the story must be viewed as the poor creature saw it.

Telling the story from the heroine's point of view, Lubbock concluded, is 'the readiest means of dramatically heightening a reported impression'.[4] Alan Boon recalled that the first book he recommended for publication as a new employee in the early 1930s was called *Unconditional Surrender* (not, presumably, the Evelyn Waugh title). But it was told from a man's point of view. It did not sell—and Boon learned a lesson he would never forget. Clearly, reader identification with the heroine would become one of the key components of a successful Mills & Boon romance.

The 'Alphaman' was based on what Alan Boon referred to as a 'law of nature': that the female of any species will be most intensely attracted to the strongest male of the species, or the Alpha. Mills & Boon heroes always fit this category. For fictional heroes, of course, this was not a new concept: among the many influences and role models for the dashing, mysterious, slightly dangerous hero were Darcy in *Pride and Prejudice*, Heathcliff in *Wuthering Heights*, Rochester in *Jane Eyre*, Rhett Butler in *Gone with the Wind*, and Maxim de Winter in *Rebecca*.

According to Alan Boon, the special attraction which Mills & Boon novels held for women during this period was their 'wholesomeness', a quality which his father promoted. This is not to imply that the novels never took risks. Rather, they were not explicit, nor what one would class as 'immoral'. They were 'romantic' in the way they dealt with relationships, and they always ended happily. 'Father was very careful about the moral line, about the boundaries you could not cross,' Boon said. 'But he was not very hesitant of sex. In a curious way, the novels were more permissive in a sense than today.' These so-called 'sexy' books were written by Louise Gerard, Denise Robins, and Elizabeth Carfrae, among others. 'Mary Burchell wasn't sexy, but she showed an awareness of it,' Boon explained. 'I always thought that Mary Burchell's books, and Sara Seale's, in the early days had the most sex in their books. But it was a pretended form of sex, not suggestive in any way at all. It was instinct, not participating.' The same could be said for most of the women who wrote for Mills & Boon during the 1930s, and Charles Boon undoubtedly chose them well. 'Jan Tempest was immensely successful for us in the 1930s, but there was no sex in her books at all,' Alan Boon said. 'We never published her in paperback. With titles like, *Take Me! Break Me!* I'm afraid the readers would have been disappointed.'

※

During this decade the characteristics of the archetypal Mills & Boon heroine and hero began to fall into place. The heroine is a virgin, aged 18–20, somewhat clever, and almost always an orphan, which lent sympathy (and freed the woman from family obligations). The hero is significantly older, aged 30–40, enigmatic, and rough-edged. He is often the heroine's employer. The setting could be an English office or factory, or a foreign country. There is always a happy ending. The couple marry or, if already husband and wife, settle their differences and make a better start.

Beauty in the heroine was optional, perhaps to enhance reader identification. She could be plain, or a stunner, and authors were often precise in their descriptions. In Denise Robins's *Sweet Love* (1934), Tanya, an exotic dancer in Cairo, possesses 'a face of maddening beauty, ivory pale with wide-set eyes of velvet brown under curving jet-black lashes. She had a wide scarlet mouth with a short upper lip, exquisite hands and small, arched feet with pink, polished nails.' In *The Greatest of All* by Philippa Preston (1936), Audrey Merivale, 20, a stenographer and fashion model, 'stood out in all the fresh, well-bred youth that was so essentially a part of her fascination'. In *The Girl With the X-Ray Eyes* (1935) by Mairi O'Nair (Constance M. Evans), private eye Joe Ballantyre sized up platinum blonde Pamela Wynne in his own terms: 'The great criteria of womankind—in a man's eyes, at least—her feet and ankles, were slender, too, and perfectly formed.' But in *Little Brown Girl*, Drusilla is clearly ugly, with her crooked mouth, 'slightly aquiline nose', and skin tanned 'almost to a gipsy brown. . . . Her bare arms looked like small brown sticks, and the V of the frock showed her collar-bones.' The dashing hero, Sebastian, who 'never noticed a girl at all unless she was pretty', decides to be chivalrous and 'play the gigolo', since he 'occasionally had generous impulses. He never passed a beggar without parting with a shilling, and he invariably presented stray cats with saucers of milk':

> 'Oh well, if you're not a beauty, I expect you're frightfully nice,' Sebastian said cheerfully. 'It wouldn't do for every girl to be purely ornamental like Cousin Eva. Probably you're the type who can darn socks and sew on buttons and make a decent cup of coffee.'
>
> 'Oh, yes! I can sew and cook.'
>
> 'Well, there you are! That's jolly useful. Every man likes a girl to be able to cook and sew.'

Not only could she cook and sew, but Drusilla is an heiress, so beauty, in this instance, did not really matter.

If handsome (and he usually was), the hero, like the heroine, was exceedingly so, even god-like. There were never any short heroes in Mills & Boon romances. 'What a difference height made in a man!' Claire remarked of Dall in *Life for Two* (1936), Jean MacLeod's debut. In *Little Brown Girl*, Drusilla begins to take more than a passing notice of Sebastian, as he repairs his broken-down car. Sebastian has a playboy reputation:

Every now and then, her glance strayed to Sebastian. She admired the lean, graceful lines of his figure. He had god shoulders, nearly as broad but not as heavy as David's, a pronounced waist and slim hips. There was a pleasing air of vitality about him. His every movement was quick and sure. He'd rolled the sleeves of his jacket up and she could see his lean, muscular-looking arms.

She said suddenly: 'I don't think you look in the least like a gigolo. You're much too strong.'

'Thanks, baby!'

More often than not, the heroine was ostensibly middle or lower-middle class, and working for a living—situations that readers would have found familiar. Nicola Beauman has observed how, from the 1920s, it became 'less and less remarkable' for a middle-class woman, married or not, to work outside the home, which offered a degree of independence. Readers could therefore identify with a heroine who worked for a living. An escapist storyline, moreover, which promised marriage and (presumably) an end to work would have been very appealing indeed.[5] Mary Burchell admitted that she took her characters and situations from life:

> I always take a nice, ordinary girl and put her into a smarter world. But I let her retain her former simplicity. I don't think the Cinderella idea ever goes out of date. My heroine always belongs to a profession I feel I really know myself. She may be a home girl, sometimes a shorthand-typist, which I have been, or someone on the fringe of the operatic or stage world—which again applies to me—so that I know her reactions exactly.[6]

The most common occupation was secretary to the boss. Elsa Feldick in *Single Ticket*, Juliet Armstrong's debut (1938), is secretary to Madame Loubonova of Loubonova et Cie, society dressmakers. When jilted by her fiancé, Elsa, no shrinking violet, decides to defy convention and flee to India, alone, on a single ticket, to live with her Uncle Tom. In *The Greatest of All*, Philippa Preston's first novel (1936), Audrey Merivale, 20, is head stenographer 'in an agency that supplied secretaries at a minute's notice' in Manhattan. Audrey, who successfully earns her own living after both parents were drowned, finds work as a manikin with Madame Jane's Gown Shop, a chic Fifth Avenue salon catering to wealthy women.

But heroines also held more important, even unusual occupations. In Joan Blair's *Sister of Nelson Ward* (1937), one of the first 'Doctor-Nurse' novels, Nurse Carol Ross is in charge of the children's ward of Gray's Hospital in Edinburgh, 'the youngest Sister the hospital had ever known. . . . Her voice, when she spoke, was low and quiet, with just a hint that it could, if need be, give commands which were unlikely to be disobeyed.' In *The Strange Young*

Man (1931) by Louise Gerard, Ann Carmichael, 'the only child of a distinguished savant and explorer', saves the life of the hero, Roy, and is enlisted as his personal bodyguard, at a salary of $5,000 a year. In this fantastic novel, Roy and Ann are chased by a gang of killers through Siam, China, and Hawaii. Ann rescues Roy when a cobra, planted in his bed, bites him. She injects the antidote in a moment of great passion ('"My goodness, Ann," he cried, his racked face illuminated. "I'd have cobras bite me every day if I can be your 'darling'"').

Older and married heroines were commonplace at this time, although they would increasingly fall out of fashion. In *Secret Joy*, Celia Halstead is married with three children. She falls for her artist mentor, while her husband, George, lies dying from infantile paralysis. In *Painted Lady* by Helena Grose (1933), Kit is a wife and mother, who rebuilds her marriage to Jock, despite temptation. One of her suitors, Ques, expresses the charms of an older woman:

> It was not merely Kit's looks that attracted him. She had her share of them, and knew to a nicety the styles and colouring that best enhanced them. But she did not forget that she was forty-two, and never made the mistake of dressing to look younger, or following pastimes too strenuous for her years. She was proud of her age—maturity, she called it— because in her case it was proving the happiest period of her life. Two brilliant men were seeking her in marriage, an achievement she had never won in her youth. She wisely concentrated on charm rather than looks, put dignity before athleticism, and found it easier and more diplomatic to be a listener than a chatterer.

Clearly, in her description Helena Grose was reaching out to a particular segment of the Mills & Boon readership.

Without exception, heroes were, indeed, 'Alphamen', usually in an important profession, and sometimes with a mysterious or suspicious past. The hero did not have to be rich or famous. In all cases, however, the hero was recognized for his strength, integrity, and potential for providing a secure future, with security defined in financial terms (important for Depression-era readers). In *The Strange Young Man*, Roy T. Burney, 'one of the richest young men in the world', is a self-made success after a childhood in an orphanage in New York. 'Don't get the notion that I'm only a paper millionaire,' he tells heroine Ann. 'I've got five million dollars in gilt-edged securities. A nest egg for the wife and family.' In *Sister of Nelson Ward*, Dr Gregor Lothian is a 'brilliant' resident children's surgeon, the model of respectability. In *Life for Two*, Randall 'Dall' Barclay is a passionate sculptor, who marries Claire, moves to Naples, and sets up his own studio.

Power and brute force in a hero endured, a legacy of the dashing sheiks and explorers of Gerard, Sutherland, and Hull. In *Be Patient With Love* by

Guy Trent (1937), Joan encounters her brother-in-law Tom Shawn (and her future husband) whipping an errant farm boy. Joan calls Tom 'an enigma of a man' and could see why he was feared as well as loved by employees:

> 'What had the boy done to make you so mad with him, Tom?'
>
> Tom's blue eyes were like blue fire.
>
> 'He's been drinking again. His father had to complain to me about it before. Still, I think we have him in hand now; they don't like the whip—'
>
> Joan was dumbfounded. Was it possible that in the twentieth century men still brought their erring children to the lord of the manor to be beaten if they misbehaved?
>
> She questioned Tom, pointing to the whip he was still carrying:
>
> 'Do you often have to use—<u>that</u>?'
>
> His firm mouth was grim.
>
> 'Only once—thank God—'
>
> 'Was the boy drunk?'
>
> He shook his head.
>
> 'No. He was making himself unpleasant to a young girl.'

The hero had integrity, although sometimes it was deeply concealed, requiring the heroine's love to bring it to the surface. In *The Greatest of All*, Shane Carter is an artist, fashion designer, and a boxer. He also knows how to commit burglary and evade the police, and has a chequered past with a number of women. Ace stenographer Audrey is his path to reform.

Romance in the Mills & Boon novels in the 1930s took many forms. While the overall intention was, as Alan Boon has noted, 'wholesomeness', authors tried, within the limits implied by 'wholesomeness', to make their storylines as erotic as possible. A common scene, usually at the beginning of the novel, was the moment when the heroine senses an unmistakable attraction to the hero. 'Electricity' was often in the air. For example, in Mary Burchell's debut, *Wife to Christopher* (1936), Vicky senses that 'spark' on seeing Christopher for the first time:

> It is the simplest and most primitive way to the meeting of two spirits. Independent of sight, it is a spark that even a blind person can strike. Wordless, it can spring to life between people who know no word of each other's language. And, like all things primitive, it is inexplicable, instinctive—and passionately exciting.

In Gerard's *Jungle Love* (1924), one of her most popular novels, the description is even more explicit, when dashing Australian gold miner Mark sweeps jungle nurse Dorothy off her feet:

> All the passion and the power of the man vibrated through her. His quick breath fanned her cheek. The heat and tremor of the hand holding her struck through the thin silk of her gown. Every particle of pride rose up at his embrace. Everything was forgotten but his audacity.

From the first spark came the so-called 'punishing kiss', the first passionate kiss between hero and heroine that readers anxiously awaited. When Sebastian kisses innocent Drusilla for the first time in *Little Brown Girl*, she remembers her favourite romantic novels: 'He'd kissed her firmly and without hesitation. A phrase she'd read in some novel flashed into her mind: "It was a real lover's kiss, hard, passionate, and possessive." A faint tremor ran through her. She didn't feel like crying any more. She felt curiously excited.' Denise Robins was the recognized mistress of the punishing kiss device. In *The Boundary Line* (1932), for example, Dr Blaise Farlong kisses his 21-year-old bride-to-be, Terry:

> He lost his head for an instant, and bent to the generous red mouth she lifted to his, and kissed her. It was not the light caress he had intended. Her young, slender arms curved about his neck, and her eyelids closed in rapt surrender. The kiss was long and deep and infinitely satisfying to them both. It seemed to Blaise Farlong that there must, after all, be such a thing in life as recompense. He had tasted the dregs of bitterness, of suffering, and now this amazing and unexpected cup of rapture was lifted to his lips by this girl. . . . She, body, soul, and brain on fire for him, thought: 'Now I know that I love him — terribly. Now I know what it is to be in love.'

This description clearly has cinematic qualities. Kissing between married hero and heroine could be more dramatic, even more passionate. In *Life for Two*, Dall literally sweeps Claire off her feet in a fit of passion:

> She made a little involuntary movement towards him, and then, without word or sign of any kind, he had stepped forward and taken her into his arms, covering her hair and her eyes with eager, passionate kisses, bending her head back until his lips reached her mouth and clung there in one long, time-effacing kiss—
>
> She lay back in the circle of his arms, letting the sweetness of his caresses sink down into her heart, heedless of time or place, knowing only that she was here in the arms of the one man who would ever matter to her out of all the world. She gave him back kiss for kiss, infusing into her own all the pent-up love and longing of her young life.

In novels at this time 'lovemaking' referred almost exclusively to kissing of this nature. Pre- and extra-marital affairs were naturally discouraged and, if attempted, brought wicked consequences to the hero and heroine. Mills & Boon authors (and, indirectly, Charles Boon) appear to have been issuing life lessons all the time to potential readers. 'I truly don't think I have ever let a girl of mine do anything that I wouldn't like to see a girl of that age do, or if she does, she's punished,' Mary Burchell said. Jean MacLeod agreed:

> You know perfectly well that a lot of girls think that it's very clever and it's the done thing—as soon as they meet somebody they go and live with them. Well, in our day it wasn't. I mean, if you did, then you were absolutely beyond the pale. The only decent boy and girl wouldn't want anything to do with it.

Neither would Mills & Boon heroines, who defended their honour. Ann, Roy's personal bodyguard in *The Strange Young Man*, laid down the law as they travelled together through the Far East: 'If we are to stay together, you must behave in a sensible manner. I'm doing a man's work and you must treat me as if I were a man. And not try and make love to me at every turn.' In *The Greatest of All*, when the hero, Shane Carter, is blackmailed into marrying evil murderess Elma Beverley, he pledges to the heroine, Audrey, that his old apartment would be retained as a love nest for them. Significantly, Audrey rebuffs Shane, as such behaviour would be immoral. Shane admits his weakness:

> 'Yes, I suppose you are right, and I suppose with masculine stupidity I have refused to see where I was going and trying to take you with me. It was selfish, too—my coming back to seek you out, but you must forgive me. Men are not quite so strong as women when it comes to fighting for what they desire, or holding back from it because it is the better thing to do.'

Audrey's sister, Sonia, has no such morals. For years she has conducted a secret liaison with Leonard Peters. They meet at a midtown Manhattan hotel in rooms 'taken just so that we could be happy together—deliriously happy—without busy-bodies knowing anything about us'. Leonard blackmails Sonia into marrying him and they flee—but a car crash leaves him a cripple, his come-uppance.

Intimacy could be titillating, even if nothing happened. Here the famous bedroom scene in *It Happened One Night* was often repeated to dramatic effect. In *Little Brown Girl*, Drusilla and Sebastian spend a day in the New Forest, but on the way home, his car runs out of petrol. They stay the night together, in the car, huddled close under blankets. The result was quite innocent, but none the less thrilling to readers:

It was the strangest night Drusilla had ever spent. She dozed fitfully. So did Sebastian. Once she woke up to find him asleep with his head on her shoulder. It gave her a curious thrill to feel his dark hair brushing her cheek, and to listen to his quiet, regular breathing. Very gently, so as not to disturb him, she kissed his squarish chin.

What a strange thing love was! she reflected. She was cold and stiff, cramped and aching, yet she was happier than she'd ever been in her life before. Why? Because for this hour, while Sebastian was asleep with his head on her shoulder, he was hers. They were together, and it was easy to pretend that they belonged together. This night had given her something which couldn't be taken away from her. Sebastian didn't love her—he would never love her—but no other girl except the girl he married would ever see him asleep like this, or herself fall asleep in his arms.

Naturally, Drusilla's relations call Sebastian 'an unmitigated cad', and feel Drusilla has been hopelessly compromised by a man who wants her money. They insist she marry Sebastian—and Drusilla proposes to him.

What we would call today 'marital rape' was quite common in Mills & Boon novels at this time. So long as the hero and heroine were married—even if in name only—strong, violent bedroom scenes were allowed to enhance the passion. Denise Robins often used this tactic in her enormously popular romances. In *Sweet Love*, for example, Tanya, the exotic dancer in Cairo, marries upright engineer Gordon. But they separate, and Tanya is tricked into a bogus marriage with the rogue Victor. Gordon is furious, abducts his wife, and repeatedly rapes her:

'You're worse than any Eastern slave-driver!' she flung at him fiercely. 'You forget you're living in the year 1933 and that I'm English, and so are you. You can't go on forcing me to live with you—lock me up—I—'

'You shall stay with me—for just as long as I want you, Tanya,' he repeated against her ear. 'You call me a slave-driver. Ah, well, my Tanya, out here, do you know what the Arabs do with a faithless wife? They strangle her—so—'

His brown, supple fingers closed over her throat. Tanya gave a choked cry:

'Gordon—Gordon—for God's sake—'

'I'm not going to strangle you, my dear,' he laughed. 'But I am going to show my little 'slave' that she is mine—and that ten thousand dagos can't take her from me.'

'Gordon—' She was crying bitterly now. 'Please—' ...

He bent his splendid head and kissed her shoulders, slipping the narrow silk strap down her arm. Picking up an Eastern shawl of fine, thin texture, he wrapped her in it, then laid her against the pillows, pinioned her with one strong arm, and laughed down at her.

After running away, Tanya finds herself (rather like Scarlett in Gone with the Wind) pregnant with Gordon's child. Before the novel ends, a baby girl, Mary Tanya, is born, and Tanya and Gordon are reunited, with Gordon noting, 'Mary Tanya was, thank God, born in wedlock.' Similarly, in Mary Burchell's Wife to Christopher, Christopher, compromised into marriage by Vicki, rapes her, 'collecting' her beauty which she sold him, like 'any street girl':

> He bent his head and kissed her deliberately and insultingly.
>
> 'I'm going to collect what you sold, Vicki. And I'm not at all sure that it won't be rather sweet doing it.'
>
> 'No!' She made another quick movement, but he put both his arms round her and held her still. And as she lay there in his arms, staring fascinatedly up at him, he suddenly showered kisses on her: on her angry, bruised mouth, on the little hollow at the base of her throat, and lower, where the warm whiteness of her skin showed through the lace of her nightdress.
>
> Then he swung her clear off her feet. With an abrupt movement of his shoulder he knocked out the electric light, and as he did so, darkness seemed to swing down on her like a stifling curtain.

Once again, like Scarlett O'Hara, Vicki awakens the next morning in 'sweet ecstasy', noting, 'if he came with something of the terror of an avenger, he came with the glory of a lover, too'. Vicki learns she is pregnant, but the child is stillborn—perhaps a condemnation of the violence, and of her duplicity. Burchell's novel, her debut, was hardly the typical boy-meets-girl romance, but Burchell got away with it, as it was a best-seller. 'Charles Boon, certainly, and Alan, were prepared to publish whatever I wrote. And so they must have believed in me,' Burchell said. 'I think Alan probably knew, as did his father, that a little early on I was already, without knowing it, exploiting a rather bolder form of romantic novel.' Certainly Charles Boon felt the same way about his other best-selling authors.

The goal of all heroines in Mills & Boon romances is a happy ending, which means companionate marriage, motherhood, and financial security. This, no doubt, was the dream of most of the women who read the novels in the 1930s. In *The Greatest of All*, Audrey proposes to Shane, who pledges his commitment: 'He loved her. It was not merely a physical attraction; she had everything that was needed for companionship as a friend, as well as the affection that made a wife and mate.'

Helena Grose's best-seller *They Meant to Marry* (1934) is a study in marriage, motherhood, and divorce. Alannah Wingram, 20, is romanced by four men. She spurns a proposal from the noble but penniless hero, John Delwood, a struggling artist, on the advice of her mother and stepfather, and in spite of the palpable attraction between them:

> She broke off, startled by a sudden vision of John's arms round her at night, John's brown head beside her in the morning on the divan bed, John painting happily while she cooked his food, and the sun poured through the window panes—Across her breast crept a strange, sweet thrill. She swayed nearer to him.

This was the marriage dream. But the £5 a week existence promised by John was, to her, untenable. On a holiday cruise to Norway, Alannah is seduced by a mysterious Austrian, Max Langen. Max's sallow complexion and red hair are not attractive, but he is a charmer, and after her £4,000 inheritance. To escape from her stepfather and from the hero, Alannah elopes with Max to Austria ('Oh, Max, be good to me!' Alannah pleads). But Max is far from good, keeping Alannah in poverty, and forcing her to re-evaluate her feelings: 'Was this romance? Love? Adventure? This dreariness? This indefinite loneliness in an alien country?'

Alannah's tryst with this mad 'Prussian' provided Grose with fodder for strong opinions on marriage and motherhood. When Alannah suggests they start a family, Max is firmly opposed:

> 'No babies, Alannah. Not until the world depression lifts. Only selfish people would dare to bring fresh lives into this overcrowded world.'
>
> 'I see,' she said, but she felt cheated and disappointed.
>
> 'No babies!' Max had said, and from that moment their marriage had collapsed.

Significantly, the hero, John, loves children and would like to have a large family, despite his meagre earnings. Although Alannah is unhappy in marriage, she never considers divorce. Her mother stayed married with her wicked stepfather out of respect for marriage, and Alannah intends to do the same:

> At times he seemed a monster. Yet in the very moment of stealing away from him, she would be cloaked by her own ideals. Good wives did not quit. Pauline had never left Clifford, though to live with him must have been far worse than Max. And there were things of his to remind her of her wifehood; a pair of socks needing to be darned, or a shirt minus a button or two. So she stayed on, living one day at a time, and never daring to look ahead.

At the time this novel was written, women could obtain a legal divorce only on grounds of adultery; in 1937 the new Divorce Act would add insanity and desertion. No wonder Alannah ponders how women could rush into marriage lightly: 'Even when they knew of drunkenness, immorality, even dishonesty, they still went through with the wedding, preferring matrimony to lonely spinsterhood.'

Eventually Max deserts Alannah, and he is exposed as 'a professional bigamist', with wives in New York and Australia. Alannah wonders if men will now find her 'second hand'. She is reconciled to her stepfather, and receives a proposal from the wealthy Hugh Malvern. Hugh, however, is murdered. He leaves his £30,000 fortune to Alannah, who embarks on a wild spending spree with a carefree dandy, Sir Kimpton Brierlow. 'Kim' exposes her to a fast life, gets her drunk, and spends her money. All this flirting disgusts John, who calls Alannah 'Any man's girl'. In the end, virtually penniless, Alannah rekindles her love for John, who says, 'What's poverty against happiness? I'll always be able to give her enough to eat.' Naturally, since this is an escapist romance, John and Alannah are not penniless for long, as John becomes an overnight success as creator of a new comic strip.

In *The Boundary Line*, Denise Robins also tackled the horror and shame of divorce in a fantastic story of seduction and betrayal. Terry Manstone, 21, longs for the simple life, away from her society mother and fancy home in Wimbledon. Addicted to the new 'hiking' fad, she sets off alone on a trek across the Sussex downs. In a violent storm, Terry twists her ankle, and seeks shelter in a country cottage, where the housekeeper reluctantly lets her spend the night. Asleep in the hero's bed, she is awakened by him, Dr Blaise Farlong. Blaise is unhappily married, and his wicked wife, Ruth, wants a divorce. Ruth concocts a story that Blaise and Terry have spent the night together (thereby charging adultery). Terry is named as co-respondent in the divorce case, which brands her a 'bad woman', while destroying Blaise's practice. Though the accusation is false, Terry's mother throws her out, and Terry moves in with Blaise. Blaise contemplates suicide; he's about to inject morphine when Terry saves him. Blaise's lawyer suggests Terry see several doctors to prove she did not sleep with Blaise and is still a virgin; Terry responds, 'It makes me feel absolutely beastly and cheap.' But love blossoms, and they admittedly 'live in sin' until the divorce is granted. The day after the divorce, Blaise and Terry marry, and spend a busy wedding night: 'The passionate fulfillment, the beauty of those hours, had given Terry a fuller and sweeter understanding of life. The laughing child had become a woman who laughed for love in the arms of her lover.'

Pointedly, the couple does not live happily ever after. They lead a nomadic existence, settling in a town until rumours force them to move on. Blaise's divorce and Terry's involvement cripple his practice; they are broke. 'It doesn't matter how decent we are—or how much we love each other—or how far circumstances are against us,' Blaise laments. 'Nothing will be taken into consideration. We shall be boycotted.' But, as this is a romantic novel, the truth of Terry's innocence is published; she is reconciled to her mother; and one of Blaise's patients dies, leaving him a legacy of £20,000, which arrives in time for the birth of a son. Seemingly all of the suffering and hardship paid off in the end.

Marriage was twisted and tested in other ways. Sophie Cole's *Secret Joy*, for example, is a shocking novel. Celia Halstead, the heroine, is married with three children. But Celia falls for her artist mentor, Marcus Searle, at the same time her husband, George, is diagnosed as having infantile paralysis. George knows how Celia feels, and wants to depart:

> There was, he told himself, no sense in keeping alive to be a burden on his family. If he were dead Celia could marry the man who addressed her as 'beloved'. She had always been addicted to sentiment and the reading of silly novels, and <u>this</u> was the result!

George decides to kill himself, in an act couched in heroic terms by Cole: 'In this moment George Halstead, a commonplace, unimaginative man, rose, all unconsciously, to heights of heroism. It was not a coward's part he was going to play, but, according to his lights, a well-reasoned act of humanity.' Marcus knows of the suicide plan, but conceals it from Celia:

> George had died that they two might live. 'Greater love hath no man than this—that he lay down his life for his friends.' Strange to think of George in that light! The sick man was not influenced entirely by the desire to escape suffering. He had done the deed to save his family the torture of witnessing his long-drawn-out agony. His craft in hiding the fact proved this. So thought Searle with conviction . . . In death George had attained a dignity he had never possessed in life—perhaps in that last tragic act he had escaped from the trammels of mediocrity.

Love conquered all, even the suicide of the husband, in this novel. The agreement of all parties, however, seemed to legitimize the action.

Finally, Elizabeth Carfrae's 1929 novel *Payment in Full* is a fantastic multi-generation saga that seemingly pushed Mills & Boon to the moral limits—and certainly helps to explain Carfrae's immense popularity. John Alloway, kindly rector of St Augustine's, is abandoned by his promiscuous wife, and heads to America for a new life with his baby daughter, Elizabeth. On her eighteenth birthday, Elizabeth, now a great beauty, is orphaned and left penniless. She loves Christopher 'Kit' Mallory, son of the wealthiest man in town, but his father forbids a liaison, given the scandal concerning her mother. In her grief, Elizabeth accepts a proposal from George Hutton, a Jamaican sugar plantation owner twenty-five years her senior. She does not love him, but he stood 'between her and starvation'. They live in Jamaica, where Elizabeth is shy and withdrawn. After three pregnancies and three still-births ('If I had loved him, his children wouldn't have died. . . . I didn't care enough to keep them alive.'), George takes the doctor's advice and sends Elizabeth away, alone, for a restorative cruise to Havana. There she meets Kit again, now a dashing US naval officer, and they rekindle their romance. Despite her married state, Elizabeth convinces Kit to spend two weeks together, largely in bed. Her ulterior motive: to bear Kit's child, which would make her miserable life in Jamaica more bearable. Their lovemaking is endless:

> 'I'm a rotter and a cad, and I ought to be shot, but—oh, gosh, Elizabeth, I'm so happy I could stand on my head. Here and now. We'll play "let's pretend" to the last second and the final curtain. . . .'
>
> He knew nothing the world could ever give him could, for one moment, equal the marvel of Elizabeth's selfless, glad surrender or touch of mystery of the love they found together in these miracle-laden 14 days.

On her return to Jamaica, George finds his wife a changed woman, informing the doctor she's even happy to make love: 'She's extraordinarily pleased about it herself . . . It's the first time she's appeared even interested.' No wonder: Elizabeth is pregnant, and has an 'unusual' eight-month baby girl, Elinor, nicknamed Nona. Because George is overjoyed by Nona, and their plantation home, 'Content', is truly a happy one, Elizabeth justifies her actions and her adultery:

> She'd perpetuated what every one would consider a perfectly scandalous and hideous sin, and, by doing so, had supplied Content with the one thing it needed to reach perfection in George's eyes, and George himself with the greatest joy he'd ever had in his life.

This being escapist romance, Carfrae tied up all the loose ends. George is thrown from a horse and paralysed. Elizabeth prays for his recovery (although she admits, 'Don't—please, dear God—let me want George to die'). But he does, and in the final scene, Kit and Elizabeth, both now in their mid-forties, are enjoying their honeymoon. Amazingly, pangs of conscience are dismissed by both:

> 'If we did something that the world would call a sin, we've had to pay for it. In all these years of loneliness. In the fact that I can never claim my own daughter. That I had to give her to another man. But poor Hutton worshipped the ground she walked over, Elizabeth . . . Ethically it was all wrong, of course. We knew that at the time, but we <u>did</u> make Hutton happy, Elizabeth. If you ever look back now, you can always remember that.'
>
> 'Yes,' she said, 'it's just that, Christopher, that has made the looking back even possible. Even bearable. Only—need we <u>look</u> back any more,

Kit? . . . I'd so much rather remember what George said to me once about being happy after he died and look forward, Kit.'

Carfrae's novel, a best-seller, was an unusual, even heterodox novel for Mills & Boon to publish in 1929. The rigid 'formula' that governed the future Mills & Boon romance was still quite loose.

❧

Since most of the women who wrote for Mills & Boon during the 1930s were young, they were likely to be fairly closely in touch with their potential readers and in tune with changes in style. They were certainly sympathetic, for instance, to the single working life and the concerns about money, finding a husband, and starting a family. Especially the first. 'You will notice in all the books in those early days the troubles which the girls have almost always stem from little money around,' Mary Burchell recalled. 'These girls have immense temptation to fritter; it's an age of frittering of course. The fear of not being able to make your own way was a very, very strong one indeed.'

This fear explains the concern Mills & Boon heroines place on marrying 'well'. The heroine in Barbara Hedworth's *How Strong Is Your Love?* (1938), Claire Vickers, 19, says her ambition is, 'Any woman's . . . I'm not a bit original. I honestly believe I have the makings of a good wife and mother.' But she adds, she's not 'all pious and good works; I like comfort and luxury and having money as much as most people.' In *They Meant to Marry*, Alannah inherits a £30,000 legacy when her boyfriend Hugh is murdered. She's delighted with the cash and has no reason not to accept it, despite John's misgivings:

> She quickly discovered that wealth brought great responsibility, and certain status. She was as yet too stunned to derive any pleasure from it. She still could not realise she need never again fear poverty. Independence was hers; freedom and wealth . . . She was free to travel, buy all the things she had always longed for, marry whom she wished.

In *The Strange Young Man*, Ann finds Roy physically unattractive, but his self-made wealth is rather seductive:

> If she married him, she would do her duty by him. Make his home happy and comfortable, look after his health, give him those children he had made such careful provision for. Ann's future, a day or two ago so meagre, suddenly grew full and rosy. A soft light invaded her eyes as she sat meditating in the prospect of being Mrs. Roy Burney.

Interestingly, Ann accepts the engagement even though she knows little about this strange young man: 'For all she knew Roy Burney might be America's prize criminal. Already he might have been married and divorced half-a-dozen times. He might be a bootlegger. The head of a White Slave Syndicate.' Upon their engagement, Ann tastes 'the sweets of unlimited money. Whatever she expressed the least fancy for, whether it was a $20,000 pearl necklace or a bunch of flowers that cost a few cents, the boy bought for her.' Naturally, all of these novels end happily. In *The Strange Young Man*, for example, tough guy Roy is revealed to be the son of the Countess of Mooring and heir to a vast (and thereby legitimate) fortune.

Apart from an obsession with money, Mills & Boon authors also cast a critical eye on the young generation of the 1930s, sometimes sympathetically, though usually not. Heroines are mostly defensive when it comes to their class and station, and the value system normally associated with the middle classes was championed. There was no substitute for good, hard, honest work and an independent life before marriage. Shop-girl Kitty, for example, in *Anchor at Hazard* by Ray Dorien (1935) is repelled by her greedy upper-class mother-in-law, who is shocked that she worked for a living:

> 'You were in a shop?' gasped Mrs. Lewis.
>
> 'I was in the office. I didn't stand behind the counter, not that it makes any difference,' said Kitty, amused at the other woman's prejudice.
>
> She did not think it necessary to explain that the girls had to present a high standard of education and appearance to be considered at all by the firm . . . Although she had always earned her own living, she had discovered that her attitude to it was very different from that of people who in her opinion had not worked for money, and yet seemed to expect it as a matter of course. She felt the chill of this self-absorbed nature.

Other characters in this novel agree. Rose is amazed that Kitty's marriage is viewed as a come-down by her husband's family: 'Nonsense! Hasn't the world moved since then?' Similarly, in *Be Patient with Love* by Guy Trent (1937), Joan resents her husband Phil's contentment over his unemployed status, and their subsequent dependence upon his family. When accused of indolence, she reacts: '"I don't ask anyone to keep me," she flared. "I've earned my own living before, and I can do so again". . . . She was Joan Thomas who had earned her own living since her seventeenth birthday. She wasn't used to being dependent, and she resented owing her bread and butter to comparative strangers.'

So-called 'modern girls' were put under a microscope by Mills & Boon authors. Heavy make-up and poor manners were usually bad signs. Claire, 19, in *How Strong Is Your Love?* is a 'modern' with modern habits, vices, and a rebellious nature for a young lady, as she displays to her mother:

> 'I suppose you have to spoil your pretty mouth with that sticky rubbish. When I was young, if a girl had gone to an engagement party made up like that . . .'

Claire laughed:

'In your young days, it would have been a crime to do this.' She took a cigarette from the case lying on the dressing-table and lit it. 'But Time marches on, you know.'

Similarly, in *The Boundary Line*, Blaise Farlong considers Terry, who rebels from her society life and good home, a refreshing change: 'He did like simple and natural people. No permanent waves and lip-stick or any kind of artificiality here. Just a sun-browned, human young woman, with brown hair, straight as God intended it to be, except for that one delightful wave tumbling across her flushed cheek.' Terry's innocence about sex and relationships, unlike her sister Barbara, are also regarded favourably by the author, Denise Robins:

> Barbara—so prim, so proper, so conventional on the surface—had at times shown an overwhelming curiosity about sex matters—read forbidden books in secret, lain awake at nights probing into matters best left alone—which Terry had thought rather nasty. Essentially a natural, healthy-minded person herself, she had learned the facts of life in rather academic fashion, just as she learned anything else, and thought no more about it.

In *Little Brown Girl*, Sebastian, the reformed gigolo, decides Drusilla is quite 'kissable', despite her lowly status:

> Drusilla was eminently satisfactory to kiss. Perhaps it was because she was so young and unspoilt. She had none of the pretty tricks, the deliberate provocativeness of girls like Daphne and Linda. Perhaps one grew tired of treating love as a game. There was a refreshing novelty in knowing that the girl you were kissing had never been kissed before and took you deadly seriously.

Together, Drusilla decides, they are Beauty and the Beast. 'You know, handsome men often do choose plain wives,' she says, presumably offering hope to some readers.

In *Payment in Full*, Elizabeth Carfrae devotes long passages to condemning 'modern' girls and their predatory instincts, even though her heroine, Elizabeth, is less than pure, having cheated on her husband and borne another man's child. That child, Nona, grows to be a beautiful but wild teenager, who unknowingly tries to seduce her real father, Captain Kit Mallory. Elizabeth ponders her wayward daughter and her wild circle:

> They were, she thought, watching Nona, like hunters tracking an unwary animal. Padding behind it. Waiting to pounce. Revolting almost in the dogged persistence of their trail.
>
> It didn't help matters either that Nona wasn't the only one. They all

did it, these modern girls, in one way or another. Either in their clothes or their manners or the shameless invitation of their eyes. It wasn't, Elizabeth told herself bitterly, to be wondered at if trouble followed so swiftly on the heels of these hunts.

When Kit's ship docks in Jamaica, Nona meets and falls hard for him, but not before Elizabeth tells Kit that Nona is his daughter. Nona smuggles herself aboard the ship and into Kit's bed; he finds her and erupts, calling her friends 'a selfish, soulless, heartless, brainless set of little idiots who ought to be whipped and sent to bed'. In a long soliloquy, Kit ponders the immorality, pitying men who are trapped by such 'minxes':

> The way she looked at him. Didn't she realize, the utter little fool, that she couldn't play that game with men and get away with it? Without leaving a stain in her freshness somewhere? . . .
>
> The little minx. So wrapped up in her own egoism and supreme self-assurance and impudence that she could dare play any sort of damfool game. And if things went wrong, it'd be the man who'd be blamed. Who'd be a blackguard and a swine and an unmitigated scoundrel to take advantage of a girl's innocence and trust in him. When, after all, he'd only done what every bit of her, except perhaps her voice, had asked him to try to do, and then let Nature get the upper hand and drown her cries of protest.

Clearly, the romantic novels which Charles Boon published in the 1930s were free from the editorial restrictions which would dominate the decades after the Second World War. At this time, Boon's experimentation with styles gave authors a certain autonomy. If Joan Sutherland and Louise Gerard were masters of romance and passion in the 1910s and 1920s, it was Denise Robins who took it to the next level, combining high romance with an intricate, fast-moving plot that inspired other Mills & Boon authors. One of her most popular novels, *Sweet Love*, covered all of the vices—rape, bigamy, suicide, illegitimacy, divorce, stabbings, poisoning, and more violence—in setting up the premise that mother love is the fiercest and greatest of all. Tanya and her husband Gordon endure endless hardships but are reunited, with child, in the end, cleansing all evil.

But there were still taboos. We have seen how authors scorned the behaviour of 'modern' girls. Drinking was also frowned upon, or seen as an indicator of bad tidings. Dr Gregor Lothian, the hero in *Sister of Nelson Ward*, initially dates wealthy but unsuitable Pearl Carluke, who enjoys a tipple:

> Gregor poured out a weak whisky and soda for Pearl and another for himself. He did not approve of women drinking whisky, but Pearl was

accustomed to be a law unto herself, and he knew that if he did not mix her a drink she would mix one for herself, so he took the opportunity of making it a weak one and offering it under protest.

They did not keep company for long. Both Mary Burchell and Jean MacLeod also shied away from spirits. Burchell blamed her demanding, staunchly Presbyterian editors at D. C. Thomson, which serialized her novels in *My Weekly*: 'In those days a Scottish publisher wouldn't have had anything at all. I mean, if at the end of Chapter Three (the heroine) had had a second sherry, I would get a telegram saying, "Cut out the sherry."' MacLeod said that explicit drinking was not allowed: 'It's not essential to the story; you just say, well, a second round of drinks or something like that. You needn't say they had six sherries or two.'

One change from the style popularized by Gerard and Sutherland was the greater tolerance for foreigners, the significant toning down of prejudice and jingoism. Foreigners might be criticized but earn respect, often at the expense of British pride. In *The Fortunes of Felicity Anne*, Felicity, a dancer, performs a professional tango, watched closely by the hero, Dick Norton, a Rhodesian farmer:

> A tall, dark, rather swarthy individual, a 'dago' as Dick summed him up, contemptuously, with the Britisher's usual cheery intolerance of foreigners.
>
> However, this foreigner showed himself no mean exponent of his art, and their dance evoked considerable applause.
>
> Dick was impressed in spite of himself. *He* could not have done it in a hundred years.

In *The Strange Young Man*, Ann Carmichael will not tolerate rudeness or foul language, when Roy criticizes her old Peking friend, Dr Cho Bem Ling:

> 'Say, who's this Chink?' he asked quickly.
>
> There was a suppressed note of jealousy in his voice which Ann was too tired to notice.
>
> 'Don't call him a Chink,' she said in weary protest. 'He's an Oxford M.A. as well as M.D. A most highly cultured man ... Oh, dear, why will you use that objectionable word?'

However, when a foreigner is evil, an author did not mince her words. In *They Meant to Marry*, Alannah supports her Austrian husband Max, in spite of the objections of her family:

> 'I am a foreigner, and you English distrust foreigners. You think we are all terribly immoral.'
>
> 'Oh, not since the war,' she said, laughing merrily, for she knew there was a germ of truth in his joke. 'You people will think _me_ a foreigner.'

But Alannah's trust is misplaced, as Max mistreats her, threatens her with violence, then deserts her when he is exposed as a bigamist: 'Her whole world was tumbling about her ears. Things she had believed in all her life—chivalry, sympathy, and love—were all proving so much mist.'

The attention to taboos is important when one considers that some titles were banned, a fate which was to haunt the firm in later years. In November 1939 a Mills & Boon novel, *How Strong Is Your Love?* by Barbara Hedworth, made the Irish Government's list of prohibited books, on the grounds that it 'advocate[d] the unnatural prevention of conception', a provision of the 1929 Censorship of Publications Act. Other titles on the list that month were of a non-fiction nature: *Morals, Manners and Men* by Havelock Ellis (Watts); *Sex and the Love-Life* by William J. Fielding (Blue Ribbon Books, New York); and *Every Woman's Book of Love and Marriage and Family Life* (Amalgamated Press).[7] The very fact Mills & Boon attracted the attention of the Irish censors is a tribute to the firm's popularity, but it would also learn a lesson here, as in later years the fear of offending the Irish—and jeopardizing sales in the lucrative Irish market—would become a cornerstone of editorial policy.

Mills & Boon published this novel, the 'first' by Barbara Hedworth (another pen-name of Mollie Seymour Pearson, who had also written as 'Guy Trent' since 1934), over a year earlier, in August 1938. Splashy advertising for this title billed it as 'an absorbing romance' and 'a love story that will delight everybody'. Apparently not: it is not surprising that this title was banned, since the heroine's father, a village doctor, is an abortionist. He decides to help Rose, unmarried but pregnant, by performing 'an illegal operation'. The abortion (never called such by name) is a success, but a blood clot kills Rose. To spare his family the shame and scandal, Dr Vickers shoots himself. Claire Vickers's sympathetic mother tries to explain the doctor's actions to her daughter:

> 'Rose and Mrs. Withers came to your father, they begged him to save them. So he decided to risk his own reputation, everything he had built up, all he stood for in this town to help an honest, decent family out of their trouble. He couldn't bear to see an essentially good girl like Rose pay such a violent price for a moment's folly and trusting generosity. He couldn't bear to think of a baby coming into the world with no one to care for it.'

> So father had *helped* Rose. He had done something which mother had tried to make sound like an act of self-sacrificing heroism.

> Claire had said deliberately:

> 'You mean, father performed an illegal operation on Rose.'

> The words burned her tongue and her shame was like a thick fog blotting out all other emotions. She thought it would have been easier to have said: 'You mean father killed a man?'

Mother admits that the news was 'a great shock at first, but he made me understand—it was for humanity's sake'. But Claire is resentful ('She was never going to feel 19, lighthearted and young again'), and angry at Rose, as she believes Rose should have known better:

> Claire couldn't find it in her to be sorry for Rose. In these days girls weren't without knowledge ... and if a man really loved you, in the way Max loved, he didn't ask what Rose's lover had asked ... he was patient, he waited because he loved you so much.

This was an obvious lesson for 'modern' girls. None the less, the father's shame costs the Vickers's family their standing in the community, income, and friends. Claire's engagement to Max Himley, whose newspaper magnate father is 'one of the richest men in the country', is broken off, since marriage to Claire would 'ruin' Max's career. This snobbishness sets Claire off:

> 'Not that my father committed any crime,' her tone rose. 'It's you people with your ugly minds who are the sinners ... you with pitiable lack of charity ... your smug little crowd that goes singing in church and opens bazaars and gives hefty donations to the hospital, but who haven't it in you to give the benefit of the doubt to a man who was your friend.'

Max defies his parents and sets out to win Claire back. He nearly succeeds— and she is tempted by his offer that they live together first. But, her 'prudish inner self dragged forward ugly terms like "living in sin"', and Claire realizes she could become like Rose: 'No one had ever told Rose sanely, strongly, the facts of life, why chastity mattered to women? So she gave herself, just the same as I am going to give myself to Max.'

In the end, Claire realizes she loves Fred, the kind and gentle doctor who worked with her father. That love changes her outlook, and buries the anger she initially felt towards her father. Claire can now face the brave new world, which is somehow kinder and gentler, as she tells Fred:

> 'You aren't rated a spoil-sport and visualised as grim and pince-nezed with a horrible sort of hat, just because you've a yen to make the world an easier place for those who haven't all your luck; in the same way that a girl doesn't have to be ostracized and damned to all eternity ... because she has had a bad break over a man and is mother to a child which hasn't the right to a surname. What I am trying to say,' she puckered her face into a frown while her lips were smiling eagerly, 'is that, in spite of the misery in the distressed areas, the hopeless poverty and the wars raging all round us, the world has become a kinder place.'

Clearly, Mollie Pearson (perhaps enjoying the anonymity as 'Barbara Hedworth') had strong opinions, and her novel is actually a celebration of life. But we cannot be surprised that the Irish blocked this novel and its unconventional expression of a controversial subject. The ban does not appear to have affected Hedworth's career—or Guy Trent's—at Mills & Boon. Pearson wrote seventeen novels as Barbara Hedworth for Mills & Boon from 1938 until 1944, when she (and Guy Trent) moved on to Hutchinson.

&

By the outbreak of the Second World War Mills & Boon's transformation as a 'library house', supplying romantic fiction to the circulating libraries, was complete. Charles Boon had amassed an impressive list of prolific authors who sold well. As we have seen, Boon's instincts were good. He was inclined towards experimentation with his new authors, letting them test the waters, develop a style, and build a repertoire. All of this was conducted within a 'moral' framework, although the boundaries were sometimes blurred. So long as a happy ending—defined as companionate marriage, motherhood, and a degree of financial security—was provided, some latitude was allowed.

What the firm lacked, however, was a focus which would define the genre and establish a house style. That would come as a result of the Second World War, when authors were united in their work to boost morale and influence their readers. The unusual wartime market, which sold out existing stocks, would lead Mills & Boon on to a more standardized path. The novels of the 1930s would remain as an example of a freer style. One can only wonder how the genre would have developed had the Second World War not intervened.

Chapter 7
The 1940s: Flying the Flag

*'I'll have you know that you've entirely revolutionised all my old ideas on naval offi-
cers and their wives. I used to be firmly convinced that the only place for a naval wife
was at home waiting for her husband to come home on leave every three years or so.
But you've changed all that for me, Lucy.'*

*'A good thing too — it certainly needed it,' she murmured with an attempt at
severity. 'This is the fundamental power of women, really . . . to be able to change all
a man's pet theories and have him like it!'*

Marjorie M. Price, *The Power Of Women* (1941)

*'I can't make you out, darling. I believe you'd <u>rather</u> go dropping bombs on Germany
than spend an evening with me.'*

*It was quite a shock when he didn't immediately deny it. Instead he seemed to be
pondering the suggestion as though it deserved his most serious consideration. Finally
he shook his head.*

*'No, Mandy, it is not so. But until ze Germans are finally smashed zere can be no
lasting happiness for us and millions like us.'*

Barbara Stanton, *W.A.A.F. Into Wife* (1943)

THE Second World War provided Mills & Boon with its first opportunity
to shape what would become a formal company editorial policy. Charles
Boon, fiercely patriotic, was well aware of the addictive nature of the romantic novels and the likelihood that they influenced readers. Now, the novels
were specifically targeted to current events, shortened (due to paper
rationing restrictions), and promoted even more vigorously as a list under
near-impossible trading conditions. The imprint was firmly established due
to record demand. After the war, Alan Boon could build on the foundations
set by his father, and maintained after his death by Joseph Henley.

In a time when reading increased along with the desire to escape from the
harsh everyday reality, Mills & Boon's romantic fiction sold well. The firm
went to war with the typical romance but added a strong dose of patriotism

and social commentary. John Boon believed that Mills & Boon has not been given sufficient credit for maintaining morale with its novels during the war. On one occasion the Ministry of Supply refused to give Mills & Boon its paper allocation. 'The Publishers' Association protested on our behalf, saying quite rightly that these were the sort of books which were read by the women in factories and all that,' Boon said. 'They gave way.'[1] Mass-Observation reflected the mood when interviewing a middle-class woman from Chelsea in 1943: 'Well, I like a nice sentimental love-story, something that makes you feel really absorbed. When I get hold of one I really like, I don't believe I'd notice the sirens.' She added a preference for Ursula Bloom, Denise Robins, 'and that sort. I don't like anything highbrow or unpleasant. I don't like books that make you feel life's worse than you think.'[2]

Mills & Boon authors would have agreed. Mary Burchell regarded romance novels as an excellent escape from reality, particularly during the Second World War. 'Of course we all like make-believe, particularly when things are not going awfully well, naturally,' she said. Berta Ruck recalled how popular her novels were during the war, common on library and Red Cross Hospital shelves where she was listed under ' "Light Love" . . . On which shelves, I'm told, it's never left for long. Well, it's something to have been of some entertainment value to the sick and wounded.'[3]

In all respects the basic tenets of the fledgeling Mills & Boon editorial policy—Lubbock's Law, the Alphaman, the happy ending, and a wholesome moral theme—were retained, even reinforced, by wartime. But in terms of background and social detail, Charles Boon initially encouraged writers to leave the Second World War out of the romances, because it dated the story and discouraged the novel's reprint potential. 'We couldn't really publish a reprint of a book (in which) guns and bombs were falling all over the place,' John Boon said. Jean MacLeod recalled that this reluctance to accept wartime romances was part of the common belief at first that the war would not last very long. 'They thought that the pre-war stories would carry them through a short war,' she said. 'But then of course after two years, three, four—they realised they had to acknowledge the fact that boy was meeting girl during the war, just as anything else. The war probably made better, more truthful plots.' Magazine editors agreed, notably Winifred Johnson of *Woman's Weekly*. 'When writing in the war years it was easier to have a hero in a reserved occupation,' Esther Wyndham recalled, 'hence Miss Johnson's plea to her authors after the war, "*Please*, no more farmers or doctors." '[4]

Wartime did not diminish the need for heroines to be strong, spirited, and (usually) beautiful. In fact, it enhanced it. When Boots undertook a 'Literary Course' on 'Light Romance and Family Stories' for its library staff in 1948, the firm offered insight into the genre and how it had evolved. Heroines who used to be 'very well-bred indeed' and 'delicately nurtured' had changed during the war:

> Women to-day are quite capable of taking care of themselves, so that instead of attracting the attention of the hero by their helplessness, they usually meet and win him through a joint interest in some occupation. It becomes a juxtaposition of secretary-marries-boss, nurse-marries-doctor, landgirl-marries-farmer, etc.

There was also a new emphasis on the heroine's career, obviously a reflection of the more prominent role of women in society and their conscription for war work.

Certainly, Mills & Boon heroines in the 1940s are stronger, more responsible, and more independent. Doctors and nurses were commonplace. Dr Janine Destry, the heroine in *Give Me New Wings* by Elizabeth Hoy (1944), lives in Morocco. In *Lamont of Ardgoyne* by Jean MacLeod (1944), Lorne MacDonald is dispatched to Egypt with the Queen Alexandra Imperial Military Nursing Service, where she runs a mobile hospital unit. There she cares for 'Montgomery's men', 'men who had known the fire and fury of the Alamein break-through, the men of the spear-head which had allowed Alexandria and Cairo to breathe freely again and had sent Rommell back across the desert in ignominious defeat'. Careers are important, and second nature. In *Healing Touch* by Margaret Malcolm (1942), Elizabeth Vereker is a physiotherapy nurse in the Massage and Electrical Department of 'world-famous' Queen Eleanor's Hospital. She is surprised when an elderly patient expresses envy at her position, which Elizabeth takes for granted:

> 'You see, you girls have so much with which to fill your lives nowadays,' Miss Pettigrew explained. 'Now, when I was a girl, nearly fifty years ago, there was so little one could do. One could be a governess. Or a dressmaker — if you did not mind being looked down upon. But nothing else, except learning to keep house and hope for — for a husband so that you could put your teaching to good purpose. And sometimes, of course, he never *did* come, and there was nothing at all,' she smiled and sighed in one breath. 'So you see, my dear, you *are* to be envied.'
>
> 'Yes,' Elizabeth agreed soberly. 'Yes, I suppose we are.'

Elizabeth, like most Mills & Boon heroines, was orphaned quite young, and so working and earning a living comes naturally to her. Elizabeth's dream is to 'find happiness': 'Finding my niche — finding a place where I want to be and where people want me to be.' Indeed, when a young ruffian steals her handbag, Elizabeth insists he be released without charges — and throws him two half-crowns.

If Mills & Boon heroines appear to have matured in the 1940s, heroes were still Alphamen. Boots claimed that romantic heroes had not changed much since the days of Charles Garvice, Florence Barclay, and Ethel M. Dell. The hero remained 'strong and silent', with an impressive physique but a dour temperament: 'He usually comes from a good family but owing to some misunderstanding has cut himself off from society to brood about it in the outposts of the Empire.' Significantly, Boots added, 'The popularity of James Mason on the screen proves that feminine taste in heroes has not changed very much.' Indeed. 'Thirty-four might not be a great age, even in the eyes of eighteen, and with his tall, broad-shouldered figure he had an air of latent strength,' Judy gushed of Godfrey in Juliet Armstrong's *Frail Amazon* (1941). Soldiers, airmen, and reserved workers abounded. Judy in *Proud Citadel* admired Glenwell (a smuggler aiding the Resistance in Fascist Morocco) in the desert sunshine: 'bronzed dark with sun, his casual clothing proclaiming the splendid carelessness she loved; bare ruffled head, bare muscular arms, the open necked shirt revealing the powerful chest'. *W.A.A.F. Into Wife* by Barbara Stanton (1943) follows Mandy Lyle, 19 and never been kissed, as she joins the war effort. Mandy fantasizes about Hollywood film stars Robert Taylor and Tyrone Power. She falls hard for Count Alexei Cziskiwhizski, leader of the Polish Squadron attached to Mandy's aerodrome outside London (when he kisses Mandy's hand, it 'set her whole being aflame').

Wartime settings and characterizations enhanced the romantic possibilities for Mills & Boon authors during the Second World War. Some novels were set overseas, others on the home front, and many had a nursing theme, reflecting the Doctor-Nurse plotlines that were growing in popularity. And in most cases, the heroine saved the day for Britain.

In *Give Me New Wings*, Dr Janine Destry has moved to 'Fascist' Morocco, having fled a broken love affair in England. Morocco is a place where 'The English ships scarcely ever docked now, never had time to stay. Brave English ships coming out of their blitzed ports to keep the trade flag flying!' There the Spanish resented the English for their attitude and pride, as one officer mused:

> The English were full of arrogance; not the 'put-on' kind of arrogance displayed by the Germans who sometimes visited the Señor Capitan Ruiz. The English had been proud for so many centuries that it was second nature to them now to look down their noses at the rest of the world. You could bomb their cities flat and threaten them with utter defeat and they went on quietly looking down their noses at you. Just as they had looked down their noses at the Spanish Armada in 1588.

Janine saves the life of 'world-famous' RAF pilot Kerry Travington, who bails out of his doomed aircraft and lands on her cottage. Janine could not help but be impressed by this unconscious bundle dropped from the heavens: 'He was an exceedingly long and well-built young man, and must have weighed every bit of twelve stone in sheer muscle and bone.' But Kerry, awakened, wants to get back to camp, and tries to leap off the operating table:

> Janine pushed him gently down on to the table again. She took his hands in her own and held them warm and close. 'Listen, my dear,' she said softly, but with arresting firmness of tone. 'You can't crawl over the mountains to-night. As soon as you're able to do it, I'll help you. *I'll* get you back to your base. I won't let the Spanish put you in a concentration camp. I'm English, too, remember.'
>
> 'You mean you can hide me, here?'
>
> 'Yes,' Janine answered recklessly. 'I mean just that.'
>
> 'They'll make things hot for you if they find you out—'
>
> 'That's my affair.' A wave of sheer exaltation swept over her. She had given a promise unthinkingly, but, heavens above, what a glorious chance had come her way! She was in the war now in all truth, right up to the neck in it. She'd get this boy mended and whole again and send him safely back to his squadron if it cost her her life.

They fall in love, Kerry saving Janine from becoming 'one of those lonely spinster women who cannot bear to be stirred out of their usual little ways'.

Love also conquers all in the aptly titled *W.A.A.F. Into Wife*. The hero, Count Alexei, speaks in an absurd accent laden with 'zees' and 'zoos'. He seeks revenge on the Nazis who murdered his family in Warsaw and confiscated their lands. Stanton (a pen-name for a joint effort of two authors, one male, one female) never minced words, as when Mandy is told about the Count's plight:

> 'Freddy says he's never known anyone hate the Nazis quite like the Count. He'd raid Germany every night, rain, snow or fog if only they'd let him. His eyes light up, Freddy says, when his Squadron's detailed for night ops. Can you wonder at it? His family killed—or worse. His Castle in the hands of those filthy Nazis. All his property seized. He used to be frightfully rich, Freddy says, but now he lives on his pay.'

This being an escapist romance, Mandy fantasizes about being called Countess, and living half the year in Poland, in 'that Castle snatched back from the barbarous Nazis. It'd be marvellously furnished, with lovely high rooms, superb pictures, priceless tapestries, spacious grounds.' But theirs is not an orthodox courtship. War work constantly interrupts their lovemaking:

> 'I can't make you out, darling. I believe you'd <u>rather</u> go dropping bombs on Germany than spend an evening with me.'
>
> It was quite a shock when he didn't immediately deny it. Instead he seemed to be pondering the suggestion as though it deserved his most serious consideration. Finally he shook his head.

'No, Mandy, it is not so. But until ze Germans are finally smashed zere can be no lasting happiness for us and millions like us.'

While the Count is off bombing Europe, Mandy remembers to say her prayers at night:

Since joining up she had got into the lazy habit of saying her prayers <u>in</u> bed rather than outside. It wasn't that she was ashamed, just that there seemed no special point in making oneself conspicuous. Besides, when one shared a hut with fifteen other girls—as at the training camp—it was embarrassing to them—they might be laughing and joking at the time—if one suddenly knelt down beside one's bed.

Too, she couldn't really believe that God was more likely to listen to and answer one's prayers because one was kneeling on the chilly floor instead of lying warm and snug between the blankets.

Nevertheless to-night—Peggy was on duty—she got out, knelt by the side of her bed and prayed:

'Oh, God, I do love him so terribly. Please take care of him and bring him back safely.'

God does, and Mandy and the Count decide to marry and eventually settle in Poland, in spite of their obvious cultural differences and the objections of everyone around them. Stanton concludes the book by addressing the reader directly:

Life and love are full of risks, in peace-time almost as much as in war. To run away from them is no recipe for happiness. Where did that deadly slogan 'Safety First' ever get anyone—nation or individual?

We're perfectly aware that Alexei and Mandy will have to face all the problems and trials—yes, and the disillusionment—of life. We've yet to discover these are any more difficult to bear <u>after</u> you're married than before. Rather the reverse. And even if the worst should happen, just think what lovely memories they'll have to look back upon.

These outright expressions of fierce patriotism were common. It is not surprising that, at a time when Mills & Boon was forced to reduce the length of novels due to the paper shortage, room was still made for long patriotic disquisitions. In *The Gold and the Dross* by Valerie K. Nelson (1945), Clova Caseton leaves Rhodesia for England to seek her true love. 'England—Home, she called it, as most colonials did, though she had never yet set foot in it—sang to her with a siren voice that would not be stilled.' In *Autumn Bonfires* by Nan Sharpe (1944), David Test, a New Zealander demobbed from the RAF, tells his hostess, Scottish farmer's wife Pat Cardillyn, about the 'extraordinary' effect 'your little England does to one'. What follows is a stirring endorsement of the host country:

'It's in your old villager with his tankard of beer and his glorious stubborn disbelief in anyone but himself; in your ancestral halls with their tradition of service and responsibility. It's in your homes, and your hills and your hearts,' said the man from New Zealand. 'It's something that's mixed up with honour, and humour and history, it's—it's indefinable, but it's a potent heritage.'

'God grant that we may never lose the sense of it,' Pat answered. 'Sometimes in the chaos and confusion of this mechanised life you wonder if the echo from the past won't be permanently drowned.'

'England means a lot to you too, Pat, doesn't it?'

'It means the happiness of my family,' she answered slowly, 'and the trust of my friends. It means stout walls that will withstand the tempest and keep out the cold winds of Chance; it means warm hearths and warm hearts, and the great humanity of Churchill. It means the peace of its valleys, the strength of its great trees, the passion of its seas. It means courage and toughness and tenderness, and loyalty and laughter and love.'

'Almost a religion?' he suggested.

'Surely when you're ready to fight and die for anything, it becomes one,' she answered.

Sharpe's passions continued, as Pat Cardillyn muses about the 'brave boys' as they slept:

These boys, sleeping the sleep of exhausted children, were the men who were saving the world: it was a fact so simple and so staggering that the mind found difficulty in accepting it. On the threshold of life, with their youth a nightmare of rumours and lies, of intrigue and unrest, from where did they get their 'ready mind and steady nerve', their unfaltering gallantry and iron resolve? Was it from a faith in the future or the faith of the past? From vision or hereditary instinct? No wall of steel was as impregnable as their courage, no line of fire as deadly as their determination. That their service to mankind should ever become a matter for common acceptance, that lip service alone should be the reward of their valour, was unthinkable. No task was too difficult to be undertaken, no objective too far or too fierce to be stormed, no selfless height of glory too unobtainable for the wings of Liberty to reach. To the stars and beyond, undaunted, undefeated, undismayed—faithful unto death was the Royal Air Force.

The Ministry of Information could not have been more pleased. David Test is filled with hate over 'not only the beastly savagery of war and the concentration camps, but the cruelties of peace as well'. He tells Claire, Pat's daughter and a Wren, that all those killed so far in the war will have died in vain unless selfishness, greed, jealousy, even 'the frightened and neglected babies' and 'the chained and beaten dogs' are tackled next:

> 'You feel strongly, David.'
>
> His glance was very direct.
>
> 'Don't you?' he asked.
>
> 'It's a pretty big undertaking, this hate of yours,' she said slowly.
>
> 'It's a pretty big undertaking to give up your life,' answered the rear-gunner.
>
> 'You mean it's the only way we can—repay?'
>
> 'The only way,' he replied more quietly. 'Millions have died to give the world another chance. If we forget this time what they have toiled and bled and sweated for we've no right to hope for salvation.'

David's bitterness is typical of war; he feels himself 'a grandfather in years': 'The bitter, aching resentment of youth that had had its wings clipped, its hands stained in blood, and its heart bruised by a horror and tragedy it should have never known.'

Sympathy for soldiers and victims of war was also apparent in *This Much To Give* (1945) by Jean MacLeod. Sister Lindsay Hamilton works in St Ronan's Hospital with mentally upset war veterans, whose plight stirs her maternal instincts:

> Lindsay's heart was suddenly beating fast and high in her breast. Here was the chance she had always wanted, the type of work she had long sought. She thought of the men in the wards where she was going, men broken mentally by the stress and strain of war, but not altogether for-lorn hopes, men who might benefit from this new treatment ... That she might have some small part in their recovery was her earnest prayer.

Disturbed pilot officer Douglas Harvey, whose brother Richard is a hospital doctor, is Lindsay's new charge. 'Can't they see that all I want is to get back inside a 'plane again!' he rages at Lindsay. She urges him to believe in miracles: 'Miracles of science are happening every day, and there are miracles with which science has nothing to do. Even in this hard, modern world we are often confronted with them, perhaps more in the operating theatre than anywhere else.' But Douglas rails that she and women in general cannot appreciate the horrors of war, and especially his invalidity:

> 'You don't know what you're talking about. A woman's life can't be cut up like this. It's foolishness attempting to make comparisons.'
>
> 'Not always.' She stooped to pick up some magazines and a newspaper which had fallen from the paper-rest on his chair. 'Some women have achieved great things—some of them in this war—and known frustra-

THE SPIDER'S WEB

ISOBEL CHACE

30–2. Isobel Chace, *The Spider's Web* (1966), Eleanor Farnes, *The Stepsisters* (1966), and Margaret Rome, *Bride of the Rif* (1971). Mills & Boon's book cover designs evolved with the changing social attitudes and bolder marketing techniques of the late 1960s.

THE STEPSISTERS

ELEANOR FARNES

BRIDE OF THE RIF

MILLS & BOON

Margaret Rome

33–5. Violet Winspear, *c.* 1966, and two novels, *Lucifer's Angel* (1961, her debut), and *The Pagan Island* (1972). Winspear's mildly erotic style set a new standard for Mills & Boon novels. Her larger-than-life heroes, Winspear claimed, must be men 'capable of rape'.

36–38. Constance M. Evans, the star guest (second right) at the Darlington Writers' Club meeting, February 1973, and two novels, *A Lover from London* (1940) and *The Five-Shilling Holiday* (1964). Evans, who wrote 112 novels between 1932 and 1972, serviced the enduring segment of the Mills & Boon readership which preferred old-fashioned, 'wholesome' romantic novels.

Mills & Boon's Paperbacks

"More like selling magazines than books!"

That's what one retailer told us about our paperbacks; whether he was right or not, each month he bought from us six certain sellers, even bestsellers by some standards. Steady sales like this come from reader loyalty, and over the years we've built up something like a personal relationship with our readers. They come from that large group of people who are bored with tales of sex, violence and sadism and just want a pleasant book. Once they came to the libraries each fortnight and asked for "the new Mills & Boon's", now they come each month and buy the new paperbacks. With this backing it's extraordinary how sales have snow-balled, largely by word of mouth, without much advertising or ballyhoo. Unless you profit from it, you are missing steady business if you don't stock our books. Write for our lists now.

Mills & Boon

50 Grafton Way, London W.1

39-40. Trade advertisements, 1968 and 1971. Mills & Boon's publicity at the close of the 1960s was bolder and provocative, flaunting reader loyalty and satisfaction, 'pleasant' stories, and record sales.

Holiday reading
throughout the year* from MILLS & BOON

* World sales are now running at over 25,000,000 copies a year

MILLS & BOON
Paperbacks
that please
20p net
17-19 Foley Street
London W1A 1DR

tion, and others have faced what you are experiencing now by just the loss of someone near and dear to them. It isn't an individual experience, as I see it. Unhappily, in war, it's almost universal.'

Lindsay urges Douglas to overcome his hardship and 'live to the full. Perhaps in a different way than that in which you had planned it, but it is not always by our own choosing that we achieve completeness in life.'

Even in wartime, Mills & Boon novels ended happily, with a kiss and the promise of a future together. In *Give Me New Wings*, Dr Janine marries Captain Kerry, and they expect two months together before he is sent off again. The ending to this novel:

> 'Two months!' she whispered. 'Oh, Kerry, think of it!'
>
> It didn't occur to them that it was tragic ... two short months of happiness snatched from the cauldron of war. Two months before Kerry would be called away again. Two months' reprieve from danger, or from death. But they didn't think of it like that. Lovers never do.
>
> Beyond the apple trees the river flowed, somewhere a night bird called in the warm, still darkness, and over their heads the stars shone small and bright. They would always be there, these timeless stars. And in the hearts of men and women who love there will always be faith. That is why war and all things cruel are so much more unimportant than they sometimes seem.
>
> When Kerry took Janine in his arms and kissed her that autumn night the war and all it might yet mean to them was very unimportant indeed.

Similarly, in *Proud Citadel*, Judy defies her family to be a partner to her unorthodox smuggler husband, who is aiding the Arabs in their Resistance. Whatever danger lurks, Judy will stand by Glen, as she tells her father:

> Glen, the lonely indomitable with a vision in his flashing eyes that urged him on even to death itself. On the mountain peaks he trod there was no place for the domestic and tame convention of a marriage devoted to the comfort and safety of the home. Not a wife to cling and hamper he needed, but a companion to stand shoulder to shoulder— that's what he had said to her. Shoulder to shoulder. The feeling of exaltation returned to her, the trumpets once more sounding in her ears.
>
> 'Dear,' she said gently, 'Glen isn't the wage-earning sort of husband you have in mind. He's the kind of husband a Martha Washington might have understood—or Mrs. Oliver Cromwell,' she added quaintly. 'The splendid, uncomfortable men just a very few women have been privileged to help. I—wouldn't want him any other way.'

A similar commitment is made in *The Power of Women* by Marjorie M. Price (1941). In Hong Kong, Lucy Lynward, 25, breaks her engagement to marry

Naval Admiral Francis, war hero and an escapee from a Japanese internment camp. She vows to travel wherever he goes; she will not sit at home and roost in Hong Kong:

> 'I'll have you know that you've entirely revolutionised all my old ideas on naval officers and their wives. I used to be firmly convinced that the only place for a naval wife was at home waiting for her husband to come home on leave every three years or so. But you've changed all that for me, Lucy.'
>
> 'A good thing too—it certainly needed it,' she murmured with an attempt at severity. 'This is the fundamental power of women, really . . . to be able to change all a man's pet theories and have him like it!'

But sometimes romance took on a military, no-nonsense air. In *Trial by Gunfire* also by Price (1941), Captain Martin Domax issues a marriage ulti-matum to his recently jilted secretary Charmain Bell, and promises a real commitment:

> 'You needn't run away with the notion that ours is going to be one of those sentimental brother-and-sister relationships. You know, separate bedrooms and a chaste good-night kiss on the brow at eleven-thirty, so to speak. We'll begin as I mean to go on, see? I'm not getting any younger, and I want some children before I get too stiff in the joints to beat 'em. So don't run away with the idea that I'm a chivalrous novelette hero con-tent to get nothing in exchange for the honourable protection of my name. Quite the contrary.'
>
> 'But—but—' Charmain's face was pink and eyes wide with embar-rassment and distress.

※

Despite the war, there were still certain taboos for authors to avoid in their novels, including drinking, sex, and foreigners. Interestingly, some novels are also filled with life lessons for lonely women who might be tempted to give all for a soldier. Temptations for extramarital or premarital sex in wartime were strong, but Mills & Boon authors were ready with warnings.

In *Trial by Gunfire*, Charmain Bell is disappointed by a cad who breaks their engagement. He's going away to war; she nearly sleeps with him. Clearly chastity was less important to the men (except for the hero) in Mills & Boon novels than for the women, especially the heroine. Her boss, Captain Martin Domax, decides the only solution to her broken heart is that they marry. Martin is tough, even brutal, chastising Charmain for her foolishness:

> 'You damned little fool, you. . . . And he'd have gone off to-day, prob-ably leaving you in the family way or something if I hadn't happened along just then. God! Some of you modern girls make me sick. And I

thought you were different, credulous ass that I was. . . . It's better to walk proudly, with your pretty head up, able to look the world in the face, than to do something you'd regret all your life, just for a minute's satisfaction. Don't be unhappy, my dear, be glad—and proud.'

Charmain bowed her fair head on her clasped hands and broke into the piteous tears which had been so long pent up within her sore heart.

But married heroines were no less at risk. In *Away From Each Other* by Fay Chandos (Jan Tempest 1944), Maive, in charge of the newsagency while her husband, Clifford, joins the Fire Service, is seduced by Shaun, an Army captain and a married man billeted in her home. Shaun tells her: 'We haven't time for prolonged discussions in ethics and conventions. . . . Haven't you heard there's a war on, darling? And I may be sent out East any day now.' Maive recalls her father telling her mother the same thing in 1916, and realizes, 'Only a romantic little fool falls for that old plea.' None the less, Maive does succumb in the end (in a nod to realism, perhaps), but Shaun is exposed as a rogue and a bounder in time for her to rekindle her 'indestructible' love for Cliff.

In *Autumn Bonfires*, Pat Cardillyn laments the fact that the fire has gone out of her marriage to farmer Luke, 56, made even more apparent by the appearance of a nubile land girl, Beth, 19. This story of a middle-aged couple and the strains on their marriage presumably appealed to a particular segment of Mills & Boon readers:

> Dear, inarticulate funny old Luke, who took so much in his world for granted—including his wife! If only the lover refrained from relinquishing his role in favour of that of the complacent husband, how much happier and easier the state of marriage would be, thought Pat whimsically, but to so many men it was just a role to be discarded as swiftly as possible after its mission was accomplished. If only they would realise what a little tenderness meant in a woman's life, how many fewer heartaches and lonely hearths there would be. It was so little to ask; perhaps that was why it was so seldom given.

Both Pat and Luke are tested and tempted by their wartime visitors: Pat by the New Zealand airman David, and Luke by Beth. Pat is fearful, after twenty-three years of marriage, of 'the spectre of the Other Woman'. She muses, 'No, Luke would not want to lose his land girl—now, not when he was just beginning to discover again the quickening pulse, the brightness of the morning.' When David challenges Pat to stand up to her husband, she resists:

> 'You could, if you chose, be a stunning-looking woman, but you won't take the trouble. You've let yourself go to seed because of the babies who have had to be fed, and the chickens who've had to be hatched, and the

hundred and one miserable little household chores that have had to be done in order to keep one man complacent and satisfied.'

'You surely haven't forgotten that a woman's place is in the home,' murmured Pat with a mischievous twinkle.

David looked at her with exasperated resignation.

Eventually Pat leaves Luke and lives in a hotel in Edinburgh. There she meets David and enjoys his company—but no more. Suddenly she is happy, coiffed and dressed, 'A woman who was *soignée* and sophisticated from the highest curl to the tip of her slim, neat brogues.' Luke eventually swallows his pride and realizes his love for his wife (and his wife's abilities):

> Quite suddenly Luke knew he didn't want to go back to his empty house, to its loneliness and desolation; didn't want to go on any more doing his own chores, didn't want to live the life of a monk. He wanted his wife, wanted her as he had never wanted her before, not just because he was sick to the soul of washing up, but because he loved her— because at last the mists were lifting and the truth was breaking through. It had taken the thought of separation to drive the fact home, but now he knew.

Indeed, men are often chastised for their behaviour and mistreatment of women. In *The Power of Women*, Lucy is engaged to officer Robert Dardraye. Robert's wicked mother Melissa wants the wedding to obtain Lucy's dowry. But Melissa scolds her son for his infidelity, keeping a Chinese mistress and carousing with his fellow officers. He claims it's nothing; she's 'just one of the girls':

> 'You filthy, disgusting little cad,' she ejaculated with a whole world of icy scorn in her glance. 'You've no more sense of decency than a pariah dog. You dare to risk your chances of a good marriage with a respectable girl for a—a creature of this type. I'm utterly ashamed of being your mother. God knows how your father would have taken this but I hope he'd have thrashed you within an inch of your life.'
>
> 'Oh, come, Melissa—' Robert protested, genuinely distressed at the nauseated expression in her eyes. 'I'm not such a pariah as all that. She— she wasn't a bad type of kid, really, and all the chaps, nearly all of us, step out a bit occasionally. And I put an end to it directly I became serious with Lucy, honestly I did. You surely are enough woman of the world to understand that a chap of my age can hardly be expected to live like a monk.'
>
> 'You are expected to live like a gentleman,' she told him with a cutting scorn which made him wince. 'I have no excuse for weakness and lack of self-control. Such things as I've found out about you to-day sicken me, and when I think you're my own son I feel as if I could take a carbolic bath to try and scour away our relationship.'

Retribution is swift, for Robert has his arm blown off in enemy action, and the engagement is broken.

Apart from sex, drinking remained a demon. In *April's Doubting Day* by Margaret Malcolm (1945), Beverly Vereker is praised by her father when she gags on a glass of spirits. 'Thank goodness there is none of the sophisticated, cocktail drinking modern girl about you,' he says. In *The Gold and the Dross*, Clova Caseton is assaulted by the intoxicated hero, Dr Rory Fondrane: 'The man who stood before her was very drunk. Even she, inexperienced as she was in such matters, could not doubt it.' When he grabs her and plants a kiss, 'the reek of spirits sickened her and the scream died in her throat'. But when Clova starts to fall for Rory, she looks beyond the reek: 'She thought idly that, despite the dissipation and despite the scowl, he was a very handsome man.' Rory has a good reason to be drunk: his wicked brother has wrongly accused him of manslaughter, and stolen his research of a new wonder drug. In the end, Rory's reputation is restored—and he pledges to stay sober.

Financial security remained a concern, especially in wartime when rationing prevailed. Heroines are responsible with money, if still obsessed with obtaining it. In *April's Doubting Day*, when Beverly notices a pound missing from her household accounts, she panics and frets, to the ridicule of her wicked mother, Cherry:

> Cherry laughed ... 'Anyone would think you were on the verge of bankruptcy, the way you worry over a mere tuppence ha'penny!'
>
> 'But it isn't tuppence ha'penny,' Beverly pointed out. 'It's a whole pound and I don't feel in the least bit happy about it.'

No wonder Cherry laughs: she stole the pound to pay her gambling debts. She does the same with Beverly's jewellery, and eventually 'sells' her daughter in marriage to Paul for a £250 cheque. But Cherry does get her come-uppance in the end: she's killed in a car accident while driving with another man.

Good fortune befell heroines, even in wartime. In *Trial by Gunfire*, Charmain Bell, an orphan, is—if one can believe the puns—secretary and typist to the junior partner of Messrs Wayes, Means and Company, solicitors, of Dull Court in the City of London. She's a 'voracious reader' in the bus and tube of romantic novels, preferring those in which the heroine comes into an unexpected legacy, 'enabling her to wend her triumphant way through incredible and deliriously exciting adventures to a suitably romantic ending on page two hundred and sixty-three'. Of course, this happens to Charmain, when she wins £500 in the weekly football pool. She certainly can use the money:

> She had to support herself on her tiny weekly pay envelope and so her clothes were neither expensive nor lavish, but a natural good taste, plus

a figure which many society debutantes might envy, served to give her the appearance of being much better dressed than she actually was.

In *Anne Finds Reality* by Frances Braybrooke (1940), when working-class Anne receives an unexpected inheritance, she is determined to become a philanthropist and help the needy: 'Suddenly Anne realised the power of the wealth that was now hers.'

But an over-obsession with money was regarded as unhealthy and impure. In *I'll Never Love You* (1945), Frances Braybrooke created a most disagreeable heroine, Shannon Rillerton, who despises her Cockney background and family (who run a popular pub, the *Ring O' Roses*), and is determined to keep them a secret as she climbs her way to the top of the acting profession. Shannon uses her relations until she is rich and famous, then ignores them completely. Once she loses everything, and is forced to assume an alias and work in a third-rate repertory company in Millingtown, she has a revelation. She now admires her fellow actors, living together in a fleapit boarding house:

> She admired their dogged courage and, quite by accident had learned of the ill luck that had brought them to what they now were. They never spoke about it, never grumbled. Now that she really knew them all—living on small salaries—for the first time she realized how much she owed to her aunt and uncle. She had been spared that. She had always had enough to live well. The fear of unemployment that haunted others who were not so fortunate had never been one of her worries. Listening to them talking, she learned that none of them had anything but what they earned—nothing put by for illness. Most of them had no relatives on whose help they could depend in an emergency. They lived literally from hand to mouth. She could afford many little extras that were beyond their reach. She had never been afraid of hard work, but she had never had to slave as she was doing now.

In the end, Shannon loses her money, and her acting job, and opens a roadside café, where she finds happiness at last—like her pub-owning family. She comes full circle. When the stage beckons again, she turns it down: 'It's almost unbelievable, but I've come to believe that fulfilling one's ambition and being a great success, does not make up for other more important things.' Like the hero, Bruce Canova, a racing car driver who loses all, swallowing his pride to work as Shannon's chauffeur, Shannon learns the lessons of love. As her father notes, 'She has discovered that love and happiness are worth all the fame and money in the world.'

Wartime novels also recognized Britain's allies in praising other countries and peoples, teaching tolerance, and, in some cases, criticizing Britain. One cannot fail to notice the many comments on caring and sharing. In *The Gold and the Dross*, for example, Clova Caseton finds the welcome in Devonshire quite unlike her adopted country Rhodesia. Clova's hostess and cousin, Vere Ravensheugh, asks her to pay for her stay, even though she was invited.

> She had received a shock. It was useless to deny that. But hospitality was different here, she reminded herself. In Rhodesia, life had been so lonely in the early days that you had welcomed guests for your own sake, rather than for theirs. And so, with the years, hospitality had grown to be a sacred thing, almost like it is in the East. But Mrs. Ravensheugh didn't think of it like that.

Her relations in Devonshire are snobs and resent Clova's free-thinking and attitudes towards servants, whom she regards as friends and confidantes. Vere laments the difficulties of moulding Clova:

> She was telling herself that it was really an uphill job trying to teach this pretty barbarian anything of the management of servants and of a large house. She had lived in the uncivilized places of the earth so long that she herself was practically uncivilized.
>
> They had all been highly amused before Clova came, when Ralph had enquired whether their guest from Africa would be black. But now one could almost think that there might be greater problems connected with such a visitor even than colour.

The colour question and tolerance were also raised in *Proud Citadel*. Judy, a product of a narrow-minded father and privileged upbringing, is initially repelled by the women in Morocco, where she has fled to be with her fiancé (then husband) Glenwell Grant:

> 'They've never heard of Oxford and the Sorbonne. Their manners are frightful, and in fact, Glen, they're little better than a bunch of nice childish savages.'
>
> Glen was rather angry with her for saying that. 'They're just *different*, Judy. They have their own culture, their own traditions. You'll get used to them in time, but I won't have you referring to them as "savages".'
>
> Judy gave in at once. She couldn't bear to quarrel with Glen, and her hand on his arm tightened anxiously as she glanced up at his dark, displeased profile.

But Judy matures in Tetrablanca, thanks to a gentle Arab teacher named Sayed Ibrahim, who tells her, 'We who are Moslems are interested only in the progress of the spirit. For the Western peoples progress is measured in terms of cruelty and might.' She also sees first hand the suffering of North African peoples at the hands of the Italians and Germans, and defies her father, who says the Arabs are bound for extinction like the American Indians ('The Arab is doomed, as the red man was before him.'):

Something had swept her away for ever from the narrow backwater and she could feel the flood waters of a great ocean about her. Selfishness must go, not because it was wrong so much as because it was suffocating, the blindness of her father's outlook must give way to the far-sightedness of fellowship. Privilege would wither, might crumple. Love, faith, comradeship, these qualities would rise and triumph. The unheard cries of the suffering Arabs were but the prelude to the deeper cries which would one day engulf the whole stupid, suffering, struggling world. And out of the chaos right would emerge—not from any crude machinery of class revolution, but from the incalculable processes of adjustment which govern the passionate will to survive.

A brave new world indeed. Judy flees 'Fascist Morocco' with her husband for 'the most beautiful oasis in Algeria', where they are called 'the chosen of God'.

A similar revelation for the heroine occurs in *April's Doubting Day*. Beverly Vereker, 18, born in Kenya, is overwhelmed by London and its drabness; the city, she decides, 'could do with a good scrub'. She also noticed that 'there was something peculiar about the people—something missing, and she had reached Oxford Circus before she realized what it was. All the individuals that made up this crowd of passers-by were white—there were no dark skins or even dusky ones among them.' Beverly is upset when the hero, ace inventor (and RAF veteran) Robin Maxted, tries to tell her the ways of the world, and that she should beware of strangers and the evil that lurks around every corner:

> 'I can't bear it when people start doubting other people—I mean, you see, I've never had to be frightened of anybody in my life and so it hurts when anybody talks about there being so much evil in the world. I don't believe it!'
>
> He was silent for a moment and then he said gently . . .
>
> 'You know, when I joined up, I was an absolute kid. I'd never been away from home and all the people I knew were decent and kindly. Well— you meet all sorts in the services. Splendid chaps and rotters and all shades in between. And sometimes, you found that the chap you thought was so fine had a weak streak in him of which he was heartily ashamed and other times, you'd find the rotter doing something decent—people are mixtures, you know. But, until you realize that there is really such a thing as evil, I don't think you can properly appreciate goodness. Heavens, I'm preaching but—well, that's the way I've found it. Does it help?'
>
> She shook her head.
>
> 'I'm afraid not,' she said regretfully. 'I want to believe that everybody is fine and splendid—'

Robin's young face grew very serious and very tender.

'But, Beverly dear,' he said gently. 'We aren't living in fairyland. We're living in a world where even the kindest and best people blunder along and make mistakes. Isn't it better to face up to that?'

'No!' she said with sudden passion. 'No—I can't—I've got to believe—oh, please, don't let's talk about it any more, I can't bear it!'

Northerners also have a thing or two to say about the South and London in particular. Judy Farrish, 18, in *Frail Amazon*, is not ashamed of her modest upbringing. Forced to leave her Northern village of Burlester to support her widowed mother in London, Judy is constantly put down by her relatives, with whom she lives. Judy is the junior typist at Starfield & Morbett, whole-sale designers of sports clothes. Her jealous cousin, Brenda, also works there. Judy is in love with Peter Shend, the famous motorist and businessman, but Brenda disapproves, as he is related to the boss's fiancée. But Judy is from proud Northern stock:

> 'It's going to be pretty sickening for me,' Brenda went on, 'if Judy starts making a fool of herself, trying to climb out of her proper sphere. I shall begin to wish I hadn't got her into the firm at all.'
>
> Judy's flush deepened. It was pretty mean of Brenda, she thought, dragging Peter Shend's name up at the family breakfast-table.
>
> 'We're more democratic, up North,' she declared stoutly. 'If I wanted to make friends with Peter Shend, the fact of his being rich and famous wouldn't deter me—nor the fact that he's a second cousin of the girl my Chief plans to marry. After all, Miss Litarre, as she calls herself, is only a crooner—and a pretty poor one at that.'

The author, Juliet Armstrong, though born in India, was also from proud Northern stock: she was a descendant of the famous border raider Johnny Armstrong, hanged at Caerlanrig in 1529. Judy complains to Peter, 'You don't know what a treat it is to be with someone who doesn't make me feel as though I were something out of the Zoo.' When the boss, Godfrey Starfield, tells Judy that the business is bankrupt, but would like her to help him, she is his ray of hope:

> 'I mean to rebuild the business, just as I built it up in the beginning—from practically nothing.'
>
> Her eyes sparkled. 'That's the talk,' she exclaimed. 'If I didn't know you for a Southerner, I'd call it real North-Country grit.' And then, feeling that she had been guilty of a shocking breach of decorum, she began to stammer an apology.
>
> 'That's all right, Miss Farrish.' His eyes were grave, but there was a quirk about the corners of his mouth. 'I shall need honesty and bluntness

far more urgently than prim manners in the struggle that's before me—
and the will to work all out on any job that comes along.'

Judy agrees to become the fashion model for the fledgeling house, Starfield
correctly sizes her measurements as 'thirty-five and thirty-seven': 'I estimate
human figures just as an architect calculates the measurements of a building.'
Together, hero and heroine set out to change their world.

When Alan Boon assumed the editorial reins of Mills & Boon in 1945, succeeding his father (and, after a few years, Joseph Henley), he built on the
foundations laid for editorial policy before and during the war. Boon, like his
father, was an active editor, and worked closely with authors. In the difficult
post-war years for publishers, it was imperative for Boon that he consolidate
the firm's successes as the premier romantic fiction imprint. With his return,
we begin to have documentary evidence of the role of Mills & Boon and the
close relationship between publisher and authors.

Alan Boon's reactions and advice on synopses and manuscripts reveal the
emerging Mills & Boon style. He was an active editor eager to advise authors
on the smallest of details. For example, in 1947 he wrote to Ann Deering
about her new novel, *Journey to Romance*. 'Ann Deering was a lady who was
ultraromantic,' Boon recalled. 'She wrote in an excessively romantic style.
She breathed passion, as they might say, in the sort of books she wrote.' But
in this instance, Boon urged her not to reveal the hero's feelings for the heroine until much later in the novel. 'When the reader knows all the time what
Vanessa thinks of Andreas, and Andreas thinks of Vanessa, the reader also
loses some interest in Vanessa's romance. The reader knows in advance that
she is "batting on a good wicket".'

In this novel, Vanessa Hallard is a woman who has 'everything'—looks,
money, social position—but love: 'Romance—she had read of it, seen much
of the sordid intrigues which continually surrounded her, if they were anything to go by, but as yet she had never been touched by its magic hand.'
Vanessa meets the hero, her old flame Andreas Grieder, in Switzerland, only
to discover he is engaged to a blind woman, Anneliese, whom he does not
love, but will marry out of duty.

On Boon's advice, Deering switched a crucial scene from chapter 1 to
chapter 9. When Andreas professes his love in chapter 9, about two-thirds
of the way through the book, it is clearly meant to be an episode of high
emotion:

> 'Yes, there is someone I adore, I worship, someone who though she is
> near to me now, in my arms at this moment, is as far away as the moon
> itself to reach, as the faint stars above a weary earth. And her, I want
> more desperately than I have ever known or wanted before.' His eyes

were tormented as they looked at her. 'Oh, Vanessa dearest ... loveliest Vanessa, whether it is right, or whether it is wrong, I love you and only you. I will do so until the end of time and beyond even that! For without you, life is all darkness, all desolation, all duty. Oh, Vanessa ... I love you so ... I love you so ...' His voice broke, thinking of that love that could never be, burying his face against the softness of her, anguishedly as though his heart too would break within him.

For a moment she stood perfectly still, mute, glorified in that knowledge she had never thought it possible to hear from his lips.

'I love you too, Andreas,' she said simply, her eyes like misted stars, lingering tenderly on that sleek bent head.

We can imagine the impact were this scene to have remained in the first chapter. Needless to say, as this was a Mills & Boon romance, a miracle cure for Anneliese's blindness is found (by a kindly German doctor who had escaped the Nazis), and she encourages Andreas to break their engagement so she can marry someone else—and he can regain his true love with Vanessa.[5]

At the root of Mills & Boon's editorial policy was one cardinal rule: do not offend the readership, which is the lifeblood. 'Our readers don't want to read about the unhappy side of life,' Alan Boon said. 'Our readers are not really interested in good literature. They are only interested in what effect it has on them.' Boon made this point strongly to one of his oldest authors, Jan Tempest, in an exchange of letters in 1949. The correspondence is especially interesting in Boon's admission of just how much his firm had changed since 1908.

At issue here were two 'taboo' subjects: politics and religion. Boon was concerned over derogatory references to Russians as 'Bolsheviks' in Tempest's latest novel (as Fay Chandos), *For A Dream's Sake*:

> It has always been our policy, as publishers, to try not to step on anybody's toes in politics or external affairs—your readers and ours being of so many manifold varieties. We wonder whether it would be possible for you to make a slight revision where these passages occur. ... From your experience of us you will know that we do not make a habit of interfering with our authors' works, but only to do so where we think there is a definite 'case'. We do genuinely believe that it would be to our mutual advantage for this alteration to be made.

It is odd that Boon should have been so sensitive of Russian feelings, since Russia was no longer an ally of Britain's. In any event, Tempest, who published her first novel with Mills & Boon in 1935 and often wrote six novels a year, should have known better. But she refused Boon's request: 'About the mention of Bolsheviks—if Fay Chandos has any readers with "Red" tendencies, the sooner she loses them the better. She may also have readers who are thieves or murderers, but does not propose to spare their feelings by condoning theft or murder! I am sorry, but I cannot compromise where my principles are involved.' In his reply, Boon was forced to admit that things used to be far different at Mills & Boon:

> We have of course in the past played our own part in political, religious controversy, etc. On our files today, such famous books as 'The Conservative Mind' by Harold Begbie, 'My Life for Labour' by Bob Smillie, 'The Iron Heel' by Jack London, 'Life Changers' by Harold Begbie, etc. are a few of the dusty witnesses to our more controversial past. Today we regard ourselves more as publishers of entertaining novels, in the same way that many firms set out frankly to entertain. As a minor line of policy, we have sought to avoid 'red-rag' controversial problems—two of which traditionally are politics and religion. I will not say that this has been anywhere near the main reason for any success that yourself and ourselves may have achieved together. Of course, it hasn't! But we do get wonderful and frequent tributes, which mean sales in these days of difficult trading conditions, from the Trade and private people.

One such tribute, Boon proudly related, was from Thomas Joy, then Chairman of the London branch of the Booksellers' Association, as well as Librarian of the Army & Navy Stores. This 'fine public tribute', in Joy's forthcoming book, Boon noted, said that Mills & Boon 'specialize in light romance, and if a library has a demand for this type of book, it may be confidently obtained from us'. Apparently, the appeal worked, as Tempest altered her text, removing all 'Bolshevik' references.

As we have seen, one of Alan Boon's first steps as editorial director was to link Mills & Boon even more closely with the fortunes of the weekly magazines published for women, including *Woman's Weekly*, published by the Amalgamated Press, and *My Weekly* and the *People's Friend*, published by D. C. Thomson. Winifred 'Biddy' Johnson, editor of *Woman's Weekly* and other AP titles, was a demanding editor who often called on Mills & Boon authors for revisions to their serials. Johnson demanded realism and relevance in her serials, and was known for having a keen knowledge of her middle-class readers. Among Mills & Boon authors, she favoured Sara Seale, with whom she sparred often. In 1945, for example, she insisted Seale incorporate changes in her latest serial, *Folly to be Wise*, as a result of the election of a Labour Government. Among these were her insistence that the hero had done some war service as a Wing Commander, a change from 'the ancestral hall atmosphere', a good dose of reality (rationing and restrictions), and a more grown-up, less 'schoolgirlish and immature' heroine. 'I was trying to produce a story on the lines she originally suggested, and don't feel it's my fault if, in the meantime, a Labour Government intervenes and changes her ideas!' Seale complained to Boon, adding, 'I am delighted that you have got a good price for the story, and congratulate you, but I'm beginning to feel I earn my money with the A.P. as they seem a trifle dictatorial from the poor author's point of view.' None the less, Seale fell in step. For example, her hero, Max Soames, who lives in a grand estate on Dartmoor, was given a mysterious past, which included war service 'in Intelligence'. For months, heroine Tessa Lovaton is told, Max was lost and feared dead—and the experience 'changed him'.[6]

Magazine editors were as concerned with the romance in a serial as they were with the 'realism'. In their opinion, it was important to provide tender scenes to keep the romance 'hot'. In 1949 Alan Boon passed on the 'reader's notes' from D. C. Thomson to Ann Cameron, regarding the new novel she was writing, *Life Begins Tomorrow*. The main problem: Thomson editors felt it was 'not sexy enough', and required more tender scenes between the heroine, Morag Harrison, and the hero, Robert Sternleigh. Among the specific comments were: 'P. 35. Bigger build up of Morag's first meeting with Robert? P. 46 Opportunity for Morag to think of Richard in some way. P. 56 Slightly more romantic picture of Robert? P. 87 Slightly more detailed observation of Robert by Morag?' Cameron liked the pointers and planned a revision: 'It may take a little time, but I <u>know</u> I can improve it by letting my romantic rein go a little freer. And for the future I will try and incorporate a bit more "hotting-up" to the Scottish brew!' Indeed, when Morag, 25, who has left home in Scotland to work as companion-housekeeper in the London home run by Robert's old matron mother, first meets Robert, 'her heart turned over in her breast'. The 'more romantic picture' of Robert is provided after mother scolds Morag:

> She felt the colour rising to her cheeks, and wondered why. Her fingers touched his arm lightly, and the touch was a bond which surprised her.
>
> 'Please don't say anything more about it, Robert,' she replied gently. 'Your mother is a remarkable woman, and you know how glad I am to do anything for her.'
>
> 'I know. Thank you, my dear.'
>
> They stood for a moment looking at each other, and she saw again in that split instant of time the flash of his manhood illuminate the deep-set eyes. Saw, through the armour in which he encased himself, a glimpse of the deep, fast-flowing river of the man he really was.

Alan Boon zealously protected his authors, and in Jean MacLeod's case, stepped in to advise when D. C. Thomson overwhelmed her. MacLeod's novels had been serialized in Thomson publications since 1936, and she had placed twenty-nine serials. In 1947, on D. C. Thomson's prompting, MacLeod wrote an historical romantic novel, *The Wild Macraes*, for the *People's Friend*. Since, as an historical romance it was out of character among the typical contemporary romantic serials, D. C. Thomson suggested MacLeod use a pen-name, which she did: 'Catherine Airlie' (although she thought the idea dishonest to readers). Alan Boon approved, but told MacLeod, 'We are most anxious that you shall not be forced to overwrite.'

But D. C. Thomson's demands on MacLeod started to interfere with Mills & Boon's needs, and in the fraught post-war publishing climate, Alan Boon stepped in to MacLeod's defence. In 1947 he advised MacLeod to write in the 'Mills & Boon style'—contemporary, not historical, romance—for her next book, not according to D. C. Thomson's demands for a sequel:

> We are not keen that the sequel—if a sequel <u>must</u> be written—should take the same form as THE WILD MACRAES. What would suit us more than anything would be a typical, modern Jean S. MacLeod story. We are quite certain that no harm would be suffered by 'Jean S. MacLeod' if you were to do this: other authors do exactly the same thing. . . . Say, one strong romance between hero and heroine running throughout, dominating the story, with its finale at the end? We believe this is in your best interests. The book rights are today more valuable than the serial rights.

To drive the point home, Boon noted that a previous novel, *House of Oliver*, earned MacLeod 'nearly £350 in royalties <u>without</u> taking into account the cheap edition which will later follow, and which should add considerably to this figure. Barring the unforeseen, RAVENSCRAG should earn you between four hundred and five hundred pounds (again without the cheap edition).' These numbers were impressive, since D. C. Thomson paid only £200 or so for serial rights.

But D. C. Thomson was insistent, since *Macraes*, MacLeod was told, had been the most successful serial they had published for some time, generating 'letters from many of the colonies'. In 1948, Boon and Henley were mulling over the *Macraes* sequel: 'Although as a general rule we do not publish sequels—one of my father's 10 Commandments!—and we also do not favour publishing stories which may be out of character with the rest of our list, we have decided we will publish this projected novel. We have had the honour of publishing all your work to date, and we do not wish this record to lapse.'

Although *The Wild Macraes* and its sequel, *The Restless Years*, were big sellers for Mills & Boon (both published under the new Airlie name), Boon was reluctant to distract MacLeod from her main forte: contemporary romance. D. C. Thomson were tough customers, Boon recalled: 'These editors enjoyed power. They wanted all the authors for themselves. You accepted their terms or nothing. I think [they] . . . ruined Jean MacLeod as a writer. She was very pedestrian in her writing, to conform with what they required up there.'

The plot and background of a Mills & Boon romance were often suggested by the author, who would select according to her own interests or curiosity. Sometimes an author would go to great lengths in her research for a novel. In 1948, for example, Juliet Armstrong was excited by her new manuscript, *Sky Steward*, and its 'authentic' aviation background. Armstrong gathered most of her information from stewardess friends, and went behind the scenes at RAF Northolt. Via her agent, A. P. Watt, Armstrong wrote:

> Will you please tell Mr. Boon of the interest there is—according to your own information—among women and girls in the career of air steward. So far as I gather from B.O.A.C. and B.E.A.C., I am first in the field with a novel with an air steward heroine. So I do hope he will be able to get the book out before anyone else does.... I have been so careful to say nothing in the least derogatory about <u>my</u> imaginary airline—the reverse, in fact—I don't see that there can be any snags. For instance, I have not had any plane accidents.[7]

The pilot-stewardess romance would become a popular storyline in the 1950s, with horizons opening and more people travelling overseas. Consequently, interest in foreign locations also increased. When Alan Boon in 1948 praised Jean MacLeod's *Chalet in the Sun* and its Swiss skiing background, he noted, 'The story has made us feel what we are missing just now, in these days of limited travel and austerity.' MacLeod elaborated:

> You see, we couldn't travel during the war at all. So after the war I started to travel in a big way, and my location started to be different. And the women's magazines in London always wanted one Scottish story, one background of Scotland, per year perhaps, or six months. But they wanted one in between all these. Generally when I came back from holiday I wrote that background.

In *Faith For My Banner* by Betty Stafford Robinson (1948), Cara Chisholm, aged 21, evacuated for eight years in America, returns to England where Punch, her RAF beau, was killed in 1944. Cara recalls life among the Yanks with the greatest fondness:

> Of course being in America was great fun ... the gay, carefree life ... campus parties ... skating picnics in the clear blue mountain air ... sunbathing on golden sand ... laughter and brittle wisecracking nonsense at soda fountain bars ... an interesting job to help the war effort ... a sky so vividly sapphire, rivers so wide, buildings so tall, violent clean colours and speed and slickness, a pulse that beat out life loud and strong and virile. So different from this grey shabby land.

No wonder Cara is homesick for America. Similarly, with rationing remaining in place for years after the end of the war, heroines are often treated to elegant meals or given the opportunity to buy nice clothes. In Marjorie Moore's *What of Tomorrow?* (1950), Joyce is delighted to be invited to lunch in a smart restaurant:

> Joyce just sat back and relaxed. It seemed futile to protest, a short time back she'd been wondering what it would be like to lunch here with a wealthy escort, now she knew; she only hoped that as it was merely a chance meeting she wouldn't be expected to pay her own share. The omelette alone would have made her housekeeping a problem for a week to come; the lunch Nigel Chayne had ordered would have left the housekeeping accounts in chaos for months!

Perhaps many of Mills & Boon's readers would have sympathized.

❧

Mills & Boon continued to pay extreme attention to names and settings in novels so as to avoid any potential libel action. This obsessive attention to detail, which seems amusing at times, was always regarded as essential. In 1948, for example, Alan Boon and Valerie K. Nelson confronted a name problem in *After the Ball*:

> We are in rather a quandary over the name WINTRANT, which appears on page 228. If there is an American officer of this name, it might be extremely dangerous for us also to use the name in AFTER THE BALL. We have no means, however, of ascertaining whether there is or is not a WINTRANT in the American Occupation Forces. We wonder whether you could suggest any way out of the difficulty? . . . It is true that the character Wintrant in the story dies, but this would not be likely to save us.

Nelson checked all directories, with no luck, and offered to contact the American Embassy. She and Boon thought of alternatives, including Venpule, Badenys, Pannarton, and Kantrope. Eventually, the character was rechristened 'Adrian Venpule'. For *Tomorrow's Bargain* by Jean MacLeod (1948), Boon advised new names, 'to be absolutely safe', for The Flower Pot shop ('as there are several shops with similar names in London'), Frogman & Mortons solicitors, and the town of Guildford. The alternatives: The Garden Gate, Dennise and Blanders, and Metford.

By 1950 Mills & Boon readers were a loyal—but vocal—group. When a novel offended, or pleased, Mills & Boon heard about it. In 1947, for example, Frances Braybrooke received bad news. A Hertfordshire reader of *Loving You So* (a Cicely Colpitts title) complained, 'Never in all my experience of reading have I ever read such a load of junk all in one go. Please, do try and draw the line somewhere.' On the other hand, a fan of *Love Knows No Death* expressed her pleasure to Mills & Boon:

Tonight I started to read a book that you wrote, it is called 'Love knows no Death'. The heroine is name [*sic*] Monica and I have just read how she died. Never have I read anything so real and beautiful on paper. If all your other books are as good as this one I'm <u>sure</u> they will be a success.

Oddly, *Love Knows No Death* by Deirdre O'Brien was published in 1931— attesting to the longevity of Mills & Boon novels and of their reprints in the circulating libraries. Letters of gratitude like this were not uncommon.

One reason why Mills & Boon took great care in editing manuscripts was because they knew readers would write in and complain when they spotted errors. In 1949, for example, an invalid reader from Gloucestershire, who called herself 'a severe critic' and who insisted her library books 'come up to standard', wrote to condemn *A Stranger Intervenes* by Errol Fitzgerald. 'I have just been reading one of your publications, and it will probably be one of the last unless the standard of fiction in the others is much, much better,' the writer threatened in her own crudely written letter:

I make a mental note of anything that offends or pleases, and I can usually tell after a couple of pages if its [*sic*] rubbish or otherwise.

May I point out one or two instances in 'A Stranger Intervenes' which stands [*sic*] out, on page 6, it says 'the soft September sunlight' later on page 14 — its [*sic*] still the same afternoon by the way — it says, the October sunlight glowed.

On page 124 the blackthorn blossom is gleaming white, celandines are out and snow is still on the ground. To a town dweller that probably reads all right, but anyone in the country would laugh themselves hoarse, celandines and snow.

There is a very bad slice of grammar on Page 203 it says 'Old Threadbin sent for me his own self', whew it gave me the creeps.

There are several other bad bits of writing besides the slushiness of the whole M.S. The heroine is supposed to be courageous but by jiminy she always seems to be flooded with tears.

I hope you won't think me very rude writing to you like this. I think I should be a Book Critic what a thrill that would be.

And yet *A Stranger Intervenes*, in spite of the unusual lapse in editing standards, was one of the best-selling Mills & Boon titles in 1949, with sales exceeding 7,000 copies.

The legacy of the Second World War on Mills & Boon and its authors was strong and lasting. After the variety which characterized the Mills & Boon list in the 1930s, wartime brought a new purpose and maturity to the romantic novels and, especially, to their heroines. Women joined the war effort and, while still seeking a husband and companionate marriage, made a bid for their sex's stature and independence in a changing world. While the novels retained their escapist purpose, there was less frivolity and a degree of realism, which served only to enhance reader identification. In the 1950s Alan Boon would build on these new strengths, while following the lead and advice of the editors of the popular women's magazines, who understood their reading audiences well.

Chapter 8
The 1950s: Preserving the Legacy

> *Alan, I'll certainly watch out in the future, and you can hurl bricks at me any time you like, as I'm not easily offended when it's for my own and the FIRM'S good. I never intended to write pornographic fiction: I try to make my first old-fashioned point that the virtuous are unassailable by the forces of evil and right is might in the happy ending.*

Anne Vinton to Alan Boon, 1958

> *In this novel we have the situation that a woman is the mistress of a doctor, who is in turn the lover of his own niece. None of these goings-on is described in any detail or spoken of with approval, and the heroine is particularly horrified and disgusted; but I cannot help feeling that in view of the touchiness of our Irish market, it would be well if Jane Langford could keep off such situations altogether. Further, though the doctor's misdeeds catch up with him, Madeline's do not, as she lives all her life in wealth and rates two highly satisfactory marriages. I feel sure that Christian charity would wish to see her copping it a lot fiercer than this!*

Joan Bryant to Alan Boon, 1958

WHEN Alan Boon became Editorial Director of Mills & Boon in 1945, he inherited an imprint and publication list which had been created and refined by his father since the early 1930s (and administered somewhat distantly by Joseph Henley after Boon's death in 1943). This rich inheritance was both a bane and a blessing. On the one hand, the Mills & Boon name was well established among readers and librarians as the pre-eminent supplier of 'quality' romantic fiction. Although there was some competition (namely Collins and Hutchinson), Mills & Boon stood alone with the largest list, and a growing readership enhanced during wartime. Charles Boon, as we have seen, was a master of the art of author relations, and of nurturing new and highly prolific talent to supply the list.

But there were disadvantages. Alan Boon was entrusted with the Mills & Boon imprint, a kind of Holy Grail which was somewhat inflexible. For a young man anxious to make his mark, this left little room to be creative and innovative. The system was set, the market identified, and it was left to Boon to act as shepherd. As such, he was no revolutionary. 'To be successful,' Alan Boon said, 'you have to be a salesman, to see the market.' Indeed, with the commercial libraries under threat and production costs reaching exorbitant levels, Mills & Boon could not afford to take risks during the 1950s. The status quo ruled, and innovation was postponed until the 1960s and the paperback era.

The fact that Alan Boon maintained the system amid the extraordinary changes of the 1950s, with such success and diplomatic flair, is surprising, given his lack of experience as a publisher and editor. By all accounts, he was a 'natural'. His energy and commitment, evidenced by the voluminous correspondence in the Mills & Boon archive, were impressive, and he was his father's son when it came to charming the authors. By the end of the decade Alan Boon had put a personal face on the firm—and was justly earning a reputation as the father of the Mills & Boon romance.

Editorial policy in the 1950s remained a personal affair. As we have seen, Mills & Boon did not have a formal, published 'style' manual as exists today. 'No formula was written down. There were no tip sheets,' Boon recalled. 'Because all the books had the same basic appeal and standards, the readers could rely on buying the imprint.' And the guarantee of the imprint was escapism. 'I think that's the basic appeal of our books,' Boon said.

During the 1950s Alan Boon, along with his trusted (and clever) assistant, Joan Bryant (who was at Cambridge with John Boon), maintained Charles Boon's legacy and the imprint. They built upon the already established foundation of editorial policy (Lubbock's Law and the Alphaman), while remaining receptive to changes and suggestions from their 'outside' readers, the editors of the weekly women's magazines.[1] Archival evidence reveals what has long been suspected by literary critics and historians: these books were managed, and managed carefully, with an eye on protecting—and satisfying—domestic and foreign (especially Irish) markets. The reader was paramount, and the concern was not to offend, but to entertain. At the same time, Mills & Boon did maintain a moral code with boundaries that could be approached but not crossed.

The heart of the Mills & Boon romance in the 1950s remained, naturally, the hero and the heroine, their relationship, and the happy ending. The hero was, as ever, an Alphaman, larger than life. The heroine still searched for Mr Right while asserting her independence as a 'career girl', or by supporting her parents or siblings. In 1954 Margaret Malcolm shared her views on love, romance, heroes, and heroines with the London *Evening Gazette*. With fifty-five novels written since 1940, Malcolm noted that heroines were getting older (24 instead of 20). 'Sophistication is never a desirable quality in heroines,' she explained. 'That is always an attribute of the villainess, and goes with hardness, selfishness, and greed. After all, they are the most troublesome faults in real life, aren't they?' She also noted that lately heroes were clever and aggressive, but not rich: 'Brains now take precedence over wealth.'[2] Betty Beaty, who specialized in the aeroplane pilot hero, agreed. 'The hero is the strong but basically kindly man that most women want to meet, no matter how independent they might be,' Beaty said. 'I think it's archetypal, and I think that Nature dictates that attitude for the survival of the species. Modern living adapts and modifies it, but I think it's still there. However the man has to have real strength, not to be the snarling beast that is sometimes portrayed.'

More often than not, the heroine was still a Cinderella. 'What chance could there be for "a little brown linnet" like Lynette?' asked Vera May in *Lovers of Lynette* (1952), when the hero, Nicholas, 'was a man of experience, who worshipped beauty, and especially beautiful women'. Mary Smith, in Jane Arbor's *A Girl Named Smith* (1960), describes herself as shy and 'no oil painting in the way of looks'. In *Amber Five* by Betty Beaty (1958), Captain Richard Sutherland of Lancing Airways likes Sally, the new stewardess, because she's 'kind and polite and pleasant and unobtrusive. And best of all, *homely.*' But all Mills & Boon heroines know how to sew, cook, clean, and look after children, whether they have been trained or not. In Joyce Dingwell's *The Girl at Snowy River* (1959), set in Australia, the English heroine, Prudence, rises to the occasion to impress the local hero, Smoke Lawless:

> In spite of her statement to Smoke Lawless that she could not cook, the statement that he had waved impatiently aside, Prue was sufficiently woman to feel a challenge in the situation, to determine to answer the challenge and to emerge with flying colours. She supposed no true member of her sex, however sophisticated, really cared to be marked as zero when it came to culinary art. But how, when you had no culinary art, could you not be given bottom marks? . . . In the flat, she and Clare had seldom bothered. A quarter of ham when one was too tired to dress, a can of spaghetti, but most times they had gone across the road to the Bun and Butter and had a served meal instead.

Newer authors updated the image, making the heroine more independent, high-spirited, and fashionable. In 1958 Joan Bryant complimented Anne Weale, writing, 'May I say how heavenly it is to have a fashion-conscious author? You wouldn't believe how many are still sending their heroines out to quiet little dinners in groundlength skirts!' Similarly, in 1958 Bryant called Phyllis Matthewman on a 'tiny' point in *Cupid in Mayfair*: 'Sarah's only tolerable dress. I couldn't understand how high-necked black, almost a uniform for the over sixties, could be referred to as too <u>young</u> for a sub-deb, and finally reached the conclusion that your typewriter had betrayed you and you meant too <u>old</u>.'

A distinctive change in the Mills & Boon heroines in the 1950s is evident in the new emphasis on leaving home and family for a 'career', often in a foreign setting. The choice of career or location was often suggested by the author, who would go to great lengths in her research. Betty Beaty drew on her own experiences in the RAF and commercial aviation for her novels. Most Mills & Boon authors of hospital-based stories had nursing experience themselves, including Marjorie Moore, who was a hospital radiographer. Jean MacLeod relied on her cousins, who were doctors and nurses. 'I had that knowledge behind me. I rang them up when I needed to know,' she said. Or, as in the case of *Air Ambulance*, MacLeod tagged alongside the doctors, nurses, and pilot—even breaking her leg in the process. Anne Vinton, another nurse who spent time in Africa, drew on her own experiences in *The Hospital in Buwambo*. When Dr Sylvia Phillips is rebuffed by the bush hospital chief David Carroll—he was expecting a man, since 'Africa is no place for a woman'—Sylvia erupts: ' "I never expected to meet that particular bias in *our* field," she said, curtly. "We do everything nowadays, fly planes, drive taxis, plough straight furrows, but Mr. David Carroll will not tolerate a woman surgeon in his hospital!" '

If the heroine was evolving in the 1950s, the hero remained tall, dark, and handsome, an imposing physical presence. In *A Girl Named Smith* (1960), Clive Derwent, an agricultural engineer, has 'a rugged profile of outsize features, and an obstinate contour of jaw'. Pete, the stable boy who is secretly a famous veterinarian in Phyllis Matthewman's *Romance Goes Tenting* (1956), resembles Frank Sinatra ('the famous crooner') and has a distinctive grip: 'The strong, virile feel of his fingers gave her rather a shock. The unexpected strength of his grip made him somehow more formidable.' In fact, heroes often have impressive hands. In Betty Beaty's *Maiden Flight* (1956), the heroine stewardess admires the Captain, and 'the sensitive strength of his large hands'. In Bethea Creese's *The Chequered Flag* (1953), Fort Hazzard, playboy racing car driver and head of Hazzard Motors, possesses 'a sinewy strength in every line of his alert, upright figure'. Caught in the rain, Fort rescues Rosel Vermont, receptionist for Flick Distributors, the West End agents for Hazzard cars, and helps her to undress, giving her cold feet a warm rub with his own sensitive hands:

> Without ceremony, he went down on his knees and began to rub her feet, not gently but with such powerful vigour that she was obliged to put her hand upon his shoulder to prevent herself from overbalancing. A glow went through her. Here was she, the unimportant girl of the reception desk, seated upon a Windsor chair with the head of the firm at her feet, engaged upon homely administration to her own comfort!

Whereas the heroine is often clumsy and insecure, the hero cannot show weakness, either in appearance or in actions. The hero could have a disability—Sara Seale often used a blind man (who regains his sight in the end) or a disfigured man to great dramatic effect—but he still had to be 'handsome'. In 1955 Joan Bryant warned Valerie K. Nelson that her heroes needed improvement:

> We are wondering if they would not have a greater appeal if the heroes were more attractive in appearance. We noticed that in nearly every case they are all rather small and narrow-featured and pale and colourless, particular stress being laid on the absence of colour in their hair and eyes, and this does somehow build up in one's mind a picture of someone rather unhealthy and, if you will forgive my saying so, actually repulsive.
>
> It is hard to believe that, in view of the facts we are given, they can actually have so strong an attraction for the heroines and other women. We do not, of course, suggest that you should go to the other extreme and make them startlingly handsome, but they might be given something of the attractive ugliness of, say, Gregory Peck or James Mason. We do hope that you will not mind our making this suggestion and that you will be willing to give it your consideration.

Nelson accepted the advice curtly: 'I note what you say about the physical appearance of the heroes of my books and will bear it in mind when writing the next story. I do hope I have covered all your points satisfactorily.' Clearly Nelson's heroes were not cast from the Alphaman mould. In *Who Is Sylvia?* (1954), Piers Tresaith, a Welshman, has 'hard, unsmiling grey eyes'. In *Disturbing Stranger* (1956), Kit has a standard man's silhouette: 'tall, and broad, yet slender-hipped—and there were many such'.

Being an Alphaman meant having an important job, too. Kurt St Pierre in *The Golden Peaks* by Eleanor Farnes (1951), for example, owns a successful mountaintop hotel in Switzerland. Anne Vinton, who wrote many of the popular 'Doctor-Nurse' romances in the 1950s, believed the medical profession was best. 'You don't want to have a coal miner as a hero, or for that matter a carpenter,' she said. 'You're looking for somebody in a position. The best position is a doctor. A doctor is more glamorous, and nurses were noble.' But in *Craddock's Kingdom* by Jan Tempest (1958), the hero, Alan Maitland, has the highest job of all: clergyman. He's no stooped cleric: an Oxford rugby blue, 'so good looking', with 'such a fine physique . . . he might have posed for a St. George, setting out to kill the dragon, in a stained glass window'. In this novel the heroine, Pamela Craddock (daughter of the most powerful man in Calnbridge, a man who regarded Calnbridge as his 'kingdom'), admires the hero as a stranger on a train. 'For a moment, their eyes met—and Pamela's pulses quickened perceptively. His were the deepest, clearest blue she had ever seen, a real cobalt blue.' When the stranger takes off his hat and overcoat, Pamela is shocked:

> The door of his compartment was open. He was standing just inside, removing his scarf and raincoat. For a moment Pamela's eyes rested approvingly on his thick, fair, attractively wavy hair. With hair like that, he ought never to wear a hat, she thought critically. Then, as he turned from adding his scarf and raincoat to the rack, where his suitcases and hat already reposed, her grey eyes widened in sudden dismay. He was wearing a clerical collar. He was—of all things—a clergyman.
>
> Something clicked in her brain, and she only just succeeded in stifling an ejaculation of vexation at her own lack of perception. This young man must, of course, be the new curate. Hadn't she heard that he was expected to preach at St. Mary's on Sunday? She ought to have guessed who he was, from his well-modulated voice.

The curate reminds Pamela of the heroism of chaplains during the war, and concludes, 'It takes rather more courage to be a clergyman than to tackle many other jobs.' But Mills & Boon was careful with heroes of foreign extraction, drawing the line, for example, at German heroes, in spite of the popularity of Mills & Boon romances in post-war Germany. In 1959 Iris Danbury apologized for the delay in completing *The Rose-Walled Castle*, since she had to make extensive changes:

> As you know, I have set this on the shores of Lake Constance and first chose the German part. Halfway through the novel it began to creep on me more and more strongly that it might be prejudicial to let the heroine marry a German, even though he is, I hope, all that an M. & B. Hero can be. So I have put the castle back where it originally belonged—on the Austrian side of the frontier, and he is an Austrian. This has involved a lot of re-writing of incidents and delayed me.

With foreign travel expanding in the 1950s, interest in foreign locations also increased—with the exception of Germany. 'The development of backgrounds increased the appeal of our books,' Alan Boon said. Alex Stuart's debut, *The Captain's Table* (1953), was set on an ocean-going liner, the *Claymore*, bound for Hong Kong. 'To sit at the Captain's Table is an honour eagerly sought after; not less so, certainly, when the Captain is handsome, distinguished, and young for so important a command,' ran the blurb. In this novel, Captain Robert Blair falls for Catherine Duncan, who represented Great Britain in skiing at the Winter Olympics at Oslo. When Catherine sees the Captain, 'her heart began to beat painfully':

> A tall, broad-shouldered man, with an austere, tanned face and a pair of the coldest blue eyes Catherine had ever seen. It did not need the four

straight gold stripes on his sleeves, nor the lace on his immaculate cap, to tell her that this was the Captain.

But the Captain hates women: 'No woman had ever held his heart as his ship held it—none had offered a greater attraction than the sea offered him.' Until Catherine, that is.

Heroines travelled far and wide. 'Love affairs in the aviation world have a special character,' ran the blurb for *Amber Five*. 'Attractive young people are thrown together by the vagaries of the roster, then as suddenly snatched apart, whirling off to destinations hundreds of miles asunder. And all the time the busy grapevine is complicating things with its speedy and fantastic rumours.' Jean MacLeod set her 1956 novel *Hilary French* in the South of France and Monaco, she said, 'in view of the fact that much is to be made of the Grace Kelly–Prince Rainier of Monaco wedding'. Joyce Dingwell was one native author who made good use of the Australian setting. *The Girl at Snowy River*, for example, was set in the Snowy Mountains of New South Wales. Australia was definitely an 'Alpha' country, described as 'a man's place. Stimulating, challenging, a place to discover', with a 'virile, cosmopolitan air'. In this novel, Prudence is the only woman at the construction site of the new dam. She wins the heart of the hero, Smoke Lawless (he has smoky-coloured eyes), but marriage to Smoke meant marrying the land:

'This is no valley beautiful,' he said harshly, 'but this is my country. If you are my woman you must understand now that here I belong.'

If you are my woman . . . The five words thrilled through her.

She turned and looked at him, seeing for the first time the quiet intent of his smoky eyes.

He looked at her and waited. He had asked no actual question but still he waited.

'I am your woman,' she declared slowly, wonderingly, exultantly.

'I am your woman, Smoke Lawless, so here *we* belong.'

Anne Vinton's debut, *The Time of Enchantment* (1958), was set on a cocoa plantation on the Gold Coast of Africa, a setting which allowed for a literally steamy romance. Triss Wayne, 23, a nurse, meets the hero, Stephen Graham, plantation owner, on the cruise out from England. Triss works at the clinic on Stephen's plantation where she treats the Ashanti. Stephen in the bush is transformed: 'In the primeval setting of the bush he appeared acutely masculine, a creature capable of sudden, sweeping, natural urges.' A car crash forces Triss and Steve to spend the night together in a cabin in the bush (although Stephen is a gentleman, turning his back as Triss changes into one of his bush shirts).

But as foreign settings became more common in Mills & Boon novels, so did the risk of error. Alan Boon recalled that Mills & Boon's star author of the 1950s, Lillian Warren (as Rosalind Brett), earned the wrath of Canadian readers when her heroine, while paddling a canoe in a Canadian lake, dropped her oar, and it sank. 'I understand all self-respecting Canadian paddles float,' Boon noted. Similarly, in 1957, Mills & Boon received a letter from Miss L. O'Dea of New South Wales. 'When I go to the library I always choose a Mills & Boon book because I know that, although light reading, they are enjoyable,' she wrote. She proceeded, however, to dissect *More Precious than Gold* by Olga Gillman, which was set Down Under. Especially galling to O'Dea was the heroine's lightning tour of Australia:

> All goes well for a while until she goes on a picnic on page 137, and in half a day reaches the seaside, which, if there was a direct road (and there isn't) is at least 360 miles from Bourke. Not being satisfied with having reached the coast so quickly, they swim (in the Pacific Ocean) around a cliff (completely unafraid of sharks—and knowing English girls I cannot believe that one of them isn't afraid of sharks, as that is one of the first things they will ask an Australian in England when talking about surfing—'aren't you afraid of the sharks?', or being bashed against the rocks), then, along the rocks they go to find a pool of coral—which belongs entirely to the warm waters of the north coast of Queensland.

Gillman, a South African, was horrified by the criticism: 'I <u>do feel</u> deflated!!' she told Boon. 'Criticism is good for one . . . In future I will leave Australia alone.'

Not surprisingly, authors took an almost passionate interest in their writing, and both Alan Boon and Joan Bryant displayed remarkable patience as authors submitted synopsis after synopsis of proposed novels. Boon worked closely with each author, trying to maintain a certain tone and style. He acted as confidant, friend, and script doctor. When an author started to stray outside the 'boundaries', he responded quickly. As editor, he often suggested ways to spice up the plot, or the style of presentation, or the characterizations. When a criticism was especially strong or detailed, he often had Bryant relay the bad news.

In 1953 Vera May, a schoolteacher from Northamptonshire who had joined the firm a year earlier, provided three, 200-word synopses for new novels, each a variation on a familiar theme. In one, entitled *Melisande*, the 18-year-old heroine, leaves the orphanage to travel abroad and work as an *au pair*. But she leaves behind the village boy who loves her; she will return. In another synopsis, explained May, 'Father tells daughter that the small factory for which he has worked all his life and which he loves, is failing. He hints gently that there is one way of saving it—by his daughter marrying a certain man whom she does not know very well, but has always disliked.' They find true love in the end. This second synopsis appears to have been published as *Faithful Heart*, but changed into a 'Romeo and Juliet' story, as described in the following blurb:

> For generations the Grants had owned the flourishing sawmill by the river, and for an equal length of time the Lovesays had been their most skilled and trusted workmen. There was a strong bond between the two families—but there was a gulf too, a social gulf. Marriage between a Grant son and a Lovesay daughter, for instance, was unthinkable, said the parents on both sides, but they had to think about it all the same, and think hard, for Timothy Grant was spending more and more time with Faith Lovesay ... and the predatory gaze of Marilyn Lovesay's beautiful eyes was beginning to be fixed on Timothy.

The third proposal, and the one which May said she preferred to write, was called *Success Girl*. Sally spurns her 'old faithful lover' in order to attract 'the most popular young man in the neighbourhood', who 'worships success and girls who are in the limelight'. So Sally sets out to become 'the greatest success of all'. She does so, 'against all setbacks', but ultimately 'she has realised his worthlessness and knows that she loves the old faithful lover, the one who has never failed her'. Interestingly, May added:

> It ends something like this, 'Perhaps she ought to have felt a failure, but instead she felt the greatest success in the world. New curtains for the kitchen windows, a strip of lino for the bathroom, planning, scheming, building a little home of their own—that was success.'

In his reply, Boon was appreciative of the ideas but firm in his verdicts. The factory story, in his opinion, had the best prospects, given its 'Alphaman qualities'. Nothing was said about the orphanage plot, but it would appear that its Alphaman possibilities were slim. Lastly, in Boon's opinion, *Success Girl* was fraught with problems:

> On the whole novels where nice docile heroes play second fiddle until the final scene do not have the same punch as where the hero is the dominant character. We are not quite sure how you intend to portray the hero of this story. If he is a dominant personality well and good, but if he is rather milk and water and all the exciting adventures are with the man she does not marry, then we do not think the story will be effective. We feel the hero should always be the most attractive male character in the story, and also the most prominent. Where throughout a novel the heroine hankers after another man and then at the end is married off to a nice worthy character, the result is not so effective ... if you tackle SUC-CESS GIRL you should be very careful with your hero, that is, the man who ultimately marries the heroine.

Without exception, Boon insisted, the hero had to be the Alphaman. It does not appear that May attempted to write this novel, but she did write forty novels in all for Mills & Boon.

Similarly, in 1953 Boon wrote a three-page letter to Valerie K. Nelson, a veteran author first published in 1936, outlining everything that was wrong with her current manuscript, *The Prize is Romance*. The theme was a familiar one: the poor, plain typist heroine, Rosemary Dacourt, wins a newspaper competition, earning £5,000 and a holiday for two on the French Riviera. She longs for the love of the local boy, Jim Trembourse, but once in France, meets the enigmatic hero, Jean, Marquis de Theonville. Boon's main concern was that Nelson's novel was not romantic ('hot') enough, which would diminish its commercial appeal:

> There is no doubt that what the readers of Valerie K. Nelson's novels require above all is a strong romantic interest, in which the heroine's romance dominates the rest of the story. In THE PRIZE IS ROMANCE, the romantic side of the story is virtually non-existent, as the story stands at present, until about page 135. In the story it is stated (pages 12, 13, 14, for example) that the heroine has loved Jim Trembourse all her life; but there is, as the story stands, little other evidence that the heroine gives much thought to Jim.
>
> After careful consideration we would very much like you to give thought to the idea that more should be made of the heroine's feelings for Jim until such time, much later in the story, when Jean can take over. This would have the effect of keeping the romance 'hot' in the reader's mind.
>
> We appreciate that you cannot go too much off the deep end concerning the heroine's love for Jim, because of the later transfer of her affections to Jean, but we do think that by, for example, every now and then allowing the heroine to think of Jim you could add to the romance of the story. For instance it would be possible on occasion for Rosemary to wonder what sort of wife Amy would make for Jim, and feel unhappy about it . . . On page 97 when the 'weight of sadness dragged at Rosemary's heart' the reason might, for instance, be that she had longed to have golden hair, etc. to have won Jim's affection.

'As you are aware,' Boon concluded, 'we do not make a practice of writing to authors about their stories unless we feel it is absolutely necessary, and we would be very appreciative if you would examine the points we have raised.' In other words, follow orders, which Nelson did, replying to Boon, 'I am more sorry than I can say that so much revision has been necessary for this story and I will certainly bear in mind for future stories the fact that the romantic interest should be stressed above any other aspect of the story.'[3] Indeed, in the published novel, Rosemary forever daydreams about Jim, who's engaged to Amy, 'the prettiest girl in Raylorne':

And again came the thought of Jim, her mask-like little face glowing into life, as she did so. He might be Amy Reynolds's fiancé, but he was the person who meant more than anyone else to Rosemary. She had loved him for so long—ever since the first moment that she had met him, she sometimes thought—though of course he knew nothing of it. The sight of him each morning, going to his office, when she was on the bus gave her a warm feeling in a heart that so often felt cold and chill because no one cared about her.

Once in France, Rosemary is still tortured by thoughts of Jim: 'These lovely surroundings had brought to life once again those old yearnings for romantic passion—had brought a reminder that she wasn't the cool, bread-and-butter miss that even her closest friends thought her to be but an ardent, vital young woman.' But soon she transfers her affections to the French hero, who was a prisoner of war in Nazi Germany. Rosemary, who had always heard that Frenchmen 'were great lovers', gives the Marquis 'full marks'.

In addition to 'hotting up' manuscripts, Boon often advised authors to provide exciting 'emotional scenes'. 'Emotional excitement is much more important than a purely dramatic sort of excitement (for example, the heroine hanging from a precipice by her teeth),' Boon instructed Elizabeth Gilzean in 1957. For the best sales, Boon added, it was important to have a tender scene between hero and heroine, and then introduce conflict:

> Having now got the heroine and the hero towards each other, it will presumably be necessary to consider the advisability of 'breaking it up' between them a little. Two of the classic gambits for this, of course, are (A) the hero sees the heroine receiving an unexpected (by her) peck from someone else and misunderstands, and (B) the heroine or hero overhear a conversation and misunderstand.

Indeed, these gambits were appearing more often in the evolving Mills & Boon formula. Gilzean, a journalist and nurse born in Canada but living in Birmingham, was grateful for the advice, noting, 'Part of my difficulty is that I'm afraid to use emotion enough because I'm trying to avoid being "sloppy" sentimental. I shall have to try and let myself go and see what happens.'

A final example showing the careful attention which Mills & Boon paid to synopses is an intriguing one, submitted in 1959 by new author Nerina Hilliard, a stenographer born in Ilford but raised in Australia. In her three-page letter posted from Sydney, Hilliard wove an outrageous plot. The setting is present-day Algeria. The hero is a Muslim, raised by Frenchmen, but secretly a nobleman and a member of the Tuareg tribe, descendants of a lost European Crusader army. He has, Hillard noted, 'a "lord of creation" air' which 'would fit in well with the aloof and somewhat infuriating type of hero you seem to like'. The English heroine travels to Algeria with her fiancé to seek out her mother's Tuareg roots. She meets the hero, falls in love, is released from her engagement, and they marry.

Hilliard admitted her proposal could cause problems. For one, the Tuareg, 'although of course deeply suntanned are supposed to be a Caucasian or "white" race. I mention this in case there might be some colour prejudices among some readers.' As for the Muslim religion, she noted the Tuareg treat their faith with 'only the most casual type of lip service', so religion would not intrude. In his reply, Boon said he liked the plot, but 'one of my readers is against it'. That reader was Joan Bryant, and her reader's report is a classic document for its statement of all the cardinal rules that were broken by Hilliard. 'Sorry to be a wet blanket,' Byrant wrote to Boon, 'but I feel we must discourage this novel, for the following reasons':

a) Colour bar. Miss Hemming's account of this race as originally Caucasian would do for English readers, but we have to think of our South African market, too, and I don't believe they'd stand for it.

b) Religion. If the hero is a Moslem, I don't think it helps much that he is a lax one! The Eire readers would find much matter of offence here. If, on the other hand, he is made an RC (because of his French upbringing) then we must expect roars of rage from the manse.

c) However carefully the scene is set, the story is surely bound to recall the sheikery of the <u>Garden of Allah</u> and <u>Desert Song</u> periods. This is hopelessly unfashionable, and so much mockery has been slung at that particular genre that I very much doubt whether it will ever share in the revival that other vogues of the 20s and 30s have been enjoying.

d) Algeria. This link-up is the reverse of an advantage. Our readers have shown over and over again that what they like about romance is that it takes their minds off the troubles of real life. Algeria is one of the nastiest things happening today, and fortunately it is one that we can put out of our minds with a clear conscience. This does seem to me a most excellent reason for <u>not</u> writing about it.

In closing, Bryant wondered why Hilliard did not follow the example of her fellow Australian authors (such as Joyce Dingwell) and write about her home continent, 'one of the countries of the future'. Boon wrote to Hilliard, suggesting such: 'So far you have not done an Australian story which deals with the subject, say, of an English girl emigrating to Australia. . . . There is a strong interest in this type of story at the present time, and quite often it has translation possibilities because of the European interest in Australia as a country for emigrating.' Hilliard barely had time to read Boon's letter before her death in 1960, and the Tuareg novel was never written.

Undoubtedly during the 1950s Mills & Boon kept their readers (both at home and abroad) and sales in general in the back of their minds when editing manuscripts. As before, the firm kept a tight watch on potential taboos and controversies. However, in most cases, Mills & Boon did not act as censor but as adviser, attempting to defuse problems in a creative way, without sacrificing the dramatic power.

The most common problems revolved around, not surprisingly, sex. Passion was acceptable and encouraged; 'sex' or titillation were not. For example, Anne Weale's debut, *Winter is Past*, was a best-seller; it seethed with passion. The heroine, Alex Murray, is spunky and spirited, the setting, exotic yet dangerous, the hero, a brute. Alex arrives in Malaya to discover her father, a rubber planter, has been killed by Communist terrorists. She is left in the hands of a guardian, Jonathan Fraser, and impresses the soldiers:

> 'Oh, I'm stifling.' Forgetting her earlier shyness Alex slipped off her cotton jacket and accepted the lemonade Tom handed to her. Her bare shoulders and arms gleamed pale and satiny in the soft glow of the oil lamps. The tight bodice outlined her young breasts, her narrow waist. To both men, had she known it, she was the tantilizing personification of their secret longings, the warm lovely creature who haunted them on those long nights when the frogs croaked unceasingly in the lallang and the rubber forests seemed alive with menace.

Jonathan teaches Alex how to fire a revolver and rifle; 'he told her coldly that if the bungalow was ever attacked she would have to fend for herself as neither he nor the police guards would have time to look after her.' She accepts Jonathan's marriage proposal as expedient; when her bus is hijacked by terrorists and she refuses to hand over her opal engagement ring, she's brutally pistol-whipped. That kindles Jonathan's love:

> 'Kiss me, Alex.' His voice was husky.
>
> 'What a fool I've been,' she said presently. 'But you always seemed so aloof . . . as if you despised me.'
>
> 'Aloof! Great heaven, if you knew what a curb I had to keep on myself not to make love to you months ago! It was intolerable having to play the stern guardian when every time you smiled at me I wanted to crush you in my arms and never let you go.'

Mills & Boon heroes—like their heroines—faced temptation, but authors carefully curbed these (natural) desires to maintain the moral line. Indeed, careful editing of manuscripts kept passion within acceptable levels. In 1958 Alan Boon wrote to the literary agent Peter Janson-Smith about revisions to *House of Lorraine* by his client, Rachel Lindsay (Roberta Leigh), one of Mills & Boon's most popular authors. Boon was anxious to proceed with publication; but wanted Janson-Smith to know about 'one slight suggested amendment':

On page 153, 4 lines from the bottom, we would wish to delete, 'Her body aching with desire', and for the paragraph beginning line 2 of 154, we would suggest the reading be: 'Then there was no need of words, for all his passion and longing was in the depth of his kisses. Unashamed, she clung to him and returned kiss for kiss, touch for touch, until, withdrawing a little, she lay quiescent in his arms'.

Subtle changes, perhaps, but the effect is softer and less erotic.

Alan Boon's most loyal authors were passionately opposed to physical sex and, as such, against the trend in popular fiction (set by best-selling 'racy' novels such as 1956's *Peyton Place* by Grace Metalious). In 1957 Olive Norton, new to the list as 'Kate Norway', heaped scorn on romance authors such as Sheila Reid, who, she claimed wrote 'positively obscene' stories, 'all about seeking lips, and tongue tips, and the perfume that rose between her breasts, and chaps getting all hot and bothered fairly gnashing their teeth with desire'. She added: 'I wouldn't dare. I could make it very D. H. Lawrence if it was just a <u>book</u>, but when it's a Mills and Boon book, or a serial, you don't feel you can.' Boon trained, and picked, his authors well.

Not surprisingly, kisses represented the extent of lovemaking in the 1950s. According to Boon, the 'punishing kiss' remained the crucial dramatic moment, usually midway through the novel. In *Lovers of Lynette*, for example, Nicholas plants one on Lynette's 'soft, unrouged lips', unexpectedly, as he bids goodnight:

> He was gone, and the car was gliding away as she still stood there, stunned and thrilled and bewildered by the magic of that kiss. It had been so quick and unexpected. She felt herself trembling as she turned away and let herself into the hall. He had kissed her, Nick had kissed her, Nick, who had seemed like a god out of reach, had kissed her. Kissed her. The words made music for her, and her eyes were like misted jewels as, her weariness vanished, she ran noiselessly up the stairs.

No one wrote kisses like the acclaimed mistress of the genre, Lilian Warren (Rosalind Brett), who was the top seller for the firm in the 1950s. Warren's sexy style as Brett, with its hint of violence, often had to be watered down by the firm and the women's magazines. In *And No Regrets* (1950), the impact of the kiss was powerful:

> 'If you were smaller, I'd spank you. As it is, big girls get kissed.'
>
> He bent his head, brought her face close to his and possessed her lips, crushing her to him from her shoulders to her hips. When after endless, savage moments body and mouth were free of him, when at last he moved away from her, all she could do was look furious and fluffed. Her lips stormed with colour, her eyes with the rage of abused love.

'Go ahead,' he leant against the chest of drawers, looking aloof and unmoved, 'call me a brute. It's another classic from you females.'

There still could be no suggestion of pre- or extra-marital sex, either by the heroine or hero. Secondary characters were another matter, and if they engaged in 'immoral' behaviour, they were 'punished' in some way. For example, in 1951 Alan Boon expressed concern to Vera May over *Lovers of Lynette*. In this confusing novel, Toby is the best friend of the hero, Nicholas; 'Rachel', the other woman, is engaged to Nicholas; Lynette is the heroine, engaged to Toby:

> There is one aspect of the new story (which we liked). It concerns an incident where, as things stand at present, it appears that Rachel spent the night at the flat of either Toby or the hero. I do not know what your ultimate intentions are, but we think it advisable that it should be made clear that Rachel did not, in fact, spend a night in a man's flat. This is a precaution we have to take, bearing in mind the views of certain sections of our public.
>
> At the same time (as you may remember, when we discussed such things on your visit to London), I am not anxious that you should weaken the power of any future writing you may do for us, for fear of offending people. If, in our opinion you do ever fall through the ice, we will draw your attention to it.

In her reply, May wrote, 'I do remember all that you said on the subject, but I think I must have made the mistake of thinking that, while the hero and heroine must be spotless, it was not so important about the other characters.' She decided to change the name of Rachel to Olga, since Rachel, 'has a Biblical flavour and is not suitable for the glamorous type such as the girl in my book. I think "Olga" is more indicative of the sophisticated type.' But although innuendoes were removed from the published book, *Lovers of Lynette* still contained some fairly strong scenes. When Lynette confronts Toby on his infidelity with Olga, and returns his ring, Toby forces it back on her finger. 'There it stays,' he commands:

> 'Let's forget it, my darling, let's kiss and be friends.' He took her in his arms and kissed her half-savagely, her eyes, her hair, and lastly her tight, unwilling mouth. She turned and twisted and struggled, but he held her ruthlessly, his kisses bruising her lips and throat.
>
> She was amazed at the tempest of revulsion that swept over her as she was in his arms.
>
> 'Let me go,' she said furiously . . .

But fantasizing about sex was permissible, so long as the betrothal of heroine to hero was clearly on the cards. For example, in Anne Vinton's *The Hospital in Buwambo* (chosen by Harlequin as its first paperback title), Dr Sylvia Phillips and Dr David Carroll endure hardships in their bush hospital, and in the end, decide to marry. But they nearly sleep together before marriage: David longs for her, 'his soul bounded to enter the world of woman. He was impatient: 24 hours was too long to wait to know more of her.' Sylvia's ready; but after feverish kisses, 'Glorying in her trust, her love, her complete surrender, David gathered the tatters of his patience around him like a threadbare cloak, and gently put her from him.' No sex before marriage for this couple, Vinton decided. But the best of heroines often put men in their place when they crossed a line. In *This Time, it's Love* by Fay Chandos (Jan Tempest, 1951), the heroine Celandine is shown around Florida by the caddish Randolph. While she admits that, 'Randolph had an uncanny knack of making a girl feel herself lovely and desirable', Celandine has her limits. When Randolph professes he's 'hungry' for Celandine, she rebukes him, saying nice men do not use such language:

> 'Do you then know so much about men? I don't think you've had a great deal of experience, little one. Men may have admired you, but I'm certain that no man has yet possessed you.'
>
> 'Well, of course not.' Her colour deepened. She forced a laugh. 'What extraordinary things you say, Randolph! If it's a line, I don't care for it.'
>
> 'Are you so shy and prim that you are shocked by my desire for you?'
>
> 'I think you're talking nonsense and I don't like it. I suppose you're trying to make me rise. It's not very clever.'
>
> 'Come into my arms. I want to play with that fair, silky hair and stroke your creamy skin.'
>
> 'Oh, don't be silly!'
>
> '*Silly?*' His eyes narrowed. 'Is it silly to make love?'
>
> 'It's silly to talk in that extravagant fashion. If you're showing off to impress me, you're wasting your time.'
>
> 'Oh, no! I don't intend to waste any time. I'm going to make you mine, before you have a chance to elude me.'

Randolph wants to compromise Celandine and force her into marriage, but she breaks free, running wildly into the swamp. The hero, Steven, rescues her.

Affairs had no place, nor did the intentional break-ups of engagements or marriages. In 1959 Joan Bryant advised Anne Weale on the issue of affairs with regard to her latest novel:

> We are not altogether happy about the situation in which the grandmamma had an extra-marital love affair. If one puts in a thing that might shock some readers, it should, I feel, 'earn its keep' by contributing something positive to the story; giving a twist to the plot, enhancing dra-

matic values or amplifying character. For instance, in CASTLE IN CORSICA the sinister atmosphere of the night-club put the heroine in an alarming predicament and justified the hero's rather piratical intervention, and was therefore worthwhile.

But the grandmother's story doesn't have this quality; one feels straight away that it is improbable that a woman of that type would tell a grown-up granddaughter such a thing about herself at their first meeting, and there is ample explanation for John's jealousy without her and David Lovell having gone quite as far as that. So would you be willing to modify the relevant bit of text, to make them very much in love but not going the whole way?

Bryant added, 'It seems so petty and prudish, yet instinct (often a better guide than reason in such cases) has been saying to us, All right, be prudish, for goodness sake!' Weale apologized, and made amends: 'Sorry about the grandmother's wicked goings-on. I must have had a slight moral black-out or something.'

Another taboo concerned cousins marrying—quite unlike in the 1930s, showing perhaps how time and sensitivities had changed, and how much more censorious Mills & Boon had become in the 1950s due to a greater focus on foreign markets in particular. In 1958 Bryant warned Jean MacLeod on her latest, *Red Lotus* (by Catherine Airlie), set in the Canary Islands:

When (p 165) Felicity mentions her cousinship with Julio as an additional reason for not marrying him, Philip says that this would almost be considered as an asset on Tenerife. Well, we recently sold the Italian rights of a novel where a girl was in love with her cousin; he did not return her feelings and they were never married or even engaged, but the good nuns insisted on changing the story, in translation, so that she was only a childhood friend. I can see that on some remote island, where cousin marriages must sometimes be inevitable, there might be a more lenient attitude, but do you know it as a fact?

MacLeod was horrified: 'I think it is very important that we should change the "cousinship" remark when the Roman Church is "agin" it . . . I did not know about Roman Catholic Cousins! The Pope has been "having a go" at quite a few things recently!'[4] Indeed, in the published novel, Felicity and Julio remain cousins, but marriage is never discussed.

For Mills & Boon, the market in Ireland remained a large and lucrative one, so important to the firm's fortunes that it often cramped writers' styles. Whereas we have seen that in the 1930s Mills & Boon authors had more freedom, and their novels were occasionally banned in Ireland, times had changed. 'We have to be very careful indeed that there are no complaints about the novels in this important market,' Alan Boon advised authors in 1958. 'The possibility of being banned in this market is a very serious matter.' Ireland, he added, 'objects strongly to divorce, bedroom scenes, illegitimacy, or seduction in novels, even if in the context the comment is unfavourable to such." Joyce Dingwell, for one, recalled Boon's concern over Irish readers:

> Alan wrote out to me that he was not sure about an MS I had sent in that had a divorcee in it. He thought the Irish readers would not like that. Could I think of a way out? It was hard. At last I wrote back in desperation, 'I have killed her: she died peacefully years before, much revered, and the wedding can go on.' The theme of 'everything stopping at the bedroom door' was very true then. The nearest we ever got was 'a look came into his eyes'.

Mills & Boon tried mightily to identify potential problems before they could reach the Irish audience. Editors relied on readers and sales representatives for advice, and when there was a problem, acted quickly. 'One of our travellers has recently spent 17 days in Eire touring the country and speaking to librarians throughout the length and breadth of their land, and he, in his report, has emphasized the utmost importance of suiting the market in the way I have described,' Alan Boon told veteran author Constance M. Evans (first published in 1932) in 1958.

As usual, Boon's manner with an author when she crossed the 'Irish line' was gentle, yet persuasive. For example, in 1951 Boon told Jan Tempest that the Irish were concerned about *Without a Honeymoon* and the issue of illegitimacy: 'As you may be aware, the Irish are more than usually sensitive on some matters, and our representative thinks that the fact of Clarinda's infanticipating before her marriage would be viewed in Southern Ireland with disfavour, to say the least.' He proceeded:

> We should not, in the ordinary way, ourselves mind about one book getting into trouble, although since our representative has pointed this out to us we should, in your interest, have drawn it to your attention. The difficulty about it lies in the probable consequences. At the present time the Irish market accept without question any of your books without reading them, and indeed any of the books we publish. They do this with confidence because none of them for a very long time has got into hot water.
>
> It is our view that no great adjustment would be required if Clarinda merely went away from Garnet because of the strain of being continually in his presence when she was in love with him. In view of the fact that Garnet was always attracted by the unobtainable, this would be

most convincing. Perhaps if necessary, when Clarinda had her fall she could break her ankle, or something like that.

In this novel, Clarinda is the sister of the heroine, Romola, who is married to the hero, Dion. Dion's half-brother is Garnet. In her reply, Tempest agreed, 'It would be a pity indeed to disturb the present happy position in this market,' and she revised as suggested. Clarinda does indeed plan on going away; she wants to marry Garnet, 'but she wanted even more to be sure of the depth and strength of his love for her. She had thought that her absence would put it to the test.' But she swoons and falls; Garnet rescues her, and the hospital performs an emergency appendectomy: 'She had thought that her tendency to nausea and dizziness had been due solely to unhappiness and over-strained nerves. How stupid she had been not to realise that there was something wrong with her!' The nausea, one notes, was *not* due to pregnancy.

Not all authors were as understanding in their revisions as was Tempest. Evans had to rewrite her 1959 novel, *Second Blossoming* (as Mairi O'Nair), because the heroine, herself an illegitimate child, proceeded to have one. 'Don't you tell me that in Ireland people are so good and ignorant of the facts of life!' an irate Evans wrote to Alan Boon. 'I've known several Irishmen, and they don't give me at all that idea! <u>And</u>, they only paid £10 for a serial!' Nevertheless, Evans did change her manuscript to satisfy the Irish market: the heroine, Anne Berison, becomes an orphan, raised by her aunt and uncle. She marries a dashing Italian engineer, Dr Michael Alassio, and moves to Florence. But Michael is exposed as a murderer and is killed; Anne can then marry an American tourist, Alan Fyson (she admires his 'good set of strong white teeth'). Their marriage will be a 'second blossoming . . . much better and happier than the first'. At the book's end, Anne is still childless.[6]

Anne Vinton often fell out with the Irish with her hospital romances. 'There was no actual sex [in my novels], only the promise, and I was once blue-pencilled for allowing my couple to marry and actually enjoy the first night experience of pure love,' she recalled. 'But my making love caused trouble with the Irish censors. "He undid the buttons on her blouse", something so trivial like that. Alan Boon told me it wouldn't "go down" in Ireland, so I had to do a retake on that. Sex was always there, but never explicit.' For example, in Vinton's debut, *The Time of Enchantment*, Triss attends an Ashanti tribal dance in an African village, and is more than impressed: 'The singing would grow wilder, the drums more fanatical, and then the splendid males would divest themselves of all but loin-cloths and gyrate in a blood-heating dance of primitive origin . . . "How easily one could discover one's primeval self in this setting!" she thought.' Triss is swayed into a trance, and fantasizes about the hero, Stephen, kissing her, 'his lips pressed hard . . . So real it was that Triss' sweet mouth pouted for a kiss, uninhibited and generous.'

Apart from sex, divorce remained a major taboo, despite the fact that divorce was becoming more common in British (but not Irish) society. In 1958 an Irish bookseller wrote to Mills & Boon about Vinton's novel *Sister Tutor's Secret*, which contained a reference to the divorce of two characters. Although the bookseller noted that, 'It is not often that I have to write to you especially on this subject,' he said that Vinton's book 'has been returned to us by a couple of libraries here with the remark that they do not consider it a book which they feel they could put up for general circulation'. The problem: 'They might take exception to the episode on pages 42 and 43, and in these circumstances I should be pleased if you would allow me to return it for credit, and it seems very unlikely that any other librarian will order it.'

Given the pages in question, it is a surprise that Mills & Boon did not receive more letters of complaint from Ireland. The heroine of *Sister Tutor's Secret*, Fran, is forced to leave her post at Duke's Hospital because of a romantic scandal. She had fallen in love with a married man, Rod. To obtain a divorce from his wife Elaine, Rod asks Fran to feign an overnight stay with him at an inn, so that Elaine's 'private eye' can obtain incriminating pictures. 'It was all so insane, yet so right seen through the eyes of a deep and senseless love,' Fran agrees:

> She successfully smothered all her conscience's promptings that what she was doing was wrong. As they took a few drinks in the hotel lounge together it became easier to be convinced that she was helping both Rod and Elaine by such a night's work. After all the evil would only be in people's minds. Rod had promised not to harm her. Nothing could override conscience's conviction as to the sanctity of marriage and the natural consummation that followed—never preceded—the ceremony. Rod knew and shared her views, she was sure.

But he did not, and while attempting to rape her ('Scream, then, you blasted little prude'), Rod has a heart attack. Fran is forced to contact her hospital, as well as Rod's wife:

> The rest was all rather horrible. Elaine was not at all grateful to Fran for helping her secure a divorce.
>
> 'My dear kid,' she said, as they waited together. 'I have enough evidence for a dozen divorces. Rod does this sort of thing at least once a year. He can have a divorce any time he likes. I do hope for your sake he had his attack before—before—'
>
> 'Yes,' Fran said tensely, seeing herself stripped of all innocence and decency in this woman's eyes. 'I'm sorry, Mrs. Bart.'
>
> 'I'm sorry for you,' Elaine replied airily. '*I'm* the one Rod married, remember!'

Although Vinton presented this situation as an act of foolishness and naivety on a girl's part, and showed how she suffered in dignity and status, the Irish still did not regard this as a morality lesson. To Boon's letter, Vinton's reaction was swift: 'It has given me a jolt indeed to find that instead of receiving an accolade from you I look like "getting the sack"!' She (rightly) placed some blame, 'on the part of your reader(s) who passed the story in the first place knowing your markets, which I, until now, did not'. But in the end, Vinton promised to be good:

> Alan, I'll certainly watch out in the future, and you can hurl bricks at me any time you like, as I'm not easily offended when it's for my own and the FIRM's good. I never intended to write pornographic fiction: I try to make my first old-fashioned point that the virtuous are unassailable by the forces of evil and right is might in the happy ending.

> I also wonder if the libraries of Eire have put the same ban on ROOM AT THE TOP and the works of SOMERSET MAUGHAM, or is it only the unknowns who must watch their moral step.[7]

Winifred Mantle, who wrote as Jane Langford (and, in real life, was a university lecturer), was also called on the carpet by Boon in 1958, for her novel *Happy Return*. Joan Bryant revealed the touchiness of this situation in a confidential memo to Boon:

> In this novel we have the situation that a woman is the mistress of a doctor, who is in turn the lover of his own niece. None of these goings-on is described in any detail or spoken of with approval, and the heroine is particularly horrified and disgusted; but I cannot help feeling that in view of the touchiness of our Irish market, it would be well if Jane Langford could keep off such situations altogether. Further, though the doctor's misdeeds catch up with him, Madeline's do not, as she lives all her life in wealth and rates two highly satisfactory marriages. I feel sure that Christian charity would wish to see her copping it a lot fiercer than this!

Indeed, *Happy Return* dealt with some strong issues. The heroine, Susan Gilchrist, lives in Saint Faustin, a 'little Riviera resort'. She works as a companion and secretary to Madeline Egerton, a wealthy widow who believed that 'the acquiring of husband or lover was the only conceivable occupation for an attractive woman'. Susan dislikes the sly Dr Tullio Toselli, who ministers to Madeline's invalid stepson, the hero Neil (for whom Madeline has considered euthanasia). Dr Toselli's 'niece', Lina (her parentage is questionable: 'She may be—the family swarm like flies . . . But what is certain is that she is his mistress'), is Neil's nurse, and schemes to drug him, marry him, and then kill him. But Madeline arranges for Susan to marry Neil instead.

The draft letter to Mantle, probably written by Bryant, read as follows:

We have been somewhat worried of late at receiving complaints from Eire about the existence of objectionable (by their standards) situations in some of our novels. In one instance, a single protest by a reader about a book in which divorce was talked of as a practical proposition (though it did not actually take place) caused a librarian to cancel orders, not only for books by the particular author concerned, but for all Mills & Boon titles whatsoever; so you can see that we have to take the matter seriously and to be sensitive to opinions which are not our own.

None of your books has so far come in for censure, but we have been rather doubtful about THE HAPPY RETURN, in which, you will remember, Dr. Toselli is the lover of his niece or alleged niece, Lina, and of Madeline Egerton. It is true that all this is described in the most unexceptionable way, and with marked disapproval, but all the same, it is there—and Madeline, instead of coming to the bad end which the pious would have [been] saving up for her, goes off at last to a happy future with an agreeable husband.

We do not share the standards which could object to such a book, and we have in the end sent it off to the printers as it stands, but we would appreciate it very much if you could construct the plots of future novels without any fracture of the seventh commandment, even by unsympathetic characters. Both the Irish and Australian markets have shown a marked increase in strictness during the past two or three years, rejecting books which at one time would not have caused an eyebrow to be raised, and they are so important we feel bound to consider their views.[8]

The fact that Mills & Boon would bother publishing an 'offensive' novel is a credit to the firm's commitment to its authors' craft. At the conclusion of *Happy Return*, Madeline snares a kind and wealthy American as her next husband, while Susan struggles to make her (not yet consummated) marriage to Neil a success:

Susan found herself lying awake thinking about Madeline Egerton. She was not anything Susan wanted to be, except a woman who had made her husband happy. She was vain, deceitful, immoral, but—she had made her husband happy. Susan wondered what stiffness in herself, what inexperience, or inhibitions, prevented her from giving way to her love for Neil. Was it only that she had been brought up to expect that romantic love in both of them must come into existence first? She had supposed that she knew better.

Susan and Neil pledge to be husband and wife, and remain 'faithful, trusting and affectionate to the end of their days'.

Not surprisingly, Irish Mills & Boon authors such as Jean Herbert were smarter in avoiding potential disaster. In 1956 Herbert, a university lecturer and member of Irish PEN, wrote to her agent, Juliet O'Hea of Curtis Brown, to reassure Boon on his query concerning *Dangerous Valley*, and the 'hero's scoundrel of a brother' who smuggles weapons to the Middle East. 'I never thought of touching at all on Arab/Jewish relationships,' Herbert insisted. 'The only value of any situation in a work of this kind is as a peg on which to hang a romance. The question of Israel <u>vis-a-vis</u> her neighbours is one I would wish to keep off, not least because a good friend of mine, whose library in Dublin is one of the best of the Mills and Boon "shop windows" here, is herself of Jewish origin.'

Novels with a religious background were popular in Catholic countries like Ireland, so long as Christianity was presented with respect. *Craddock's Kingdom*, for example, is filled with Christian teachings and moral advice dispensed by the hero, clergyman Alan Maitland, who sets out to rid his parish of moral decay and corruption. 'Without Christ, no life is worth living, no job is worth doing, no so-called amusement is worthwhile,' he preaches. Consider the ending to this novel, where the once-bitter Pamela has now married the new vicar. He has persuaded her to forgive her jilted suitor, who ran her down with a car:

> To follow Christ Who said: 'Father, forgive them, for they know not what they do', was the only life worth living, the only security, the only certainty in this changing and often harsh world of ours . . .
>
> When the congregation stood to sing the closing hymn, 'The earth shall be filled with the glory of God', her eyes met her husband's, and it was as though their hands and hearts touched and were linked together in 'one increasing purpose'.

Significantly, when Alan Boon passed on some positive fan mail to Jan Tempest in 1958, he added a caveat: 'There is no doubt that stories like . . . CRADDOCK'S KINGDOM do appeal especially to some readers, but it is also a fact that there are other readers who are not so happy about them. We think it is a good thing to publish a Jan Tempest story of this type occasionally, but not to concentrate on it exclusively.' In her reply, Tempest agreed, 'It is not to everyone's taste.'

Throughout the 1950s Alan Boon and Joan Bryant erred on the side of caution in analysing every manuscript for potential problems, screening for taboos of one sort or another. The Doctor-Nurse plotline, possibly the most successful type of Mills & Boon romance in the 1950s, was fraught with potential problems. Medical details and situations, no matter how minor, had to be carefully checked. On *Bid Me Love You* by Valerie K. Nelson (1956), for example, Mills & Boon inquired, 'Virginia flings herself on her knees by Andrew's bed and proceeds to talk to him for a considerable time.

Hospital beds are very high and kneeling by them is not a good way to establish communication with a patient.' The scene was removed.

Despite the authors' repeated insistences that these hospital romances have a harder, realistic edge, nothing could interfere with the happy ending, and illness was often avoided as a plot device. In 1958 'Joan Blair' (a collaboration of two authors, Anne Pedlar and Helen Rees) and Alan Boon came into conflict over a work-in-progress, initially titled *I'll Never Marry*. Wisely, Pedlar and Rees (whose 1937 debut, *Sister of Nelson Ward*, was one of Mills & Boon's first Doctor-Nurse novels) were not risk-takers. Pedlar presented their plot idea to Boon:

> One of the ingredients is the heroine's determination that, because of her family history, she will, in fact, never allow herself to become engaged to be married. This resolution has been strengthened by the tragedy of a disastrous car crash in which both her parents were killed, and her only sister, Lorraine, very seriously injured. Jennifer feels that now she and Lorraine are alone in the world, she must put Lorraine before any question of her own personal happiness.
>
> There are, as far as we can make out, two possibilities in the way of illness which could be considered a barrier to marriage: melancholia, or some form of mental instability in the mother's family, or the rare disease called haemophilia, which is carried by the women but is taken by the men, whose blood will not clot.
>
> My own feeling is that mental instability is much the more effective barrier, but it does occur to me that you might prefer the rarer disease, because of the sort of hoodoo there used to be about mentioning insanity. Would you, therefore, prefer us to avoid the mental trouble and use the haemophilia, to which there can surely be no objection from public prejudice?
>
> Of course, after nearly wrecking her life and that of the men she loves, the heroine discovers that she is no blood relation, but that she was adopted as a baby. Good friends come to the rescue with the offer to take care of Lorraine, and all ends as it should.

In his reply, Boon could barely contain his horror, but replied in his characteristic diplomatic manner: 'We feel not too happy about either of the barriers you mention for the heroine not marrying. In an escapist form of fiction there could be no danger of a gloomy note creeping in, but we do not doubt that you will be well aware of the possibility.' He continued:

> Is it absolutely necessary that these are the only two possible barriers? Would an unhappy love affair of the heroine, or some memory, not be strong enough? We would like you to give this your careful thought as to whether some other barrier could not be used.

The question has been raised as to whether with a family history of mental instability the family would be permitted to make an adoption. Perhaps in these circumstances haemophilia would be the alternative, but if you decide to use this we know that you will do it as carefully as possible in view of the type of novel you are writing.

The duo admitted 'Joan Blair' never thought about the marriage angle: 'The mental instability factor must now be considered out. The point that no family with such a record would be allowed to adopt had not occurred to us. But it is certainly a good one.' Pedlar continued:

> I don't think that the haemophilia complication need cast a gloom over the story if we're careful. Lorraine is very much in the background, and even for her, things turn out pretty well. We could, if necessary, find another barrier, I think, to separate the two young people, but we rather liked the twist by which it was circumvented by adoption. I should think that there could be no objection to adoption because of such an obscure blood condition, don't you?

Within months, the novel was finished. 'I know you'll be pleased to hear that we have taken your suggestion and eliminated all inherited insanity or haemophilia from it, using the emotional situation resulting from a car crash for which the heroine thought herself to be responsible instead,' Pedlar wrote. 'We think it is really much better, and makes the medical complications unnecessary.' Boon was pleased, and the title was changed to the more positive *Lonely No Longer*.

Since marriage was a sacred ceremony (at least to Mills & Boon and its readers), it had to be held in a church, although no denomination could be mentioned. Elopements and registry office marriages were forbidden. Phyllis Matthewman tried to fight this aversion to registry offices in *Imitation Marriage* (1952), as she complained to Alan Boon:

> I said that Val came out of the registrar's. This has been altered to 'unfashionable little church'. Well, I am sorry but this just will not do. The marriage was an entirely formal one. Val would certainly not have consented to a church marriage because she would not swear to love honour and obey the man she was marrying. She would not, in fact, have taken a religious vow instead of merely a civil declaration. Larry, whose only wish was to marry her with as little publicity as possible, would certainly have chosen a register office. Any marriage in a church would be more public, something highly undesirable in the particular circumstances. I have therefore altered this back again.

But Matthewman lost her battle; in the published book, 'Val came out of the comparative gloom of the unfashionable little church into the clear, pale sunshine of late December.' Similarly, in 1955 Alex Stuart came under fire for suggesting a registry office marriage *and* a mixed marriage in *Gay Cavalier*. In her initial draft, the secondary characters Sean (who is Catholic) and Penelope (a wealthy Protestant heiress) decide to elope to escape the objections of Penelope's parents. 'The mixed marriage problem is one I am very conscious of when I read the story, as I am of Ulster origin but have a lot of Catholic friends,' Joan Bryant told Stuart. 'It is noticeable that in all the discussions between them, neither alludes to the fact that the other is in love with a heathen.' Stuart, in her reply, admitted she 'was skating on thin ice here' (and noted she wrote *Gay Cavalier* for serialization in *Woman's Illustrated*, edited by 'an R.C. editor,' R. J. O'Connell). She was happy to revise, cutting mention of the registrar, and having the wedding in church ('denomination unspecified . . . leaving the R.C. reader to draw her own conclusions, and the C of E likewise'). 'My sole aim is to keep out of trouble in these matters: I hold no strong views,' Stuart concluded. In the novel, Sean and Penelope are married in St Wilfred's, a small but 'very quiet and peaceful' church, by a 'priest'.

The close attention of Alan Boon, Joan Bryant, and their assorted readers to detail in editing manuscripts was astonishing, and often bordered on the ludicrous. Nothing was sacred, and Mills & Boon could never be too careful. Here Bryant especially brought to bear her scientist's mind and Cambridge training, in the quest for a libel-free, logical manuscript. Mills & Boon also relied on outside freelance editors such as 'Miss Wood' of Burnley, described as the 'North Country reader'.

Judging from the volume of correspondence in the Mills & Boon archive, the firm, like most publishers, took the greatest pains to change names and settings so as to avoid any potential libel action. The obsessive attention to detail was always regarded as essential. For example, in *The Half-way House* by Winifred Mantle (1956), Joan Bryant altered the surname of Nurse Peggy Downes to 'one that does not appear in the Register of Nurses. Basically of course Peggy is really rather a nice person, and by the end of the story I had grown very fond of her, but in her first few appearances she is a bit silly and tiresome, and it seemed wiser to reduce the chances of identification.' And so to uphold the esteem of the nursing profession.

Sometimes names were changed to prevent a book becoming too dated, and avoid a costly revision if the title were reprinted. In 1951 Alan Boon asked Leonora Starr (Dorothy Rivers, wife of the Mayor of Southwold, Suffolk) about *The Wings of Youth*: 'On page 58 there is mention of Gary Cooper and Noel Coward. This of course is liable to date the book at some indefinite date in the future . . . We are sure THE WINGS OF YOUTH will be read for many years to come.' But in 1950 Boon and Barbara Stanton locked horns on changing names in *Gone is the Thrill*. 'It seems far better (and with-out any possible danger) to write of a character, "She longed to dress and act like Vivien Leigh, to own a Rolls, to stay at the Ritz" than to substitute "a famous actress", "a luxury car" and "a West End Hotel",' Stanton wrote. In his reply, Boon admitted 'we are far less despotic now than we were with Charles Boon', but stood firm:

> We should wish to leave the Rolls and Ritz in, but the question of Vivien Leigh would be an interesting point. The Rolls and Ritz will probably endure for ever, but Miss Leigh, more be the pity, in the nature of things may not do so, and this might date the book in years to come if there were a question of reprinting it. However, as I have said, it is an open question.[9]

Although Mills & Boon's caution with names can seem silly, it has paid off on several occasions. In 1955 the firm's worst fears were realized with Anne Weale (Jay Blakeney) and her debut novel, *Winter is Past*. As the novel was being serialized (prior to publication) in *Woman's Own* (under the title, 'The Heart In Torment'), one of Blakeney's fellow journalists at the *Yorkshire Evening Press*, Bill Lang, took notice, and offence, to a character in the story called Captain Bill Lang. The real Bill Lang wrote to Mills & Boon:

> I realise that this is a well-written story, but I had no inkling whatsoever that Mrs. Blakeney was going to use my name. Her excuse was that she introduced the name before she ever knew me, but in view of the fact that she was checking it off in the office one Saturday afternoon while I was there (although I knew nothing of my name being in the story) she had ample opportunity to make a correction. This has caused both my wife and myself great distress, and I have no intention of being lam-pooned at the office and in York, where of course there are scores of readers of Mills and Boon.

While Lang insisted that a correction be made in the book proofs, he added his hope that 'this will not prejudice you against any future work which Mrs. Jay Blakeney may submit. We do not wish to spoil her literary career.' Needless to say, Weale was horrified, and pleaded her innocence to Alan Boon: 'The description of this character bears no resemblance whatever to Mr. Lang but although I have explained that the name was used quite acci-dentally he insists it was a deliberate "dig" at him and refuses to be placated . . . Unfortunately the rest of the staff seem to find his attitude amusing and tend to "rag" him about it. Naturally this fans his wrath.'

In the end, Boon changed the character's name in the published book to Captain Harry Bax, but not before having to answer a request from *Woman's Own* that Weale describe the character and the real man to ensure that there was no coincidence. She complied:

Mr. Lang has never been in the Army. He is of slight physique and has neither ginger hair nor a moustache. His complexion is pale and even his worst enemy could not deserve to describe him as 'a trifle stupid-looking' as he has a thin, rather sensitive face. His wife's name is Mary and she has never been an actress nor does she use heavy make-up or have a marked disdainful manner.

Boon wrote to Lang that, following careful examination, 'there is no resemblance, except the name, between "Captain Bill Lang" of THE HEART IN TORMENT and your good self', but 'in view of your special request', Mills & Boon would change it. A rather sheepish Lang replied:

> Please don't think I have been taking a high-handed attitude in this matter. The point I have made all along, and which my solicitor continues to make to 'Woman's Own' is that I work in the same office as the authoress, and in my view, the coincidence of names is a little too much. I am very grateful to you for this settlement, which is quite satisfactory to me.

The Weale experience left Mills & Boon shaken, and even more determined to check manuscripts carefully. In 1956, when Joan Bryant asked Phyllis Matthewman to change the name of a disagreeable character in *Safari With Wings*, she explained why: 'Mr. Alan Boon is a bit worried about the disagreeable character, Dave Rankin. Could you just confirm that the name does not belong to anyone you know, in or out of an airline? Sorry to worry you with this, but a quite experienced author got us into a jam recently by using an acquaintance's name in this way, so we're all a bit nervous at the moment.'

Apart from proper names, situations and facts were checked carefully. In 1958 Bryant questioned Marjorie Lewty about her debut novel, *Never Call it Loving*. 'Are you sure that tea is grown in Nyasaland?' Bryant asked. 'I've no doubt it is climatically possible, but I'm not conscious of having ever drunk African tea or seen it advertised . . . I know it seems utterly trivial, but it is just the sort of thing that, if it *is* wrong, readers tend to pick on.' Yes indeed, Lewty replied, her husband's nephew managed a tea estate there: 'I certainly don't think the point trivial. Ever since I began writing for magazines I've tried to check every little point. I've always understood that readers will go to no end of trouble to draw attention to anything incorrect.'

Character actions, major and minor, were subject to close scrutiny. In 1959 Mills & Boon offered a rare suggestion to Lilian Warren on her latest Rosalind Brett novel. 'In Chapter 1, Lisa arrives off the plane in a brown suit and does not change for dinner—surely, after a long trip?' In 1955 Bryant presented a laundry list of problems with Matthewman's *The Beckoning House*, including,

p. 5—Roger's loss of memory. No quarrel with this in itself, but later in the book we have Keith losing his memory too. Somehow, though I can't justify it logically, two amnesias seem to me excessive.

p. 233—Gerry says he has asked Julie to keep the news of the broken engagement to herself. Isn't this inconsistent with his having sent an announcement to the newspapers?

Matthewman agreed to remove Roger's amnesia, despite the damage to the plot ('I doubt if the reader will question the fact that he apparently didn't bother about being born an English child and being brought up American. Anyway, we can risk it.'), but she resisted the other change: 'He didn't want Julie to talk to Coralie about the broken engagement. Coralie might not notice the announcement in the papers.'

Authors often challenged Mills & Boon's editorial changes, but the firm won most of its battles. In 1950 Barbara Stanton complained about Mills & Boon's editorial readers, who 'naturally tend to over-caution since they get the kicks if allowing anything libellous or suggestive to slip through'. While Stanton (in reality John Hunt and a female partner) appreciated that 'all Mills & Boon novels must be wholesome in tone', he insisted:

> Surely in 1950 an occasional 'Blast!' or even 'Damn!' under provocation is permissible even from the nicest of girls! Yet, in the proof of NEVER STOP DREAMING when the heroine at one stage 'let out a heart-felt "Blast!"' this had been changed by your reader to 'uttered an oath', which, surely, sounds more rather than less reprehensible.

Needless to say, the 'expletives' remained expunged.[10]

Chapter 9
Women's Magazines: The Outside Editors

The Johnsonian formula for glamorous unapproachability is worked out along the following lines: the hero should not be too kind and easy going. There should be a feeling of tension, the heroine not knowing whether she is pleasing him or not. The contrast of a tender scene is better secured if it is contrasted with a certain coldness. The hero should not show too much personal interest in the heroine early in the story, and it must not be made palpable that he is falling for the heroine.

Alan Boon to Jean MacLeod, 1952

I wish you would just tell me, from the Johnson etc. point of view, how far one can go with a) drinking, b) swearing, etc. I gather she deletes My God, and To Hell with it. It seems a bit odd that she can't stand that, and yet she wants it all sexed up . . . I specially want to know about drinking because I plan to let Bruce take Trudi to a country pub for a quick one in Chapter 2. Do Johnson women go to pubs? I always think 'country inn' sounds so ingenuous, especially if they go for <u>supper</u>, even if it's bread and cheese and a gallon of wallop . . . we can always make it a milk bar or something when we approach Johnson. (<u>Not</u> that I can quite see a milk bar in the middle of Middleton Woods — but there, maybe an itinerant one.)

Olive Norton to Alan Boon, 1957

WHEN he rejoined the family firm after the Second World War, Alan Boon freely admitted, 'I didn't know a great deal about romantic fiction. I thought that most of the successful romance authors seemed to be in women's magazines. So, if I got hold of these authors, we should be O.K.' How right he was. For Boon's linking of his firm with *Woman's Weekly* and other popular magazines represents a turning point in the development of Mills & Boon, the romantic novel, and editorial policy. From their offices in Fleet Street or as far north as Dundee, the editors of women's magazines became Mills & Boon's unofficial outside readers, an extension of the firm's editorial department. Indeed, much of what Boon learned as an editor (revealed in the last chapter) was gleaned from his conversations with the magazines.

The women's weekly magazines in Britain emerged from the war with an enhanced readership and circulation. As such, they were an excellent shop window for Mills & Boon authors (whose serials appeared weekly) as well as a source for new authors. It was essential for Mills & Boon to maintain its existing relationship with the magazines, given the financial rewards. As its library markets were increasingly threatened during the 1950s, Mills & Boon needed the magazines to bolster readers, and keep its fiction lively and up-to-date. Mills & Boon's hope was that readers, attracted by a weekly serial, would proceed to borrow or buy the book, which evidence shows they did. The association between book and magazine was further enhanced by the magazines' use of illustrators and artists, who subsequently designed dust jackets for Mills & Boon.

Because the magazine editors understood Mills & Boon's dependence, they did not hesitate to demand changes and dictate policy. They acted from a position of strength, given the high fees (up to £1,000) they could pay for a serial, and wielded their blue pencils freely. In most cases, Alan Boon respected their advice, based on proven sales experience. They could craft a serial that sold, and hence a book that sold. Boon was in good hands. The symbiosis worked, and, with few exceptions, Mills & Boon and the magazines served the needs of the same audience. 'Serials speeded up our own techniques,' Alan Boon said. 'The hero and the heroine met more quickly.'

But the relationship between Mills & Boon and the women's magazines, though mutually beneficial, was never easy. Whereas Alan Boon perfected the art of diplomacy and charm in coaxing his authors to make revisions or recast the direction of a plot, the magazine editors could be brutal. Some editors, including Winifred Johnson of *Woman's Weekly* and Mary Grieve of *Woman*, had strong views of relationships and morality which were starting to be decidedly old-fashioned at the end of the 1950s. Boon often found himself as referee in a shouting match between magazine editor, author, and (sometimes) agent. To his credit, Boon defended his authors vigorously, and often two versions of a novel were published: the serial form for the magazine, and the original manuscript for the library market.

⚓

Like Mills & Boon, the editors of weekly women's magazines respected their readers, and nurtured contact to maintain their circulations. According to James Drawbell, who achieved legendary status in the industry as editor of *Woman's Own* (and who later published three novels with Mills & Boon), the reader was the only boss in publishing: 'You have to know who your reader is, be identified with him, know how to attract and hold him in bondage to the almost unbreakable habit (and habit is everything) of buying your product.'[1] Editors could take advice from readers, but could also use reader loyalty (and gullibility) to make suggestions and promulgate values and attitudes. They were respected as 'gatekeepers of the female world'.[2]

Three magazines dominated the market during the decade. *Woman*, published by Odhams, was the largest, with a weekly circulation of 2.2 million in 1950, rising to 3.2 million in 1959. With readership estimated at three people per copy, up to 10 million women were reading *Woman* every week in 1959. *Woman's Own*, published by Newnes, was second, at 1.8 million in 1950 and 2.4 million in 1959; and the Amalgamated Press's *Woman's Weekly*, third, hovering between 1.6 and 1.8 million throughout the decade. Another Amalgamated Press title, *Woman's Illustrated*, sold around 500,000 copies per week. On a smaller scale, D. C. Thomson (and its affiliate, John Leng) published two weekly magazines which had a loyal following in Scotland and northern England: *My Weekly* and the *People's Friend*; both sold around 200,000 copies per week.

Although Mills & Boon sold serial rights of coming novels to all of these titles throughout the decade, it negotiated most often with *Woman's Weekly*. Of all the weeklies, *Woman's Weekly* had the best reputation for 'quality' fiction, and attracted readers from the same social groups as Mills & Boon novels. Cynthia White has noted how the mainstays of *Woman's Weekly* were knitting and fiction, and 'their continuing reinforcement of the old values. They are strong on happy memories, humorous real-life experiences, warmth and companionship' Mothers and daughters read *Woman's Weekly*, which maintained an almost 'compulsive following ... which has withstood changes in women's lifestyles and life-chances'.[3] Indeed, Mary Grieve respected *Woman's Weekly* for transcending its drab letterpress appearance: 'With none of the benefits of modern production *Woman's Weekly* made so close a connection with the readership that it held its own by the strength of this communication, and against all the expertise, promotion and glamour of the big publications.'[4]

Alan Boon negotiated directly with the editors or fiction editors of the magazines. Often a manuscript was shopped around title to title, until it found a serial berth. Book publication followed a month or two after the multi-week serial ended its run. Initially, the serial and book versions had different titles, for obvious reasons, but reader ire ended this practice.[5] Wherever possible, Mills & Boon enlisted the illustrator for the serial to prepare the dust jacket for the novel. Colin Orme and Jack Faulks, for example, worked for *Woman's Weekly* as well as Mills & Boon.

Mills & Boon authors visited London regularly to see the magazine editors as often as to consult Alan Boon. Since the authors were under contract to Mills & Boon, correspondence from the magazine editors was funnelled through Alan Boon, or through the agent if the author had one. The effort was certainly worth while.[6] In 1951, for example, *Woman's Weekly* offered to renew serial options for three Mills & Boon authors: Eleanor Farnes (£500 for the first serial; £550 each the for next three), and Marjorie Moore, and Sara Seale (£550 each). Mills & Boon usually kept 10 per cent of these payments, which were a windfall to the author. Sara Seale, for example, earned £1,200 a year for ten years from two serial options. Anne Weale recalled that in 1958, her third year as a Mills & Boon author, she earned £811 from Mills & Boon (representing advances on two books, and royalty payments), but £552 in serialization payments from *Woman's Illustrated*. 'At that time a thousand a year was most young achievers' target income, and to my delight I'd exceeded that with spare-time writing,' she said. 'It was time to retire from journalism and start a family.'

To Mills & Boon, like other fiction publishers, serial contracts provided cash flow, free publicity, and increased book sales. 'If a serial had been especially successful, the readers would write in and say, "Can I have the book?"' Alan Boon recalled. 'In a way it was one of our forms of research. The readers who write in and say, "I really like this, which I read in," etc.' Fan mail confirms this. In 1957, for example, Sara Seale received a long letter from Miss Elsie I. Alexander of Preston, a fan and magazine reader:

> As I am lame—I'm always glad that reading doesn't need legs! ... I do want to tell you how I simply <u>love</u> your books. I want to thank you for them and to ask you please to go on writing ... It was lovely to open 'Woman & Home' and find a new Sara Seale serial running in it—I'm <u>so</u> enjoying it—I can hardly wait each month and if 'I Know My Love' is on sale by next Christmas, I shall have it.

Although the majority of Mills & Boon readers borrowed rather than purchased their novels, an increasing number asked to buy copies of favourite books, as a keepsake for their home libraries. In 1958 Alex Stuart reported that she received fan mail, 'of the type usually sent to Elvis Prestly [*sic*],' from a teenage reader of *Woman's Day*, who 'begs for "more stories like Governor's Daughters" because they're different'. In 1960 Miss Wendy Robson, 16, of Belfast wrote to Jean MacLeod about *The White Cockade*, her historical novel about Bonnie Prince Charlie. 'When I read your book when it was being serialized I was so excited over it that my family was nearly driven mad on the day before the magazine came out. Your book made the entire period come alive for me ... I bought the "White Cockade" recently because I liked it so much.'

It comes as no surprise, therefore, that Alan Boon encouraged his authors to write in as 'serial-genic' a fashion as possible, to achieve the 'biggest box office' for their work. Betty Beaty, who started as a serial writer for *Woman's Weekly*, noted that book chapters were like serial installments. 'You've got to have a "hook" at the end,' she explained. 'Imagine a book is a train. Each of the carriages has to be connected to the other.' It was also important to maintain suspense, so the reader would return week after week. The larger magazines, such as *Woman*, would run a serial over six weeks; Woman's Weekly could take up to twelve. 'The serial writer's principal problem is to keep the heroine and the hero apart for the length of the book,' Boon advised his authors. 'One of the most usual ways of doing this is to establish "conflict" between the heroine and hero, rather like a boxing match where there is a great deal of sparring, with an occasional clinch (quickly broken up), which proceeds to the final knock-out.' Of this, Jean MacLeod lamented, 'It's awful trying to keep two people apart for 258 pages, let me tell you.' To Sara Seale in 1959, who was writing a serial for *Woman's Illustrated*, Boon reminded her that tension was essential for a good serial: 'No doubt as you continue you will bear in mind the possibility of using the bitch vis a vis the heroine to stir up tension—at which you are a past mistress.'

In case after case, magazine serialization influenced Mills & Boon's editorial decisions, and usually for the better. In 1961 Boon contacted Hilary Wilde in South Africa, regarding her new novel, *Red As A Rose*. Although he liked it very much, he offered a suggestion:

> to give it as wide a serial chance here as possible, it would be advisable to take out the part which deals with the fact that the hero and his mother are not on loving terms. I think some of the editors here would feel that this would strike a jarring note from the point of view of some of their readers. From our point of view as a novel, we should not mind; but if it is at all possible we should like you to deal with this matter, to give the work every possible chance.

And so Wilde did, in a single passage: 'Kit had returned with the chairs. He grinned as he sat down, and Elinor saw, with something of a shock, how very much he loved his mother.'

In the same year, Boon wrote with advice to Joyce Dingwell in Australia. Dingwell's novels were not being picked up by the magazines, so Boon asked a magazine editor for help:

> I think it is always valuable to know what is in the mind of the editor when you are writing a prospective serial, so I think you would like me to be quite frank as to her opinion. She said she thought there was what she called a masochistic element in the hero–heroine relationship— that the hero was too unrelievedly tough and rude, and he did not, in general, show enough kindness. I hasten to say in this respect that this is the editor's opinion, and that your work has always been very popular with our readers; that we have been quite satisfied with them as they have come to us, but that in the event of your trying to get into this ser-

ial market it might be advisable to see whether you can do anything to answer this criticism.

'This was the editorial feeling,' Boon concluded.

The popularity of the women's magazines in Britain and the demand for quality fiction among competing titles prompted the publication of 'how-to' books and articles. In 1960 Anne Britton and Marion Collin published *Romantic Fiction: The New Writers' Guide*, which included several chapters on writing serial fiction. Britton was fiction editor of *Woman's Own* and *My Home*, and later wrote for Mills & Boon as 'Jan Anderson'. 'It is absolutely imperative that authors realise from the outset that in dealing with romance you are handling a quality or a state of mind which enters the lives of the majority of people in some form of another,' Britton and Collin wrote. However, they added, there were certain taboos to avoid:

- Drunkenness. 'Certainly the heroine is never "tipsy" and rarely does the hero spend his time propping up bars.'
- Deformity. 'Never a heroine with one leg. No one will buy *that* story.'
- Divorce. 'This offends so many readers and especially Eire, which could mean the loss of several thousand copies.'[7]
- Illegitimate children. 'Never.'
- Mixed race and colour bar. 'To make a mixed marriage the central situation in a story is to invite a definite rejection at the present time.'

'Authors may protest that all these tragedies are happening in the modern world at this very moment, but this cannot alter the fact that the women's magazines are aiming for the highest possible circulation, that is to appeal to as many readers as possible,' the manual continued. 'They are designed to entertain. Therefore they must respect the prejudices existing in the minds of large sections of the reading public, and avoid any subject which might make somebody, somewhere, discontinue her subscription.' Unsurprisingly Mills & Boon offered the same advice to its authors.[8]

By far the strongest editorial presence of the decade was Winifred 'Biddy' Johnson, editor of *Woman's Weekly* and recognized by Alan Boon as having a major influence on the genre. Johnson began her career on another Amalgamated Press title, *Forget-Me-Not*, and edited *Woman's Weekly* for over twenty years before she retired in 1961 at the age of 69. 'The dominant note throughout is usefulness,' Johnson told her troops. 'Our one desire is to please the average woman.'[9]

Johnson cast a long shadow on romantic fiction. She may not have invented the genre, but she did help to perfect and popularize it. As fiction editor of a number of best-selling weekly magazines, she was in a powerful position. She recommended serial purchases for other Amalgamated Press titles, including *Woman and Home*, *My Home*, *Woman's Illustrated*, *Home*, *Home Chat*, and *The Oracle*.[10] Her range was vast: from the passionate, sexy novels of Lillian Warren ('Rosalind Brett,' *et al*) to the more mundane, domesticated fiction written by Mary Burchell, and Johnson's favourite mainstays, the Doctor-Nurse romances.

Woman's Weekly and Mills & Boon 'were sort of brother and sister at this time,' Alan Boon said. 'All their serials usually were published by ourselves.' In 1953, for example, Mills & Boon serials were scheduled to begin running on 17 July (by Esther Wyndham); 28 August (Sara Seale); 11 September and 25 September (both Kathryn Blair); 9 October (two: Eleanor Farnes and Rosalind Brett); and 23 October (Alex Stuart's debut, *The Captain's Table*). Throughout 1959 Mills & Boon had two serials running concurrently in *Woman's Weekly*, including three by Brett, and one each from Jane Fraser (the pen-name of Rosamund Pilcher), Joyce Dingwell, Wyndham, and Iris Bromidge. (Iris Danbury)

'Miss Johnson wanted first choice of everything,' Alan Boon recalled. 'She had the magic touch. She had a good idea of what appealed to the public, which was always a strong romance, with never any suggestion of sex. Her idea was to have everything very cosy indeed, without any jarring. The characters wouldn't speak with an accent.' She frowned, moreover, on swearing and drink, and 'the unhappy side of life. Miss Johnson would never have the word "cancer" in her serials.'[11]

But there were definite rules, which some authors found hard to swallow. 'Alan Boon encouraged his authors to write in a way which would please the formidable Miss Biddy Johnson,' Anne Weale recalled. 'Miss Johnson had arbitrary ideas about what her readers—mainly "housewives"—wanted, and the magazine's circulation proved she knew what she was talking about. She and the other editors of women's magazines made the rules and heroines' behaviour was usually several years behind what was happening in the real world.' Among these old-fashioned ideas: a girl couldn't call at a man's flat to deliver a parcel. Since Weale had earned a living since she was 17, she admitted she had no time for 'prissy' heroines. But Johnson, she claimed, was 'spot on about the conflict between the hero and heroine' as well as the ultimate goal of the story, to secure a husband.[12]

Esther Wyndham, who had ten serials published in *Woman's Weekly* and *Woman and Home* (including her best-seller, *Black Charles*) recalled Johnson as demanding and precise, insisting the hero and heroine conform to her own romantic formula:

> Lady Diana Spencer would never have qualified as a Johnson Heroine, except that she was a virgin and loved children, for she was far too beautiful, too rich, and had too easy a life . . . The spirited heroine must not

only have a wonderful way with children and old people but some previous tragedy or hardship in her life. And, of course, she had to work hard for her living. It was her character rather than her looks that attracted; she became beautiful only at rare moments, preferably when the hero was looking at her without her knowing it. Naturally, she became permanently beautiful at the end when irradiated with requited love.

The Johnsonian Hero, Wyndham added, had to be strong, brave, 'frantically busy' and rich, 'best if he was self-made'. Prince Charles would have passed muster: 'In spite of being a prince he worked hard, had had rumoured involvements with other girls, and had not declared himself until the last instalment; however, there was a quality of mystery lacking in him.'[13]

Johnson was a demanding editor who often called for several rewrites. But not all authors had difficulty with her. Betty Beaty recalled fondly her contacts and meetings, and said Johnson was generous in her praise when she liked a serial. 'I went up to London several times and had tea in her office,' Beaty said. 'She always sent for a plate of delicious Fuller's cakes to accompany the tea. She also took me out to lunch once or twice—to Fortnum and Mason's because she said she found waiters somewhat overpowering and much preferred the waitresses. She introduced me to champagne cocktails.' Johnson tried to persuade Beaty to write more often. 'She upped my fee to unprecedented levels for that time, suggested I get someone to look after the girls and concentrate on writing, saying that if I did I would be a very rich woman,' she said 'I didn't, of course. David was doing very well, translated world-wide, and we preferred to go on as we were.' The most Beaty ever wrote, under pressure from Johnson, was two serials in one year.

To Biddy Johnson, the hero was the most important character in any romantic serial. 'It was generally accepted that Miss Johnson should fall in love with the hero,' Beaty recalled. 'She always insisted that heroes be very tall. In one serial, when I described the secondary hero as tall, she inserted in parenthesis after my description, "but not so tall as Captain Wainright", who was the hero.' A dash of French or Italian blood was also preferred. Overall, Johnson's views fit in well with the Alphaman concept. 'The hero is the strong but basically kind man that most women want to meet, no matter how independent they might be,' Beaty said. 'However the man has to have real strength, not to be the snarling beast that is sometimes portrayed.'

Johnson's editorial policy towards the hero was known in the trade as 'glamorous unapproachability'. In other words, the hero had to be exceedingly handsome, but 'five times larger than life' and aloof—so much so, that he appeared initially out of reach to the wayward heroine, and therefore the reader. When Jean MacLeod ran into some difficulty with her second *Woman's Weekly* serial, *Cost Price*, in 1952, Boon gave a lesson on Johnson's theory:

> Her basic formula in my opinion is that the heroine should not know whether she is pleasing the hero, although generally speaking it is her object to do so. The reader also should not know whether the hero is getting interested in the heroine. The Johnsonian formula for glamorous unapproachability is worked out along the following lines: the hero should not be too kind and easy going. There should be a feeling of tension, the heroine not knowing whether she is pleasing him or not. The contrast of a tender scene is better secured if it is contrasted with a certain coldness. The hero should not show too much personal interest in the heroine early in the story, and it must not be made palpable that he is falling for the heroine. The hero–heroine relationship might be considered a little unorthodox for this quarter, especially as, when the story develops, the hero is patently very human and considers bailing out to Australia when he gets a bit tired of things. The average glamorous unapproachable hero in this quarter always calls the tune and never seems to be at a loss.

Similarly, in 1950 Johnson said she liked 'very much indeed' the Eleanor Farnes novel, *The Golden Peaks*, except for one fault which in her opinion, could easily be put right:

> The hero Kurt is too kind and easy-going all the way through. There should be a feeling of tension — the heroine not knowing whether she is pleasing him or not. (In passing, I think it would be better for her to continue calling him Monsieur St Pierre, rather than Kurt — and so should Anneliese. It makes him so easy otherwise and he becomes too approachable. This slight alteration we can make ourselves.) I should also like our author to run through these chapters toning down the friendliness somewhat. You get the contrast of a tender scene better if it is contrasted with a certain coldness. For this reason I would like very much a scene written in, early on, where our heroine makes a gaffe and St. Pierre is severe about it. All the rest is quite charming and the story is delightful — but I do think, as I say, that Pierre needs a certain glamorous unapproachability.

Farnes complied, almost to the letter. In *The Golden Peaks* the heroine, Celia Dorrelson, travels to Switzerland with her young niece for a rest-cure. They stay at a mountain hotel owned by Monsieur St Pierre; his secretary is Anneliese. To 'eke out her foreign currency', Celia takes a job as a waitress in the hotel. Celia is constantly reprimanded by her boss for her behaviour — being too friendly and chatty with guests, for example ('You were acting as if you, too, were a guest. And that will not do.'), and often runs off in tears.

When a waiter knocks down Celia, and her arm is injured by broken dishes, the hero takes her aside and bandages the wound, 'with hands that were gentle in spite of their firmness'. When Celia won't stop crying, St Pierre shows his 'tender' side:

> He removed the cloth and the bowl, and put them aside. He came back to her, and standing a little behind her, put his hand on her shoulder, firmly, reassuringly. 'Now, now,' he said, 'don't do that.' His other hand offered a clean, white handkerchief, which she took gratefully, and held to her eyes. Suddenly, wearily, she felt at peace. Her shaking had stopped, her feeling of humiliation had drained away, and under the touch of his hand on her shoulder, she felt content.

Thereafter Celia is forever daydreaming about Monsieur ('to smell the smoke of his cigarette, even to feel it wafting in front of her face'), even though she has decided to settle for Geoffrey, a kindly Englishman. Only when St Pierre professes his love for Celia, rescuing her from atop a golden mountain peak, does she call him by his Christian name.

The Johnson heroes, moreover, reign supreme in the story and dominate the heroine, not vice versa. Esther Wyndham recalled that Johnson made her rewrite her first serial because the hero portrayed weakness. 'I had made the hero say that he was feeling ill in order to get away from a party,' Wyndham said. 'She wrote indignantly, "Who can have respect for a man who feels ill at a party?"' In 1953 Boon wrote to Jean MacLeod with bad news of *Nobody's Child*, which Johnson found 'not quite right for her papers'. The reason for the failure was MacLeod's weak hero, quite unlike the heroes in her past novels:

> In general I find that her [Johnson's] heroes usually command Fate and the ball bounces the right way for them. If we compare, say, Stuart of THE SILENT VALLEY with Grant and Charles, one feels that Stuart is not inconvenienced by Fate, but that Grant and Charles have their difficulties. In THE SILENT VALLEY it is poor Jane who does all the worrying, and in general this, I should say, is the Johnsonian formula, i.e. the hero is 'five times larger than life' and the heroine spends her time not knowing whether she is pleasing him or not. This of course is a very broad generalisation because there are spirited heroines as well as downtrodden heroines in the Johnsonian orbit. It does necessarily mean, however, that the novelist's scope tends to be diminished.

Indeed, Dr Stuart Hemingway in *The Silent Valley* is a true Alphaman unshaken by operating room drama; 'The impervious set of his jaw as she tied his mask only served to confirm her belief. It was like iron, the whole man cast in iron.' Similarly, when Johnson rejected Hilary Wilde's latest, *Red as a Rose*, in 1961, Boon surmised it was due to her change in heroes: 'When

I was talking to [Johnson] recently she told me that one of the things she liked about THE GREEN PARAKEETS was the De Gaulle-like character of the hero. It may be that the present hero may not appeal to her quite so much, as he does a great deal of drawling, and it is hard to imagine De Gaulle drawling!' In *The Green Parakeets* (1961), the hero, Henri Revoir, is half-English, half-French, like the heroine: 'He was very good-looking but there seemed not a single thing wrong in that perfect face ... smooth, sun-tanned skin with his perfectly even white teeth and straight nose.' He makes a grand entrance on horseback—'She knew instantly that it could only be "Himself", as the Islanders called the Seigneur, Henri Revoir':

> As Annette watched him, the man rode down towards the little house slowly. Her awe mounted as she saw him clearly, and she understood why so many people feared him. She even shivered a little at the thought of ever finding herself facing his anger. Yet how good-looking he was. Never in all her eighteen years had she ever seen such a handsome, impressive-looking man.

Throughout the novel, Henri is forever staring and 'looming'. At the end, Annette kisses him, and proclaims, 'I'm not afraid of you ... And I grew up the day I met you.'

Clearly, the romance between hero and heroine remained paramount. Betty Beaty, as one of Johnson's students, captured the glamorous unapproachability of the hero in *Amber Five* (1958), perhaps the best-known of her aeroplane romances. When stewardess Sally Matthews survives a crash, she professes her love to Captain Richard Sutherland, who replies, 'I've loved *you* longer':

> 'This ordering around so *brusquely*'—obediently she lifted her knife and fork—'that's why I never guessed that you ...'
>
> 'But that's how I'm made. That's me. And you love *me*. Don't forget that. And you're going to marry me. Don't forget that either! And a good husband does order his wife around and look after her. Because sometimes the two mean the same thing. And to *husband* is to *care* for.'
>
> And she had laughed, and touched his hand with hers. And that was the only reality—their two hands joined to one another.

In 1950 Sara Seale sent to Alan Boon revisions for her latest *Woman's Weekly* serial for, as she wrote, 'Miss Johnson wanted an added bunch of heart-wringing goo!!' The suggested insertion, 'on the third or fourth page from the end', in Seale's ragged handwriting, is revealing. The hero exclaims, 'Only don't wring my heart like this,' and the narrative proceeds:

> For the first time she was aware of the pain in his voice and of the warmth and protection which at last flowed from him unchecked. She was weak under the urgent touch of his hands and her resistance and her

pride ebbed away leaving her only a suppliant. Her hands groped blindly for his shoulders, met and clasped tightly behind his neck.

As far as the heroine was concerned, Johnsonian was careful to make her as 'realistic' as possible, to promote reader identification. The Johnsonian heroine was hard-working and independent. Beaty recalled that, in her novels, the heroine 'usually tended to have what they call in Yorkshire, gumption, and is not a swooning violet'. Johnson would not tolerate poor discipline or an 'unrealistic' atmosphere. In 1954 she criticized Sara Seale's latest serial draft, the tale of 17-year-old Tansy, the ward of the hero, Gavin:

> I do deprecate a heroine who does nothing but moon about. I think Gavin should have made it clear that he was taking Tansy into his home for three months while they think of what she can do for a living. Why should he support her—an able bodied young woman who should be learning to support herself? She is intelligent and should make it plain that she has every intention of training for something. Also I feel readers would like her better if she tried to do something useful when she was staying in the house.

In 1956 Johnson called Seale's latest, *Sister to Cinderella*, 'Such a sad waste of time . . . It is so entirely lacking in common-sense. How a shorthand typist could possibly afford to run a home and keep two other people, and a servant living in, on her salary is surely too miraculous to believe.' But reader identification also had its limits. In 1958 the heroine of Jean MacLeod's *The Gated Road* caused concern in serial circles. Alan Boon reported that R. J. O'Connell, editor of *Woman's Illustrated*, 'has said that THE GATED ROAD will not do for his paper, as he "is not happy about a crippled heroine"'. The other weeklies also rejected the serial, but eventually *Home Chat* purchased the rights. In this novel Jane Thornton, 'pieced together again' after a tragic accident, wonders, 'Is it going to be like this always? I'll never be able to run or walk quickly or—dance again?' Needless to say, she does.

What was perhaps Johnson's greatest (and most pervasive) contribution to romantic fiction was a plot situation nicknamed 'MINO'. In this case a man and woman could live together in a contrived but unconsummated marriage, for a variety of social or professional reasons. This was a 'Marriage In Name Only', or MINO. This created a potentially 'sexy' situation, as the reader waited anxiously for the moment when love would blossom and thaw the frost between the characters. As such, it broadened storyline possibilities within the acceptable moral line. According to Esther Wyndham, the Irish market convinced Johnson to remove the slightest hints of impropriety. MINO did that; situations outside of marriage did not:

In one story when my hero was in Washington with the heroine, his sec-retary, and I had allowed her to sleep in the sitting room of his hotel suite because all the hotels were full (a situation helpful to romance), Miss J. sent me a telegram, for I had gone abroad between instalments: 'Please make another effort to find Elizabeth a room of her own.'

One of the masters of MINO in popular romantic fiction was Lilian Warren, writing as Rosalind Brett. 'She really had sex in her books in the late forties, but she also had the qualities which Miss Johnson could see would make a good serial writer for *Woman's Weekly*,' Alan Boon recalled. The solu-tion: remove the unacceptable sexy situations from her books, through a MINO storyline. 'If you read *And No Regrets*, by Brett, the theme of the story was a trial marriage,' Boon explained. 'It may seem now rather innocuous, but it was quite bold in those days. The man and the girl agreed to go and live on an island somewhere for "X" time and then part, with no regrets.' Since Johnson could pay well, she persuaded Brett to rewrite the story, so that the couple were married before setting off. 'We published the MINO version of it ourselves, but not the original, because at that time our readers also would have objected.'

And No Regrets, first published in 1948, tells the story of Clare Meriden, an orphan, and Ross Brennan, a lonely coffee plantation manager in Nigeria. Clare regards him as a mysterious and arrogant stranger: tall and lean, with 'a hard, tanned face; there was a certain charm about it, and also the arro-gance of some one who had gone through life getting exactly what he wanted of it'. Ross senses Clare is 'mad to get away from this small, slow town for a while'. He desires companionship but not marriage, as 'a lifetime's a long time to spend with one woman.' Clare disagrees, so long as love is present:

> 'You're not in love with me, are you?' he demanded.
>
> Instinctively she hung on to her pride. 'I . . . don't think so.'
>
> 'Good. If you were, it would complicate matters. My suggestion is this—that we become husband and wife for eighteen months.'
>
> 'And when the eighteen months come to an end?'
>
> 'A clean cut, Clare, and no regrets.'
>
> She sat still and quiet, trying to take in what he was offering her. Travel at last, to a part of the world she could never hope to visit without a man. And marriage, too. With Ross.
>
> 'You're not in love with me either, are you?' she said with certainty.
>
> 'No, there's nothing soul-rending in what I feel for you. It's easy to imagine oneself in love with an attractive girl, but liking your looks and contradictions is a long way from death-defying love.'
>
> The hurt of those bald phrases. But in the silence that followed them,

her thoughts leapt into the future. Married to Ross, living alone with him in the bush, she might teach him to love and need her.

In Nigeria, Ross sets up a camp-bed for Clare in his bedroom — 'I don't want it all along the bush grapevine that my marriage is strictly a platonic one' — and they spend many so-called 'monastic' nights together. Chapter by chapter, in the heat of the moment, many kisses are stolen. Closer and closer the 'couple' is pushed to the brink:

> 'Have you got every step of your future planned, Ross?' she asked. 'Doesn't it ever include a proper marriage, or am I overstepping the boundary line in touching upon such a personal matter?'
>
> He put her a little way from him then, gripping her wrists with work-roughened fingers and treating her to an unsparing appraisal that drove heat to her cheeks. She saw the shimmer of angry fire beyond the flint of his eyes, and she thought his anger aroused by the substance of her question — until he said: 'That boundary line was laid for your protection, not mine. It's easier for a man to forget himself, and to forget afterwards what he had done in the heat of an aroused moment.'
>
> 'A moment that might easily have tied us together for life, is that it, Ross?'

When Clare falls ill with a raging fever and reveals her love for Ross in her delirium, it's all over: '"Take a long look at me," he smiled wryly and held her a little away from him. "I inhabit this body no longer. It has been taken over by a dark little slip of a thing . . . a rather beautiful slip of a thing, I might add." '[14]

Boon frequently recommended MINO storylines to Johnson, especially involving her favourite author, Sara Seale, who often had two serials running in *Woman's Weekly* each year.[15] In fact, her most popular novel, *The Gentle Prisoner* (heralded by *Woman and Home* as 'the romantic novel of the year' in 1949), had a MINO plot. In a play on *Beauty and the Beast*, the hero, Nicholas Penryn, is disfigured, living alone in a mansion: 'Nicholas, badly scarred, was convinced that no woman could ever feel anything but revulsion for him.' He 'buys' Shelley Wynthorpe from her father, to forgive his debts. Shelley, though 18, looks like a schoolgirl; she's had a sheltered Catholic convent upbringing. Penryn marries her and takes her home as a 'collector's piece', another gem in a house full of treasures, a gentle prisoner. Shelley eventually convinces him, 'If you love enough, there is no such thing as ugliness.' Similarly, *Wintersbride*, serialized in *Woman's Weekly* from November 1950 until March 1951, was another MINO effort by Seale. Adam Chantry, a dashing surgeon, rescues a waif, Miranda Clare, from a travelling circus. He's a widower with a young daughter and a house on Dartmoor ('Wintersbride'), complete with unfriendly staff (shades of *Rebecca*). To rescue Miranda and appease his loneliness, he agrees to marry her.

Over the course of several months in 1958, Johnson offered changes and suggestions to Seale on her latest MINO serial, *Lucy Lamb*. In this story, another variation on *Rebecca*, Lucy agrees to marry Dr Bartlemy Travers and live at his gloomy mansion, Polvane, surrounded by hostile servants. Travers does not love Lucy, but she has loved him since she was 14, when he rescued her from drowning. Lucy mothers his young son, Pierre, but Travers is inattentive and cruel, haunted by memories of his dead wife, Marcelle, who did drown. Against Seale's wishes, Johnson demanded a crucial change in Seale's original plot, in which the young son is killed accidentally while in Lucy's care, a tragedy which nearly destroys her marriage. 'We all hate the idea of the little boy dying,' Johnson told Alan Boon. 'It spoils the story and makes Lucy seem so inadequate. She should be able to bring father and son together.' In the changed ending, Pierre lives, but he and Lucy are lost in caves by the sea. Travers rescues them, but Lucy falls deathly ill and is delirious. In her usual, abrupt fashion, a busy Johnson offered Seale her notes on the ending—which Seale followed to the letter: 'The scene where he nurses her—and she must say she knows she will never be to him what his first wife was and he tells her briefly that the marriage was not a happy one,' Johnson wrote, to which she added, 'Finale'.[16]

Biddy Johnson kept a long list of subjects that were not permitted in serials during her tenure at the Amalgamated Press. In some respects, these represented personal preferences (editing was nothing if not personal), in others, a reflection of the largely middle-class readership. 'Miss Johnson set great store by readers' reaction, and I know that *Woman's Weekly* had a vast response,' Betty Beaty noted. '*Woman's Weekly* was thoroughly middle class. They were a little timid about offending or worrying—they said, readers sometimes think of this as a newspaper, and rely on this so much they accept it as being true. You mustn't have anything in that that worries them too much.'

Johnson preferred Doctor-Nurse romances, so long as they promoted the profession, and upheld doctors as the perfect heroes. In 1952 she informed Alan Boon that Jean MacLeod's *The Silent Valley*, a hospital story, 'has rung the bell' for *Woman's Weekly*, MacLeod's first serial success. But Johnson, as ever, demanded revisions, especially about 'the fatal operation':

> We decided that the fatal operation was too poignant. People simply could not bear it. We have given a good deal of thought to it and we feel it would be better to make the result of the operation itself successful. But let the Matron still reprimand Jane for negligence, and ask for her resignation. The Nursing Home cannot afford to have people who make careless mistakes.

MacLeod agreed, and Johnson expressed her gratitude to Boon: 'It was the greatest relief to be able to bypass that upsetting operation, and I am old-fashioned enough to feel it rather frightful to undermine one's faith in doctors.'

But here, as in many instances, two different versions of the same title were published, one for the magazine audience, the other in book form for Mills & Boon readers. In the novel version of *The Silent Valley*, published in 1953, the 'fatal operation' was restored. At the Conyers Park Nursing Home, a doctor gives the heroine, Sister Jane, the wrong bottle of blood plasma for a patient's transfusion. The surgeon (and hero), Stuart Hemmingway, who 'abhors carelessness', catches the error and sends Jane for another bottle. By the time she returns to the operating theatre, the patient has died. Although Stuart reassures her that, 'Nobody can really be held responsible,' Jane is horrified, as is wicked Matron Agnes Lawdon, who demands her resignation. No matter that the other doctor, Tom Sark, was responsible: Matron says Jane must take the responsibility: 'What is your future compared with that of a rising young doctor?' In the end, Jane resigns, but Stuart hires her to nurse a private patient in Switzerland.

In the serial version of *The Silent Valley* (run in *Woman's Weekly* from October 1952 until January 1953), the entire theatre episode was cut, so as to remove the sad tone. Instead, Matron, with her 'dark eyes' glinting, asks for Jane's resignation because she has 'seriously antagonised a patient of importance'. Mrs Carter wished to sit in a chair while her bed was being made, and Jane had refused, since she was forbidden to sit upright. None the less, Jane is fired. Johnson's advice was followed to the letter, and Jane does not display carelessness.[17]

Jean MacLeod ran into a similar taboo with *Woman*, and its editor, Mary Edmonds. In 1959 Edmonds rejected *The Little Doctor* for a number of reasons, including a heroine who was 'more than a little prissy and old-maidish'. But the real problem lay in presenting illness and suffering. She told Boon:

> Did you not feel yourself that it is bad to have a character suffering from disseminated sclerosis, which is described as 'a slow killer' with no hope held out for a cure? There are so many people who have this disease and, incidentally, she [MacLeod] has got some of her facts wrong. I had two close friends who have been suffering from d.s. for several years, and I know quite a bit about the symptoms.

MacLeod was upset over 'the rather vicious criticism', telling Boon, 'I do want you to know I have checked my facts.' She did her homework with some of the best doctors, who agree that the condition is incurable. The 'slow killer' remark is fitting, she added, because it is made privately between two doctors; 'They *could not* cloak it in a hopeful aura of vague phrases when they were talking together as professional men. It would be laughed out of court if read by a member of the profession, I'm afraid.' While Boon reassured MacLeod that he believed her, Edmonds stood firm.

In the end, Mills & Boon capitulated, no doubt because it was dealing with the best-selling woman's magazine in Britain. Joan Bryant broke the news to MacLeod, not Alan Boon:

> While we don't question your facts here (on the contrary), we feel that the book as it stands is likely to cause distress to sclerotics and their relations. Our books are very popular in hospitals, as you probably know, and one can't exclude the possibility that some people so afflicted may read it and see their illness baldly labelled as a killer whose victims have no hope. It is, surely, one thing to know such a fact about oneself (and some of them may not know it), quite another to see it in cold print. So could we just suppress the actual name of the disease, referring to it as a deadly one and leaving just an implication that Maxwell tells Jane exactly what it is? Alan and I have talked about this and we realise that what we suggest weakens the impact of the announcement. But it is a sacrifice we are hoping you will make, not on grounds of accuracy or policy, but to spare the feelings of people who already have enough to contend with.

Naturally, MacLeod agreed: 'I see your point about d.s. sufferers, and expect it would be best to soft pedal the actual words.' This is how the passage in question appeared in print (1960). Even with the disease name suppressed, the dramatic power of the scene was not diminished:

> Suddenly he was looking straight at her. 'Jane, Valerie is incurably ill.'
>
> He spoke the name of the disease, and the fatal words dropped into a terrible silence. Jane felt the icy grip at her throat tightening until it seemed that her brain would no longer function, even to grapple with the significance of what she had just heard. A dark and widening void seemed to be gaping in front of her in which she and Max and Valerie were doomed to wander for ever.
>
> 'It can't be true!' she heard herself saying, at last. 'There must be some mistake—some way out.'
>
> Max continued to look at her steadily as he said:
>
> 'You know there's no way out, Jane.'

Jane, the heroine, realizes that Max married Valerie to shield her, to protect her when the disease took its toll: 'There was nothing they could do; nothing that medical science had yet been able to devise which would give Valerie back the full, adventurous life she longed for once this slow, insidious killer had taken complete hold.'

Thomson-D.C also favoured Doctor-Nurse serials for its two magazines, *My Weekly* and the *People's Friend*. J. D. Davidson, managing director, told

Boon in 1958, 'I have a theory that fiction must never disturb the faith and trust a woman feels for doctors and/or nurses. Women are in their care more often than men and are more emotional towards them, giving them an aura.' Therefore, graphic detail was preferably avoided. In 1958 Davidson objected to Elizabeth Gilzean's debut, *On Call, Sister!*:

> From our point of view, Mrs. Gilzean is perhaps <u>too</u> knowledgeable about medical matters! . . . I feel Mrs. Gilzean, from her knowledge, and from her obvious enthusiasm for nursing, does tend to let medical exactness swamp her actual 'story'. A big section of the reading public appears to lap up the swift progress of an operation: but there must be just as large a section which finds it too strong meat. As far as we are concerned, romance, human relationships and emotions must come first.

A nurse herself, Gilzean's response was cutting: 'He had the typical male reaction to medical scenes (far more medical students faint in theatre than ever a nurse).'

Johnson also kept careful checks on strong language and strong drink. In 1957 new author Olive Norton asked Boon for lessons in the Johnson style for her Doctor-Nurse books. 'I wish you would just tell me, from the Johnson etc. point of view, how far one can go with a) drinking, b) swearing, etc. I gather she deletes My God, and To Hell with it. It seems a bit odd that she can't stand that, and yet she wants it all sexed up,' she wrote:

> I specially want to know about drinking because I plan to let Bruce take Trudi to a country pub for a quick one in Chapter 2. Do Johnson women go to pubs? I always think 'country inn' sounds so ingenuous, especially if they go for <u>supper</u>, even if it's bread and cheese and a gallon of wallop . . . Anyhow I shall write it that way for the book, and we can always make it a milk bar or something when we approach Johnson. (<u>Not</u> that I can quite see a milk bar in the middle of Middleton Woods—but there, maybe an itinerant one.)

In his diplomatic response, Boon advised, 'I can only estimate what Miss Johnson does or does not like but on the whole I would say that it is better, so far as possible, to keep strong drink out of the stories, although a sherry quite often appears in Sara Seale's stories. I do not think that public houses are much in fashion in that quarter. Swearing is not popular, but the expression "good grief" is quite often used.' Norton did avoid pubs in her novels but not 'strong' language. In her 1959 novel, *Junior Pro*, the heroine, junior nurse Lindsay Wood, is surprised when the hero, Dr James Bereford, explodes under pressure from a gathering crowd while tending an accident victim in the road:

> I heard James behind me say, 'Blast those confounded photographers!' I realised that until tonight I had never heard him anything but polite and

gentle, and never thought him capable of swearing. His voice was no longer mild. He sounded very angry.

ℒ

Settings were a key element of romantic serials, and the foreign and exotic always appealed, especially after the harshness and austerity of wartime, and as more people were going on overseas holidays in the 1950s. In 1950 Alan Boon wrote to Jean MacLeod, 'You are quite right that there is a vogue in our local magazines for stories with foreign settings, and many of them which run two serials at the same time have one with a foreign setting and one with a home setting.' Far and away the most popular destination was the African continent, no doubt due to the success of serials by Lilian Warren (as Rosalind Brett and Kathryn Blair). For example, *The Foolish Heart* by Marjorie Warby, serialized in *Woman's Weekly* in 1950, was set on a coffee plantation in Kenya.

But foreign settings and characters raised concerns about accuracy and political controversy. 'Violet Winspear, going to Venice, describes a scene where the heroine had a romantic session on the balcony of one of the bridges there,' Alan Boon recalled. 'Loads of *Woman's Weekly* readers had been to Venice and knew this was an enclosed bridge.' Hundreds wrote letters. Similarly, in 1950 Johnson rejected *This Time, It's Love* by Fay Chandos (Jan Tempest) since, Boon reported, 'She says that she cannot quite believe in the American atmosphere.' Not that there was much American atmosphere to believe in, in this tale of Celandine, who travels to Florida to stay in the huge mansion left to her in a bequest by 'Great Uncle Rollo'. Miami is 'a fabulous city out of a fairy-tale'. There Celandine falls for a lawyer, Steven, 'a pretty good specimen of the American male' and not 'at all like the usual conception of a lawyer. With his deep tan, rugged features, and broad shoulders, he conveyed the impression of an out-of-doors man.' Celandine eats her way through this novel in what would have been a fantasy for rationing-deprived readers in Britain. As she devours turtle soup, followed by 'a roast, peas and mushrooms, and a salad of crisp iceberg lettuce, radishes, chopped cucumber and pineapple, dressed with thick sour cream', Celandine ponders men and her own fate: 'She was nibbling a slice of walnut cake. It was rich and delicious, but it seemed to stick in her throat. She was acutely conscious of Randolph's proximity; of his lithe figure, unfathomable dark eyes, and curious magnetism.'

Like Mills & Boon, *Woman's Weekly* and other magazines avoided certain countries and settings, to be on the safe side. When Johnson turned down Hilary Wilde's *A Romantic Safari* in 1961, Boon surmised it may have been the African setting: 'I find there is a certain nervousness in some serial quarters about using the African background. I think some of the editors may be

worried that there might be political trouble just as they are running the serial. In my view, it would not matter if that did occur. You may be sure I urged
this view on the editors.' Mills & Boon published these books none the less.[18]

In 1962 Boon liked Jean MacLeod's *The Black Cameron*, and wanted to offer
it to either *Woman's Weekly* or *Woman and Home*, provided MacLeod could
amend the American military background and nuclear disarmament theme.
Joan Lee, one of Johnson's former assistants now with *Woman and Home*,
explained the concerns of Jean Twiddy, Johnson's successor and fiction editor:

> Miss Twiddy, who is Scottish, has a very strong feeling against the
> American base background because it immediately brings to mind
> nuclear disarmament. She does not like the idea of our heroine willingly
> coming to Scotland to soften up the Scots into accepting the American
> invasion and giving up their houses. It makes Fiona an unsympathetic
> heroine to many people. Could Fiona be specially interested in ornitho-
> logy?... This suggests a possibility for the presence of the American ship
> in Scottish waters. Could the Americans be doing a scientific oceano-
> graphical survey? The girl comes up as a secretary because she wants to
> revisit her native land and then is asked by Homer to find billets.
> Unwillingly she agrees.

MacLeod drew on personal experience in writing this novel. During the war
she was stationed as an air raid warden near her childhood home on Holy
Loch, guarding the British submarine base. She was willing to 'change the
Yankees from nuclear disarmament targets to harmless biologists or zoolo-
gists', who are doing a survey, and therefore require a base. In the final version, the heroine, Fiona Malcolm, is enlisted as a secretary to assist the
American Institute of Oceanography in conducting a survey of Loch Torran.
Their vessel is the USS *Atalanta*, which Fiona observes is 'scarcely noticeable'
and has not spoilt the loch. But this 'American invasion' is resented by the
natives, including the black-haired laird, Roderick Cameron, who distrust
foreigners. Fiona's ally is the (romantically named) John Kennedy, the school-
master of neighbouring Scoraig.

Mary Burchell learned first hand a lesson in using a controversial foreign
background. In 1956 R. J. O'Connell, editor of *Woman's Illustrated*, invited
her to write two serials based on her own experiences in Germany and
Eastern Europe before the Second World War. The first, *Love Is My Reason*
(which Burchell told readers, 'This is the story I always wanted to write'),
dealt with displaced persons and refugee camps. The second, *Loyal In All*, was
set in Hungary, around the recent uprising and the Soviet invasion, at the
suggestion of O'Connell, as Burchell recalled:

> O'Connell said to me, 'Well, of course there's only one place where you
> can start the next serial, and that is in Budapest.' So I said, 'Well, you
> understand I have never set foot in Budapest in my life, and this isn't the

moment to start.' He said, 'All the same, I would like you to do it.' At least I knew the awfulness of the police knocking on the door at five in the morning, you know, and your father or your husband dragged away in front of you. And so I did it. I got a letter from one woman, and she said, 'The description of the escape was so exactly what happened to me that I can hardly believe you didn't know me.' I was very gratified.

In real life, Burchell and her sister had recently 'adopted' two Hungarian refugee families in a Displaced Persons' Camp in Bavaria. In this serial, Marika Stevens is a young nurse in a Budapest clinic, where she assists the dashing and mysterious Dr von Raszay to escape from the evil secret police. Marika's mother is Hungarian, and her father is English. With a friendly journalist, Rodney Dering, in tow, they witness the uprising ('The Revolution has begun') and the brutal Soviet invasion. The trio, along with a gaggle of orphans and elderly, flee the city and head for the Austrian border, helping the injured along the way. Amid the snipers' bullets and bomb explosions, Marika and von Raszay fall in love. Wading through the swamp marshes, they face danger:

> They all stopped then and listened intently, gripped by a common instinct which told them danger was near.
>
> For some time all they heard was the night wind stirring the rushes. But then—horribly near—came the sound of a shot, and Marika was near enough to Rodney to hear the sleeping child on his back stir in her slumber.
>
> 'The guards are shooting!' she thought, and an icy chill dried the perspiration of exhaustion on her face.
>
> Then two or three shots followed in quick succession, and away to the right of them they heard a cry.
>
> Pity and terror were drowned in the overwhelming realization that they were not the target this time. And though she was ashamed that the stark will to live crowded out all other considerations, Marika felt sick with relief.

Marika 'has lived through enough strain to kill most people'. But the group makes it safely to Austria, and is reunited with Marika's parents. Marika accepts von Raszay's proposal in the obligatory happy ending:

> He bent his head then and gave her a long kiss on the mouth. She forgot then that her parents were looking on. She forgot that there were still problems to solve and arguments to settle. She only knew that this was what she had wanted during all the dark and terrible days of her adventures.
>
> 'I'll do—whatever you say,' she repeated in a whisper.

Readers of *Woman's Illustrated* and Mills & Boon novels, however, were not happy, despite the ending. Burchell's novel intertwined strong political sentiments and somewhat graphic violence with a traditional love story, and the recipe unsettled readers. 'We received letters of complaints—"We don't like Mary Burchell now, she's gone over to horror stories,"' Burchell recalled. 'You see, they didn't want that. They wanted romance. Both of my books ended happily, but they didn't like the feeling of a very disagreeable reality.' The rebellion of her core readership was something that Burchell would long remember. 'I wasn't dying to write any more like that,' she said.[19]

An important point is made here. Although reader reaction to Burchell's novel was negative, Mills & Boon none the less published it, as it was a good story, respecting the author's craft. Herein lay the dilemma which the firm often faced in the 1950s and illustrates its seriousness as a publisher. As authors grew in prominence, their independence increased, and their dependence on the magazines (and serial money) lessened. The magazine editors resisted this decline, as they required a regular supply of 'quality' fiction. Mills & Boon was often caught in the middle—but to the firm's credit, sided mostly with its authors. The bonds between Mills & Boon and the magazines would be loosened further with the growth of retail paperbacks in the 1960s.

One of the best examples of a situation in which Mills & Boon encouraged an author, and her independence, concerned *The Persistent Lover* by Eleanor Farnes (1957). When serialized as 'But Love—She Dared Not' in *My Weekly* in 1956, Boon regarded this novel as a milestone:

> My considered opinion is that the serial acceptance of THE PERSISTENT LOVER is the most significant event in serial history since the war. In my opinion THE PERSISTENT LOVER breaks away from many serial conventions, and I feel that its appearance ... must increase the scope of all writers of serials. I feel that it must have an effect on other papers, and I shall be very interested to observe the future. I am sure that your contemporaries will be also tremendously interested in its success.

This book was indeed a departure (even a risk) for the firm and for Farnes (who published her first novel with Mills & Boon in 1935), who admitted she had removed her usual 'rose-coloured spectacles' to write this one. The heroine, Jessica Marlowe, 26, is a widow with two children: frail and sickly Stephen, 7, and robust Antony, 5. A dashing stranger, Mark Richardson, arrives in Biddecombe Bay with his 'spectacular-looking London friends'. Fun-loving and fond of parties, Mark has little in common with the sad Jessica, who was 'too young to have gone through so much experience'. Naturally, they fall in love. The punishing kiss in this novel takes a new twist when Mark kisses Jessica's *hand*: 'In the small hall she leaned against the door, fighting down the wild emotion Mark Richardson's kiss had sent surging through her whole being.' The children love Mark, and Jessica believes she can find happiness again. But the hero and heroine quarrel, and in a horrific accident, Mark backs his car over Antony, killing the child. Not long afterwards, Stephen also succumbs to a fatal illness. Jessica flees to Switzerland, saying, 'My life is empty. I have had it all. A husband, children. And nothing is left.' Against all odds, by the end of the novel, Jessica rekindles her love for Mark. In a twist, she gives *him* a punishing kiss:

> Why should she be shy with a man who thought of her like that? So she leaned down and kissed him on the mouth, a kiss that started softly and gently and then became ardent as her longing for him surged up in her.
>
> 'And what,' asked Mark, his eyes very close to hers, 'was that for?'
>
> 'It was my declaration of love,' Jessica said. 'You see how brave I am.'

Mark promises Jessica that they will have at least ten children; 'He knew he wanted her to have his children, to wipe out, for him at least, the memory of another man's children.'

When she wrote *The Persistent Lover*, Farnes was on a hot streak, having just landed a plum *Woman* serial appearance for her novel, *Secret Heiress* (serialized as 'So Fair The Day'), which earned her more than £680. *Secret Heiress* had a fairly standard romantic plot: the heroine, Fiona Chard, is the daughter of a wealthy steel magnate. Her father wants her to learn about the world, and she takes a job as secretary to an engineer, Peter Webber. Fiona's wealthy pedigree is kept secret, much to the confusion of Peter, who suspects she's a kept woman, given her expensive clothes. In the end, they marry, and Peter joins the family firm as the son Mr Chard always wanted in the business.

Small wonder that both *Woman* and *Woman's Own* turned down this very different romantic serial. The problem was, as Boon noted, *The Persistent Lover* did break away from many serial conventions. Farnes enjoyed the change but knew the reaction would be mixed; she worried that Boon himself would disapprove: 'I can almost hear you groaning in despair because, having got me into "Woman", you will think this one will flop. Boon strongly disagreed: 'It is a novel which I shall remember when I have forgotten a hundred others. We shall feel proud to publish it.' While he also believed the Farnes public would like it, despite the fact that it was written along different lines, Boon was concerned that the magazine editors might find the plot too 'harrowing'.

They certainly did. Mary Grieve, editor of *Woman*, liked the story, but felt that the death of two children 'makes too great an element of sadness' for a successful serial. Irene Josephy of *Woman's Own* believed a heroine with two children was 'not the sort of heroine' she liked to provide for her readers.

There is no evidence that the serial was sent to *Woman's Weekly*—but given Johnson's obsession with death, it most certainly would have been turned down. When Helen Annan of *My Weekly* said yes, Boon was generous in his praise to Farnes:

> Many congratulations on your new success. There is no stopping you now! I feel that the success of THE PERSISTENT LOVER at My Weekly is epoch-making, and marks the beginning of a new trend in serials. The situation is extremely interesting, and I feel you have struck a blow for freedom.

My Weekly paid a paltry (in serial rights terms) £250. As the serial unfolded, Farnes worried about 'a flood of protesting letters' to *My Weekly*, but none was offered in print. Farnes did report to Boon of Annan's response: 'The "reader reaction", she says, "was extremely good and all who wrote enjoyed the story tremendously, so it really is true that women enjoy having their feelings torn by the stories they read and the films they see."'

Alan Boon believed in his authors and nurtured their growth, although the author had to be a 'star' or of long-standing service to merit such attention and independence. In 1954 Lilian Warren, through her agent, Dorothy Daly, was infuriated by the 'unauthorised' changes Biddy Johnson had made to *Sweet Deceiver* by Rosalind Brett. 'Miss Johnson's amendments to the novel will not be mine, and it is quite possible that by making the background more stilted and Victorian—which is her aim—she will present what is really a false picture of a governor's house in these times,' Warren wrote. 'Believe me, today's colonial governors cannot risk upsetting the natives by displays of autocracy and splendid imperialism.' She continued:

> In a serial, this point has not much importance, but I would not care for a story of mine to go into book form giving a picture which is not genuine and up to date. SWEET DECEIVER is a good story as it stands and, except for serialisation, I can see no reason why it should be altered.

Daly (who confided to Boon, 'I put my foot in it well and truly') assured Warren that Mills & Boon 'would not have dreamt of using Miss Johnson's amendments without consulting you'. Boon agreed, in a reply to Daly:

> I found Mrs. Brett's letter very interesting because recently there have been one or two occasions where a novel has been altered for serial purposes. I suppose it is inevitable that editors and book publishers must see things differently from time to time, and in each case we have preferred the author's version as being stronger and more true for the purpose of book publication.

Boon was being modest in citing just 'one or two occasions'. In any event, he predicted *Sweet Deceiver* 'is going to have an extremely good innings' as a best-seller, and it did when published in 1955, without Johnson's changes. In this novel, the setting is Bolani, capital of the Tunak Islands in the South Seas, governed by Sir Henry Penlan. Julian Stanville, 33, Chief Commissioner, wants to advance his career by marrying Sir Henry's daughter Amanda. But Amanda is not keen ('Instinctively, she knew he was aware of his attraction for women, and unreasonably she disliked him for it intensely'), and asks her friend Elizabeth Mayne, accounts clerk in a City office, to trade places while her father is away. Sir Henry is a fair man when dealing with the chief, or raja, of each island, he tells Elizabeth:

> 'Julian has always had a strong aversion to my habit of travelling the islands informally and almost alone. He's tried many times to persuade me to take a military guard, but I've clung to my old methods in a changing world because my endeavour has always been to inspire confidence rather than fear.'

Indeed, when the Governor is taken hostage by a renegade raja, Julian seeks him out without soldiers, so as to prevent a war.

Alan Boon frequently intervened to support his author when she was overly badgered by the magazine editors. In 1953 Alex Stuart complained to Boon of her distress when Johnson rejected her latest manuscript, *Forsaken by the Great Winds*. Her confidence fell 'by Miss Johnson telling me that the story had "flopped" and in her view couldn't be saved':

> An editor of Miss Johnson's standing can make or mar an author of mine: her rejection of WINDS, coming, as it unfortunately did, when I'd written only the first 16,000 words, was a blow which wrecked my writing for months afterwards. (I have often wondered what started the prevailing belief that authors write better if discouraged.)

But in her next letter, Stuart praised Boon for restoring her confidence (a talent, we have seen, that Boon used often with his authors). 'By telling me you like WINDS . . . the value of that cannot be assessed in percentages and I don't think it should be,' Stuart wrote. 'Serial writing, as you once told me, is good for discipline but just occasionally one has to confess to finding it irksome.'

Similarly, Anne Weale recalled Boon's role as mediator at luncheon meetings between herself and R. J. O'Connell. 'Alan controlled those meetings,' she said. 'If he felt the editor was being too stern, he stepped in. He was our agent in a way. It was lovely.' The magazine editors appreciated Boon's loyalty, although it often got in the way. In 1953 J. D. Davidson wrote to Boon complaining about Sara Seale and other authors who did not take serial writing 'seriously'. 'It seems to me a great loss of time and opportunity for authors just to be content to hit or miss with a serial just because they know, in any case, that you will publish the book,' Davidson said. 'They ought to be made to feel the serial side is very important both for money and prestige and publicity.' Davidson tried, he told Boon, to convince Seale otherwise: 'She thinks it less wearing to write as she wants and just hope a serial comes out of it. That may be the right way for her, I don't know. But it seems a waste.' Boon, who was well versed in Seale's battles with the D.C. Thomson editors, joked to her in a letter, 'I doubt whether after some of your recent experiences you will be impressed by his argument.' Similarly, Boon backed Jean MacLeod in 1950 when she was pressured by D.C. Thomson's partner, John Leng to write sequels to her serials. 'The book rights are today more valuable than the serial rights,' Boon reminded her:

> We feel ideally there is no doubt you should always use the plots you wish, and we ourselves prefer that you should do so. At the same time, the serial market would not have the same guaranteed security which Messrs. Leng have offered in the past, and, therefore, as we have said before, we are most anxious that you should do what you think best. If necessary, of course, it might be possible to compromise—to write one 'agreed' serial for Leng's and another one off your own bat at the same time.

MacLeod did just this, but incurred Dundee's wrath when she sold a serial to their competitor, *Woman's Own*, in 1951. 'They regarded MacLeod as their author, actually, and when she wrote one or two books for *Woman's Own*, a rival magazine, they accused her of being ungrateful,' Boon recalled. 'They said they'd made her what she was. Actually, Jean MacLeod's Scottish books on the whole were more staid.'

In 1965 another star author, Essie Summers, wrote to Boon from her New Zealand home, with the plea that she retain her freedom and creativity. 'I seem to think, breathe, live my stories for many weeks, constantly jotting, before I ever sit down to the typewriter. In short to let the story possess me,' Summers said. 'I know writing is only about one quarter inspiration—the rest is sheer hard work and discipline—but the inspiration is <u>necessary for the start</u>.' Summers asked if she could disregard plot suggestions from *Woman's Weekly* and write what she wanted:

> I feel (regretfully) that if I continue writing to a certain pattern—I mean the serial pattern—I am going to lose a little something . . . Would it be all right with you, Alan, if I continue to write novels to please myself— my readers—you? And if the odd one does find favour serially, just to look on it as an extra.

Boon was very sympathetic, given the fact that Summers was one of the top authors in the 1960s. 'As publishers, we do not mind at all if our authors do not compete in the Serial Stakes,' he reassured her. 'Most of our authors do not "serialize", although I must say this is not always through choice!

Therefore, Essie, if you feel that it is best for you, I suggest you just write and if a serial comes along, so much the better.'

By the mid-1960s, times had truly changed, thanks to the paperback revolution. The financial success of paper-bound novels would finally release Mills & Boon from the iron grip of Fleet Street and Dundee.

Chapter 10
The 1960s: Change and Experimentation

I try to keep abreast of our changing world, like to be realistic—yet at the same time idealistic. I could not bear to write a story with the heroine cherishing an undying regard for a married man. I feel it is quite possible for her to be tempted into a situation like that—in fact for all heroines to be above temptation of straying affection is too hard to swallow—but with me it wouldn't be possible to involve her more or less permanently. I didn't use that incident ... merely to form a basis of misunderstanding, but to reach readers with the idea that though one may slip a little, it is then that the things we live by, come to our aid and give us the necessary courage to make a decision that costs us pain.

Essie Summers to Alan Boon, 1962

I know there is a lot said about 'reader identification' but it isn't really possible in the fullest sense. If so, then one would have to write about young scrubbers, tired housewives, ailing grandmothers, etc. And who on earth can truly identify with a sardonic Spanish Don, a handsome surgeon, a dashing Italian, or a bittersweet Greek? The real aim of romance is to provide escape and entertainment, not to dish up 'real life' and 'real life people' on a plate with egg on it!

Violet Winspear to Alan Boon, 1973

THE sweeping changes inflicted on Mills & Boon during the 1960s had a significant impact on editorial policy. Paperback publishing, a way of life for the firm by the middle of the decade, freed Mills & Boon from the editorial strait-jacket of the women's magazines. The firm and its authors could be more aggressive and responsive to the social changes of the 1960s, while maintaining something like a conventional morality. The standard formula was stretched and moulded into forms unseen since the days of Joan Sutherland and Louise Gerard. Although certain basic elements remained— the happy ending, the 'Alphaman', and the virginal heroine—the novels become more daring, even explicit, in the depiction of romance. In this sense, Mills & Boon recognized the competition posed by the erotic novels

of Harold Robbins and Jacqueline Susann, for example, as well as the popularity of television serial dramas. Mills & Boon novels retained a degree of
'wholesomeness', but the romance was definitely 'hotter'.

The priority, as paperbacks became more prominent, was to publish what
the readers wanted, and therefore what would sell best. 'Our policy has never
been radical, or controversial,' John Boon said. 'We wouldn't offend or
shock. First of all, commercially, it would be a bad decision. Everyone would
say we're just in it for commerce. Well, to some extent we are, and, why not?
I think that we are following tastes, following what the public wants, what
our sort of readership wants.' It is Mills & Boon's flexibility and willingness
to change which would prepare the firm for unprecedented success.

Mills & Boon's modest willingness to go with the times, however, increasingly clashed with Harlequin Books and the old-fashioned opinions of Mary
Bonnycastle. Indeed, a significant change in the 1960s, as opposed to our
1950s and women's magazines discussions, can be seen in Mills & Boon's
growing independence, assertiveness, and confidence. Now, the firm will
publish a bolder book first, and then offer it to the magazines or to Canada.
Alan and John Boon were independent publishers again, thanks largely to the
financial strength offered by paperbacks. Their position was a charmed one.

❧

As an introduction to the 'Swinging Sixties', it is instructive to examine two
novels, one from the beginning of the decade and one from the end, which
represent the changing style of the Mills & Boon romance. The authors in
question, Rachel Lindsay (Roberta Leigh) and Violet Winspear, were among
the firm's most popular and successful. Both were also as influential on the
style of the romantic novel in the 1960s as Lilian Warren and Esther
Wyndham were in the 1950s.

In 1961 Anne Weale wrote to Alan Boon to express her concerns over
recent changes in the women's magazines and the style of fiction which they
were publishing. She worried that her own writing (successfully serialized in
Woman's Own and *Woman's Illustrated*) was not keeping pace with the latest
trends, and might be considered 'old-fashioned':

> One can't help feeling that Miss J's [Biddy Johnson] influence is waning
> rather fast in *Woman's Weekly*, and the other magazines seem to be taking
> a marked swing over to stronger stuff. I've been particularly impressed
> by this since reading the Rachel Lindsay serial in *Woman's Illustrated*. After
> wading through Lady C. [*Lady Chatterly's Lover*] without a qualm, I was
> quite shocked to find *W.I.* accepting a heroine who is in love with a mar-
> ried man. And the [Netta] Muskett-ish goings-on in New York, followed
> by a pregnant corpse, have been even more staggering. Of course the

whole story is awfully well written, but it does seem a striking departure from the established moral code.

I don't mean by this that I want to become a Metalious [Grace Metalious, author of *Peyton Place*], and naturally I'm guided by your views which are far more knowledgeable than mine. But I am beginning to wonder if my plots are a shade old-fashioned and ought to be adjusted slightly. I suppose I've been assuming that because I'm a bit younger than most of the other romancers, I must be in key with the times. But in fact it's well over ten years since I was actively engaged in romance, so to speak, and there's quite a gulf between my generation of girls and the present one.

Boon, in his reply, was non-committal, but did encourage Weale to remain in the serial game, even if that meant changing her style: 'I am sure that you are very much capable of writing nearer to the "SONG IN MY HEART" beat if this is what is required.' Indeed she was: Anne Weale evolved into one of the 'sexiest' authors Mills & Boon published in the 1960s and 1970s, adapting her writing style to the lower threshold of permissiveness when necessary.

But *Song in My Heart* by Rachel Lindsay, published by Mills & Boon in 1961, was indeed a departure for the firm. This novel stretched all of the conventions of the age and dared to mention several of the taboos which Alan Boon and Joan Bryant worked so hard to suppress. Like *Peyton Place*, *Song in My Heart* treats sex, adultery, and violence with a frankness that would have shocked some readers. But the fact that Boon allowed its publication is testimony to his instincts as an editor and his faith in his author and her readers. In this novel, Sara Lister, a budding opera singer, agrees to work for the Combined Television Company, a rival to the BBC, to help her gambler brother pay his debts. She is 'discovered' while performing on a quiz show by Philip John Stafford, the 'Big White Chief' of the network, who promises to make her 'the greatest pop singer of the century'. Gone were the days when Mills & Boon worried about mentioning real names: Doris Day, Maria Callas, and Connie Francis all make an appearance. Sara is an overnight success, and she and 'P. J.' head to New York to appear on the *Eddie Benfield Show*, 'the ambition of every British singer'. Needless to say, Sara and Philip fall in love—even though Philip is married to Tina. Sara fantasizes about Philip while soaking in her hotel bath:

> Instantly she thought of Philip and found herself hoping, with an intensity that frightened her, that she would see him again while she was here. Heat invaded her body, a heat that had nothing to do with the temperature of the water.

Clearly the reader shares in Sara's fantasy, and is not offended by the fact that she is in love with a married man (although she never sleeps with Philip, she wants to). After a party and too much champagne, Philip kisses Sara: 'Sara closed her eyes and gave herself up to an ecstasy she had never believed possible.' But Philip breaks away, in tears, as Sara pleads, 'If you want me, I'm yours. What's the use of pretending any more?' For the heroine to play the aggressor role was something new for Mills & Boon. Philip professes his love, but says he can never divorce Tina since, in a car crash caused by his careless driving, Tina was injured, and now cannot have children. Racked by guilt, Philip decides to remain married in name only; 'We've never lived together in the normal sense of the word,' he tells Sara.

Upon their return to England, Philip says he cannot condemn Sara to a secret liaison, and she erupts: ' "Damn my career!" she said passionately. "Do you think I care whether I'm a success as a singer? I want to be with *you*, Philip." ' Soon Tina is found dead, and revealed to be three months' pregnant, by her lover (who was also the murderer). This sets up the 'happy' ending, as Philip and Sara can now marry. 'You haven't any guilt at all. Tina would want you to be happy,' Sara tells Philip.

It is not surprising that Anne Weale was shocked by this novel (which sold well), as it was a departure from the 'established moral code'. Although Sara pursues the relationship with a married man, she is also portrayed as a victim of circumstance. She preserves her virginity (just), until the obligatory marriage can take place. Clearly, with the proper qualifications and clarifications in place, Mills & Boon could extend the boundaries of the romantic novel at a time when readers were adding more spice to their romance (*Peyton Place et. al.*).

Another author, Violet Winspear, regularly shocked the old-timers in the Mills & Boon readership, as often as she delighted the younger generation. In 1970 she submitted to Alan Boon her latest manuscript, *The Tawny Sands*, which she called 'a love story in the Blair–Brett tradition but with a dash of the desert added to the personality of Don Raul':

> I have always been intrigued by the desert island theme, and decided to place a man and girl almost alone in the desert itself. This gave me the chance to air my dialogue and to build up tension when Janna, a little nobody, finds herself thrown by the winds of chance into the keeping of Raul Cesar Bey — one of my 'beloved tyrant' type of heroes.

Tawny Sands was one of Winspear's most popular novels, although it is yet another retread of the *Rebecca* storyline. Janna, 20 and an orphan (parents remain non-existent in Mills & Boon novels), is secretary and dogsbody to a wealthy lady author on the Côte d'Azur. There she meets Don Raul Cesar de Romanos, a mysterious Spanish nobleman. Janna is instantly attracted to this 'dangerous' man: 'The face was a little cruel — a lot of it passionate with some suppressed emotion, such as would be present if such a man was not given the free rein that handsome, arrogant, supple creatures demanded. He reminded her, somehow, of a panther in a cage.' In the hotel pool, Don Raul swims naked, watched intently by Janna (who, quite unlike Mills & Boon heroines of the past, does not blush): she finds him 'bronzed from his throat to his heels, naked as a statue of Apollo in a pagan garden . . . rippling with tight-coiled muscles as one of those superb jungle creatures'.

Don Raul convinces Janna to accompany him to Morocco as his 'fiancée' to appease his family. There he dresses her in silks and jewels, while Don Raul is transformed into an Arab sheik ('The faint slant to his dark eyes was intensified here,' Janna observes). Suddenly Janna discovers her conscience and tries to resist Don Raul's lecherous advances, suffering many bruising kisses. Growing angry, he ridicules her 'vocation of spinsterhood', to which she retorts, 'I'd sooner be a spinster than just an object!' They openly discuss sex:

> 'I expect you've sown quite a few wild oats.'
>
> 'It's in the nature of a man, *nina*. And in the nature of a woman to prefer a bit of the devil to a lot of self-righteousness.'
>
> 'I know that.' She broke into a smile. 'I'm not an absolute prude, though you keep harping on my innocence. I am twenty years old.'

They sleep side by side in the desert, endure dust storms, and survive a swarm of locusts. Ultimately they fall madly in love and marry, Janna 'lost in the arms of her desert lover'.

Winspear's fans could not get enough of her passionate romances, which were usually set in exotic foreign lands. Reader response to *Tawny Sands*, Winspear told Boon, was incredible. 'I believe in their hearts that quite a few men like to think of themselves as sheiks in disguise, and quite a few women would enjoy being carried off to where the dishes are washed in the sand and there are no beds to make!' she wrote. Maybe so, but soon after *Tawny's* publication, Winspear aroused considerable controversy by her remarks on the BBC *Man Alive* programme, and in a companion interview in the *Radio Times*. Winspear, described as possessing 'man mania' and having sold 700,000 novels in the US and Britain to date, got carried away in revealing her vision of the archetypal romantic hero:

> I get my heroes so that they're lean and hard muscled and mocking and sardonic and tough and tigerish and single, of course. Oh and they've got to be rich and then I make it that they're only cynical and smooth on the surface. But underneath they're well, you know, sort of lost and lonely. In need of love but, when roused, capable of breathtaking passion and potency. Most of my heroes, well all of them really, are like that. They frighten but fascinate. They must be the sort of men who are capable of rape: men it's dangerous to be alone in the room with.

The reference to rape would haunt Winspear for the rest of her career, even though her (crude) description spoke for generations of brooding and threatening Mills & Boon heroes. 'I hope my image at the Woman's Weekly has not been damaged by the vitriol,' Winspear told Boon. 'I <u>did</u> say that heroes of romantic novels, in the Rhett Butler, Rochester tradition, should be capable of rape. If the girl is not virginal there is no danger.' Winspear claimed to know exactly what her readers wanted in their heroes, as well as in their heroines:

> As these girls are rarely in the running for the Miss World prize it seems rather foolish if they go around presuming that some tycoonish guy is panting to kiss and fondle them, and it rather robs the girls of pride if they are continually in a state of heat. I prefer that romantic heroines should have pride if not stunning beauty, and they should be as mystified by the hero's intentions as the reader of the book.

Alan Boon, not to mention Biddy Johnson, would have agreed.

Both Roberta Leigh and Violet Winspear expressed in their novels several themes which characterized Mills & Boon romances in the 1960s. As society was changing, along with attitudes towards love, sex, marriage, and children, so did Mills & Boon authors reflect these changes in their novels. This is not to imply that Mills & Boon no longer imposed certain restrictions on its authors and upheld a 'traditional' moral standard. Boundaries remained—primarily, premarital sex—that authors could not cross, no matter how successful Harold Robbins and other racy authors had become. The primary reason was, as always, not to offend the readership. Readers wanted their fiction to be lively and up-to-date—Peter Mann's survey proved as much—but the emphasis remained on 'clean' and 'wholesome' stories, with the occasional vicarious thrill and touch of fantasy.

One of the hallmarks of the Mills & Boon romance in the 1960s was an emphasis on new and exotic backgrounds, in the form of a trendy occupation or a foreign country. The latter was increasingly popular (and an interesting return to the 1920s romances), with many novels set in Greece, Spain, Italy, and North Africa (thanks to the success of Winspear, whose ideas were copied by other authors). Further afield, foreign-born authors from Australasia and South Africa offered what Alan Boon called 'Great Open Spaces' stories. Since readers may have travelled to these destinations on holiday (or dreamed of so doing), Mills & Boon novels often resembled travelogues in their descriptions of local customs, food, and (especially) men. When *The North Devon Journal-Herald* reviewed *Jacaranda Island* by Iris Danbury (1972), a tale of a secretary who travels to Tenerife and meets the rich man of her dreams, the newspaper noted, 'It makes a pleasant enough guide-book to Tenerife and some readers may go there for their holidays with a good fore-knowledge of places of interest, while some more working girls may be persuaded to travel to the Canaries in search of romance with hand-some, rich foreigners.' In 1962 Joan Lee of *Woman's Weekly* suggested to Alan Boon 'fuel for a good emotional story' set in Australia which Hilary Wilde might wish to write. Lee provided a detailed synopsis:

> A girl travels to Australia with her family which consists of her mother, her new step-father and his daughter who is much the same age as the heroine, or perhaps a year or two older. The step-father is a very difficult man, ruthless, accustomed to having his own way, and the mother has only recently married again.

> The heroine must have had some very good reason for accompanying them. Perhaps to escape from an unhappy love affair. But suddenly she begins to realise that her step-father resents her. She meets the hero on board ship. He is very eligible and the step-father tries to promote a romance for his own daughter.

> Such a situation would give plenty of scope for the step-father's machi-nations. Somehow the heroine finds herself continually being shown in the wrong light. A misunderstood, put-upon heroine is usually very popular, as you know.

This shipboard romance, with an English girl setting off to a foreign land, future uncertain, was a common storyline in the 1960s. Wilde took up Lee's idea, and wrote *Red as a Rose* (1963). But her version was considerably dif-ferent (no room for a family), as illustrated by the dust jacket blurb:

> Setting off in a luxury liner for a new life in Australia, Elinor should have been enjoying every moment of the voyage. But all she could think of was how much she loved Kit Anderson—who, unfortunately, regarded her as nothing but a stupid little nuisance.

Australia and New Zealand remained popular settings, and most of the new Mills & Boon authors in the 1960s, inspired by the success of Joyce Dingwell and Essie Summers, came from this part of the world: Peta Cameron, Dorothy Cork, Margaret Way, Audrey Willson, Mary Moore, Nora Sanderson, Karin Mutch, and Gloria Bevan. These authors generated much fan mail from satisfied readers. In 1964, for example, Essie Summers heard from an admirer in Chippewa Falls, Wisconsin (who had written to Harlequin Books, the publisher of her paperback edition). She claimed to have read each of Summers's books 'at least six times over':

> Your books have really made new Zealand a place to me, not just a squig-gly little mark on the globe ... The more I re-read your books, the more I have felt an urge to know you personally. To find out if you are like your heroines, so refreshing and yet mature with such a solid background and staunch moral principles.

The reader identified with Summers's domesticated heroines: 'I particularly enjoyed fixing up Mary's old homestead, baking sponges with Prue, and have wiped many a brow in sympathy with Judith on ironing day.'

Although Ann Britton and Marion Collin in *Romantic Fiction: The New Writers' Guide* (1960) urged authors, '*Never* set a whole book in a country you have not visited. By doing so you will kill it before the second chapter', many successful Mills & Boon authors did just that. Violet Winspear, mistress of the Greek romance, never left the south-east of England,[1] and Ethel Connell ('Katrina Britt') had never been away from Blackpool when she wrote about Venice in *A Kiss in a Gondola*, her first novel. But Connell was often challenged over her use of foreign words and phrases. In 1972 a Mills & Boon manuscript reader asked of Alan Boon:

> I would be grateful if you could drop a tactful word to Katrina Britt about her use, or rather misuse, of foreign languages in her stories. She is very fond of doing this, but unfortunately does it so badly that I have to do an enormous amount of searching in dictionaries and correcting. It is obvious from the basic mistakes she makes ('Frauline' instead of 'Fraulein' throughout A SPRAY OF EDELWEISS) that she has no knowledge whatever of any other language, and as she must be aware of this I feel she might emulate Violet's [Winspear] praiseworthy example and check these languages herself with the aid of a local library or dictionary, or get a more knowledgeable friend to vet them for her.

Winspear did, indeed, know how to use a phrasebook. 'There is some Italian in STRANGE BEWILDERMENT and we should be grateful if you could inform us of its authenticity,' Boon responded to Connell. 'Our own Italian expert is away at the moment and we have no-one else here who can manage the lingo.' In her defence, Connell claimed she used the *McGraw-Hill Pocket Travel Guide* and *Hossfeld's Method of Italian Grammar* in using, for example, *bello* [sic] *bionda* to mean 'beautiful blonde'.

Sometimes authors took their research of foreign backgrounds and customs to extremes. In 1960 Joan Bryant wrote to Phyllis Matthewman about her latest novel, *Cupid Under Capricorn*, set in Rhodesia:

> This business of the phallic symbols at Zimbabwe. I suppose there's nothing improper about a young man's mentioning such things to unmarried girls, but I really don't think he ought to stress the reason for their being so called! It is rather, as it were, inviting their attention to the original object. So I've deleted the words 'from the shape' (Page 119). I do hope this will be all right with you.

Matthewman, sheepishly, apologized for her explicitness: 'Why I stress the phallic symbols I can't think! I suppose because I was interested in the whole subject of Zimbabwe, which of course I read up. But I'm sure it's better to pipe down on the subject. What on earth would our old lady readers think if we didn't!' In this novel, Gail and Philippa work as stewardesses for Rhodesian Airways. On a stopover they meet dashing engineer/metallurgist Rick Fraser. Together they tour the ancient ruins known as the Acropolis on Zimbabwe Hill. In the offending passage, as published in 1961, Philippa asks Rick a question, which is answered quickly:

> 'I say, that's an odd-looking building, a kind of cone-shaped tower, isn't it?'
>
> 'It is. Almost certainly something to do with the worship of whoever inhabited the place. Some kind of phallic worship, I suppose. Had enough of the temple now?'

So-called 'hot spot' countries were usually avoided as backgrounds, or handled with special care. In 1967 Alan Boon was concerned about Iris Danbury's latest novel, set in Spain:

> In view of the situation at Gibraltar, we would like to change the title of THE SPANISH DOCTOR. I feel confident that the Spanish Government does not want any serious trouble, but just in case something went wrong, we would prefer to take precautions in advance. It's the 'Spanish' bit, of course, that we would like changed. Can you think of a way round, retaining the suggestion of the sunshine and the medicine?

Wisely, Boon hoped to continue to sell this novel should public opinion turn against Spain and all things Spanish. Danbury, a former secretary who ran her own typing bureau, agreed, suggesting *Doctor in the Sun*, *Doctor at San Cristobal*, *Doctor at Villa Ronda*, *Doctor Sebastian*, and *Gracias, Doctor*. Boon picked *Doctor at Villa Ronda*, but informed Danbury that she could keep the references to Spanish cities in the manuscript: 'I think it reasonable to retain the name Barcelona in the new opus and the same could have gone for Majorca . . . It was just that we thought it advisable to keep the Spanish out of the title.' Similarly, in 1966 Gladys Fulbrook wrote to Boon, agreeing with Joan Lee's comments on *One-Man Girl* and its 'risky' Cyprus setting: 'In view of the steady crumbling of the old British Empire, no one would bat an eyelash if we walked out of Cyprus to-morrow—and no woman would want to identify herself with that background.' But she disputed Lee's charge that the setting would date her novel, predicting British troops would remain there for years. In *One-Man Girl*, Nurse Polly Worsley, 23, a Lieutenant in the Queen Alexandra Royal Army Nursing Corps, heads to Cyprus to join her boyfriend soldier, Patrick. There both are tested and tempted by other lovers. Although armies are stationed in Cyprus, no explanation why is provided, and the novel is essentially a travelogue.

⚘

The development of the hero, the heroine, and their relationship intensified in the 1960s. Generally, the heroine became more assertive and independent, willing to follow the hero to a foreign land without much thought for her own safety. In turn, the English-born hero faded into the background, superseded by a brutal, dangerous, but fascinating Greek, Italian, or Spaniard. The romance certainly became 'hotter', but still within limits. A loyal following remained, however, for Doctor-Nurse novels, which continued to thrive, and for the slightly old-fashioned, cosily domestic romances written with flair by older authors such as Mary Burchell and Jean MacLeod. Variety was the spice of the ever-expanding Mills & Boon list.

Alan Boon continued to rely on his authors to keep his heroines up-to-date and encourage reader identification. 'I try to keep abreast of what young girls are thinking and doing and what they're dreaming,' Margery Hilton, a professional dancer from Newcastle, told *Woman's World*. Hilton's debut was *Young Ellis* (1966). 'I think their dreams are not so different than mine were. There's lots of bravado, they are so afraid of being thought not "with it". But I think marriage and a family is too basic an instinct built into women for it ever to be eradicated.'[2] Jane Donnelly, a crime-story writer who made her debut with *A Man Apart* (1968), noted that heroines were smart and independent, a reflection of the age:

> They are rarely dim. They make mistakes and they often started off falling for the wrong man but as any agony aunt would tell you there's still a lot of that about . . . The heroine is still basically moral, loyal, and a good friend, very bright in the head and super sexy with the right man. She can still make an idiot of herself but she can laugh at herself too. Now she shares the action, out of bed as well as in; you don't get them cowering in corners any more while the hero deals with the opposition.

A career remained important to the heroine. 'Governesses and secretaries turn up less often,' Donnelly noted. 'All the professions appear. Often they are high powered and exotic.' In *Cupid Under Capricorn* stewardess Gail tells the hero how much she enjoys her job, the travel, and the 'luxurious' hotels. She has no immediate plans for marriage: 'I don't think I *could* go back and settle down to the same thing day after day. I'm sure I couldn't . . . I don't want to get married, not for ages. It means giving up too much.' Famous last words for a Mills & Boon heroine.

The Mills & Boon hero remained an 'Alphaman' in every sense of the word. In *Keeper of the Heart* by Gwen Westwood (1968), Dr Stephen Nash is described as 'an advertisement for cigarettes'. In *Merlin's Keep* by Olive Norton (1966), Nurse Rosemary Hurst is staggered by Welsh hero Michael Guise: 'I swung round and confronted a Viking—or my childhood image of one. Sea-coloured eyes and a golden beard.' In Wynne May's *The Highest Peak* (1966), set in Portuguese East Africa, Laura, who works for the Broadcasting Corporation in Johannesburg, is impressed by the sight of uniformed passport officer Manoel de Castro, and 'the wonderful shape of his hands and of his well-cut lips':

> She was also attracted to the way he always seemed to have superb control of his mind and body. There seemed to be a hidden strength in him. He was supremely male and this was expressed in every line of his body, and yet, as she looked at his severe profile, she knew that it was not only something physical that she felt towards this man, although his physical nearness had the power to overwhelm her.

A hint of danger surrounded the 1960s heroes, particularly Violet Winspear's Greeks. In *The Pagan Island* (1972), Hebe is attracted by Nikos Stephanos, who considers women as 'flighty as birds'. He is prone to displays of violence:

> 'To Fate, *kyria*, who arranges whom we shall meet, to love or hate.' He tilted the glass to his lips. 'Drink with me!'
>
> It was an order and she obeyed—and immediately afterwards she was shocked when he deliberately smashed his glass against the edge of the table.
>
> 'Why did you do that?'
>
> 'Only because I felt like doing it.' He lifted his knife and fork to attack his dinner. 'Don't you ever give way to impulse, or does British restraint hold you back?'
>
> 'I should hope my impulses are not so dangerously untidy.'
>
> 'A very British attitude . . .'

Indeed, when Hebe meets rich American tourist Daphne, Daphne tells her why she is entranced by Nikos: 'He throws you, eh? It's the first time you've met a man with a streak of ruthlessness. You're young and sort of innocent, so perhaps you don't know that women are just a bit fascinated by the men who make them feel afraid.' Similarly, in *A Man Apart*, Libby Mason, 19 and well-off, is instantly attracted by the gardener/bricklayer, Adam Roscoe. He kisses her suddenly: 'hard on the mouth and her blood caught fire. She wanted nothing, needed nothing in the world but him.' But her Uncle Graham considers him a crook and a wastrel, and forbids Libby to continue seeing him:

> 'I can see that a young girl like yourself might think it all very romantic to be wandering around the country like a gipsy, but I won't have this man in my house, and I won't have you going to that shack of his on the hills either. For God's sake, girl, can't you see the sort of risk you're running?'

Libby said bluntly, 'What do you think he's going to do? Rape me?'

'I wouldn't put it past him.'

'Well, I would. And I do know him a little better than you do.'

'You're not to see him again, Libby.'

'You can't stop me!'

But it turns out that Adam is a writer who pens a best-seller, *The Loner*. In the end, Uncle Graham admits that Adam's talent shows 'a touch of genius'.

The theory of 'reader identification' so cherished by Mills & Boon for thirty years was put to the test in the 1960s with these newfangled heroes. Although the heroine remained an approachable figure with all her faults and insecurities, the heroes became more obscure, daring, and even fantastic. Violet Winspear wrote of this to Alan Boon in 1973, when she submitted her latest, *Palace of the Pomegranate*:

> I was rather worried that Mills & Boon might not like the idea of a Persian hero. I know there is a lot said about 'reader identification' but it isn't really possible in the fullest sense. If so, then one would have to write about young scrubbers, tired housewives, ailing grandmothers, etc. And who on earth can truly identify with a sardonic Spanish Don, a handsome surgeon, a dashing Italian, or a bittersweet Greek? The real aim of romance is to provide escape and entertainment, not to dish up 'real life' and 'real life people' on a plate with egg on it![3]

Escapism, we have seen, has always been a priority for readers of romantic fiction, although heroes had been more recognizable (and therefore more acceptable) when depicted as an office boss or airline pilot. Hilary Wilde would have agreed. Writing to Boon in 1966 from Swaziland, she mused about her heroes:

> The odd thing is, you know, that if I met one of my heroes, I would probably bash him over the head with an empty whiskey bottle. It is a type I loath and detest. Yet I can remember (quite a long while ago) practically swooning over the Sheik, and Ethel M. Dell's (was it?) The Way of a Man (Eagle?), so I imagine that in all women, deep down inside us, is the primitive desire to be arrogantly bullied. Personally, in real life I can imagine nothing more distasteful but then we all of us need, at some time or other, to retreat into fantasy and I suppose this is a good way in which to do it.

Of course exceptions abounded, and often tended towards the other extreme. For example, a blind hero was a possibility, sometimes regaining his sight with the heroine's help, sometimes not. In 1967 Gladys Fulbrook shared with

Alan Boon a fan letter from a blind man who had enjoyed a Braille version of her novel *The Seeing Hands*, which had been endorsed by the Guide Dogs for the Blind Association:

> Certain passages do ring a bell. It does bring out the great point of the possibility of a full life to anyone blind. I do hope it sells well. It should inspire a lot of blind folk. So many, on being first deprived of their sight give way to despair. If some are lucky enough to have this book read to them it might show them the road to follow.

The Seeing Hands tells the story of Caroline, 19, a junior typist who volunteers in a puppy-walking scheme for the Guide Dogs for the Blind. In a park she meets the hero, Graham Harding, 31 and blind. As a soldier in Bahrain, Graham contracted an eye disease, and lost his sight, as well as his fiancée. Caroline rescues him when he falls in the park, and soon she falls for him. They agree to marry, despite her youth and Graham's handicap. The ending: '"Graham, I'm so happy," she sighed. "And of course you won't need a guide dog, with me around."'

Reader identification also extended to the happy ending. This, however, sometimes raised concerns. In 1972 a Mills & Boon manuscript editor disagreed with Betty Neels over an 'endorsement' of motherhood in Neels's latest novel, *Uncertain Summer*. In this romance, the hero and heroine plan to marry, and have children, with the hero happily announcing he would like a 'large' family of at least four boys and four girls. The Mills & Boon editor altered the reference to four children to two. In doing so, she admitted, 'It is the first tentative attempt I have made to introduce a slightly different editorial line. In this I am backed up by everyone at Mills & Boon except [Alan] Boon, who is still rather nervous about it!' Acknowledging Mills & Boon's 'unique position' as regards reader identification, she added that she was 'one of the growing number of people who are desperately worried about overpopulation', and was personally convinced that Mills & Boon could do something about it:

> It is for this reason as well as personal conviction that we never allow such topics as divorce, adultery, drugs, abortion and permissiveness generally to appear or to be upheld. Our readers don't want this sort of thing in their own lives — and why should they? And we are reassured when our authors state opinions that they feel to be the right ones. For this reason I am increasingly reluctant to let any suggestion creep in that every nice girl ought to want as large a family as possible; I think it's as irresponsible as suggesting that there's no harm in soft drugs.

She added that some readers 'may even feel slightly guilty' if they don't happen to have as many children: 'Although I personally would like to, I don't propose to actively suggest that no more than two children is the number to aim at, or to offer a packet of pills with every paperback—but I <u>am</u> very anxious to tone down the opposite idea.'

In her masterly reply, Neels (whose old-fashioned style of romance was light years away from Leigh and Winspear) believed that, provided there was enough money to bring up and educate children, 'a large family is a marvellous thing (You've noted that my heroes are always well-heeled!).' Neels admitted she deplored birth control when used 'for purely selfish reasons . . . I find it just as unforgivable for a couple to decide on a second car instead of a baby . . . I also feel that if birth control is pushed too far, the coming generations are going to lose their sense of responsibility and family life, as such, will disappear.'

But the passage, as published, was none the less toned down by Neels. It appeared on the penultimate page of the novel. Nurse Serena Potts agrees to marry her Dutch doctor, Gijs van Amstel; they plan to honeymoon in Scotland:

> 'Oh, Gijs, I'm so happy I think I'm going to cry. Laurens told me once that you were very good at letting girls cry on your shoulder.'
>
> 'Not girls, dearest—just you, and later on, our daughters.'
>
> Serena said gently: 'No, little boys, all like you.'
>
> 'There is such a thing as compromise, my love,' said Gijs on a laugh. 'How about an equal number of each?'

❧

Alan Boon maintained his role with authors as their expert script doctor, offering advice where necessary. Increasingly in the 1960s he was forced to comment on extreme statements or situations in manuscripts, usually of a 'sexual' nature. Here the context was very important; if appropriate to the particular novel and setting, Boon appeared more willing to relax his normal restrictions. But Irish readers as well as the objections of Mary Bonnycastle and Harlequin Books were always at the back of his mind. When an author strayed from Harlequin requirements, Boon was quick to act. 'Our Canadian associates have a basic requirement for a fairly simple, straight forward romance,' Boon advised Nora Sanderson, a New Zealander married to a Methodist minister, in 1967. 'They have felt that recent N.S. novels have [not] been their sort of story. This has cost you a good deal of money . . . For the record, not that you are likely to deal with such situations, they do not like heroines to be in love with married men, or married heroines in love with other men, or unhappy married situations, and no touching on differences of colour.'

Certain subjects remained taboo, such as excessive drinking. In 1963 Boon wrote to Ivy Ferrari on changes to her debut manuscript, *Sister at Ryeminster*.

'The hero we would like also to be pretty above board and not to have been involved in a car crash while under the influence,' he said. 'I don't want you to feel that we are clamping down too hard on realism but after talking to you I think you understand our position.' The incident was removed. Divorce, too was still forbidden. In 1959 Boon wrote to the literary agent Peter Janson-Smith about *A Time to Love* by Janey Scott (Roberta Leigh):

> As you know, in this story there is a situation where the hero is engaged to a girl in circumstances that he believes his wife has divorced him. It is stated that the wife's country had made those wives who were married to citizens the other side of the Iron Curtain, divorce their husbands. In view of the Irish situation, where divorce is concerned, we would prefer the situation to be that the government had decided on annulment of the marriages, rather than divorce. We would be glad to have the author's authority to make the one or two alterations in the story to change divorce to annulment.

Published in 1960, *A Time to Love* tells the story of Tanya Kovacs of the fictional nation Petrovia and her former husband, Adrian, an Englishman and ex-diplomat now running for Parliament. Adrian becomes engaged to Diana, daughter of wealthy Lord Biddell. When Adrian tries to discover whether Tanya is still alive (or still his wife), he pesters the embassy: 'He had been told that all Rovnians [of Petrovia] who had married Britons had been given decrees of annulment, so that in the likely event of his tracing Tanya, she would no longer be his wife.' Problem solved. Similarly, in 1961 Joyce Dingwell crossed the line with *The Third in the House*. While Boon liked the novel, and said it was 'admirably written', 'a problem which has been raised concerns the basic situation, i.e. that the heroine marries a divorced man while his first wife is still alive':

> I think that this situation is one that would worry a number of our readers. It would be very difficult indeed in this country to find an Anglican minister to perform such a service, and the Roman Catholics would be very hostile to the idea. We have, of course, a large number of Roman Catholic readers, and the Southern Irish market is very important to us. . . . Do you think it would be possible for you to revise the book so that Keir's first wife is dead before the story starts?

Dingwell agreed, killing off the first wife.

What Alan Boon termed 'skullduggery' in novels was also discouraged. Many authors tried to inject an air of adventure or even mystery into their novels, but Boon considered these elements distracting to the romance and confusing. 'We want a story to tranquillise us,' Boon explained. 'You don't want violence brought into it.' Here he was in full agreement with Harlequin Books. In 1965 Iris Danbury suggested to Boon that her new novel 'follow some skullduggery in industrial spying that might involve my girl. The papers are full of microphone capers, and secrets of the board-room being conveyed to rivals. It need not be too involved or what women call "business-y."' This was not a good idea, Boon replied: 'We would prefer that the skullduggery was played down pretty much, no police Inspectors running around.'

To new author Roumelia Lane, born in England but living in Majorca, Boon was more specific about violence. In 1967 he wrote to say he liked Lane's synopsis for a romantic novel, except for the ending: 'We would like you to consider the possibility of altering the ending. We would prefer a situation in which Ryan rescued the heroine from a spot of danger in which there was no question of violence cutting across racial relations—i.e. the coloured houseboy attacking the white heroine.' In her reply, Lane suggested, 'How would it be if I put the antagonistic slant on the widowed hotel proprietress (who has designs on Ryan Holt herself) and kept Nabu the servant just a background character of the story?' Boon agreed, but added:

> We would prefer that human violence did not enter the story. Perhaps you could use a wild animal, or storm, or brushfire, or something you may think of in that line. The reason is that we have an important North American market which does not like human violence, and this market can be of considerable value to you.

Boon noted, 'Verbal battles between heroines and their rivals (of course, the emphasis is on the rivals being bitchy!) tend to be effective in this genre.'

Boon's mention of 'racial relations' raises another taboo. The race question was often skirted and largely avoided, especially among Mills & Boon's authors from South Africa. Wynne May noted that, given the problems in South Africa, Alan Boon advised her not to set her novels there. 'It was difficult living here, but we were determined to stay on and see it through,' May said. 'I went from island to island backgrounds. Then, I used Namibia, Kenya, Mombasa, and Zanzibar. I am fortunate to be well-travelled.' Similarly, Gwen Westwood noted that she had one dispute with Boon over race, and never repeated her mistake. 'Only once I remember Boon said he thought it was unnecessary when I had mentioned, in describing the way of life in a small South African town, that the heroine wondered how long it would go on this way,' she recalled. But her native African characters were sympathetic figures, she maintained: 'My African servants in the books were always pleasant but I suppose it always was the master–servant relationship, although the children usually played with African companions.'

Other, more established (and English) authors were less co-operative, and expressed a social activism characteristic of the 1960s. In 1963 Jean MacLeod hoped that Joan Lee and *Woman's Weekly* would purchase serial rights to

Sugar Island, set on a Barbados plantation. But Lee disliked the depiction of the native people in the novel, much to MacLeod's disagreement:

> I don't really feel that Mrs. Lee can possibly object with regard to the coloured people in the story. They are West Indians and one couldn't write without including them. On these big sugar estates there are literally hundreds of them, all happily employed by white or coloured owners. Neither Mammy nor Jake are objectionable types, I feel.

Indeed, the inhabitants of the sugar plantation to which Kay Mathieson, the heroine, returns are friendly, if depicted in a stereotypical manner reminiscent of the slave characters in *Gone with the Wind*. Upon seeing Kay, 'Mammy', the housekeeper, exclaims, 'My Miss Kathy, but you am a sight for sore eyes!' Boon supported MacLeod, and said *Sugar Island* 'has the makings of an outstanding Jean MacLeod novel'.

In 1964 Boon asked Alex Stuart for major changes to her latest manuscript, entitled *The Scottish Soldier*. In her submission letter, Stuart realized that there might be problems with this novel. 'Please understand that I <u>want</u> Mills & Boon to publish this one very much but I know your reputation for publishing "pleasant books" is of great value to you and, of course, wouldn't want to damage this,' she told Boon. The problem concerned Stuart's insistence that the heroine's father act as a crusader in race relations in Lehar, a fictional African nation. He publishes a book demanding equal rights for black people, and targets South Africa and its apartheid laws. This was hardly the stuff of a Mills & Boon novel, Stuart admitted, and at first she did offer a change in background:

> The only situation I should find almost impossible to make would be if I had to cut out the heroine's father's story, as the whole character of the heroine depends on this. But I could (with difficulty) make the father an American who got involved in the Colour Question in one of the Southern States—do we care about American sales? Personally I think that having the book banned in S. Africa because it was anti-apartheid ought to increase its sales elsewhere but this is your province, not mine. ...This is the sort of 'romantic' novel I am now hoping to be able to write (Occasionally, not all the time) as I believe it to be the kind which <u>must</u> come in the future, if the romantic novel is to hold its new, young readers and go forward, rather than backward.

Stuart's thoughts on the future course of romantic fiction are interesting since she, as Vice-President of the Romantic Novelists Association, often spoke on the future of the genre. Boon was certainly sympathetic with the subject matter and appreciated Stuart's frustrations as an author. In offering a compromise which would still make this an important work, Boon was willing to bend the rules far more than he would in the past, to salvage for his fiction 'Empire' what he called (unfortunately) 'operation asbestos':

> We feel it undesirable that the heroine's father should have written this book which brings him into conflict with South Africa and we appreciate your willingness to modify this aspect of the story. Could it not be that he had written something like THE RIGHTS OF NATIONS a la T. Paine?

> What worries us is the colour question and we would prefer that Lehar should be an uncoloured nation in the history of Israel, Cyprus, Malta, and X others. There is no doubt today, as our reader has suggested, that when even a prospective Labour cabinet minister is supposed to be in danger of losing his seat because of the ramifications of immigration, that the subject is dynamite.

> We have very many Indians, Arabs, and Negroes who read our novels and we would prefer that they were just subjects of Lehar . . . I appreciate that this could mean a different concept of the book for you, but we feel that the work could still be quite enthralling if the aforementioned amendments were executed along the lines we have suggested. Under separate cover we are sending you one of the typescripts so that you can examine for yourself the possibility of your carrying out our operation asbestos.

> Believe me we have not written in this way without considerable thought and do appreciate all the implications of your feelings. I think it would be best when next we meet to talk this matter over. We do very much indeed appreciate also the great loyalty you have shown in wishing to remain in the Empire and I can assure you that our feelings in this respect are equal to your own.

Stuart, writing 'Oh, woe is me and all that jazz', refused to make these major changes and asked to take the book elsewhere, such as Collins: 'It is with deep regret that I say I can't do as you ask.' She decided to speed up work on her next Mills & Boon novel, a standard Doctor-Nurse romance, *Samaritan's Hospital*: 'SAMARITAN'S won't upset any Arab, Indian, Negro or S. African readers—it's a safe Mills & Boon straight-jacketed [*sic*] novel.'[4]

✣

The flourishing Doctor-Nurse genre was ripe with potential problems, and, again, Harlequin's objections were always taken into consideration since Harlequin was the major customer of this 'product'. In 1966, for example, Mills & Boon advised Nora Sanderson in her latest manuscript, *The Patients in Ward Seven* (which became *Junior Nurse on Ward Seven*), to avoid 'jarring episodes or mentions'—in this particular case, the mention of abortion. 'This genre of story has sometimes been described as cosy, escapist if you like,' Alan Boon wrote, 'and while we feel that gradually more can go, it is still desirable to steer clear of what is sometimes called [the] kitchen sink.' Boon elaborated on Harlequin's—and therefore Mills & Boon's—requirements:

> They require a fairly straightforward love story with heroine and hero dominating the story (and without an excess of back-chat between subsidiary characters) which, above all, can be read by young Canadian girls in their teens without any words or incidents occurring which might be considered to strike a jarring note. Please do not think that we are suggesting that young girls in their teens cannot read the N.S. books but I am sure, for example, the very mention of the word 'abortion' would worry our Canadian associates from the point of view of what they feel their teenage girls should read.

But certain violence was, apparently, tolerated if central to the dramatic plot. In *Junior Nurse on Ward Seven*, for example, a pyromaniac stalks the hospital, setting several fires and injuring patients. Other Mills & Boon authors fought for a greater degree of realism in their hospital stories. In 1970 *Woman's Weekly* rejected *Casualty Speaking* Olive Norton, in which, they complained, 'the baby bashing is too shocking (even though neither of the babies was killed—and one would have expected at least one to be)'. In her reply, Norton, a nurse, refused to compromise and eliminate the violence: 'Baby-bashing is all too common a feature of Casualty life, and I was indeed trying to show that it goes on all the time. One must leave <u>one</u> door open for the reader to go on thinking about—life isn't neatly tied off at the end of a specific story: it goes on. And on.' Indeed, in the published novel (1971), Norton offered a graphic account of an inner-city hospital, not unlike the medical drama programmes currently in vogue on television. Nurse Min Westwood, who 'thoroughly enjoyed the hurly-burly of her work in the casualty department of a big city hospital', expects the unexpected, including drug pushers who attack her. The 'baby bashing' concerned two children, aged 2 and 3, beaten up by teen thugs with bricks outside the local fish and chip shop. The attack, Min is told, is a consequence of having fewer policemen on the beat, due to 'budget cuts'.

Although Mills & Boon accepted greater realism in its Doctor-Nurse novels, it insisted that the main characters uphold the highest standard of the profession. In 1964 Welsh novelist Jane Ray asked Alan Boon's opinion about the changes *Woman's Weekly* requested to her debut novel, *Mary into Mair*, specifically 'That Hugh should be a medical student who doesn't complete his course (editorial policy—they don't like denigrating the medical profession by showing an irresponsible doctor).' It is surprising that *Woman's Weekly* was so concerned, since Hugh Trevor, a medical student and 'rather wayward son of the local doctor' in the Welsh village, is not the hero but a cad who compromises Mary into an engagement ('What right had he to talk about marriage? He wasn't qualified, he had yet to prove himself a doctor—it was far too soon for him to be thinking of marriage,' Mary says). Hugh criticizes the 'medical rat race' and fails his exams. But he gets his come-uppance for paying disrespect to the profession: Hugh is killed in a car crash, which allows Mary to marry her neighbour and the hero, Owen Pritchard.

Similarly, nurses had to be depicted as above reproach. Those who were not (usually the secondary characters) were often used by authors to illustrate unsavoury characteristics or actions, as lessons to the reader. In 1963 Alan Boon wrote to Hilda Nickson, a nurse and member of the Liverpool Writers' Circle, on her latest manuscript, *The World of Nurse Mitchell*. In a classic understatement, Boon expressed concern over 'the slightly controversial aspects':

> The feeling now here is that if you find it possible, we would like you to write out the Lesbian angle and the V.D. References, and we are sorry that we should have come back to you at such a late stage; but the feeling here is that it would be a good commercial policy to do this if possible.

Nickson did indeed eliminate references to venereal disease among the nurses and their patients, but the 'Lesbian angle' remained. This goes to show how flexible Mills & Boon could be, so long as the issues were couched in euphemisms—and a firm 'life lesson' was supplied.' The situation in this novel concerned two nurses (and secondary characters), Terry Marsh and Betty Shaw. Terry is tall, lanky, and gaunt, 'fingers stained yellow with heavy smoking'. Christened Theresa, the 'masculine-sounding' name suited her. Betty, small and 'giggly', follows Terry everywhere. Nurse Vanessa Mitchell, the heroine, suspects the friendship, musing, 'Terry certainly seemed to exert a strong influence over the other girl.' She is determined to help them: 'As it was, while in hospital they would be objects of derision, in the world outside they would be set apart as misfits, living in their own narrow, private little universe, only half alive, and ending their days as frustrated spinsters or worse.' Clearly Vanessa knows what these 'misfits' really are, and the reader is also left with no doubt. She tries to talk sense into Betty when Terry is stricken with the flu (and incapacitated). In this exchange, there can also be no doubt as to the author's real opinions on the subject:

> 'Really, I thought you were beginning to learn a little sense. You and Terry don't *own* each other, don't belong to each other. Can't you see the difference between a good friendship and a bad one? Don't you see, Betty? You're doing each other real harm.'
>
> Betty's eyes were wide. 'How are we? That's a silly thing to say.'

'No, it isn't. Deep down inside, every woman wants a husband and children. A happy marriage. A man to love her and to be loved by. You and Terry might be robbing each other of that happiness. That is, so long as you carry on like this.'

Apparently Betty fancies a man, Dr Moorby, but Terry is jealous. Terry confronts Vanessa and accuses her of 'trying to break us up'. Vanessa tells Terry to let Betty go:

'Why can't you love Betty enough to let her stand on her own feet, and spread your capacity for loving over a wider field? . . . I'd like both you and Betty to know real happiness. You can change, Terry, if you want to. They say it comes easier when you're young.'

In the end, Nickson provided a happy ending: both Terry and Betty find themselves (male) doctors to love, and the lesbian element in the hospital was eliminated.

The very fact that Mills & Boon published novels with mildly controversial, even 'taboo' subjects in the 1960s illustrates how receptive the firm was in acknowledging changes in society—and also how independent its editorial board had become. Paperback publishing gave Mills & Boon a certain freedom to trust its own instincts again, free from the magazine editors who so dominated the 1950s novels.

Time and time again, Mills & Boon serials were rejected by magazines in the 1960s, particularly by staid editors at D. C. Thomson in Dundee. In 1965, for example, J. D. Mackay, editor of the *People's Friend*, turned down Essie Summers's *Sweet are the Ways*, featuring a minister hero, Revd Dougal MacNab. While he personally enjoyed it, Mackay explained that he could not offend his own, mostly Presbyterian readership:

There is much in this story that would be strange to our readers, and perhaps unacceptable to them. There is the fact that two ministers are involved in the heroine's life, one of them letting her down badly in time of stress and police court publicity. Even though towards the end of the story he returns to confess his fault and reaffirm his love, the image of perfection has been destroyed, thus contradicting the Scottish concept of the ministry. In the minds of our readers, ministers are above reproach and must always be so.

There is also mystery in the heroine's past life, repeatedly referred to throughout the story, which ultimately reveals itself as an innocent involvement in a raid on a publican's premises and a murder charge. This, even though narrated in retrospect, is again not 'Friend' material.

But *Sweet are the Ways* (1965), set in Summers's native New Zealand, was one of her most successful novels, which she dedicated to her own minister husband, 'and to the readers all over the world who have asked for a story about a minister'. In this novel Elspeth is an advertising copywriter who writes romantic stories. Dougal MacNab is the minister of St Enoch's who has adopted two orphans. D. C. Thomson would certainly have had no objection to the promotion of Christianity in this novel as Summers devoted long passages to a discussion of faith and God. In courting Elspeth, Dougal professes 'friendship, liking, respect, passion. See—*I* don't flinch from the word, nor replace it with a pallid substitute like attraction!' But Elspeth believes she is an unfit wife for a minister, due to her past ('A minister's wife must be like Caesar's—above reproach!'). While engaged to another minister, Elspeth, in an act of compassion, harboured a friend and suspected fugitive, who was found, was jailed, and spoke of Elspeth's involvement. Although her name was cleared, the minister broke the engagement. But none of this matters to kindly Dougal: 'If the church depended upon being staffed with a lot of saints, it would collapse from want of workers.' They marry in the end.

Clearly Summers, one of Mills & Boon's top-selling authors in the 1960s, did not shy away from 'unusual' situations, which could explain her popularity. She was often more tolerant of character failings than were the magazine editors. In 1962 Alan Boon wrote to Summers about her new novel, *Where No Roads Go*. Joan Lee of *Woman's Weekly* wanted to purchase the serial rights but was concerned by the scenario of the heroine being in love with a married man. Boon's defence and support of Summers was remarkable but not surprising, considering her popularity:

> In the past this sort of thing has not been entirely acceptable in these quarters, because of a feeling that married readers had no sympathy for a girl in love with a married man. However, there is a 'wind of change' going on in these matters now, and Mrs. Lee asked me what I thought . . . She told me that there was a general feeling among some of the younger editors that the time was right now for more realism . . .

> I feel that this part of the story adds to the strength of the story, and you might weaken your writing by worrying about possible taboos. Of course, I would not suggest that the heroine should go in for illicit sexual relations or anything of that sort of thing.

Certainly not: in her reply, Summers expressed her delight at Boon's endorsement, and was pleased that her writing was considered 'strong':

> I try to keep abreast of our changing world, like to be realistic—yet at the same time idealistic. I could not bear to write a story with the heroine cherishing an undying regard for a married man. I feel it is quite possible for her to be tempted into a situation like that—in fact for all heroines to be above temptation of straying affection is too hard to swal-

low—but with me it wouldn't be possible to involve her more or less permanently.

I didn't use that incident (where she has determined to cut out anything clandestine—but gets involved with the hero) merely to form a basis of misunderstanding, but to reach readers with the idea that though one may slip a little, it is then that the things we live by, come to our aid and give us the necessary courage to make a decision that costs us pain.

Like all Mills & Boon authors, Summers hoped to instruct—and influence—her captive audience for the greater good. In *Where No Roads Go*, set in Australia, Prudence pines for Godfrey, who is married. The hero, Hugo, scolds her and other girls who act in this foolish fashion: 'I saw my sister's marriage break up because of a girl like you. A girl who appeared, on the surface, sweet and wholesome. I saw the happiness of a home, a whole family disintegrate.' Prudence tries to defend her actions, claiming that since Godfrey's bitchy wife has 'ceased to be a wife' (in every sense), he needed to seek solace elsewhere:

> A wife could be faithful in the strict sense of the word, yet untrue to her marriage vows just the same. She doesn't only vow to keep only unto her husband, she vows to love and to cherish him. A woman who nags doesn't keep that vow. She could be so frigid she drove her husband to seek companionship elsewhere, yet in the eyes of the law she is blameless.

But Prudence comes to her senses, deciding to part from Godfrey (helped, no doubt, by his accident in a train crash).

One of the best examples of the divergence between the Mills & Boon romance of the 1960s and the past Mills & Boon romance obsessed with pleasing the magazine editors, occurred in 1969, when Maurice Paterson, editor of D. C. Thomson's best-selling *My Weekly*, rejected Karin Mutch's *The Story of Jody*: 'I'm afraid Judy [*sic*] is too off-beat a character even for us. I don't think *My Weekly* readers would really get interested in a girl from a motor-bike gang background! I do feel sure, however, that one of the teenage magazines would surely be attracted to it.'

The Story of Jody was set in Mutch's native New Zealand, and published when the author was only 20 years old. Jody Linton, an orphan who 'liked "living for kicks", and bad luck to anyone who got in her way', is a most unorthodox Mills & Boon heroine. 'Self-destructive, selfish and willful', Jody hangs out with a Hell's Angels gang and is called 'A daughter of Satan'. On page 23 she marries Brent, brother of the hero, Adam; on page 24, drinks several vodka-and-orange cocktails; and on page 25, Brent is killed in a car crash while driving drunk. Newly widowed (and arrested) Jody is put in her brother-in-law's care and lives on his farm. Adam, racked with revenge, nearly pushes wild Jody off a cliff.

But Jody's transformation under Adam's stern gaze is a powerful story of redemption, directed by Mutch towards her rebellious young generation of the late 1960s. Jody learns to cook and clean, to rise at 6 a.m. and wash before breakfast. Jody confesses to Adam that she's cold and hard because of her upbringing by an aunt and uncle who didn't want her: 'I've never had parents who doted on me, whom I could lean and depend on, whom I could cling to. I've never had security.' But this was still a romantic novel, and Jody, who grows to love Adam, decides to make the 'other woman', Shona Barrie, jealous. She gives Adam a public punishing kiss, 'on his mouth, slowly and deliberately'. He returns the favour:

> 'Adam!' she gasped indignantly. 'Take your . . .'
>
> But her protest, weak though it was, remained unspoken as his head bent and his lips covered hers. Shock drained all the energy from her and for a few seconds she was limp in his arms. Then, slowly, her senses stirred to life as an electric current shot through her, quickening her heartbeats and pulses so that they leapt and bounded, causing a sensation that she had never before experienced to such an overwhelming extent. It was a peculiarly lightheaded—and the most glorious—sensation imaginable.
>
> As always she didn't stop to think. She obeyed each impulse and wound her arms around his neck and responded, returning kiss for kiss, her ardour matching his own.

Confused, Jody runs away, lives in a convent, finds religion, cares for children, and considers becoming a nun. But Adam locates her, and forgives her for Brent's death, since it has been discovered that Brent had leukaemia, and would not have had long to live anyway (a typical justification of tragedy in a romantic novel). Jody tries the dating game with her peers, and likes the 'normal-looking' crowd at a party:

> Jody found it a very pleasant change to be in the company of a boy who was clean, handsome and smelled of a subtle aftershave and whose hair was not greasy and covering his collar. And instead of scruffy jeans, shirt and overjacket, he wore casual, well-pressed slacks, a tan skivvy and a cream V-neck cardigan . . .
>
> Everyone verbally appreciated the trouble Glenda and her flatmates had obviously gone to cooking the savouries, cream-filled sponges and preparing the club sandwiches and cream and shrimp-topped snacks, the perfect, quickly consumed Pavlova, covered with cream and sliced gooseberries.

Jody is transformed, and, with Adam declaring his love, promises to reform herself, hanging up her motorcycle helmet forever. Clearly, there were benefits to a clean-cut, morally upright lifestyle, including the love of a wealthy husband: 'His eyes were regarding her, no longer with contempt, or impatience, or tolerance, but with a deep love—a need. To love and need Adam, and to be loved and needed by him, she would want nothing else filling the places in her heart which had been empty for so long.'

※

As we have noted, the biggest editorial influence of the decade came from overseas, and the editors—led by Mary Bonnycastle—at Harlequin Books. Alan Boon did his best to satisfy his 'North American associates', as it was in the best financial interests of Mills & Boon. In letter after letter, Boon encouraged his authors to toe the Canadian line so as to make their manuscripts eligible for the 'biggest box office' and the 'highest gross'. 'There should be no situations of girls in love with married men, no seduction, no violence, no mystery,' Boon instructed Peta Cameron in 1967. 'This does not mean to say that the story has to be milk-and-water. There can be an element of conflict between the heroine and hero which can be brought out in the backchat.'

But not even the persuasive Alan Boon could stop his authors from maturing as writers, and therein lay the problem. Violet Winspear, Roberta Leigh, Anne Mather, and other talented (and prolific) Mills & Boon authors in the 1960s developed a more openly erotic writing style which would surely send blushes to the cheeks of the Bonnycastles in Canada. 'We were building up a bank, if you like, of authors who the public really liked,' Alan Boon explained. 'They had "sex" in them. We had to publish these books. If we hadn't had the courage of our convictions and published some of these books—some of them were quite strong and shocking—the authors would have gone to some other publisher.' Given Mills & Boon's careful market research, the response from readers was positive, not negative. 'In general, we operated the way the tide flowed. We would decide which way it would flow, using information that was coming up,' Boon said. 'We had a lot of readers' letters saying, "I like this" or "I like that." That would influence our decisions. I don't think we ever pushed our authors, saying, "You have to make this more licentious."'

Not until well into the 1970s would Mills & Boon follow the trail blazed by the notorious 'sex novels' published in the 1960s, and permit premarital sex between the hero and heroine (when Mills & Boon did, it was considered acceptable at the time to the readership, and published under a special series banner.). Winspear, Mills & Boon's 'sexiest' author (and regularly banned by Harlequin), resented the sexier novels and films of the 1960s, devoid of romance but full of rape (*Last Tango in Paris*, in her estimation, was simply 'sheer mental masturbation'). 'Too much realistic sex is out of place in the romance,' she wrote to Alan Boon in 1970:

I go for the vicarious thrill . . . 'Gone with the Wind' when Gable slung Scarlett over his shoulder and marched up and up those stairs with her—symbolism if I ever saw it! It would have been spoiled if, as in today's films, he had been shown tearing her clothes off. We had a saying at my old firm—'there's a difference between scratching your back and tearing it to bits'.

She added, 'I don't agree that women like dirty books. I think that when it comes to fiction women are like men with their shirts, they like them crisp and comfortable at the same time.'[6] In her novels, Winspear was the mistress of euphemism, which enabled her to include 'sexier' situations without being the least bit explicit. At the conclusion of *The Pagan Island*, for example, the marriage-in-name-only between Hebe and her Greek god, Nikos, bursts into love in a particularly vivid description:

> With an incoherent murmur she buried her face against the hard warm muscle and bone of him. 'I want to stay to be yours, or I want to go away quickly, because I love you too much.'
>
> Firmly then he held her away from him and he searched her face, her eyes, her pleading lips. 'Life with a Greek is a bursting skin of wine; a thing of passion and sometimes pain; joy and anger; aggression and surrender. Can you take all that? So fair and slender—'
>
> 'Nikos! I am Hebe! Cupbearer to the god!'[7]

Like Winspear, several of Roberta Leigh's novels were deemed too 'advanced' for publication by Harlequin, including one Rachel Lindsay title, *Price of Love* (1967). In this novel, Paula MacKinnon is a dedicated, older doctor who is married to her work. 'Biologically I'm a woman with woman's needs. Of course I'd like to marry,' she tells the divorced doctor who pursues her. But Paula instead is pursued by Jason Scott, a rich playboy whose life she saved after a car crash. In appearance, we are told, he is 'every girl's idea of a Greek god'. In one particularly sensual scene, while Jason lies unconscious, Paula traces a path with her finger along the lines of his face and 'the full, sensual mouth'.

Jason wakes up, recovers, and vigorously pursues his doctor, despite their difference in ages. Initially, marriage is the furthest thing from his mind:

> 'What game are you playing at? Why are you interested in me?'
>
> 'Why is a man interested in a woman?'
>
> 'For marriage or a love affair,' she said bluntly.
>
> His eyes glittered with amusement, giving her a glimpse of how handsome he must be when he was well. 'I take it you're not interested in the latter?'
>
> 'You take it correctly,' she retorted. 'And neither of us are interested in

the former! So why don't you act like an adult instead of a spoiled play-boy!'

Despite Paula's realization that Jason has 'known' scores of women ('"He's used to sharing a room with a woman," she thought resentfully.'), they do marry, and head to his villa in the south of France. Their lovemaking—as man and wife—is frequent and described by Leigh with an explicitness not permitted by Mills & Boon in the past:

> The dress fell around her feet and his hands came up to her breasts, his body close against hers, then he swung her into his arms and carried her to the bed . . .

> Drying herself with a large fleecy towel, she inspected her body in the mirror, marvelling that it looked no different since last night. Memories coloured her cheeks and she savoured the joy of them. With what sensuous delight Jason had made love to her; awakening her to such tumultuous passion that everything had been forgotten except the overwhelming desire to become a part of him. No longer has she been passive and accepting. Glorying in her power to arouse him, she lived her victory to the full until, exhausted and spent, they lay side by side, his hand covering her breast, her head on his shoulder. But languor, like passion, did not last, and when their need for each other returned it brought an even greater closeness. Their loving this time was slower, each moment lingered over and enjoyed, the climax a sharing of exquisite agony.

Clearly, this was new ground for a Mills & Boon novel. Interestingly, after suffering a miscarriage (which Jason attributes to stress and overwork), Paula agrees to make the ultimate sacrifice for her man and 'for our children' by choosing to leave her beloved hospital and open a private practice: 'The doctor in her was forgotten, the woman was predominant; the way it had to be.' Motherhood still followed marriage (and transcended the heroine's career) in Mills & Boon romances.

Sex between husband and wife became commonplace in Mills & Boon novels in the late 1960s. *The Marriage of Caroline Lindsay* (1968), the first novel by Margaret Rome, 'caused a sensation', as Mills & Boon admitted in its catalogue (and was, naturally, rejected by Harlequin). Rome, who worked in a biscuit factory in a mill town in northern England, wove a dizzying tale of marriage, divorce, death, pregnancy, and deceit set amid the villas of the rich and famous in Rome. Caroline is initially shocked that her unmarried sister, Dorinda, is having a baby. But once Dorinda expresses how much she loves Vito, the Italian father, Caroline feels better: 'I haven't experienced love such as yours, but I believe loving means giving, and the more you love a man the more you must want to give. It's quite simple, really, isn't it?' But soon Vito dies, Dorinda abandons her newborn son, Vito jun., leaving Caroline as his new 'mother'. Vito's cousin arrives from Rome to claim the child. Domenico Vicari, who 'had the bearing of a gladiator', runs one of the 'largest and most famous export and import businesses in Italy'. He likes Caroline, and claims her, too, offering a marriage-in-name-only so she can help him raise Vito jun. Once in Rome, everyone's blood runs hotter. 'I am no celibate,' Domenico says. 'I can only promise you that I will endeavour to give you time before I claim a husband's privileges.' He eventually does, on several occasions, and before long Caroline falls 'desperately' in love with him.

If Mills & Boon authors wrote freely about post-marital sex, they also explored sexual problems between man and wife, which surely must have been a concern of at least some of the readership. In *Big Man at Katta Wirri* by Anne Vinton (1970), for example, the title character, Raitch Macauley, lives up to the book title: 'Gary Cooper's double . . . a big man indeed, six foot three at least and with wide shoulders.' Raitch is boss of Katta Wirri, a remote sheep station in Australia. Innocent English lass Tessa Meade answers a newspaper advertisement to tutor Raitch's invalid nephew, Wayne, 7. Needless to say, Tessa and Raitch fall in love and marry. But on their wedding night, as a rapturous Tessa 'felt herself emerging as from a chrysalis into the full realization of womanhood and wifehood', things do not turn out as planned:

> When you were giving yourself to the man you loved it was a language of emotions, of colours, of salmon pinks and vivid scarlets and a shining, blinding white flash just out of reach but you were getting nearer and nearer and it was indescribably beautiful and wonderful. Then—a thrust of rejection. No, it couldn't be! Raitch was putting her from him, drawing on his robe. 'It's no use,' he said in desperation.

Raitch cannot perform, and a bewildered Tessa 'soothed him sexlessly, wondering what she could do to wipe out his humiliating sense of having failed her'. Good woman that she is, Tessa pledges to be patient, a 'wife in name only' for several days, 'helpless to intervene in the battle of the man against his outraged masculine pride'. But true to the Mills & Boon romance—and its promise of a happy ending—Tessa does not have long to wait. Raitch, smelling of beer, sneaks home one afternoon from shearing sheep to consummate their love: 'They journeyed together that same enchanted preliminary way of lovers, and this time no one dammed the tide of discovery. They crowned their love.' And, in that moment, they conceive a child—which must have legitimized for some staid readers this afternoon indulgence!

Like Lillia Warren, Rosalind Brett and Esther Wyndham in the 1950s, the willingness to depart from the old formulae displayed by authors such as Winspear, Leigh, Rome, and even Vinton was imitated by other Mills & Boon authors, but with varying degrees of success. More often than not, however, Alan Boon had to apply the brakes. In 1970 he informed Valerie K. Nelson's agent, Michael Horniman of A. P. Watt, that Nelson had gone too far with her latest manuscript, *The Blonde Girl.* He included the verdict of Mills & Boon's manuscript reader, who was appalled by the content. 'All this is too much to load on to the basic structure of the romantic novel,' the reader wrote. 'As for the <u>dolce vita</u> party of which the Captain of Police relates, "there was drink, yes; much worse, drugs and, I am afraid, unmentionable orgies" (p. 174), perhaps the least said, the better.' The manuscript was not published, as even the 'new' Mills & Boon had its limits. Nelson, first published by Mills & Boon in 1936 and a veteran of 58 novels in 34 years, was trying too hard, perhaps, for one last hurrah.

Afterword
The Global Company and its Product

The sad thing about prose today is that people are under the impression that if you call something by a different name, it's no longer unpleasant. You know, when you all write about pre-marital sex, what you mean is fornication. If you don't know the word, look it up in the Bible — and the penalties.

Mary Burchell, 1986

Every few years Mills & Boon changes. A change is always author-led and mirrors what is happening in the world outside. We are not behind the times, at all, despite critical opinion; we are well aware of current trends and keep abreast of them. At one time we had a kiss in the middle and a kiss in the end — now full sex sometimes occurs quite early on!

Sheila Holland, 1995

THE story of Mills & Boon in the past twenty-five years is an epic tale worthy of its own history. Neither the Boons nor the Bonnycastles could have predicted the direction that the new company would take from 1972, when Harlequin Enterprises acquired Mills & Boon. In Part I of this history, we have revealed how co-operation between the two companies intensified in the 1960s, to the enrichment of both firms, as sales of Mills & Boon and Harlequin paperbacks extended beyond the United Kingdom and North America, with translations in eighteen languages. This expansion appears modest, however, when compared to the colossus that Harlequin Mills & Boon, Ltd. would become by 1998: worldwide sales of 160 million copies, in 24 languages and 100 markets, and a stable of 1,500 authors (up from 150 in 1971).

In Part II of this study, we noted how the editorial policies and concerns of both Harlequin and Mills & Boon tended to diverge, principally on the issue of sex and how it should be handled in the romantic novel (if at all). This disagreement was rapidly resolved (as the 'sexier' books achieved record sales), and today there are fewer restrictions and boundaries for authors than at any time in Mills & Boon's history. In 1998 it is not surprising to read in the pages of a Mills & Boon novel: 'He dug his fingers into her hips, lifted her up, pulled her warm silk thighs apart to open her fully. Then with a thrust of his hips, he plunged into her, deep and hard, all the way to the hilt.'

≥

When John, Alan, and Carol Boon, along with their sister, Dinah, completed the agreement to 'merge' (in reality, sell) Mills & Boon with Harlequin Enterprises in 1971, any fears for the future direction of the two companies were allayed by the presence of Richard 'Dick' Bonnycastle, Jr., a dynamic presence and a personal friend. As John Boon has stated, the deal was regarded as a solid publishing agreement, and hopes for the future were bright.

But the reality was somewhat different. Alan and John Boon effectively relinquished control of their company to a firm based 3,000 miles away. They were in a minority position on the Harlequin Board of Directors, and Harlequin executives now sat on Mills & Boon's board. The agreement, moreover, did not give Mills & Boon control over the distribution of its novels, and all of the major decisions were increasingly made in Toronto, not London. In 1975 the Boons were dealt another blow when Bonnycastle sold a controlling interest in Harlequin to the Torstar Corporation, a communications company based in Toronto (and publishers of the *Toronto Star* newspaper). Bonnycastle left the company, and Mills & Boon effectively became part of a giant conglomerate, with an accent on maximizing profits. We can understand, therefore, the disappointment of the Boon brothers as they gradually lost control of their destiny, and the legacy inherited from their father. 'We thought we might be able to influence Harlequin more than we did,' John Boon confessed. 'We did have the absolute whip hand in Editorial. But on other things, no.'

But we cannot weep too much for the Boons, as the Torstar acquisition placed both Harlequin and Mills & Boon on the road to unprecedented expansion—and profits. Torstar brought an injection of cash and rapid growth, lifting Harlequin and Mills & Boon to even greater heights. For the first time, under the guise of the Procter & Gamble-trained Lawrence Heisey, the marketing potential of romantic novels was explored and developed, with novels distributed in non-traditional ways and outlets (given away in boxes of feminine napkins, for example). In a departure from the traditional method of exporting books produced in Canada or Britain, separate publishing companies were set up overseas to publish directly in the indigenous language. Among the new companies were businesses in France, Germany, Italy, Holland, Greece, Japan, South America, Australia, and New Zealand. By 1981 Harlequin was the world's largest publisher of romances (a distinction it still holds), with 80 per cent of the world market, 18 language translations, and sales of 107 million copies in 98 countries.

The new global outlook affected everyone, especially the authors. A 'major change' from the 'old' days, noted Anne Weale (first published in 1955), 'is having to write books in a global context rather than to please the English reader and a relatively few overseas markets such as South Africa, Scandinavia, Italy. Nowadays one has to pause and consider whether a colloquial expression will make difficulties for translators in Japan, Bulgaria, etc.'

As for Mills & Boon itself, the novels were packaged and promoted as never before, with an aggressive penetration of new markets. Reader Service expanded, and direct marketing by post soon superseded retail and library sales as the principal outlet for distribution, supplying 60 per cent of profits. Whereas a reader used to travel to her local lending library with a Mills & Boon booklist in hand, to collect her favourite books, now she could have them delivered, on time, to her doorstep, along with special gifts and questionnaires on her tastes in reading. By 1980, some ten years since the Harlequin takeover, Mills & Boon achieved pre-tax profits of £4.5 million, an increase of 2,500 per cent over the 1970 figures. Today, in the UK and certain foreign markets (including Australia), the novels are still sold under the Mills & Boon brand name, while the rest of the world reads 'Harlequin Romances'.

Harlequin's global dominance was evidenced in 1989 when, to mark the company's fortieth anniversary, every one of Harlequin's 100 foreign markets published the same title on the same date: *A Reason for Being* by Penny Jordan, the firm's most popular author. The bravura act demonstrated that Harlequin could manage translation and distribution around the world. Similarly, when the Berlin Wall came down in 1990, staff from Mills & Boon's West German office handed out 750,000 copies of novels to East German women in a single day. Eastern Europe has proved a huge new market. On Valentine's Day in 1992 (an unknown holiday in Poland), Harlequin unfurled a giant banner of a heart atop the former Communist Party headquarters building in Warsaw. Harlequin sold 15 million books there in 1992.

'Mills & Boon put my books all over Europe,' Sheila Holland (Charlotte Lamb) noted, 'but Harlequin has built an empire.' By 1995 Holland had written 110 books in 22 years, sometimes finishing a book in one week, and once writing 12 in a single year. Her total sales are over 100 million copies, with translations in 23 languages. Clearly, Holland could never have achieved these figures had Mills & Boon not been acquired by Harlequin.

Being part of a large conglomerate based in Canada, Mills & Boon employees have not always meshed comfortably with the corporate lifestyle and policies. Increasingly the Boon brothers watched their firm's identity and its trademarks disappear. Author relations, for example, have become less personal and more formal, as the number of contracted authors has increased. Although Alan Boon maintained his strong presence on the editorial board into the early 1980s, increasingly younger editors with fresher ideas predominated. But Mills & Boon's editorial expertise has been preserved, and has remained the principal source for new novels, even as editorial bases have expanded within the Harlequin empire. A base in Toronto attracted authors from Canada and the United States (a rarity in Mills & Boon's heyday), and in 1984 Harlequin acquired its main rival, Silhouette Books of New York, whose titles had been distributed in Britain by Hodder & Stoughton. By 1990 editors in Toronto, New York, and London worked with more than 600 authors, and as many as 20,000 unsolicited manuscripts have been received in a single year.

Not surprisingly, with a new attention on profits and a singular focus on romantic fiction, the Mills & Boon General & Educational List, so prized by John Boon (and which achieved a degree of success), was discontinued in 1980. Several of the copyrights were sold to Bell & Hyman. 'They [Harlequin] wished we hadn't had the G&E list,' John Boon admitted. 'It didn't fit in with their marketing plans. They knew nothing about it, nothing about publishing. I insisted we should continue it, and they said all right, provided it makes a reasonable return.' But not as reasonable as the rewards reaped by romantic fiction.

✌

Alan Boon's difficulties with Mary Bonnycastle and her daughter Judy concerning 'sex' in Mills & Boon novels did not last long after the 1972 takeover. Heisey realized the difficulty in not publishing certain best-selling titles by British authors in Canada. 'Judy Burgess and her mother, being conservative people, basically enjoyed publishing "sweet" stories,' Heisey recalled. 'And the Boons were getting authors leading in a new direction. They kept putting aside these spicier books. And Alan came to me and said, "If we don't publish these books, we're going to lose these authors. They'll go somewhere else."' Heisey added that the problem did not actually lie in the Bonnycastles, as was thought. 'It wasn't that the Bonnycastles didn't think these were good books,' he said. 'They were making judgments erroneously for our readers. They felt our readers weren't up to this, just like publishers had been doing for years. Well, they haven't read anything like this because we hadn't published anything like this.'

To break the ice, Heisey arranged for four of Mills & Boon's 'spicier' novels by Violet Winspear, Anne Mather, and Anne Hampson to be published in a trial run to a random selection of North American readers and under a special banner, 'Harlequin Presents'. The books were a hit—and the spell was broken.

The experiment led to a change in the way romantic novels were mar-keted. To differentiate the type of storyline—and thereby satisfy the readers who demanded 'stronger' fiction, as well as those who required it 'softer'—Harlequin and Mills & Boon launched series publishing. Rather than one 'Mills & Boon Romance' banner for all types of novels, now there were several: romance, doctor/nurse, historical, 'Temptation' (the sexiest), and best-seller reprints, soon joined by the (generally stronger) Silhouette titles.

With series publishing, two styles of romantic novel emerged: the tradi-tional 'mild' romance (which continued to satisfy readers in Ireland and other established markets), and the contemporary 'sexy' romance. Once the floodgates were opened on the latter, new (and younger) editors pushed for stronger, bolder storylines, and thresholds kept getting lowered. Premarital sex is common in novels today, although the emphasis is on 'marital', mean-ing the copulating characters do marry in the end, or at least talk about doing so. Harlequin guidelines in 1982 advised writers that 'Sex scenes should be fairly explicit without being graphic and NEVER CARNAL.' In the age of AIDS, condoms are now common, with the hero 'turning away to attend to certain matters' before resuming his conquest of the heroine.

To Sheila Holland, who has led the charge toward more explicit fiction, these changes were perfectly natural, in line with giving the reader what she demands, and what she sees on television and in the cinema. 'Every few years Mills & Boon changes,' Holland explained. 'A change is always author-led and mirrors what is happening in the world outside. We are not behind the times, at all, despite critical opinion; we are well aware of current trends and keep abreast of them. At one time we had a kiss in the middle and a kiss in the end—now full sex sometimes occurs quite early on!' This change, as always, was a commercial decision. 'These books came out best in attracting readers,' Alan Boon said. 'That's why we did it. No one blushes any more.'

It is interesting to consider the fate of some of the authors who started their Mills & Boon careers in a more 'chaste' time, and were faced with the new requirements of the Harlequin era. 'A lot of our authors who could not handle sex started to handle it,' Boon said. 'They probably read some of the authors who could and imitated it.' Ethel Connell ('Katrina Britt') admitted that some of the older authors did just that: 'A lot of the authors used to read each other, like in school. They'd have to copy the frisky bits.' Gwen Westwood kept a list of romantic words and phrases beside her typewriter for reference and inspiration when she got stuck. These included: 'incandescent', 'savage insistence', 'hard maleness', 'drowning in depths of warm dark sea', 'chest muscles ripple beneath bronze skin', 'throbbing waves of desire', 'body like lithe spirited animal', and 'mouth hard and sure'.

Anne Weale, on the other hand, made the transition successfully. 'At that time it was right for authors to describe making love in a more realistic way,' Weale recalled. 'My own generation of schoolgirls all read *For Whom the Bell*

Tolls and were disappointed when Hemingway's exciting but fanciful description didn't happen to them. Even in the late Seventies some M&B authors were sending their heroines into ecstasies which wouldn't have happened in real life given their heroes' limitations as lovers.' Weale, whom we have seen once lamented that she did not want to write as explicitly or as sexily as did Roberta Leigh, demonstrated her newfound talents in two ground-breaking novels. *Antigua Kiss* (1982) featured Mills & Boon's first oral sex scene: when the hero, Ash, attacks Christiana, she refuses to kiss him; Ash tells her, 'There are other places to kiss.' When he does so, she is shocked, but surrenders to 'waves of ecstasy'. In *Ecstasy* (1983), the heroine, Suzy Walker, 'Britain's top secretary', longs for her missing lover at night, but finds comfort in masturbation ('Sometimes the longing for love came upon her like a sudden fever, keeping her awake at night, forcing her to an expedient which, although it eased her restlessness, left her unfulfilled emotionally, and depressed by the thought that this might be all she would ever have; this solitary, inadequate substitute for the ecstasies of a shared bed').

But many Mills & Boon authors stopped writing for the firm out of principle, refusing to participate in what they termed 'soft porn' peddling. The ones who did stop were often not very successful authors in the first place, Roumelia Lane recalled that Alan Boon and 'his editor' told her, 'You have to toe the line, you know.' 'It's a sad thing these days that you are automatically a millionaire if you don't mind writing pornography,' she said. Ethel Connell laid down her pen after thirty novels. 'I did not write any more because they changed their romantic theme to have sex as their main theme,' she said. 'I did not agree to writing about heroines who slept around and drank spirits freely.' By 1975 Violet Winspear, once at the top of Mills & Boon's charts, had also had enough, and decided to follow Barbara Cartland's example and write historical romances, set in past times when heroines were always virgins and naturally accepted as such. She wrote to Alan Boon:

> It may well be that I will find a reading public which likes an author to go rather deeper into romantic motives than certain other very pop authors go. Many readers haven't the time to probe and wonder, and are happy enough with the pulsating clinches that occur at intervals throughout the book.

Winspear was clearly disturbed by 'these sex hungry times. The sex must have gone off somewhat for people to be so in search of it. I do, indeed, get the impression that men are more in love with their cars than their wives, and that wives are more in love with their freezers and their foreign holidays.'

But some authors were more defiant, and resisted the trend towards sexier novels, with varying degrees of success. Betty Neels, for example, has baffled the marketing experts in remaining 'old-fashioned'—and staying at the top of author sales. She has never changed her style of romance, which is homely and familiar, sometimes based on the Cinderella theme (hero rescues heroine) or a family drama with lots of characters. All of her novels are the same, and hence their appeal. 'The stories I write are quite out of date as regards morals and sex but that is something readers find to their liking,' Neels said. She claimed she was once asked to put sex in her books, and she firmly declined, dismissing the current Mills & Boon romances as 'gynaecological training manuals'. Similarly, Mary Burchell continued to write what came to be known as 'family stories'. Like Winspear, she was appalled by the sexier trend on display at a *Romantic Times* conference in New York City in the 1980s:

> The rather dreadful young woman who ran it, came over first and interviewed me. She asked the most idiotic questions, like, 'Do you believe in sustained sensuality?' So I said, 'Well my dear, if by that you mean soft porn with overtones of vulgarity, no. . . . The sad thing about prose today is that people are under the impression that if you call something by a different name, it's no longer unpleasant. You know, when you all write about pre-marital sex, what you mean is fornication. If you don't know the word, look it up in the Bible—and the penalties.'

Although Burchell continued to be published by Mills & Boon up to her death in 1987, she did not sell as she once did, and clearly was published by the firm for old times' sake. Alan Boon noted that, as she got older, Burchell became more interested in the grandmother in her novels than in the heroine. 'Our readers weren't. They wanted to be chased by heroes. Our readers are reading because they're interested in the girl's experiences. In Burchell's own mind, she'd lost interest,' he said. None the less, Boon, true to his gentlemanly nature, continued to publish Burchell and a number of the old guard as a kind of charity, and with the expectation that their status as *grandes dames* of the firm would inspire the younger, friskier authors. 'I remember when Mary Burchell burst into tears because our editor felt she hadn't got it,' Boon recalled. He reassured her that she still did—and in his comforting, resembled the archetypal Alphaman hero. British publishing would not see that style again.

❧

As for the future of Harlequin Mills & Boon, and its novels, the firm has experimented with a number of new media in recent years, including videotapes, audio books, and CD-ROMs, but with little success. While book sales have slipped in the United Kingdom (a fate suffered by other publishers), sales are robust overseas, especially in Africa and Asia. In several countries Mills & Boon novels are used in schools to teach English, as they are always grammatically correct, and the interesting and exciting plot encourages reading. China is a vast new market ready to be tapped, and old novels are 'recycled' as new translations. There is an endless supply of 'product' at hand.

'I think there will be always a continuing demand for romance. It's been going for so long, it's not a genre that will suddenly collapse,' John Boon said, prior to his death in 1996. 'Whether it will be produced in books, and if so, in what sort of books, I don't know. But provided we could follow the distribution trend and the marketing trend, the future is pretty good.' The expansion of Harlequin around the world, made possible by Mills & Boon's editorial prowess, has demonstrated the international (and thereby universal) appeal of romance. Boon likened the phenomenon to a new British Empire of sorts, but added, with a broad smile, 'I hope it won't have the same fate!'

Notes

Chapter 1: *Mr Mills and Mr Boon, 1908–1913*

1. 'Sir Algernon Methuen, Baronet: A Memoir' (London: Methuen, 1925), 8.
2. Maureen Duffy, *A Thousand Capricious Chances: A History of the Methuen List 1889–1989* (London: Methuen, 1989), 8.
3. 'Sir Algernon Methuen', 9.
4. Duffy, *A Thousand Capricious Chances*, 43. According to Alan Boon, when Methuen died in 1924 he left money to current and former employees, but did not leave anything to his father, which would imply a bad parting. 'Father never forgot that,' Boon said. Alfred Boon stayed on at Methuen, and never worked for Mills & Boon.
5. Frank Boon's son, Sir Peter Boon (1916–97), was Chairman of Hoover and a renowned promoter of British manufacturing interests overseas.
6. Peter Keating in *The Haunted Study* (London: Secker & Warburg, 1989) has noted that, for a 6s. novel to recoup the costs of production at this time, it had to sell at least 500 copies. If it sold 1,000 copies, it was considered to be doing very well, earning money for both the publisher and the author. The break-even threshold rose as the cost of the edition fell. A 2s. title, for example, had to sell 3,000 copies. The fact that so many Mills & Boon titles in the early years 'sold out' attests to the firm's prosperity, enhanced by the fact that a small staff kept overheads low.
7. For the age, a £25 advance was enormous. In her autobiography, Berta Ruck, wife of Oliver Onions (like Ruck, a Mills & Boon author), recalled receiving an offer from Hutchinson for her first novel, *Her Official Fiancé*, in 1913. The advance, £20, 'took my breath away with incredulity and joy' (Berta Ruck, *A Story-Teller Tells the Truth* (London: Hutchinson & Co., 1935), 112).
8. *Punch,* in the first of many references to Mills & Boon (which attest to the firm's growing prominence), lampooned *Nerves and the Nervous* in the 6 December 1911 issue in a poem on a man struggling with low nervous energy: 'So unsettled was my brain | And so demoralised my mind's tone | I could not, for my life, constrain | My nasal organ to the grindstone; | All day, revolving in my office chair, | I found myself debating what to wear . . . If you should learn the actual reason | Of any change in me your eye observes, | Refer, my love, to Thingamabob on Nerves.'

9. *Peter Pan* was also issued in a *6d.* school edition, with an introduction by A. R. Pickles, Director of Education, Burnley. Pickles praised Mills & Boon and these 'School Readers', a 'splendid library of good literature' which, he predicted, would combat the excesses of 'an age of cheap literature and of snippety reading'. Sales were excellent: six editions were published between 1912 and 1915, with 10,879 copies sold.

10. I. A. R. Wylie, *My Life with George: An Unconventional Biography* (New York: Random House, 1940), 179.

11. *Daily Citizen* (3 Jan. 1913).

12. Ibid.

13. In 1926 Hutchinson would 'buy back' Stanley Paul, along with a number of small publishing houses.

14. On interviewing Bennett, the *Daily News* reported, 'The young author had some amusing comments to make on the literary tastes of the majority of the subscribers. "Sometimes the men knew what sort of a book they wanted to read, but women rarely did. They really depend on the librarian's taste, which is readily formed by any young person with a good memory."'

15. See *The Letters of Jack London*, ed. Earle Labor, Robert C. Leitz, III, and I. Milo Shepard (Stanford, Calif.: Stanford University Press, 1988).

16. None the less, it is interesting to note that London, notoriously obsessed with making money, checked out Mills & Boon thoroughly. In March 1913 London sent an identical letter to George Bernard Shaw, H. G. Wells, and several popular American writers asking in confidence what rates they earned from book and magazine publishers in Britain and the United States. In the letter, London boasted that he had published 33 books and 'an ocean of magazine stuff'. London must have liked what he heard, for his relationship with Mills & Boon continued unchanged.

17. *Punch* continued to lampoon Mills & Boon in its pages, a sign that the firm — and its imprint — had arrived. Under 'Literary Notes: Showing what a strong flair for topicality is possessed by the publishing trade', in 1912, *Punch* began, 'In view of the fact that KING FERDINAND of Bulgaria is a confirmed botanist, Messrs. Bills and Moon beg to draw attention to a new work of fascinating interest on English wild flowers which they are issuing.'

Chapter 2: *The Bubble Nearly Bursts, 1914–1928*

1. *The Lonely Plough* turned out to be quite famous: thanks to its selection by Oxford University Press for the 'World's Classics' series, Holme sold a grand total of 250,000 copies (although the 1914 Mills & Boon edition sold only 972 of 1,500 copies printed). Upon Holme's death in 1955, the *National Newsagent, Bookseller, & Stationer* wrote of her achievement: 'Say farewell, please, to a highbrow myth. It is this: that a writer of light fiction can never, never, never become classic. . . . Miss Holme's first publishers: Mills and Boon. Their customers, then as today: commercial libraries, and newsagent booksellers. Their stock-in-trade: light fiction.'

2. Boon's wartime exploits are discussed in *HUSH, or, The Hydrophone Service* by Lieutenant H. W. Wilson, published by Mills & Boon in 1920. Wilson wrote a personal account of life aboard the HMS *Tarlair*, captained by himself and in active service from 1917 in the North Sea and English Channel. Crew member Charles Boon is referenced in a poem penned by Wilson, entitled '15th February, 1919', lamenting the disbanding of his beloved crew: 'No longer Boon the awful burden bears, | Of giving weight to everything he hears . . .'. A footnote explained, 'Boon used to disentangle from the confused murmur, a sufficiency of sounds for a Queen's Hall outfit.'

3. Wylie, *My Life with George*, 197. In describing the publisher who essentially made her name, Wylie seemed ungrateful and uncharitable. She proceeded to say that this novel was a great success and opened doors for her in the US: 'I am not proud of much in my life but I am rather proud that I had the courage to defy advice and the wisdom to be unwise. Had I yielded to pressure, I would have continued to tramp backward and forward over the old paths until "my public" would have been as sick of me as I should have been of myself.' Her advice to new writers: 'The moment a born writer begins to think about what other people think, or wants to write what he is told other people want to read, he is as good as dead. There is only one person in the world he must interest and satisfy. It follows as the night the day that the rest of the world will agree with him.'

4. Denise Robins, *Stranger than Fiction* (London: Hodder & Stoughton, 1965), 134.

5. Dinah Boon recalled that Begbie was also a good family friend, which might have complicated business relations further. 'Sir Harold Begbie decided what would be the best schools for the boys and my Mother paid the fees from her own money', she said.

Chapter 3: *A Boon without Mills, 1929–1945*

1. Q. D. Leavis, *Fiction and the Reading Public* (London: Chatto & Windus, 1932), 6. Interestingly, Mills & Boon novels would be pitched more and more as 'nice' books or 'pleasant reading' as they gained in popularity.

2. F. R. Richardson, 'The Circulating Library', in John Hampden (ed.), *The Book World* (London, 1935), 195, 202.

3. Garfield Howe, 'What the Public Likes', *Bookseller* (19 June 1935), 580, 583. The name of the library was not given.

4. In actuality, neither was very successful—a rare Charles Boon misfire.

5. Mills & Boon books were bound in a dark red or brown cloth, perhaps heeding the 1928 report of the Commercial Circulating Libraries Sub-Committee of the Society of Bookmen, which found that some libraries 'restricted the purchase of books bound in certain colours easily spoilt by rain'.

6. Richard de la Mare, *A Publisher on Book Production: The Sixth Dent Memorial Lecture* (London: J. M. Dent & Sons, 1936), 12–13.

7. None the less, some unknowns went on to be 'stars'. In 1930 Mills & Boon allegedly published the first novel by Molly Keane, under the pseudonym M. J.

Farrell, although there is little evidence to support this claim. The novel was either *The Knight of Cheerful Countenance* or *Young Entry*. Keane recalled the experience to Russell Harty in 1982. At 17, 'I wrote this awful little hunting romance,' she said, which she sent to Mills & Boon. 'They cracked it at once, what's more, and they paid me 50 whole pounds. I don't know if they got a penny out of it, but £50 then was a terrific help.' Keane added that she wrote another book 'at once' but Mills & Boon 'thought it was too saucy and they wouldn't [publish it]. Collins published it' (Transcript, *Russell Harty Show*, 22 Oct. 1982).

8. Robins, *Stranger than Fiction*, 151. John Boon elaborated on his father's annoyance, saying he 'exploded' when Robins made her announcement, shouting, 'Go on, get out—take your money.' Ironically, in 1997 Mills & Boon contracted with the Denise Robins estate to publish some of her titles in India, where she remains very popular.

9. When Alan Boon invited 'Barbara Stanton' to lunch in 1947, Mr John P. Hunt wrote to clarify matters. 'As the late Mr. Charles Boon was, I believe, informed by Rupert Crew of the Author's Advisory Service when we signed our first contract with Mills & Boon in 1938, the pen-name Barbara Stanton represents a literary partnership which began some fifteen years ago. At that time, I was fiction editor of a London daily and for business reasons it was desirable that the names of my collaborator and myself not be revealed. . . . My collaborator who supplies the essential feminine side to all Barbara Stanton fiction is herself a very successful author of romantic novels and serials under another pen-name.' Hunt never did reveal her identity, but said she was published by Collins. She was probably Elizabeth Harrison.

10. Ida Cook, *We Followed Our Stars* (London: Mills & Boon, 1956), 102.

11. John Attenborough, *A Living Memory: Hodder & Stoughton Publishers, 1868–1975* (London: Hodder & Stoughton, 1975), 141. Similarly, in 1945 Heinemann reported that 1,600 titles in demand were out of print.

12. John Boon, 'A plague o' both your houses!' *Bookseller* (18 Oct. 1945), 498–9.

Chapter 4: *Regrouping and Restructuring, 1946–1956*

1. Interestingly, having an agent did not guarantee the best terms. Of the above-mentioned authors, only Matthewman and Bradshaw/Heeley were represented by an agent, A. P. Watt. In fact, the use of agents would diminish, in a deliberate effort by Mills & Boon to control its authors and their costs. Marjorie Lewty, who joined Mills & Boon in 1958, remembered receiving a call from Alan Boon when her agent, Peter Lewin, stopped representing her. 'Alan said, "For goodness sake, don't get another agent. We will handle your stuff." And they did very successfully, much better than an agent, who of course you pay 10 per cent for doing really nothing. Mills & Boon do the agency for you, really, and get the best prices you can get from foreign translations.' Most Mills & Boon authors would probably agree.

2. John St John, *William Heinemann: A Century of Publishing 1890–1990* (London: Heinemann, 1990), 310.

3. Richard Hoggart, *The Uses of Literacy* (London: Chatto & Windus, 1957), 278.

4. By way of comparison, in 1950 Collins issued a record 50,000-copy first edition for Agatha Christie's 50th book, *A Murder is Announced*. Christie's subsequent printings never sunk below that figure. Christie eventually was outsold only by Shakespeare and *The Bible*. She was reckoned to finish a book in six weeks, although she averaged just two books a year.

5. Bethea Creese's next novel, *Flower Piece* (1954) was dedicated, 'To Dr. John Masefield, O. M., In Deepest Gratitude'.

6. John Boon, 'Make your Readers Work for you,' *Bookseller* (19 Mar. 1955), 1016–17.

7. 'World wide, Joyce Dingwell's name is known and loved as Mills & Boon's first and maybe most popular author. . . . Joyce has achieved a tremendous ambassadorial feat for her country and she deserves a place within the list of Australian authors who have been hugely popular. She's given pleasure to millions in the past, as Emma Darcy is giving pleasure to millions now' (Marion Lennox, in Juliet Flesch (comp.), *Love Brought to Book: A Bio-bibliography of 20th-century Australian Romance Novels* (Melbourne: National Centre for Australian Studies, 1995), xix).

8. Fan mail came from overseas. In 1955 Alan Boon wrote to many authors about a grateful Australian reader, whom he helped overcome her difficulty in obtaining Mills & Boon novels. 'This reader is very grateful and in return has knitted bedsocks for her favourite Mills & Boon authors,' he wrote. Among the lucky winners: Alex Stuart.

9. John Boon, 'Venture into Westerns', *Bookseller* (12 Sept. 1953), 872–3.

10. Frank Arthur Mumby and Ian Norrie, *Publishing and Bookselling*, 5th edn. (London: Jonathan Cape, 1974), 467.

11. *Better Cookery* was the top-selling Mills & Boon publication, still, in 1968, in a listing of publishers' all-time best-sellers in *The Times* (14 Sept. 1968). Total sales: 'over 100,000' to date.

Chapter 5: *The Paperback Revolution, 1957–1972*

1. Anne Britton and Marion Collin, *Romantic Fiction: The New Writers' Guide* (London: T. V. Boardman & Co., 1960), 128.

2. But Pan did benefit from Mills & Boon. 'When Pan decided to go to three and sixpence, we picked their three launching books,' Alan Boon recalled. He picked one by Rosalind Brett, one by Kathryn Blair, and one by Celine Conway. 'They were immensely successful. I went down to Baker Street station and they had sold out.'

3. Clearly, Mills & Boon was not alone in its growing dependence on the public libraries. At William Heinemann, Ltd., such was the buying power of the public libraries in the 1960s that, without them, much fiction would not have been published. For a first novel with a print run of 2,000 copies, 90 per cent went to the public libraries. Of 4,000, 75 per cent. Only when the run was above 8,000 did library sales become less significant (John St John, *William Heinemann: A Century of Publishing 1890–1990*, 461).

4. In 1966 Dorothy Black led a walkout from the RNA of several founder members and vice-presidents. In her resignation letter Black wrote, 'Regretfully, it is sad that the R.N.A. should have gone the way of so many movements and associations run by women, and has deviated so drastically from what was originally intended, becoming simply another Writers Circle, or Mutual Admiration Society. So taken up with the details of organization, and rules and precidents [*sic*], that the original idea and spirit has gone.' That same year, Hunter Davies, in the *Sunday Times*, related an anecdote: 'BEAUTIFUL BITCHERY, overheard at a recent meeting of Romantic Novelists: "I've written fifty," boasted the First Romantic Novelist. "Is that all," said the Second Romantic Novelist. "I've written a hundred and twenty." "Tell me darling, I always forget," said the First Romantic Novelist. "You do one every year, don't you?"'

5. Sheila Holland, who, as 'Charlotte Lamb', became Mills & Boon's top-selling author in the 1970s and 1980s, recalled the first Mills & Boon paperbacks. 'I well remember the real excitement I felt on first seeing paperback M&Bs in our local W. H. Smiths at Folkestone in the early '60s. I bought the six books they had, but no more appeared for what seemed eternity; it was just a trial.'

6. Winspear lived with her mother and, like many Mills & Boon authors, never married. Judging from the small mountain of correspondence in the Mills & Boon archive, she had an intense crush on Alan Boon, whom she regarded as the personification of the Mills & Boon hero. Boon, in turn, was kind, and often chauffeured Winspear in a Rolls Royce around the English countryside to expand her horizons.

7. Westwood recalled meeting Alan Boon in London soon after *Keeper* was published, and he took her to lunch at one of his favourite spots, the Post Office Tower. There Westwood suffered from motion sickness and was violently ill. But she was appreciative of the famous Boon charm which was on full display. 'I remember that Alan waltzed us around Woolworth's where my book was in evidence. He was always enormously generous and enthusiastic. In later years we had lunch at Claridges or the Ritz and usually had pre-lunch champagne and there were always lovely flowers awaiting you in your hotel.'

8. Mann revealed other curious characteristics. Some 54 per cent of respondents preferred the *Daily Mirror* or *Daily Express* (in line with national figures) but an unusual 16 cent took *The Times*, *Guardian*, or *Daily Telegraph*. Nearly 59 per cent said they attended the cinema 'not very much', in line with the belief that movie-going was considered a young person's diversion.

9. Alan Hill, *In Pursuit of Publishing* (London: Murray/Heinemann Educational Books, 1988), 255–6.

Chapter 6: *The 1930s: A Genre is Born*

1. Jermyn March, 'The World of Fancy', *W. H. Smith Trade Circular* (19 Feb. 1927), 3–4.
2. Berta Ruck, *A Smile for the Past* (London: Hutchinson & Co., 1959), 173, 223.
3. Berta Ruck, *A Story-Teller Tells the Truth*, 405, 408.

4. Percy Lubbock, *The Craft of Fiction* (London, 1921), 5, 84, 87, 127.
5. Nicola Beauman, *A Very Great Profession: The Woman's Novel 1914–39* (London: Virago Press, 1983), 59, 226.
6. Judith Simons, 'Ideas on love have changed', *Evening Gazette* (22 Jan. 1954), 13.
7. Mills & Boon was in illustrious company. Also banned by the Irish Government in 1939 were *To Step Aside* by Noel Coward, *Brighton Rock* by Graham Greene, and *Goodbye to Berlin* by Christopher Isherwood. Former Mills & Boon authors Hugh Walpole and Georgette Heyer were also banned in Ireland at some time in their careers.

Chapter 7: *The 1940s: Flying the Flag*

1. John Boon attributed the controversy to 'some Civil Servant whose literary views probably belonged to the Left Book Club'.
2. Mass-Observation Archives, 'Reading', box 8, file F (18 Oct. 1943).
3. Ruck, *A Smile for the Past*, 178. Mills & Boon's novels, some 10 or more years old, circulated widely during the war and were read by men as well as women. One 'fan letter', from a soldier in Greece in 1943, concerned an old Denise Robins title. 'Sirs, I have read your published book Sweet Love by Denise Robins. I think that the author is a stupid over romantic twat. from a soldier in Greece. 1934 edition. P. S. Sincerely hope that robins is dead & buried.'
4. Wyndham's recollections are included in Aruna Vasudevan (ed.), *Twentieth-Century Romance and Historical Writers*, 3rd edn. (London: St James Press/Gale Research International, 1994), 738.
5. After her death in 1957 at the age of 44, an official Mills & Boon biography claimed that Deering regarded this as the best of her 21 novels: 'The theme of *Journey to Romance* gave full scope to her strongly developed sense of romance, and in this work it was as though she was pouring out all that had been pent-up within her during the grim years of war. As a novelist, her style was noteworthy for this intense expression of the romantic; indeed, there were critics who believed that at times her writing was so intensely romantic as to seem far-fetched, but there is no doubt that every word she wrote was sincere.'
6. For a closer look at Johnson and magazine editors in general, see Chapter 9. In 1946 Sara Seale expressed her exasperation over the demands made upon Mills & Boon authors by these powerful magazine editors, a theme that would be repeated many times over the next decade. In a letter to Johnson, Seale begged for mercy over criticism that her latest serial was 'too similar' to the plot of her last one: 'It does seem to me that superficial resemblances are almost impossible to avoid in present-day novels. So few situations are new and I am constantly reading things which remind me of others. There were readers who saw a resemblance between "House of Glass" and Daphne du Maurier's "Rebecca" solely on account of there being a strange housekeeper in each.'
7. Betty Beaty, who set most of her early novels in aeroplanes, noted that the two places for romance where the hero and heroine were at their most vulnerable were within the confines of an aeroplane (unlike the open spaces of a cruise ship) and in a hospital, which would explain the popularity of Doctor-Nurse romances.

Chapter 8: *The 1950s: Preserving the Legacy*

1. See Chapter 9 for a discussion of the role of women's magazine editors during the 1950s.

2. Judith Simons, 'Ideas on love have changed', London *Evening Gazette* (22 Jan. 1954), 13.

3. Clearly, there could never be too much romance, and the romantic denouement in the final chapter was essential. In Matthewman's *Romance Goes Tenting*, for example, Lois professes her love: 'Oh, Pete, don't you understand? I love every bit of you. I love your eyes, and your mouth and the whole of you. I even love you when you're in one of your horrid moods and you scowl at me. I love you whatever you're like, and I'm sure I always will.'

4. The extra effort was worth while, from an exports point of view. In 1956 Boon wrote to Alex Stuart about his recent Roman holiday. 'When I was in Rome I visited a convent where the good nuns run a magazine (very elegant, too, lots of Dior fashions and so on) and they said nice things about your work, and I hope we may make a fairly steady stream of sales there; so all the work you put in on the religious problems is worth while, though it must be a most fearful worry.'

5. Apart from the official censorship laws, in 1948 the Irish Association of Civil Liberty spoke of the 'Seven Censorships' existing in Ireland: these were, censorship by the Censorship Board; by fear; by the bookseller (on behalf of the libraries); by librarians; by library users; by library committees; and by the public (especially clergymen).

6. Barbara Stanton looked at the bright side of the Irish censors: in 1953 Stanton told Boon that getting banned might be good for sales of her latest, *The Price of Fame*: 'I'm sorry there's been so much trouble over this particular story as I still think, after re-reading the MS, it's one of Barbara's brightest for some time. Let's hope I'll teach the brazen hussy to mind her p's and q's in future, though I can't help feeling—cynically, no doubt—that if, perish the thought, the book were banned or, better still, publicly burnt in Ireland, sales over here would soar!'

7. Actually, Ireland did ban John Braine's novel, and six titles by Maugham (including *Cakes and Ale*), as well as works by Daphne du Maurier, Georgette Heyer, Hugh Walpole, and Stella Gibbons's *Cold Comfort Farm*.

8. Apparently Australian readers were also tough, although there is no evidence that Mills & Boon titles were banned there. In 1958 Bryant thanked Jean MacLeod for revisions to *Shadow on the Sun*, apparently required by Irish censors: 'I've just been reading a book about Australia from which it appears that that country, too, is strongly influenced by the straitlaced Irish form of Catholicism, untarnished by any guilty taint of the Mediterranean respect for cultural values!—which explains their fantastic system of book-banning and, alas, provides us with another reason for going warily, tiresome though it is.'

9. Some proper names were far easier editorial calls. In 1955 Joan Bryant informed Valerie K. Nelson of changes to *Change the Skies*, set in Greece: 'The journalist Oansis strikes us as being a little bit too much like Onassis who figures so often in the news. There is, of course, no question of libel here but it still looks a bit

odd, so would you mind if we called him Olleion?' In 1958 Bryant warned Olga Gillman about *The Golden Harbour*, and the bad girl character of Suzanne Clemenceau: 'Suzanne was, one feels, a victim to be pitied, still she did do something that society strongly disapproves, and Clemenceau is such a noticeable name in France. Suppose a French novel gave a fallen English maiden the name of Susan Lloyd George—wouldn't it make you think? Here the safest thing seemed to pick a name equivalent to Brown or Jones, and I picked on <u>Duval</u>.'

10. Not even Stanton's youngest characters escaped Mills & Boon's scrutiny. In 1951 Mills & Boon questioned the note written by a child in *Lonely Heart*, asking, 'Would a child of six write like this?' Stanton replied by return of post: 'If you consider this too adult for a six-year-old please delete lines 25–28 and substitute . . . His squiggly tear-stained capitals weren't easy to make out . . . '.

Chapter 9: *Women's Magazines: The Outside Editors*

1. James Drawbell, *Time On My Hands* (London: MacDonald & Co., 1968), 38–9.
2. Marjorie Ferguson, *Forever Feminine: Women's Magazines and the Cult of Femininity* (London: Heinemann, 1983), 2, 10.
3. Cynthia White, 'The Women's Periodical Press in Britain 1946–1976', *Royal Commission on the Press*, Working Paper Number 4 (London: HMSO, 1977), 54.
4. Mary Grieve, *Millions Made My Story* (London: Victor Gollancz, 1964), 219.
5. In 1950 Alan Boon informed Sara Seale that 'there is a large and growing public who like to buy your serials later in book form'. For this reason, Boon preferred that the book and serial appear under the same title. Seale's latest, *An Irish Air*, had been renamed by *Woman's Weekly* as *Flint Was His Name*. Why? 'The hero does not appear in the first installment, and mention of his name in the title will help to "carry on" readers until he makes his first appearance,' the magazine explained. Boon approved, saying the new title had more 'box-office': 'When the name of a book is different from the name of the serial, there is a dangerous tendency for the public to "lose" the book. Asked for the book under a different serial title, a bookseller is quite liable to look up your list of titles and, not finding the serial title there, inform the customer "there's no such thing".'
6. Many publishers reaped the benefits of these so-called subsidiary rights. Between 1946 and 1958 Heinemann saw its income from subsidiary rights increase by 500 per cent.
7. Mary Grieve, editor of the top-selling *Woman*, recalled that the famous 'Evelyn Home' advice page had to be changed for Irish readers, since Ireland forbade any mention of divorce or 'unconventionality'.
8. In 1963 the *Guardian*, in its analysis of women's magazines, distinguished between the 7*d.* 'glossies' such as *Woman's Own*, and the more downmarket 'blood and thunder' 4½*d.* papers (such as *Red Letter*) published primarily by D. C. Thomson. Whereas 'anything goes in the "bloods" . . . The quest among the glossies is almost exclusively for escapist reader identification stories with an ecstatic ending, boy and girl glued in each other's arms, stars twinkling.' Stories

reflected the different audiences: while heroes in the glossies had professions, such as doctors, pilots, and ski instructors, in the bloods they were shopkeepers and railwaymen. Finally, editors in papers like *Woman's Own* 'automatically return to the writer divorce, birth-control, heavy drinking and (except on rare occasions) illegitimate children' ('The ABC—and £ s d—of writing for the women's weeklies, by our own Reporter', *Guardian* (10 Apr. 1963), 7).

9. Irene Dancyger, *A World of Women: An Illustrated History of Women's Magazines* (Dublin: Gill & Macmillan, 1978), 166. Hugh Cudlipp, deputy chairman of the *Daily Mirror* Group, which purchased the Amalgamated Press in 1958, hailed Johnson as 'one of the great figures of the publishing world' and recalled her achievements; in spite of 'old worlde letterpress printing', *Woman's Weekly* sold 1.5 million copies a week and earned an annual profit of £350,000. 'Her success was entirely due to two secrets—she knew and loved her readers, and she switched her deaf-aid on to a flat battery whenever male executives ventured to tell her how to run her paper' (Cudlipp, *At Your Peril* (London: Weidenfeld & Nicolson, 1962), 192).

10. She also got through her slush pile of manuscripts quickly. Boon recalled that Johnson compared evaluating a manuscript to eating a steak: 'You don't need to eat the whole lot to know if it's tough or not', a tip Boon picked up, too.

11. When Johnson retired as a full-time editor in 1961, Boon paid her a great tribute. 'How very grateful I am to you for all you have taught me—for all that you have done for the romantic novel,' he wrote. 'Nobody has had a greater influence on the romantic novel than yourself.' He looked forward to frequent meetings; 'I shall come always as a pupil in the presence of the master.'

12. In 1956 Eleanor Farnes expressed to Alan Boon her exasperation with Johnson on her lack of originality: 'I sent her a synopsis which she did not think was strong enough, and she put forward a completely new idea (dragon aunt, put-upon niece, and wonderful doctor in attendance upon the aunt). I should have said a completely different idea, as it is certainly not a new one!'

13. Wyndham's recollections are included in Vasudevan (ed.), *Twentieth-Century Romance and Historical Writers*, 738.

14. Boon noted that Warren felt she would have been even more successful in England, if not for editors like Johnson: 'Miss Johnson bribed Brett by giving her big serial sums to take sexy stuff out of her books. Once, to get back, Brett put buggery in the story.' Needless to say, it was promptly removed.

15. In 1957 Boon reminded Johnson that 'Sara Seale feels she has <u>never</u> yet written a marriage-in-name-only story which has not been an outstanding success', including *House of Glass*; *Wintersbride*; *The Gentle Prisoner*; and *Child Friday*.

16. MINO became a household term. In 1951 *Home Chat* promoted the latest effort from Kathryn Blair as follows: 'Escape from the "everydayishness" of life lies within the covers of "No Other Haven" by Kathryn Blair (Mills & Boon: 6s.), the story of a marriage in name only, set against the colourful, romantic background of South Africa.'

17. On Johnson's advice, Beaty tried her hand at a hospital serial. 'Although I had

never written one, nor indeed ever read one, I embarked boldly and foolishly. I came to grief. My hospital had a typhoid epidemic, and I did a minor thesis on drains and the bugs that lurked therein. Miss Johnson returned the manuscript immediately and said it was no good. Back it came by return of post, with Miss Johnson's epic words—"My girls are interested in young men, NOT in drains."'

18. Wilde wondered whether 'I ought to give up African backgrounds and switch to Australian.' In any event, she was glad she moved to England from South Africa: 'The people, too, are so friendly and it is lovely to be WELCOMED to a new country, a very different attitude from that in South Africa.'

19. But O'Connell, like most magazine editors, was inconsistent in his editorial decisions. In 1954 he demanded that Alex Stuart change the opening of her new serial, *Gay Cavalier*, to remove the setting of a fox hunt. 'He thinks it would lead to violent protests from readers,' Stuart told Alan Boon, as O'Connell considered it a 'blood sport'. It was changed to a horse race. Boon couldn't see what all the fuss was about: 'We have published a few books on this subject in the past.'

Chapter 10: *The 1960s: Change and Experimentation*

1. In 1976 a reporter asked Winspear how she came to know so much about Greek men in describing her heroes. 'What a laugh!' she wrote to Alan Boon. 'I worked for six months in a place with an engineering works next door, almost exclusively manned by Greeks, and a right lot of cheeky b's they were! They seemed to fondly imagine that every female was panting to get pregnant by them. They'd actually shout it out; "Wanna baby, baby?" It's a good thing for the romances that I tone down the actual fortissimo!!!'

2. But some authors took their research of contemporary heroines too far. In 1967 Audrey Willson (actually Mr A. F. Ebert) had an interesting exchange with Alan Boon on appropriate language in his latest manuscript, *From This Time Forth*. 'My difficulty in writing this book was to write dialogue that could sound like that of a contemporary 21-year-old girl without reproducing the words she actually uses when talking freely', Ebert wrote. 'The editor is probably more familiar with the actual speech of young girls than I am. My model (for dialogue only) was a 19-year-old Croydon girl in the Civil Service. Many of the words and expressions this girl (who is a nice girl) uses would be barred by you (and would have been barred by any publisher until a few years ago, at least in a young girl's speech). I took from this girl three words which I thought would be acceptable to you, but which your editor dislikes: bloke, twit, and gosh.' Ebert objected to 'Man' substituted for 'Bloke': 'Does the contemporary 21-year-old use "man" about boys of her own age?' As for 'Gosh', Ebert lamented the use of 'grandmotherly expressions': 'Nineteen-year old girls have been using "Gosh" for more than forty years, but it may be offensive to your readers. Still, I am doubtful about "Goodness, no!"'

3. But some readers *could* identify with Winspear's exotic heroes. In 1972 Winspear received a letter and wedding photo from Charmaine da Silva Campos of Mozambique: 'Oh what wondful [*sic*], lovely and real stories you write. Romantic fiction would be dead and boring without you.' She was just married to her

Portuguese boyfriend: 'My husband's name is José Alberto da Silva Campos—
not quite so long as the lovely names you give your characters, but still. Also he
is not a Conde or Marquis or Principe, but he is the Prince of my life.'

4. Stuart concluded her lengthy letter with a personal request to Boon: 'Will you
help me decide (a) how to get the S.S. published and (b) how not to put myself
out of the Empire as a result—I like being in it, dammit, but my trouble is that
I can't write stereotyped romance any more. I wish I could.' Stuart did publish
The Scottish Soldier with Robert Hale (and under her pen-name, Barbara Allen),
and branched out into other kinds of writing, including an acclaimed biography
of Sir Henry Keppel, Admiral of the Fleet, entitled *The Beloved Little Admiral*
(1967).

5. But traditional 'family values' remained the norm. In 1964 Phyllis Matthewman
questioned Boon's corrections on *A Brother for Jane*: 'Page 159. 'You don't like
"queer", do you? But there are times when it is the right word to use, and <u>not</u>
with the meaning that has become tacked on to it of late! "Odd" won't do. It
doesn't sound right. So to avoid "queer" I've used "strange", which sounds
better.'

6. Similarly, in 1967 Hilary Wilde told Alan Boon: 'While I would never dream of
blaming any girl for being what is called 'easy' (temptation and opportunity
being what it is today) I still believe that the average girl does NOT just pop into
bed with every man that comes along. (I have discussed this with teenagers and
young twenties, of course they may have fooled me but I don't think so, but
most girls want more than the mere act, they want love, a feeling of belonging,
and of possessing.) Unless the girl is an unfortunate nympho, I think there must
be either an element of or a pretence of love otherwise she's going to feel, in
time, unclean. Of course I may be completely wrong but I do feel that men and
women are bound to view this differently. As in THE KING AND I the male view
is naturally that of flitting from flower to flower, like bees, but a woman requires
more than this if she is to retain, that most important of all things for a woman,
her self-respect.'

7. When the surgeon Dr Richard Kendall professes his love to Sister Jennifer in
Hilda Nickson's *Quayside Hospital* (1962), the nurse is ready to erupt: 'A thrill of
joy and happiness was stirring up inside her like the beginnings of a fountain
which at any moment would surge upwards with ecstatic abandon.' When
Richard proposes and kisses her on the last page, she does indeed 'erupt': 'The
fountain which had been bubbling up inside her sparkled into exuberant life.'

Select Bibliography

'The ABC—and £ s d—of writing for the women's weeklies, by our own Reporter', *Guardian* (10 Apr. 1963), 7.

ADAMS, MICHAEL, *Censorship: The Irish Experience* (Alabama: University of Alabama Press, 1968).

ADDISON, PAUL, *Now the War is Over: A Social History of Britain 1945–51* (London: BBC/Jonathan Cape, 1985).

AITKEN, JONATHAN, 'How the great whodunnit book trail led to Dublin', *Evening Standard* (2 Jan. 1967), 7.

ALTBACH, PHILIP G., and HOSHINO, EDITH S. (eds.), *International Book Publishing: An Encyclopedia* (New York: Garland Publishing Inc., 1995).

ASHLEY, BOB (ed.), *Reading Popular Narrative: A Source Book* (London: Leicester University Press, 1989).

ATTENBOROUGH, JOHN, *A Living Memory: Hodder and Stoughton Publishers, 1868–1975* (London: Hodder & Stoughton, 1975).

BARKER, MARTIN, and BEEZER, ANNE (eds.), *Reading into Cultural Studies* (London: Routledge, 1992).

BARLTROP, ROBERT, *Jack London: The Man, the Writer, the Rebel* (London: Pluto Press, 1976).

BATSLEER, JANET, 'Pulp in the Pink', in Bob Ashley (ed.), *Reading Popular Narrative: A Source Book* (London: Leicester University Press, 1989), 217–22.

BATTY, RONALD F., *How to Run a Twopenny Library* (London, 1938).

BEAUMAN, NICOLA, *A Very Great Profession: The Woman's Novel 1914–39* (London: Virago Press, 1983).

BENNETT, TONY, *Popular Fiction: Technology, Ideology, Production, Reading* (London: Routledge, 1990).

BIGG, ROLAND G., '100% Profit on Books', *Efficient Retailing* (Feb. 1955), 93.

BONN, THOMAS L., 'The Paperback: Image and Object', in Philip G. Altbach and Edith S. Hoshino (eds.), *International Book Publishing: An Encyclopedia* (New York: Garland Publishing Inc., 1995), 262–70.

BOON, JOHN, 'Book Publishing: Mills & Boon', *Publisher* (Dec. 1967), 50–1.

—— 'The Early Years of Mills & Boon', *Bookseller* (2 May 1959), 1650–2.

—— 'Make your Readers Work for you', *Bookseller* (19 Mar. 1955), 1016–17.

—— 'A plague o' both your houses!', *Bookseller* (18 Oct. 1945), 498–9.

—— 'Venture into Westerns', *Bookseller* (12 Sept. 1953), 872–3.

BRAITHWAITE, BRIAN, *Women's Magazines: The First 300 Years* (London: Peter Owen, 1995).

BRIGGS, ASA (ed.), *Essays in the History of Publishing in Celebration of the 250th Anniversary of the House of Longman 1724–1974* (London: Longman, 1974).

BRITTON, ANNE, and COLLIN, MARION, *Romantic Fiction: The New Writers' Guide* (London: T. V. Boardman & Co., 1960).

BUCHLER, WALTER, *Publishing for Pleasure and Profit* (London: Useful Publications, 1946).

CADOGAN, MARY, *And Then Their Hearts Stood Still: An Exuberant Look at Romantic Fiction Past and Present* (London: Macmillan, 1994).

CARTER, ROBERT A., 'The History of International Book Publishing', in Philip G. Altbach and Edith S. Hoshino (eds.), *International Book Publishing: An Encyclopedia* (New York: Garland Publishing Inc., 1995), 156–63.

CASTELYN, MARY, *A History of Literacy and Libraries in Ireland: The Long-Traced Pedigree* (Aldershot: Gower Publishing Company, 1984).

CAWELTI, JOHN G., *Adventure, Mystery, and Romance: Formula Stories as Art and Popular Culture* (Chicago: University of Chicago Press, 1976).

COCKBURN, CLAUD, *Bestseller: The Books that Everyone Read, 1900–1939* (London: Penguin Books, 1972).

COOK, IDA, *We Followed Our Stars* (London: Mills & Boon, 1956).

CRITCHLEY, JULIAN, 'Hope of greater rewards in the world of publishing,' *The Times* (20 Nov. 1969), 11.

CUDLIPP, HUGH, *At Your Peril* (London: Weidenfeld & Nicolson, 1962).

CULLEN, L. M., *Eason & Son: A History* (Dublin: Eason & Son, 1989).

DANCYGER, IRENE, *A World of Women: An Illustrated History of Women's Magazines* (Dublin: Gill & Macmillan, 1978).

DE LA MARE, RICHARD, *A Publisher on Book Production: The Sixth Dent Memorial Lecture* (London: J. M. Dent & Sons, 1936).

DOBBS, KILDARE, 'The Harlequin Story: Twenty-Five Years of Romance' (Toronto: unpublished manuscript, 1974).

DRAWBELL, JAMES, *An Autobiography* (New York: Random House, 1963).

—— *Time On My Hands* (London: MacDonald & Co., 1968).

DUFFY, MAUREEN, *A Thousand Capricious Chances: A History of the Methuen List 1889–1989* (London: Methuen, 1989).

EAGLETON, MARY (ed.), *Feminist Literary Criticism* (New York: Longman, 1991).

EDWARDS, RUTH DUDLEY, *Victor Gollancz: A Biography* (London: Victor Gollancz, 1987).

FABES, GILBERT H., *The Romance of a Bookshop 1904–1929* (London, 1929).

FERGUSON, MARJORIE, *Forever Feminine: Women's Magazines and the Cult of Femininity* (London: Heinemann, 1983).

The First 30 Years of the World's Best Romantic Fiction (Toronto: Harlequin Books, 1979).

FLESCH, JULIET (comp.), *Love Brought to Book: A Bio-Bibliography of 20th-Century Australian Romance Novels* (Melbourne: National Centre for Australian Studies, 1995).

FOWLER, BRIDGET, 'True to Me Always: An Analysis of Women's Magazine Fiction', in Christopher Pawling (ed.), *Popular Fiction and Social Change* (London, 1984), 99–126.

GREEN, KAY, 'Roses Along the Way', *Contemporary Authors Autobiography Series*, 11 (Detroit: Gale Research, 1989), 87–106.

GRESCOE, PAUL, *The Merchants of Venus: Inside Harlequin and the Empire of Romance* (Vancouver: Raincoast Books, 1996).

GRIEVE, MARY, *Millions Made My Story* (London: Victor Gollancz, 1964).

GRIFFITHS, DENNIS, 'Methuen and Company', in Jonathan Rose and Patricia Anderson (eds.), *British Literary Publishing Houses 1881–1965, Dictionary of Literary Biography*, 112 (New York: Gale Research, 1991), 211–20.

GRIGSON, GEOFFREY, 'Novels, Twopenny Libraries and the Reviewer', *Bookseller* (20 Mar. 1935), 286–7.

HALSEY, A. H. (ed.), *Trends in British Society since 1900: A Guide to the Changing Social Structure of Britain* (London: Macmillan, 1988).

HAMPDEN, JOHN (ed.), *The Book World* (London, 1935).

HARTWELL, LORD, *William Camrose: Giant of Fleet Street* (London: Weidenfeld & Nicolson, 1992).

HEDRICK, JOAN D., *Solitary Comrade: Jack London and his Work* (Chapel Hill: University of North Carolina Press, 1982).

HIGHAM, DAVID, *Literary Gent* (London: Jonathan Cape, 1978).

HILL, ALAN, *In Pursuit of Publishing* (London: Murray/Heinemann Educational Books, 1988).

HODGE, JANE AIKEN, *The Private World of Georgette Heyer* (London: Pan Books, 1985).

HOGGART, RICHARD, *The Uses of Literacy* (London: Chatto & Windus, 1957).

HOLLAND, STEVE, *The Mushroom Jungle: A History of Post-war Paperback Publishing* (Westbury: Zeon Books, 1993).

HOWE, GARFIELD, 'What the Public Likes', *Bookseller* (19 June 1935), 580, 583.

'Interview with Charlotte Lamb', transcript, *Weekend Plus* (20 May 1983).

IRONS, GLENWOOD (ed.), *Gender, Language, and Myth: Essays on Popular Narrative* (Toronto: University of Toronto Press, 1992).

JESSE, F. TENNYSON, 'Bedbookery', *Manchester Guardian* (22 Mar. 1954), 3.

JONES, ANN ROSALIND, 'Mills & Boon Meets Feminism', in Jean Radford (ed.), *The Progress of Romance: The Politics of Popular Fiction* (London: Routledge & Kegan Paul, 1986), 195–218.

JORDAN, TERRY, *Agony Columns* (London: Macmillan, 1988).

JOSEPH, MICHAEL, *The Commercial Side of Literature* (London: Hutchinson, 1925).

JOY, THOMAS, *The Right Way to Run a Library Business* (Kingswood, Surrey: Right Way Books, 1949).

JUHASZ, SUZANNE, *Reading from the Heart: Women, Literature, and the Search for True Love* (London: Viking Penguin, 1984).

KEATING, H. R. F. (ed.), *Agatha Christie: First Lady of Crime* (London: Weidenfeld & Nicolson, 1977).

KEATING, PETER, *The Haunted Study* (London: Secker & Warburg, 1989).

KEIR, DAVID, *The House of Collins: The Story of a Scottish Family of Publishers from 1789 to the Present Day* (London: Collins, 1952).

LAMB, CHARLOTTE, 'My First Book', *Author* (Winter 1992), 145–6.

LEAVIS, Q. D., *Fiction and the Reading Public* (London: Chatto & Windus, 1932).

LEWIS, C. S., *An Experiment in Criticism* (Cambridge: Cambridge University Press, 1961).

LIGHT, ALISON, 'Returning to Manderley: Romance Fiction, Female Sexuality and Class', in Bob Ashley (ed.), *Reading Popular Narrative: A Source Book* (London: Leicester University Press, 1989), 222–6.

LINK, HENRY C., and HOPF, HARRY ARTHUR, *People and Books: A Study of Reading and Book-Buying Habits* (New York: Book Manufacturers Institute, 1946).

LIVEING, EDWARD, *Adventure in Publishing: The House of Ward Lock 1854–1954* (London: Ward, Lock & Co., 1954).

LLOYD, NIGEL, 'Read any Books at all lately?', *Observer* (8 Dec. 1968), 14–16.

The Letters of Jack London, ed. Earle Labor, Robert C. Leitz, III, and I. Milo Shepard (Stanford, Calif.: Stanford University Press, 1988).

LUBBOCK, PERCY, *The Craft of Fiction* (London, 1921).

LUCAS, E. V., *Reading, Writing and Remembering: A Literary Record* (London: Methuen & Co., 1933).

LUSTY, ROBERT, *Bound to be Read* (London: Jonathan Cape, 1975).

MCALEER, JOSEPH, *Popular Reading and Publishing in Britain 1914–1950* (Oxford: Oxford University Press, 1992).

MANN, PETER H., *The Romantic Novel: A Survey of Reading Habits* (London: Mills & Boon Ltd., 1969).

—— and BURGOYNE, JACQUELINE, *Books and Reading* (London: André Deutsch, 1969).

MARCH, JERMYN, 'The World of Fancy', *W. H. Smith Trade Circular* (19 Feb. 1927), 3–4.

MARGOLIES, DAVID, 'Mills and Boon: Guilt without Sex', *Red Letters* (Winter 1982–3), 5–13.

MENZIES, JOHN, 'A Selected List of Popular Fiction Suitable for Lending Libraries' (Edinburgh, Apr. 1935, Mar. 1937).

MILES, ROSALIND, *The Fiction of Sex: Themes and Functions of Sex Difference in the Modern Novel* (New York: Barnes & Noble Books, 1974).

MILLS & BOON, LTD., *'And then he kissed her . . .'*, promotional cassette (London: Mills & Boon, Ltd., 1986).

MITCHELL, B. R., *British Historical Statistics* (Cambridge: Cambridge University Press, 1988).

MOGRIDGE, STEPHEN, *Talking Shop* (London: Lutterworth Press, 1950).

MULHERN, FRANCIS (ed.), *Contemporary Marxist Literary Criticism* (London: Longman Group UK, 1992).

MULHOLLAND, JOAN, 'Mills and Boon', in Jonathan Rose and Patricia Anderson (eds.), *British Literary Publishing Houses 1881–1965, Dictionary of Literary Biography*, 112 (New York: Gale Research, 1991), 221–3

MUMBY, FRANK A., *The Romance of Book Selling: A History from the Earliest Times to the Twentieth Century* (Boston: Little, Brown & Co., 1911).

—— and NORRIE, IAN, *Publishing and Bookselling*, 5th edn. (London: Jonathan Cape, 1974).

NASH, WALTER, *Language in Popular Fiction* (London: Routledge, 1990).

NEUBERG, VICTOR E., *Popular Literature: A History and Guide from the Beginning of Printing to the Year 1897* (London: Penguin Books, 1977).

NEWTON, JUDITH, and ROSENFELT, DEBORAH (eds.), *Feminist Criticism and Social Change* (London: Methuen, 1985).

ODHAMS, W. J. B., *The Business and I* (London: Martin Secker, 1935).

'On the darker side of love', *Bookseller* (16 June 1995), 32–3.

'One 2s. 6d. Novel: Library Profit — £9', *W. H. Smith Trade Circular* (6 May 1950), 22.

Orwell, George, 'Boys' Weeklies', in Sonia Orwell and Ian Angus (eds.), *The Collected Essays, Journalism and Letters of George Orwell*, i (London: Penguin Books, 1987), 505–31.

ORWELL, SONIA, and ANGUS, IAN (eds.), *The Collected Essays, Journalism and Letters of George Orwell* (London: Penguin Books, 1987).

PAWLING, CHRISTOPHER (ed.), *Popular Fiction and Social Change* (London, 1984).

PEMBERTON, JOHN E., *Politics and Public Libraries in England and Wales 1850–1970* (London: Library Association, 1977).

PICKLES, HELEN, 'Boons without Mills', *Daily Mail* (10 Nov. 1985), 36–7.

'Pooter on hidden best sellers', *The Times* (14 Sept. 1968), 17, 21.

RADFORD, JEAN, (ed.), *The Progress of Romance: The Politics of Popular Fiction* (London: Routledge & Kegan Paul, 1986).

RADWAY, JANICE A., *Reading the Romance: Women, Patriarchy, and Popular Literature* (Chapel Hill: University of North Carolina Press, 1984).

RICHARDSON, F. R., 'The Circulating Library', in John Hampden (ed.), *The Book World* (London, 1935), 195–202.

ROBERTS, THOMAS J., *An Aesthetics of Junk Fiction* (Athens, Ga.: University of Georgia Press, 1990).

ROBINS, DENISE, *Life and Love* (London: Nicholson & Watson, 1935).

—— *Stranger than Fiction* (London: Hodder & Stoughton, 1965).

—— (ed.), *The World of Romance: An Entrancing Collection of Stories, edited and introduced by the Queen of Romance* (London: New English Library, 1964).

RUCK, BERTA, *A Smile for the Past* (London: Hutchinson & Co., 1959).

—— *A Story-Teller Tells the Truth* (London: Hutchinson & Co., 1935).

The Russell Harty Show, transcript (London, 22 Oct. 1982).

ST JOHN, JOHN, *William Heinemann: A Century of Publishing 1890–1990* (London: Heinemann, 1990).

SANDERS, F. D. (ed.), *British Book Trade Organisation: A Report on the Work of the Joint Committee* (London, 1939).

SAWYER, NANCY, 'Romance and Prejudice', *Bookseller* (28 Aug. 1971), 1396–7.

SCHMOLLER, HANS, 'The Paperback Revolution', in Asa Briggs (ed.), *Essays in the History of Publishing in Celebration of the 250th Anniversary of the House of Longman 1724–1974* (London: Longman, 1974), 285–318.

SCHREUDERS, PIET, *Paperbacks, U.S.A.: A Graphic History, 1939–1959* (San Diego: Blue Dolphin Enterprises, 1981).

SEALE, SARA, 'Who Said Romantic Novel is Dying?', *W. H. Smith Trade Circular* (29 July 1950), 13, 23.

SHAYLOR, JOSEPH, *Sixty Years a Bookman: With Other Recollections and Reflections* (London, 1923).

SILLARS, STUART, *Visualisation in Popular Fiction 1860–1960* (London: Routledge, 1995).

SIMONS, JUDITH, 'Ideas on love have changed', *Evening Gazette* (22 Jan. 1954), 13.

'Sir Algernon Methuen, Baronet: A Memoir' (London: Methuen, 1925).

SLADEN, DOUGLAS, *My Long Life: Anecdotes and Adventures* (London, 1939).

STASZ, CLARICE, *American Dreamers: Charmain and Jack London* (New York: St Martin's Press, 1988).

STEAD, W. A. H., 'Best-Sellers as the Small Man Sees them', *Bookseller* (5 Feb. 1936), 115–16.

STEVENS, GEORGE, and UNWIN, STANLEY, *Best-Sellers: Are they Born or Made?* (London, 1939).

STUBBS, JEAN, 'Romantic Novels', *Books & Bookmen* (Mar. 1972).

'Subjects of General Reading: Popularity of Fiction', *The Times* (26 Oct. 1933), 11.

'A Survey of Reading', *Bookseller* (1 May 1948), 888–90.

TAYLOR, W. G., 'Publishing', in John Hampden (ed.), *The Book World* (London, 1935), 49–88.

THOMPSON, ANTHONY HUGH, *Censorship in Public Libraries in the United Kingdom in the Twentieth Century* (London: Bowker, 1975).

THOMSON, GEORGE MALCOLM, *Martin Secker & Warburg: The First Fifty Years* (London: Secker & Warburg, 1986).

TODD, JANET, *Feminist Literary History* (New York: Routledge, 1988).

TRACEY, HERBERT (ed.), *The British Press: A Survey, A Newspaper Directory, and a Who's Who in Journalism* (London, 1929).

TREVOR, MCMAHON, 'Who Buys Novels?', *Publishers' Circular* (28 May 1921), 554–5.

TURNER, MICHAEL, and GEARE, MICHAEL (comps.), *Gluttony, Pride and Lust and other Sins from the World of Books* (London: Collins, 1984).

Twenty-Five Years of Harlequin 1949–1974 (Toronto: Harlequin Enterprises, 1974).

'Twopenny Libraries and the Shops Act', *Publishers' Circular* (10 Aug. 1935), 219.

'Types of Popular Fiction: The Fast, the Sensational and the Simple', *Times Literary Supplement* (1 May 1937), 343–4.

UNWIN, STANLEY, *The Book in the Making* (London, 1931).

—— *The Status of Books* (London, 1946).

—— *The Truth about Publishing* (London, 1929).

VASUDEVAN, ARUNA (ed.), *Twentieth-Century Romance and Historical Writers*, 3rd edn. (London: St James Press/Gale Research International,1994).

WALPOLE, HUGH, 'A Letter to a Modern Novelist', in *The Hogarth Letters* (London: Hogarth Press, 1933).

WALTER, ELIZABETH, 'The Case of the Escalating Sales', in H. F. R. Keating (ed.), *Agatha Christie: First Lady of Crime* (London: Weidenfeld & Nicolson, 1977), 11–24.

WARBURG, FREDRIC, *All Authors are Equal* (London: Hutchinson, 1973).

WEEKS, JEFFREY, *Sex, Politics and Society: The Regulation of Sexuality Since 1800* (New York: Longman, 1981).

WEIDENFELD, GEORGE, *Remembering My Good Friends: An Autobiography* (London: HarperCollins, 1994).

WEST, REBECCA, 'The Tosh Horse', in *The Strange Necessity: Essays and Reviews* (London: Virago, 1987), 319–25.

WHITE, CYNTHIA L., *Women's Magazines 1693–1968* (London, 1970).

—— 'The Women's Periodical Press in Britain 1946–1976', *Royal Commission on the Press*, Working Paper Number 4 (London: HMSO, 1977).

WILLIAMS, RICHARD (comp.), 'British Paperback Checklists no. 6: Hodder and Stoughton 1926–1960' (Scunthorpe: Dragonby Press, Jan. 1990).

—— 'Pan Books 1945–1966: A Bibliographical Checklist' (Scunthorpe: Dragonby Press, 1990).

WILSON, CHARLES, *First with the News: The History of W. H. Smith 1792–1972* (London, 1985).

The Wogan Show, transcript (London: BBC, 22 Jan. 1982).

WYBROW, ROBERT J., *Britain Speaks Out, 1937–87: A Social History as Seen through the Gallup Data* (London: Macmillan, 1989).

WYLIE, I. A. R., *My Life with George: An Unconventional Biography* (New York: Random House, 1940).

Index